To Juanita Bales

From [illegible]

March 5, 2020

The Magic City

The Magic City

Ann Dudley Matheny

Footnotes to the History of Middlesborough, Kentucky, and the Yellow Creek Valley

Bell County Historical Society

Frontispiece: Aerial view of Middlesborough. Courtesy of Bell County Historical Society.

Bell County Historical Society
P. O. Box 1344
Middlesboro, KY 40965

ISBN: 096777652X

LCCN: 2002117415

For my grandchildren
Lydia
Maggie
Pence
Will
in the hope that they will learn to appreciate
all the drama, adventure, suspense,
and mystery that a study of history can offer

and

in memory of my parents,
Lydia and Dudley Brown
Who nurtured my own love of history

Contents

Illustrations

Maps

Acknowledgments

The first thing I must acknowledge is the impossibility of expressing adequate thanks to all those who contributed to this book. I owe more than I can ever say to all the people who shared their memories and memorabilia with me. A special thank you is due to the grandchildren of Alexander Arthur—Mary Stonecipher, Maggie Pickett, and Alexander Arthur II—who were most generous with their family treasures. Gladys (Mrs. Alvey) Ball spent hours talking with me, as did her daughter-in-law, Willie Ball. William H. Hoskins shared many papers and photographs of the Ball family. David Hurst allowed me access to his father's papers. The list could go on and on. I regret that space does not allow me to here acknowledge individually each person who has helped me; however, many are listed under Sources.

I wish to thank the staff of the Middlesboro–Bell County Library, and most particularly Kathy Hall, Michele Lawson, Beverly Greene, Lorene Moyers, and Jimmie Colson, all of whom were most helpful and patient. Leanne Garland, archivist for the Abraham Lincoln Library and Museum, and Carol Burkhart, cultural resources program manager for the Cumberland Gap National Historical Park, were both generous with their time and expertise. I also wish to thank the staffs of the Louisville Public Library the Lexington Public Library, the Knoxville Public Library, the Filson Club, the University of Kentucky Library, the Berea College Library, the Eastern Tennessee Historical Society, and the other research facilities I have utilized.

In a special category is Don Cole, who has spent years combing the Middlesboro library's newspaper files and has a tremendous wealth of information about the city's past, which he has always been willing to share.

My friends and colleagues at the Bell County Historical Society deserve a very special acknowledgment. Barbara and Tom Shattuck were the first to suggest a book and to offer their help. Tom, who is the author of *A Cumberland Gap Area Guidebook,* was always generous with his knowledge of the history of our area. Dr. Kenneth Smith, Tom Kelemen, and Dr.

Dwight Henn and his wife, Diane, all spent hours critiquing and proofing the book. Other members of the Society reviewed various chapters, offering their own special knowledge and perspective. The Society allowed me full use of its photographic archives, and Sam Mayes provided technical support in copying them.

I owe a huge debt of gratitude to Loretta Clark, who has been a recent source of help and encouragement. She, more perhaps than anyone else, provided the impetus to offer this book for publication. It was she who secured the services of a wonderful editor, Georgiana Strickland, who, with painstaking care, has done so much to improve this book.

Finally, and most important of all, I wish to acknowledge the large contribution made by my own family. My husband Robert B. Mathey Sr., who has been my best friend for the past fifty years, pushed and prodded me into actually writing this book. Without him, it would still be just a pile of notes residing in boxes under the bed. I also want to thank my children and their mates, Robert and Rema, Kathy Shawn and Bill, and David and Barbara. When I expressed doubts about my ability to bring this book to fruition, they were unanimous in their support and encouragement.

Introduction

Middlesborough, nestled in the valley of Yellow Creek, is a relatively small town in the southeastern corner of Kentucky, far from the seats of power and influence in the Commonwealth. A number of histories of the area are already available. So why another?

Several years ago, I was telling the Cumberland Gap National Historical Park historian a fascinating (at least to myself) story that one of the older residents had related about Middlesborough's early days. His response was that the tale was not really history but "just something that happened." I thought then how interesting were some of these "happenings" that had not appeared in any of the earlier histories or had rated only a passing note. It seemed to me that others might also be interested in these stories that could most appropriately be considered footnotes to the history of Middlesborough and the Yellow Creek Valley.

Thus this book begins with a prologue that briefly surveys the history of the area, while the main body of the book is composed of the events and personalities that could be considered footnotes to that history. Each footnote/chapter is designed to be read as an independent entity within the context of the prologue. For those accustomed to a chronological history, a timeline is provided in the Appendix.

Rather than overburden this book with source notes, I have chosen to keep documentation to a minimum. Secondary sources are generally noted only in the case of exact quotations. In the case of short quotations from contemporary newspapers or other sources that should be self-evident, no documentation is given. Much of the information for more recent history has come from personal interviews. Many of these sources asked that their names not be used, or at least not connected with a particular fact. I have made every attempt to honor that request. For this reason, some facts may not seem well documented, but I have tried to be sure everything was verified by at least two sources independent of each other.

Two other notes of explanation: Middlesborough is the official name of the city, which was selected (though with a slightly different spelling) in the expectation that the city would be an industrial steel and iron center like her namesake, Middlesbrough, on England's northeastern coast. In 1894 the U.S. Post Office Department dropped the "ugh" from most place names, and this abbreviated form is now more commonly used. Throughout the book I have used the spelling current at the time under discussion.

Another thing that might be confusing is that the term Yellow Creek Valley refers only to the basin in which the city is located, even though Yellow Creek flows another ten miles before it finally joins with the Cumberland River.

Middlesborough and the Yellow Creek Valley have had a varied and colorful past. Even those familiar with other histories of the area should find something new and of interest in this work, or at least a different slant on certain individuals and periods in the history of this unique Appalachian valley.

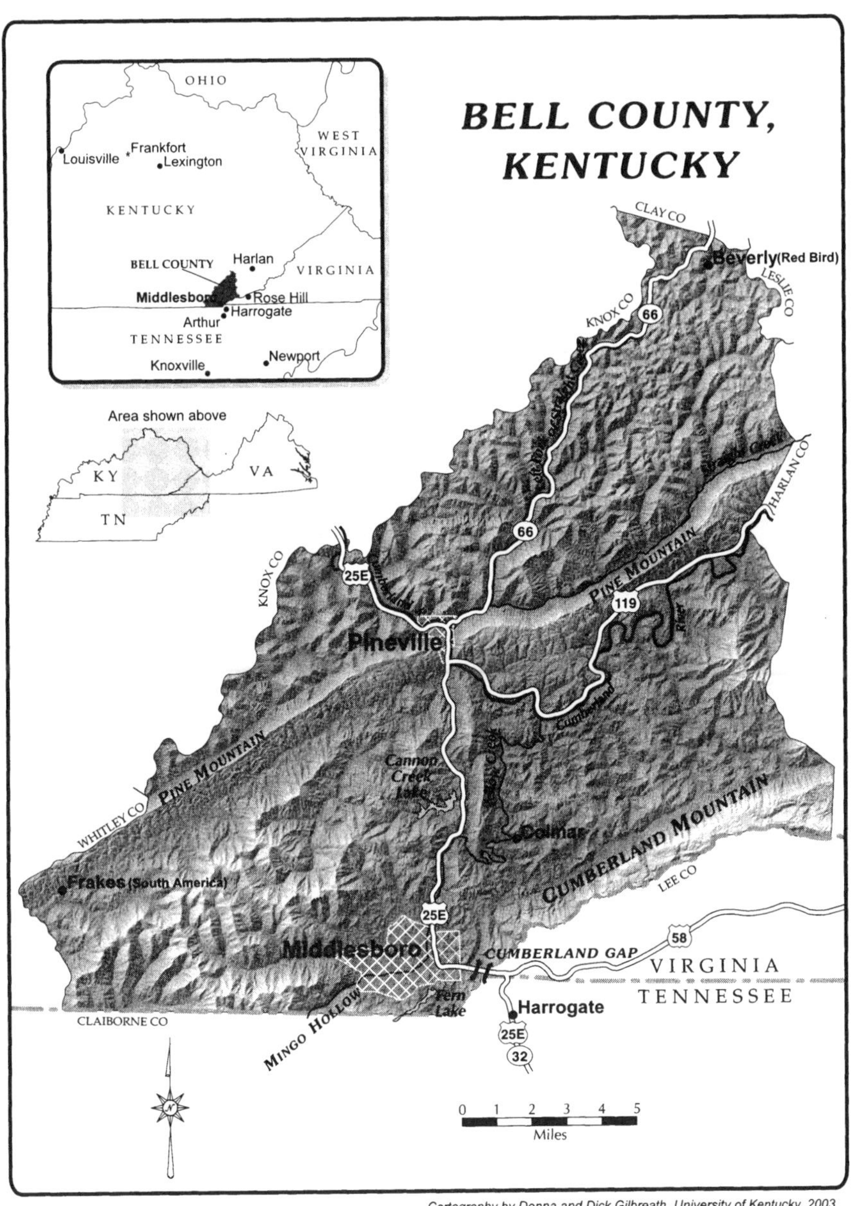

Southeastern Kentucky and adjacent Tennessee and Virginia. Cartography by Donna Gilbreath.

An aerial view of Cumberland Mountain, the Cumberland Gap at the center, the Middlesboro basin to the right. Courtesy of the Cumberland Gap National Historical Park.

PROLOGUE

A Brief History of Middlesborough and the Yellow Creek Valley

The stage on which the drama of Middlesborough's history is being played is one of truly breathtaking beauty—a wide, almost level basin encircled by magnificent mountains. To the southeast rears the Pinnacle, towering like a watchman over the historic pass known as the Cumberland Gap. Rivulets rush from the surrounding mountain hollows, gathering into branches that join to form the meandering stream now known as Yellow Creek, which traverses the valley as it flows toward its rendezvous with the Cumberland River near the spectacular Narrows to the north.

Fire or water? How was this unique valley formed? For years, geologists theorized a prehistoric swamp with such luxuriant growth that over the millennia it filled in a deep, narrow valley to form level land. Today most geologists believe that millions and millions of years ago a huge meteorite slammed into the earth's surface, creating a bowl-like crater, the stark outline of which was then softened over the eons by erosion and vegetation.[1]

Animals—first the wooly mammoth and mastodon, followed by the buffalo, elk, and deer—pounded a trail through the Gap into the valley. It was then a marshland, lush with canebrakes and salt licks, a paradise for the

[1]See Footnote One, beginning on page 1. "Footnote" as used here means one of the chapters of this book. Source notes will be found at the back of the book.

animals and later a bountiful hunting ground for the Indians who followed them through the Gap on the Warriors' Path.[2]

Although they were not the first white men to traverse the Cumberland Gap,[3] the arrival of Dr. Thomas Walker and his small band of explorers in 1750 signaled a new era, since they publicized the Cumberland Gap as the gateway through which the virgin lands to the west could be reached. Daniel Boone and his road builders followed. The Wilderness Road brought a flood of would-be settlers through the Gap. One of the first structures built in the Yellow Creek Valley was the Davis Tavern, which offered sustenance to weary travelers.[4]

Most of these early pioneers did not tarry after crossing through the Gap. Compared to the stories of the rich Bluegrass region, the swamps and hills of the Yellow Creek Valley held little attraction. The canebrakes still hid small bands of marauding Indians, and travelers usually pushed on quickly, heading for the Narrows, the second gap through the mountains. Only a few families found the valley to their liking.[5]

The first half of the new century brought two very different men to the Yellow Creek Valley. One was nearing the end of a long and adventuresome life; Arthur Campbell left only his grave as his contribution to the area's history.[6] The other, John Calvin Colson Sr., became known as the Patriarch of the Valley and sired a family that greatly influenced the history of the region.[7]

As the great western migration through the Gap slowed, the Valley slumbered. The old Wilderness Road disintegrated and was used mainly to drive livestock eastward to market. The area was relatively isolated, and the people engaged mainly in subsistence farming, along with some logging in the winter. Events and controversies shaking the country seemed to bypass these mountains.

Then came the Civil War. Both sides consulted their maps and decided the Cumberland Gap would be of great strategic importance. Troops were in the area throughout the war, the Union Army and the Confederate Army alternating occupation of the Gap several times during the course of hostilities. The armies threw up fortifications that can still be seen today. They denuded the hills of their timber and foraged for supplies from the mountaineers.[8] Despite the seeming importance of the Gap, no significant battles were ever fought in the vicinity.

---

[2]See Footnote Two, page 6; [3]See Footnote Three, page 10; [4]See Footnote Four, page 16; [5]See Footnote Five, page 20; [6]See Footnote Six, page 30; [7]See Footnote Seven, page 36; [8]See Footnote Eight, page 49.

The end of the Civil War did not bring peace to the region. The war had introduced an element of violence that had not previously been present. Guerrilla bands had roamed throughout the war years, killings had become an accepted part of life, and the conflict had made enemies of neighbors. In the closing decades of the century, the Southern Appalachians were racked by feuds.[9]

Outside the mountains, events were taking place that would influence the history of the isolated Yellow Creek Valley. With the worst of Reconstruction past, the "New South" was beginning to flex its industrial muscle. At the same time, the British Empire was at its zenith, and money poured into its coffers from economic endeavors at home and throughout its colonies. British capital created boom towns in the South, which made fortunes for both the investors and the developers. The gold ring seemed just to await anyone bold enough to seize it.

Enter Alexander A. Arthur.[10] A Canadian of Scottish descent, Arthur first visited the area in 1886. He climbed to the mountain portal from the Tennessee side and looked down upon the Yellow Creek Valley. He saw the wide basin, so unlike anything else in the mountains, where only a few families lived on widely scattered farms, and he envisioned a great city. He gazed at the surrounding mountains with their great wealth of timber, coal, and minerals and saw the raw materials for a huge industrial complex.

A charismatic salesman, Arthur set about finding financing for his vision. He first touted his plan to a group of young men, scions of rich families, who were vacationing in Asheville, North Carolina. Convinced, the young men hurriedly formed a venture group, the Gap Associates, and began securing options on land and mineral and timber rights. But Arthur's grandiose vision required far more capital than these younger sons could reasonably amass, so they financed a trip for Arthur to London, where excess capital was begging for a place to be invested and where so many had already reaped quick fortunes from developments in the southern states.

London was most receptive to the enthusiastic salesman. On January 10, 1887, the American Association, Ltd. was incorporated, and the options of the Gap Associates were transferred to the new company with a handsome profit to the original investors. Substantial sums of cash in the form of stock subscriptions began to flow in, and Arthur was named general manager and American representative of the new company, with almost carte blanche.

---

[9]See Footnote Nine, page 59; [10]See Footnote Ten, page 70.

Arthur immediately began to purchase additional lands, so that the American Association soon had title to, or at least an option on, more than 80,000 acres. He created a separate entity, the Middlesborough Town Company, to develop his city, and various subsidiary companies to provide housing and basic services. Transportation needs were addressed by new railroad lines and a tunnel through Cumberland Mountain. By means of various incentives, industries were induced to make plans to locate in his new city. Land was donated for churches, and buildings for public use were planned. Cultural and educational projects were underwritten by the Town Company. Each new venture and every new company that announced plans for Middlesborough built momentum, so that Arthur's vision for his boom town seemed already to be near fruition.[11]

As news of the mushrooming city spread, businessmen, laborers, speculators, hustlers, and adventurers of all types piled into the city that was, as yet, mostly a figment of one man's fertile imagination. A sea of tents sprang up to house the new arrivals, and people endured all sorts of hardships in order to get in on the ground floor of the "boom." By the summer of 1889 the population had swelled to an estimated 4,000.

This growing town was a true melting pot.[12] Many new residents were native to the area, living in the nearby hills and valleys and just over the Gap in Tennessee and Virginia; others were drawn from all over the United States by the lure of quick money and opportunity.[13] There was a sizable contingent of British, both established businessmen and the "remittance men" who came mostly for adventure. From southern and central Europe came many of the workmen. Those we now refer to as minorities—African-Americans and Jews—were well represented in the population mix.

Middlesborough received its city charter on March 14, 1890, just four years after Arthur first set eyes on the Valley of Yellow Creek. Already many frame buildings had supplanted tents, work on the canal and sewerage system was proceeding apace, construction had begun on some of the factories, and other industries were committing themselves almost daily. The tunnel through Cumberland Mountain had been completed in August of 1889, and the railroad now provided transportation to all parts of the country.

The seeds of the "bust," nonetheless, were already germinating, ready to bring forth their bitter fruit. First there were three large fires within two months.[14] The first two were contained, but the third conflagration, on

---

[11]See Footnote Eleven, page 102; [12]See Footnote Twelve, page 122; [13]See Footnote Thirteen, page 141; [14]See Footnote Fourteen, page 155.

May 31, 1890, consumed a large part of the town, both the business section and residences. Immediately the Town Company and the American Association poured huge sums into rebuilding, and the town soon sprang up again, "phoenix-like," as the "boomers" proclaimed, and better than before, with brick buildings instead of vulnerable frame structures. But valuable capital that was needed for development had been of necessity diverted to rebuilding.

The land sales in the fall of 1890 were very profitable, and Middlesborough was set for a new wave of ever increasing prosperity when the next blow fell. The Baring Brothers Bank, from whence had come much of the capital that had financed the "boom," failed. At first, the city could not imagine that the failure of one bank in far-off England could matter much. But the repercussions revealed a shaky foundation under the meteoric rise of the "Magic City."[15] The English investors were forced to look hard at the project, and in January of 1891 Arthur was removed as the general manager of the American Association, Ltd.

The Americans still believed in Arthur's vision, and when he returned from England they greeted him as a hero. Mass meetings were held to demonstrate their support of the man and his dream. Arthur was still president of the Middlesborough Town Company, and the land sale in May of 1891 was the most successful yet. For the time being, the town's confidence was unshakened, and it continued to be a rough and bustling boom town.[16]

In the summer of 1891, E.F. Powers arrived from London to assume management of the American Association. He proclaimed the project basically sound, though, as he dryly remarked, there had been "too much booming." He began working toward a more gradual, methodical growth for the town, with more emphasis on the development of natural resources. Although the iron ore had proven to be not of the quality or quantity originally believed, coal was abundant and of a valuable grade, and the standing timber was plentiful. Powers might have succeeded in averting a complete bust had not the general business climate in the United States turned sour. Conditions worsened, and by 1893 the country was in one of its worse panics, with business badly depressed everywhere.

The Englishmen who had not left with the first bad news had almost all abandoned ship by the end of 1893. Most of the "boomers" went off to seek their fortunes elsewhere[17] or, more likely in view of the general business climate, to quietly lick their wounds. Many of the mountaineers slipped

---

[15]See Footnote Fifteen, page 163; [16]See Footnote Sixteen, page 171; [17]See Footnote Seventeen, page 179.

back to their farms. The population declined. Businesses failed, the American Association and its subsidiary companies went into receivership, property owners defaulted on their loans, and cash money was so scarce in town that many people were reduced to barter.

The city was left owing on the bonds to which it had so optimistically obligated itself when it took over the responsibility for the various public works begun by the Town Company. With little in tax revenues after the bust, Middlesborough petitioned its creditors to allow it to defer payments and/or reduce interest. The bondholders responded by going to the Kentucky legislature and ramming through the Roundtree Bill, which mandated that bond obligations be paid before any expenditures were made for municipal officers or employees or for any improvements. This had the effect of totally crippling city services. City employees, including teachers, were often paid in warrants (essentially IOUs), which were accepted by most merchants only with deep discounts.

Some hardy souls stayed on, either because they had the vision to see that Arthur's basic premise—the promise of the natural resources surrounding the Valley—was valid, or because they had come to think of Middlesborough as home and were determined to stick with it through the bad times. They formed the sturdy nucleus of the town and carried on. Some talented professional people also remained, and the city continued to be an oasis of culture in the mountains.[18]

The grand patriotic fervor leading up to the Spanish-American War engendered great excitement and pride as Middlesborough thrilled over reports of the fiery pro-war speeches in Congress by hometown boy David Colson.[19] When their congressman vacated his seat to come home and form a mountain regiment, there was a rush to volunteer.

The city continued to suffer reverses, however. In 1898 there was a serious smallpox epidemic.[20] Then, in early 1900, city politics became so bitter that the city ended up with two competing sets of officers.[21] The general disarray allowed a lawlessness that was almost as rampant as during the earliest boom days, and Middlesboro attained unwanted notoriety in 1902 with the Quarterhouse Battle.[22]

The real turning point came with the repeal of the Roundtree Bill in 1906. Joe E. Bosworth had been elected to the state legislature with that

---

[18]See Footnote Eighteen, page 196; [19]See Footnote Nineteen, page 211; [20]See Footnote Twenty, page 225; [21]See Footnote Twenty-One, page 233; [22]See Footnote Twenty-Two, page 247.

action as his main objective. Once realized, Middlesboro regained control of its own finances and was on the road to realizing Arthur's dream.

Coal was booming, and Middlesboro was a hub not only for the producers but also for those supplying the mines and the miners. Wholesale houses had their headquarters in Middlesboro, and traveling salesmen made it the center of their operations. Businessmen were active in city government and civic groups. Reform movements brought periodic "cleanup" of the Rhine, that section of town known for its cheap whiskey and easy women,[23] and the city took on a more settled aspect. Population increased until by the census of 1910 it stood at 7,305, equaling the record it had set at the height of the "boom." Banks, retail stores, restaurants, hotels—all returned to Middlesboro in force. New industries joined the ranks of those that, like the tannery, had survived the "bust" and were now prospering.

Its third decade saw Middlesboro again in a frenzy of building. A large city hall, which also housed the police department, fire department, police court, and jail, was built at 20th and Lothbury. An impressive post office was under construction across the street from the city hall, and a Carnegie library had been secured. Roads were paved. Empty lots were suddenly in demand. World War I caused great anxiety as young men marched off to combat and as the city suffered the flu pandemic; nevertheless, the war in Europe brought a steep increase in the demand for coal, which was always good for the city.

The twenties were a time of general prosperity, although coal strikes, followed by a slump in the demand for coal in the last part of the decade, brought some economic dislocations in Middlesboro. But other industries, such as the overall factory, tannery, foundry, and bottling plant, were doing well, and retail stores were busy. A large mill serviced farmers in the area, not only grinding their grain for them but also storing it. This brought farmers and their families, including those from Virginia and Tennessee, into town on a regular basis and made it a natural center for their trade. Social life was rich with parties, dances, clubs and other organizations, and various sports and sporting events.[24] Churches and other religious organizations also served a social as well as a spiritual function.[25] Just across the mountain, Lincoln Memorial University offered concerts and lectures. The culture and interest in education that had been evident since the early days gave Middlesboro continuing rights to the title "Athens of the Mountains."

Yet there was a darker side to Middlesboro in the twenties. Bell County

---

[23]See Footnote Twenty-Three, page 256; [24]See Footnote Twenty-Four, page 262; [25]See Footnote Twenty-Five, page 268.

had been dry since 1915, antedating the Volstead Act, but the soft-drink stands on Lothbury and on 19th still did a good trade in the harder stuff, and there continued to be a certain undercurrent of violence[26] and even a connection with the gang warfare in Chicago.[27]

Almost as an omen of the difficult days ahead, Middlesboro suffered unusually severe flooding in 1928-1929. The town had been subject to periodic floods since its founding, but this was the worst and would eventually result in extensive flood control projects.

The thirties brought the Great Depression to the entire country. It was the ending of the era of speakeasies, the Charleston, and easy optimism. Middlesboro was less affected than many areas, as there was still some demand for coal, though the competitive advantage enjoyed by southeastern coal came mostly at the expense of the miners, who worked longer hours for less pay. The union wars of the thirties were felt most strongly in "Bloody Harlan," but Middlesboro was not spared its share of union troubles.[28]

As war clouds again loomed in Europe, Middlesboro boomed. Coal was in demand. The Volstead Act had been repealed in 1933, allowing Middlesboro's bars to operate legally. Gambling and prostitution became more open. Middlesboro gained the reputation of being a "Little Chicago" or "Little Las Vegas."[29] The kingpins were Alvey and Floyd Ball.

In 1940 the population stood at 11,777—not the hundred thousand that Arthur had envisioned but certainly evidence of the bustling trade, rail, and coal center he had foreseen. The area around the railroad terminal was thronged day and night. The huge Cumberland Hotel served as headquarters for salesmen and host to multiple conventions, as well as a social center. Downtown stores offered a fine selection of upscale merchandise. The movie theaters, restaurants, and nightclubs provided entertainment for all tastes. Schools were considered among the best in the state, and various cultural groups were popular. As war became inevitable, industries boomed and coal was again king.

World War II found the mountains ablaze with patriotism. In fact, the local draft board was overwhelmed by volunteers. The Middlesboro-Bell County Airport became a training center for army pilots.[30] Older miners came out of retirement to take the place of those who had marched off to war. Everyone followed the war news closely and joined in the war effort.

Unfortunately, the home front offered its own dangers, and more men

---

[26]See Footnote Twenty-Six, page 277; [27]See Footnote Twenty-Seven, page 296; [28]See Footnote Twenty-Eight, page 305; [29]See Footnote Twenty-Nine, page 319; [30]See Footnote Thirty, page 365.

died in the bars and honkytonks of Bell County during the war than did local boys on the battlefields of Europe and Asia. There was a groundswell of dismay at the wilder—and some felt immoral—aspects of the town, and many respectable citizens began to coalesce in opposition to the excesses of the Balls and their allies. Preachers railed against the activities on 19th Street. Law and Order rallies attracted large crowds.

During the forties and early fifties various reform groups organized, then faltered and disbanded, only to return in another form. When a new judicial district was formed in 1948 the political power of the Ball machine was challenged and their protection became less valuable. There was a countywide campaign against slot machines, which cut deeply into the revenues of the Ball machine. The dry forces began to win elections, though the results were overturned in court. In 1953 Middlesboro voted in a mayor-council form of government, upsetting the cozy commissioner arrangement that had allowed the Balls to dominate city politics. The following year the city voted itself dry, but court challenges delayed the actual date of prohibition till November of 1955. At the same time, reform efforts caused gambling and prostitution to go underground.

The fifties were notable for a steep downturn in the coal industry that continued into the sixties and resulted in an outmigration of population to the industrial centers of the North. The 1950 census showed 14,419 people living in Middlesboro, while the county as a whole had 43,812. By 1970 the population of Middlesboro had declined to 11,878, and in the county it stood at 31,121.

A positive step was the establishment of the Cumberland Gap National Historical Park. The idea of a park at the Gap had been around for a long time. First discussed in the 1890s as the site for a Grant-Lee memorial and later as a Lincoln Park, the idea never quite died. In the 1920s support again gathered under the auspices of the Middlesboro Chamber of Commerce and the Kiwanis Club, which initiated a corporation to pursue a national park. The Pinnacle and the road leading to it had already become a commercial tourist attraction called Skyline Drive. Numerous trips to Frankfort and Washington, along with strong lobbying efforts by such leading citizens as Robert Kincaid, Clinton Broadwater, Joe Bosworth, Tom Fugate, Howard Douglass, and Harry Hoe finally led to the appropriation of funds to begin land purchases in the early forties. World War II delayed plans, but the park was finally dedicated in 1959 by then-Vice-President Richard Nixon, the governors of the three contiguous states, and multiple state and local officials.

The sixties brought nationwide attention to the problems of Appalachia. The War on Poverty with its Operation Head Start, Job Corps, Appalachian Regional Commission, and other government programs addressed some of the problems faced by Middlesboro in the wake of the "bust" in the coal industry, but local residents also pulled together in a grassroots effort to ameliorate the economic dislocations. Joe McCauley, Glenn Denham, Maurice Henry, and numerous other citizens worked through the Middlesboro Industrial Commission to secure several new industries, most notably a sewing factory and wood products processing plant. Two new federally financed housing projects were secured. The Middlesboro School Board constructed a new high school and two new elementary schools, the latter replacing several small, deteriorating facilities.

The energy crisis of the early seventies actually proved beneficial for Middlesboro, since it sparked a new boom in coal as industries rediscovered this local source of energy. Suddenly fortunes were being made by mine operators, and coal miners were the new elite. As always before, the boom ended in a bust in the late seventies as the nation resumed its love affair with oil. Mines failed and many miners were unemployed or went to work at lower paying jobs. At the same time, concerns about pollution, in addition to the national economic condition, caused the demise of the tannery, Middlesboro's oldest industry, and the loss of several smaller industries. As the economy again faltered there was once again an outmigration of some of the brightest and most highly motivated residents, while many of those who remained came to rely more heavily on government programs and transfer payments.

By the eighties, Middlesboro had taken on that attribute of many cities, a deteriorating downtown commercial district with much of the shopping siphoned off to malls, service stations, fast food restaurants, and other businesses that lined the strip along Highway 25E. On May 9, 1988, a tornado plowed through the downtown, causing immense destruction. For a time it seemed that the city's center might die exactly a hundred years from the day of its birth.

But Middlesboro was not to be defeated. When the debris was cleared away, the damage, though in the millions of dollars, still proved to be less than originally thought, and immediately rebuilding began, much as it had after the great fire in May of 1890. Reminiscent of that earlier time when businesses bragged of rising "phoenix-like" from the ruins of that devastating fire, was one man's answer, as he stood in the ruins of his car agency, to a newsman's question as to when he might be able to reopen: "Tomorrow, unless you want to buy a car today!"

Hope also came in the form of federal funding for a tunnel through

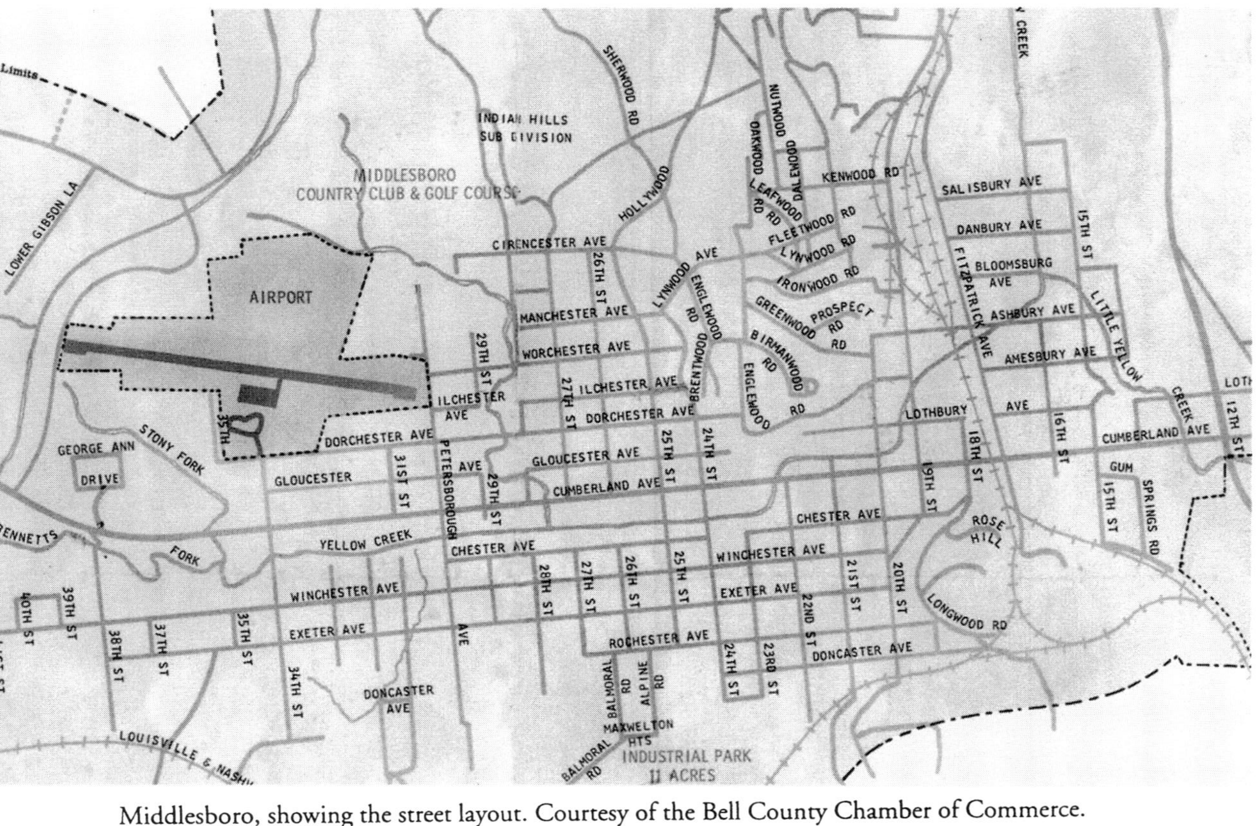

Middlesboro, showing the street layout. Courtesy of the Bell County Chamber of Commerce.

Cumberland Mountain that, it was felt, would make Highway 25E a major route, as it had once been, between the Southeast and the Midwest. That was expected to result in increased tourism as well as improvement in the general business climate.

In 1990 Middlesboro celebrated its centennial. Two years later the grandchildren of Alexander Arthur came back to see what he had wrought and to present to the city a number of his personal papers and artifacts, to be housed in the restored American Association Building.

When the new tunnel through Cumberland Mountain opened in 1996 there was a reenactment to memorialize all who had traveled through the Gap. First to emerge from the tunnel were Indians, followed by Long Hunters, pioneers and settlers, Civil War soldiers, and so on to modern times—a parade of all who had left their mark on the Yellow Creek Valley.

Newcomers and visitors to Middlesboro frequently remark on how different the city is from any other in Appalachia. They do not just note the wide, planned streets with their English names and the many impressive, solidly built homes. Nor do they speak only of the town's natural beauty, the unique basin surrounded by mountains. They also seem to refer to a certain spirit in the air, and they ask why Middlesboro is so different, what it is about the town that sets it apart from so many others. Perhaps part of the answer can be found in the city's unique past, not just its history but the "happenings" that are footnotes to that history.

Footnote One

Fiery Genesis

Trees blanket the slopes of the hilly plateau. A gold-tipped ginkgo drops a single fan-shaped leaf into the shallow pool where spiny fish laze under a clear sky and a giant dragonfly circles overhead. Here, a turtle picks his way through the mud while a small salamander scurries up a low branch. There, a Plateosaurus stretches his long neck to methodically nibble the top of a tall conifer.

Suddenly there is an unnatural brightness. The air is charged with the animals' alarm in the milliseconds before catastrophe strikes. A huge fiery ball hurls toward them with unbelievable speed, smashing into their woodland with unearthly fury. A stupendous explosion, and the very rock at the point of impact vaporizes. Enormous boulders are pulverized and thrown into the skies, and the resulting shock wave kills everything for miles around. A sheet of wildfire races outward, leaping across the already devastated landscape. Thick clouds of dust and smoke obscure the sun, and there is perpetual darkness for days on end. Nothing is left alive to see the moonscape that emerges as the clouds finally dissipate: scoured and blackened mountains scarred by a circular wound more than three and a half miles in diameter. The huge meteorite has gouged out an enormous crater at its point of impact: the area that will someday be known as the Yellow Creek Valley. What a fitting genesis for the basin that will have such a dramatic and often violent history.

Although fragments of heavenly bodies, called by the Greeks "thunder stones," have been known since ancient times, it is only within the last forty years that scientists have widely subscribed to the theory that larger meteorites have struck our planet, excavating significant craters in the earth's surface. Even today, fewer than two hundred impact structures have been documented worldwide.

Current thought is that the earth was formed 4.6 billion years ago; the oldest rock found in the Appalachian chain is one billion years old. In order to conceptualize this, it helps to imagine that the entire history of the earth occurs in one year. In this analogy, the oldest rocks on earth date back to mid-March, while those of the Appalachians form in early October. To continue the analogy, the first life organisms appear in May, and plants and animals emerge in mid-November. By mid-December dinosaurs dominate the earth, but they have become extinct by the day after Christmas. The first humans arrive late on New Year's Eve.

Geologists tell us that the earth's surface is composed of a number of rigid plates that float on the underlying mantle and are in constant motion. Over millions of years, these plates have come together as supercontinents, then broken apart into smaller continents, only to again collide. They have also migrated from the southern hemisphere to the northern and back again, so that the present-day Appalachian area was once south of the equator. The stresses and pressures caused by this movement account for much of the earth's changing topography over the eons. Thus, approximately 500 million years ago, the collision of these rigid plates caused a crumpling of the earth's crust, pushing up the first generation of the Appalachian Mountains. Erosion gradually wore these down. There followed a period, some 300 million years ago, of rising and falling sea levels resulting from the lifting and subsiding of the land mass. The Appalachian area, which was near the equator and had a tropical climate, was covered by luxuriant forests when the water was low. When sea levels rose, wide muddy lakes were formed, and layers of sediment covered decaying vegetation. The decay and compression of this flora formed coal, the Black Gold of our mountains.

Approximately 250 million years ago (early December according to our imaginary calendar), the continental plates again collided. As a consequence of this collision, the Alleghanian Orogeny, another generation of Appalachian Mountains, was born. At the same time, in the neighborhood of what would become Yellow Creek Valley, the extreme pressures generated by the clash caused a sheet of strata to break off and slide several miles northwest along a thrust fault. The leading edge of the 125-mile-long intact thrust sheet ramped upward, forming Pine Mountain; the trailing edge caused a second warp in the earth's crust, Cumberland Mountain. A major fault (a stress fracture caused by pressure and movement of rock) ran from present-day Middlesboro to present-day Pineville. Streams chiseled steep valleys in the hilly plateau that lay between the two mountain ranges. To the southeast, one of these waterways—perhaps even the ancestor of Yellow Creek—carved the Cumberland Gap where the fault had weakened the rock. Gradually, as Cumberland Mountain was pushed higher at a faster rate than the stream could erode it and, at the same time, as water pressure wore away at the fault in Pine Mountain, the stream began to drain through the notch to the north, forming the Narrows. It was after the formation of Cumberland Mountain that a huge meteorite gouged out the Yellow Creek Valley.

According to astronomers, earth is constantly being bombarded by meteoritic material, most of it no larger than a grain of sand but occasionally more like the "thunder stones" of ancient lore. None the size of the Yellow Creek meteorite has hit earth in recorded time, but scientists can deduce a model of what would happen when a large extraterrestrial body entered the earth's atmosphere. The passage would be very brief, lasting only a few seconds, and fiery as friction incinerated the mass. Even before the meteorite reached the ground, the highly compressed gas at its prow would be melting and evaporating the meteorite material, hurling blobs of rock (tektites) over a wide area. When it hit the earth, the meteorite and the impact area itself would be pulverized and vaporized by the force of the explosion. The meteorite would be completely destroyed and its material mostly dispersed in the form of vapor and tiny fragments. In the case of the well known and much studied Meteor Crater in northern Arizona, scientists estimate that the destructive energy of the meteorite was equal to fifteen-megaton bombs, twice that of the Mount St. Helens volcanic explosion and a thousand times that of the atomic bomb that devastated Hiroshima. The impact structure of the Meteor Crater has an area of 0.785 square miles. By way of comparison, the Yellow Creek Valley crater occupies approximately 10.9 square miles, a fact that hypothesizes a much bigger explosion.

Such an explosion would cause shock waves deep in the underlying rock, producing ridged, cone-shaped rock fragments called shatter cones. Very large impacts, such as the one that created the Yellow Creek Valley, have a central uplift, or rebound structure (much like what one sees when something is dropped into a container of liquid), which is caused by rocks rebounding from the initial assault. This can be seen fairly clearly in craters on the moon and is still evident, albeit much altered by erosion and development, in the hills that are now encompassed by the Middlesboro Country Club golf course. At the edges of the impact some of the rock would be flipped up and then fall back upon itself, creating an ejecta flap. This phe-

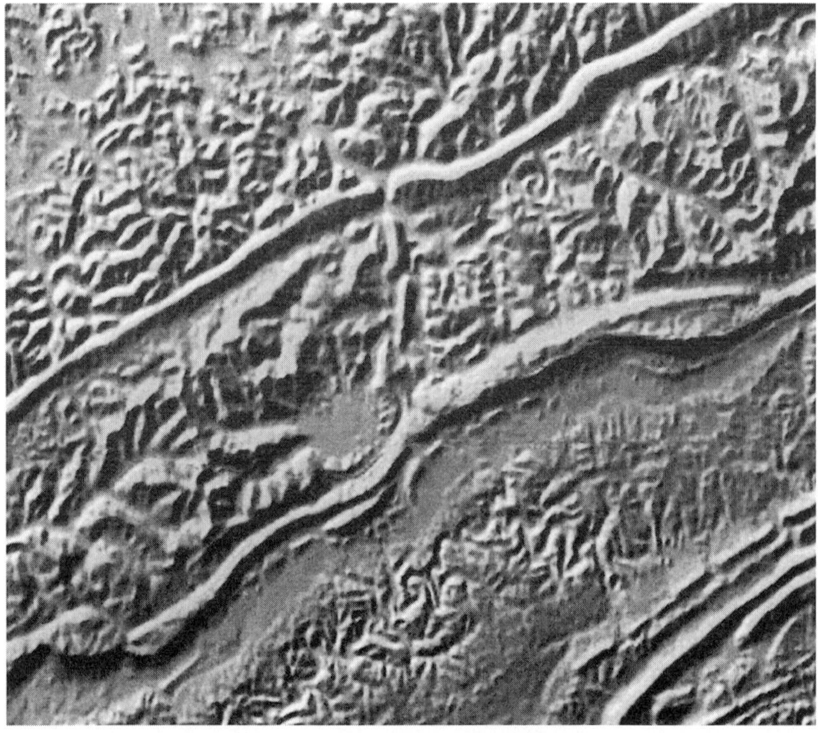

A satellite image showing the parallel ridges of Pine Mountain and Cumberland Mountain, with the circular crater site of Middlesboro at center and, directly north of the impact crater, the notch in Pine Mountain that is the Narrows. Courtesy of Ray Sterner, Johns Hopkins University Applied Physics Laboratory.

nomenon can be seen in rock at the western rim of the valley along Highway 441.

Because of the force of the impact, very few sites have any identifiable meteoritic material. Of the 116 sites that were studied by one researcher, such material was found at only thirteen.[1] The other sites were identified by the presence of what he described as "chemical and mineralogical fingerprints" and by the crater structure itself. In the case of the Middlesboro crater, three different researchers have found both shatter cones and shocked quartz grains.

Scientists estimate that the crater blasted out by a meteorite strike would be ten to thirty times larger in diameter than the body that created it, which means that the Yellow Creek Valley meteorite would have been at least 350 feet in diameter and could have been up to a third of a mile across. In discussing the Yellow Creek phenomenon, one expert explained:

> The Middlesboro Structure is particularly conspicuous, even though it is both old and highly eroded. It stands out because it is an anomalously flat area amidst a surrounding of mountains and steep stream valleys....The impact structure presently consists of encircling faults...and a central uplift. About half of the structure has outcroppings and half is covered with alluvium from several streams that cross the structure. The rocks of the central uplift are older than those of the surrounding portions of the basin and have been raised about 300 m above their normal level. The largest outcrop occurs at the corner of the clubhouse of a golf course. It consists of vertically dipping sandstone that has striations that are similar to shatter-coning. Good shatter cones are found a few hundred meters away near the boundary of the central uplift, where intensely shatter-coned siltstone has been discovered. Additional evidence of the impact origin is the presence of shock-induced cleavage and shattering in quartz grains in the sandstone.[2]

The center of the meteorite impact was not far from where the present Cumberland Avenue intersects 30th Street. The eastern rim, which has been greatly altered by both development and erosion, was near the present Highway 25E. From overlooks on the Pinnacle, the outline of the impact crater is fairly easy to discern. Satellite photographs show even more clearly the circular indentation in the mountains, which resembles a lunar crater somehow misplaced.

When Alexander Arthur built his city in this ancient valley, he did something unique. According to geologists at the Department of Interior, Middlesboro is one of only a tiny handful of towns in the entire world to be built within the crater of a meteorite.

Footnote Two

Cherokee Traditions

Hunters were pursuing their prey up Mingo Hollow, just southwest of Middlesboro, one chilly day in January of 1921. Carved by Bennetts Fork as it raced toward its junction with Yellow Creek, Mingo Hollow was the location of some of the richest coal mines in the area and was already infamous as the site of the Quarterhouse Battle (see Footnote Twenty-two). On this day, however, the hunters were simply intent on flushing out a fox.

The fox was cornered in what appeared to be a crevice, and they started the task of digging him out. As they widened the opening in the mountain, they realized it was actually a shallow cave. Inside they found the skeletons of several men, along with flint battle-axes, arrowheads, and tufts of long, coarse dark hair. There is no record of what happened to the fox as the men marveled over their find.

The report of their discovery in the national press brought forth a flurry of letters to local historian Robert Kincaid from Leaf Sixkiller, a Cherokee Indian living in Wauhillow, Oklahoma.[1] Sixkiller described himself as a full-blooded Cherokee who had been educated in white schools but had returned to the Indian territories to record the oral history and traditions of his people.

He said that his own family had originally lived in what became northeastern Tennessee not far from the Cumberland Gap, which they called Ouasioto Pass. His grandfather had traveled the Trail of Tears to the Indian Territory (now Oklahoma) where he himself had been born. Many of his letters dealt with events that had happened in the territories, but he also related oral traditions told around the campfires of times before the coming of the white men. As he said in one letter, "I have heard from the lips of an aged Indian some strange legends connected with Cherokee settlements in the neighborhood of Cumberland Gap."

Sixkiller related two different tales of events that were said to have occurred in the Yellow Creek Valley that might account for the Indian remains in Mingo Hollow.

He explained that generally to the south of the Pass or Gap there were the Cherokees, Choctaws, Chickasaws, and Creek Indians. To the north were the Wyandottes, Shawnees, Mingos, Tuscaroras, and Delawares. According to tradition, the Cherokees had once had towns in what was to become Kentucky but had been driven southward by the northern tribes, who were envious of their rich hunting grounds. At the time of the first event, which he knew was prior to 1700 (he could not be more specific because exact times were lost in the retelling of the story), there were no Cherokee settlements north of the Pass, but Indians of both the northern and the southern tribes hunted the same general area and had frequent battles over territory.

A band of Mingos led by a brave called Oogolah, the Eagle, invaded the Cherokee territory south of the Pass. It was a small raiding party, some fifty men, who silently crossed through the Gap and fell on the Cherokee settlements just to the south, killing everyone they encountered, women and children as well as braves, young and old. They ravaged the villages, plundering them of valuables, and took over a hundred scalps before turning homeward.

News spread quickly to other settlements, and the enraged Cherokees gathered all possible warriors to follow them and avenge their dead. The Mingos, burdened by their booty and in unfamiliar territory, were able to get through the Pass just ahead of the Cherokees, but they feared their pursuers would find them easy prey on the well worn Warriors' Path, so they fled westward into the marshes of Yellow Creek.

The Mingos ascended Yellow Creek as far as Stony Fork, then took the left branch, with the Cherokees in hot pursuit. Oogolah had lost few men to that point, but as they fled up the narrowing hollow he realized he had boxed his forces into an untenable position where they would certainly fall victim to the superior force of the Cherokees. Rather than allow an ignominious rout, Oogolah turned his men to face the hundreds of enraged Cherokees and raised the death chant. It was said that no Mingos survived the slaughter. Sixkiller theorized, however, that a few, mortally wounded, may have managed to find a cave in which to die with their scalp locks intact.

According to Sixkiller, this story had been told around the campfires for generations. He also related another oral tradition that could account for the Indian remains. He dated this to sometime around 1650 to 1700, but again could not be specific about the date and was not sure whether it preceded or followed the Mingo massacre.

This tradition told of a great confederation of northern Indians that had been formed to invade the south, a war party of more than 1,500 warriors led by the most noted chiefs of the various tribes. Their plan was to travel the Warriors' Path through the Gap and attack the Cherokee towns to the south in force.

The Cherokees had been warring for years with the northern tribes and had learned to leave scouts near the Gap. These tangled with the advance guard of the northern tribes, and the latter returned to the main body to report that some opposition could be expected when they passed through the Gap. It was already twilight, so the northern confederation decided to camp along Yellow Creek and make the passage at dawn.

When the Cherokee scouts realized that their enemies would not attempt the Gap that night, they hurried to the only nearby Cherokee town, which was just south of what is now known as Baptist Gap. From there runners were sent out to warn the towns to the south and to organize war parties to meet the challenge. Meanwhile, every man in the small Cherokee village, be he able-bodied or old and feeble, marched toward the Gap, determined to fight to the death to stall the advance of their enemies and give the towns to the south time to defend themselves.

That night there was a huge storm with torrents of rain. Yellow Creek, as is its wont, rose swiftly, and many of the sleeping invaders, caught in the rushing waters of the resulting flash flood, drowned. Those who managed to flee the camp scattered in the pitch black night, seeking higher ground and shelter in any crevice. Many had lost their weapons in the flood, and those who managed to retain their bows found the bowstrings had been so loosened by the copious water that they were almost useless.

When dawn came, the Cherokees who had reached the Gap looked down upon a strange sight. The camp of the northern Indian confederation had been washed away and the surviving warriors were in a state of stunned confusion. The local Cherokees were accustomed to the sudden storms of the area and had taken shelter early, keeping their weapons dry. They knew the Valley intimately, as they often hunted there.

The hunting that day was more gruesome. The Cherokees took no prisoners but did take more than a thousand scalps. Few northern Indians were thought to have escaped, but it is possible that some may have made their way up Mingo Hollow and there perished.

Sixkiller stated that he had seen in the homes of many Indians living in Oklahoma in his day tufts of hair that were said to be scalps taken during this battle.

FOOTNOTE THREE

The First White Man

Gabriel Arthur was the first white man to travel through the Yellow Creek Valley and over the Cumberland Gap and leave a record of the trip. He himself was illiterate, so his account was oral and was recorded by his sponsor, Abraham Wood.

By the mid-seventeenth century, the British colonists clinging to the eastern seaboard of the New World were beginning to look westward and explore the great wilderness. One of those intrigued by the possibilities of further exploration and expanded trade was Abraham Wood, commander of the garrison at Fort Henry (present location of Petersburg, Virginia). Wood himself led several expeditions deep into the wilderness, establishing trading relationships with the Indians to the south and west. Later he sponsored other expeditions to probe ever deeper into the mysterious lands to the west.

In April of 1673 Wood sent out a party led by James Needham, an experienced explorer and Indian trader and a successful farmer. With him he sent his indentured servant Gabriel Arthur. Arthur was young and uneducated but a hard worker and quick learner. Wood provided them with horses, provisions, and Indian guides. The party almost immediately ran into hostile Indians, however, and was turned back.

On May 17, Needham and Arthur again set out from Fort Henry, this time taking a different route to avoid hostile tribes. They had the good fortune to meet up with a company of friendly Tomahitans (Cherokees) who lived beyond the Blue Ridge Mountains and were willing to allow Needham and Arthur to accompany them back to their home village.

It was not an easy trip over the Blue Ridge Mountains westward toward the foothills of the Smokies. They lost all but one of their horses on the journey, which lasted several weeks. Finally they reached a Cherokee settlement that was built on a high bluff overlooking the Little Tennessee River and fortified with a twelve-foot-high wall of log palisades. It was one of the larger towns of the Tomahitans, populous and well provisioned, with 250 canoes pulled up to the riverbank. The Indians were very hospitable, offering them all manner of food and comfort, but they were also curious, since most had never before seen a white man or a horse. Wood related that, according to the explorers,

> they were very kindly entertained by them, even to addoration in their cerrimonies of courteies and a stake was sett up in the middle of the towne to fasten the horse to, and aboundance of corne and all manner of pulse with fish, flesh and beares oyle for the horse to feed upon and a scaffold sett before day for my two men...that theire people might stand and gaze at them and not offend them by theire throng.[1]

A few of the Cherokees had had some contact with the Spanish in Florida, and there was even one man who had learned some Spanish while a prisoner there.

Though their experience with the Spanish had engendered much animosity, the Cherokees seemed better disposed toward the English, and Needham was encouraged that profitable trade was possible. He decided to return to Fort Henry to make a report to Wood. He took twelve of the Tomahitans with him, including the man who spoke Spanish, but left behind Arthur, whom he instructed to learn the language and customs of his hosts in preparation for both trade and further exploration. Arthur made good use of his time, not only following Needham's instructions but also ingratiating himself with an old chief.

Wood was elated by Needham's report and passed it on to the Virginia Assembly. He decided that Needham should return almost immediately to continue his explorations, and fitted him out with horses and provisions, including goods for gifts and trade. Returning with him, in addition to the Cherokees, was an Occaneechi called Indian John or Hasecoll, who had been one of the guides on the first trip.

Wood eagerly anticipated the new discoveries Needham would make on this second journey. Unfortunately, instead of reports from Needham, he began to hear rumors from friendly Indians that one of his men had been killed. It was, however, many months before he learned the whole story.

As Wood later learned, Needham had difficulties from the start with Hasecoll, who was unhappy with the fact that he had so far received only half the pay he had been promised, the rest of which was to be forthcoming when he returned to Fort Henry. He complained and quarreled, becoming more fractious as the trip progressed. Finally Needham, aggravated with his constant complaints, picked up a hatchet that happened to be close by and threw it to the ground near Hasecoll, taunting him, "John are you minded to kill me?" With that, Hasecoll grabbed his gun and fired a fatal shot through Needham's head.

The other Indians became agitated, fearing what vengeance the British might exact. Hasecoll mocked them and "drew out his knife stept acrosse the corpes of Mr. Needham, ript open his body, drew out his hart, held it up in his hand and turned and looked to the eastward, toward the England plantations and said hee vallued not [at] all the English." Hasecoll then opened the packs, taking all the goods he could carry on Needham's horse. Before disappearing into the woods, Hasecoll ordered the Tomahitans to return to their town and see that Gabriel Arthur was also killed. The attitude of the Cherokees toward white men had always been ambivalent, and the frightened Indians must have argued among themselves as they returned to their town and related the dramatic murder of Needham and Hasecoll's commands.

The old chief who had befriended Arthur was off on a hunting trip. As the tribe debated, the tide of feeling in the town turned against the Englishman, and some of the young braves seized Arthur, bound him to a stake, and began piling dry brush around him. Just then the chief returned from hunting and demanded to know who wanted to kill the young white man. A brave leapt forward flourishing a fire brand, as if to light the brush, and the chief shot him. The chief then cut Arthur loose with his own knife and took him into his home, giving Arthur his protection and promising him that he would be escorted safely home in the spring.

After his close brush with death, Arthur became almost a member of the tribe. He was outfitted as a brave and taken along on a raid against the Spanish to the south. A second raid was planned on a rival Indian village near Port Royal in South Carolina. Arthur was loath to accompany them until the Indians promised that no Englishman would be harmed during the raid. The Cherokees were true to their promise and released without injury a white trader who happened to be in the village when they attacked. The band passed silently by English homes, close enough that the young Arthur could hear his countrymen discussing Christmas plans. There is nothing in Wood's account to suggest that Arthur was tempted to flee his Cherokee hosts and stay with the white men, though the thought must have occurred to him. Arthur was faithful to his charge, however, and continued with the Indians, becoming fluent in their language and ways.

Arthur's knowledge of the wilderness greatly increased when he accompanied the chief on his next journey, a friendly visit to an allied tribe to the north. The trip took ten days, passing through the mountains of Kentucky and into what is now western West Virginia, and allowing Arthur to view both the Kanawha and Ohio Rivers.

On their way home, the band of sixty Cherokees decided to attack a village of Shawnees, their long-time enemies. The Shawnees, however, not only repulsed them but captured Arthur. He had received two arrow wounds, one to his thigh, and was unable to run, so was overtaken. Luckily he had not adopted the Cherokee custom of cropping his hair, and the Shawnees suspected he was not an Indian. They scrubbed him with ashes and water and discovered that he was white. These Shawnees had had little contact with the white man at that point and were fascinated by Arthur and by his weapons. They had not yet been exposed to the fur trade and therefore had neither firearms nor metal utensils. They fed him and cared for his wounds, and he, in turn, presented to the chief his metal hatchet and knife.

Arthur watched the Shawnees bring in freshly killed beavers and singe off the fur in preparation for cooking them. With sign language, he let them know how much the white man valued those furs and how they could trade the skins for knives and hatchets just like his. He told them that if they would allow him to return to his people, he would come again with trade goods to exchange for their beaver skins. Woods reported that "they seemed to rejoyce att it and carried him to a path that caried to ye Tomahittans gave him Rokahamony for his journey and soe they departed." It was then early spring, a time when the weather is chancey, streams are running full, and wild food is scarce—not the ideal time for traveling, especially through two hundred miles of wilderness alone with parched corn (the Rokahamony) as one's only provision. Yet Woods did not record that Arthur had complained of any difficulties or of problems finding his way back to the Cherokee village.

Given the location of the Shawnee village, most historians agree that the trail they took him to was the Warriors' Path, already a well worn track that led him south, taking him through the Yellow Creek Valley, over the Cumberland Gap, and on to the Cherokee villages.[2]

The Tomahitans were excited to again see Arthur. They took him on a short hunting trip before escorting him back to Fort Henry. It was now May of 1674, and Arthur had been living with the Indians for a full year. He was undoubtedly anxious to return, especially as he was carrying with him both the furs and the information so desired by his master.

The chief and eighteen Cherokees "laden with goods" accompanied him. The trip was uneventful until they encountered hostile Occaneechis, who tricked the Cherokees into thinking their number was much greater than it actually was. The Cherokees fled, leaving Arthur behind. All night the Occaneechis searched for Arthur, who was hiding under some bushes. When they finally gave up, he ventured forth, finding that one of the Cherokees had also been in hiding nearby. Together they managed to get through the Occaneechi territory, being forced to travel at night and to live off the land. Arthur and his companion finally arrived at Fort Henry on June 18, 1674.

The chief and some of the Cherokees had managed to regroup and to save some of their furs. They circumvented the Occaneechis by making a bark canoe to travel down the James River and then traveling overland to the fort. They were joyously greeted by Arthur and by Wood, who saw the opportunity the pelts represented. The Cherokees stayed several days and promised to return in the fall.

Wood wrote out his account of Gabriel Arthur's adventures on August 22, 1674, and sent it to his friend John Richards, who was employed in London as treasurer and agent by the Lords Proprietors of Carolina, one of the English trading and colonizing companies. Notes written on the margins of the account testify that it was passed on to others in the company, but it did not receive the attention that Wood hoped it would.

Nor did Arthur's discoveries garner much attention in the colonies. Wood wrote that after Needham's first trip, he presented a report to the Grand Assembly of Virginia, "but not soe much as one word in answer or any encouragement or assistance given." Wood ended his letter with: "If I could have the countenance of some person of honour in England to curb and bridle the obstructers here for here is no incouragement att all to be had for him that is Sir Youre humble servant."

Several hunters and explorers are known to have passed through the Cumberland Gap after Gabriel Arthur, but it was left to Thomas Walker to publicize, in 1750, this gateway to the west and thus to gain his place in history.

History has noted nothing further of Gabriel Arthur. What turn did his life take after these exciting adventures? Did he parlay his hard-gained knowledge of the Indians into a profitable trading career? Did he live long enough to sit by his cabin fire as an old man regaling his grandchildren with tales of his life with the Indians? One certainly hopes so.

Footnote Four

The Davis Tavern

As the early pioneers traveling the Wilderness Road topped the Cumberland Gap and looked down on their promised land, they saw before them a seemingly endless stretch of mountain ranges and unbroken wilderness. The only sign of human habitation was a small log cabin at the foot of the mountain, close to the branching of two small streams—Davis Tavern.

No description of the Davis Tavern remains, but it almost certainly was an "ordinary," a term used to indicate that an ordinary cabin had been licensed to charge for food and lodging. The location has never been pinpointed, though several surveys and maps show the tavern, along with a mill that Richard Davis also operated in later years. In general terms, the Davis establishment was just north of the present overpass to the Cumberland Gap National Historical Park's Visitors Center.[1]

It is known that the Davis Tavern was in existence at least by 1793 and that it probably continued operation until about 1815. One early local historian asserted that Davis actually settled in the Yellow Creek Valley in 1766, but he offered no proof.[2] Although the Davis tract was alluded to in other earlier surveys, Davis did not have his own survey made of his 200 acres until January of 1799.

There is little information on Richard Davis himself. A Richard Davis was listed with the Commission for Settling Western Accounts as having been a participant in the Battle of Blue Licks on August 19, 1782. There is also in existence a certificate for military service dated 1787 for Richard Davis. The commanding officer was George Rogers Clark.[3] Although there is no proof that they are one and the same man, the age and location make it a distinct possibility.

Of the many pioneers who passed through the Gap, only a small percentage left written records of their trips. To date, only five contemporary references to the Davis Tavern by travelers have been found.

On November 11, 1793, André Michaux made a trip eastward from Crab Orchard, Kentucky, through the Gap and into Tennessee. He noted in his diary that he passed "Davissas Station" two miles before crossing into Tennessee. He and his party apparently did not stop for the night.

A Baptist minister, the Rev. David Barrow, kept a journal of his trip to Kentucky in 1795. He traveled through the Cumberland Gap on August 2 and noted that he had passed "Daviess Station on the west side of the Cumberland Mountain." He too did not tarry or leave further description. That same year the Rev. James Smith wrote of reaching the Davis cabin at the foot of Cumberland Mountain.

One who did spend the night was Moses Austin, father of the famed Texas patriot Stephen Austin. In December of 1796 he traveled the Wilderness Road on a trip from Virginia to investigate business possibilities in Louisiana. He left the following account of his stopover in the Yellow Creek Valley:

> After passing the Mountain which we did this Night we stopped at Mrs. Davis' who keeps a Tavern Down the mountain and met with very good accomodations....We took our leave of Mrs. Davis, who I must take the liberty to say may be Justly call Capn Molly of Cumberland mountain, for she Fully Commands this passage to the New World. She soon took the freedom to tell me she was a Come by chance her mother she knew little of and her Father less. as to herself she said pleasure was the onely thing she had in View; and that She had her Ideas of life and its injoyments.[4]

Austin traveled on to meet with former Kentucky Governor Isaac Shelby. One wonders if for Shelby he elaborated on the pleasures of staying over at the Davis Tavern.

Another visitor to the Davis establishment was Bishop Francis Asbury, the Methodist preacher who in 1784 had been elected the first bishop in America. For better than forty years he traveled by horseback throughout the frontier, ministering to his flock. He noted in his journal that on September 28, 1800, he stopped at the Davis establishment for breakfast. Though he made no comment on the tavern or its proprietors, he did stop there for another meal in October of 1805.

One of the many early travelers who stayed at the Davis Tavern but left no written records was Dillon Asher. His father, William Asher Jr., had

The Dillon Asher cabin as reconstructed at Red Bird Mission. Photo by author, 1997.

been one of the Long Hunters who accompanied Elisha Walden to Kentucky. William, who had served as a captain in the Colonial Army during the Revolutionary War, had moved from Virginia to North Carolina and then later to the Holston River Valley with Captain William Bean. William Asher and his wife, Peggy (also called Molly), are thought to have had eleven children. Dillon was born to them in 1777.

While a young man, Dillon accompanied his uncle on a trip to Boone's Fort by way of the Warriors' Path, a branch of which took them up Straight Creek, in what is now northern Bell County, to Red Bird Creek, where they paused to plant peach seeds before pushing on to the Kentucky River. They were attacked by Cherokees during this westward trip but managed to escape unharmed.

On their return journey they stopped at the Davis Tavern and spent the night. According to Asher family tradition, Dillon fell in love that night with one of Davis's daughters, Mary (who was also called Nancy), and soon returned to claim her as his bride. The newlyweds settled in the Yellow Creek Valley, where they lived for two years.

Meanwhile, the Kentucky legislature had, in 1797, approved funds to repair the Wilderness Road and to erect a tollgate at the Cumberland Ford.

Dillon was selected to man this tollgate. He and Mary built a lean-to house and cleared the nearby bottomland (site of the present town of Pineville) for farming. But they had lived at the ford less than a year when Dillon became involved in a dispute over a land title and decided to move.

He was enamored of the area some twenty miles north of the Cumberland Ford where the peach seeds he had sown years before had taken root and were already bearing fruit. Dillon proposed to his wife that they settle there. Mary, however, was reluctant to move to such an isolated place with no close neighbors. Finally she agreed, but only if Dillon would take her sister Sally (given name Sarah) as a second wife so that she would have a female companion and friend. At the time, polygamy was not against the law, and Dillon agreed. In about 1799 he built two log houses on Red Bird Creek, one for Mary and one for Sally. The family tradition is that "Dillon lived amicably between the two sisters and fathered a family by each of them."[5]

One of the sons of Sally and Dillon was Jackson Davis Asher, who married Margaret Hendrickson. They had twelve children, one of whom was Thomas Jefferson Asher, born in 1848. T.J. Asher early on entered the lumber business, eventually adding to his enterprises a railroad and coal interests. He founded one of the great fortunes in Bell County and earned a national reputation.

By the time of his death in 1815, Richard Davis had himself accumulated a considerable estate, which he left to his wife with the provision that she not dispose "of any of the land or Negroes, but she is to remain on the plantation...and exercise full power and control of same." Upon her death the estate was to be divided equally between his only son, Preston Davis, and one of his daughters, Susan Sims, and her husband. In 1821 the property was sold to Samuel Mark. It was later transferred to Isaac Dickinson and then to John C. Colson, who left it to his son, J.C. Colson Jr.[6] This property was identified by the American Association in 1888 as pivotal in the plan to construct a railroad tunnel through Cumberland Mountain (see Footnote Seven). Most of the original 200 acres that belonged to Richard Davis are now part of the Cumberland Gap National Historical Park.

FOOTNOTE FIVE

Early Settlers in the Yellow Creek Valley

John "Slicky" Turner was more than a hundred years old when he died in 1881. In his latter years he enjoyed reminiscing about the Yellow Creek Valley as he first saw it. He described canebrakes and marshlands teeming with wild game, laurel groves so thick as to be almost impenetrable, and little streams meandering throughout. He would tell of artesian springs that bubbled from the ground, and he remembered how one had to watch out for quicksand sinks and be careful when using the well worn animal trails, since a sudden stampede of buffalo down one of these paths was not unknown. He recounted seeing five hundred buffalo gathered at one time at the salt lick in the western part of the Valley. And he could still thrill his great-grandchildren with tales of the Indians who harassed early settlers.[1]

"Slicky" John probably did not arrive in the Valley until after 1800 and was certainly not the first to settle there, but his was one of the first families to establish a permanent home in the area. The Turners have played an important part in the history of the Valley ever since.

Although archeologists have found human artifacts dating back to 8000 B.C. in northern Bell County, they have found little evidence of any prehistoric or Indian habitations in the Yellow Creek Valley. Most of the Indian traditions seem to indicate that while the Warriors' Path was well traveled, there were no permanent settlements in the immediate area of what was to become Middlesborough.

The earliest white men to pass through the Valley left no documents. Gabriel Arthur described the Gap in 1674, but not the Valley. Martin

Chartier, a Frenchman who had helped LaSalle build the first sailing ship on the Great Lakes, is believed to have traveled through the Gap in 1692, and several other hunters and explorers traversed the area in the late 1600s and early 1700s but left few records, and none of the basin just north of the Gap. It was left to Dr. Thomas Walker to bequeath us the first written account of an overnight stay in the Yellow Creek Valley.

On April 13, 1750, his small party passed over what was to be called the Cumberland Gap and descended into the Valley. Walker wrote in his journal that on the northwest side of the Gap he "came to a Branch, that made a great deal of flat Land. We kept down it 2 miles, Several other Branches Coming in to make a large Creek, and we called it Flat Creek. We camped on the Bank where we found very good coal."[2]

Next to visit the Yellow Creek Valley were the "Long Hunters," those intrepid adventurers who spent months, even years in the western wilderness hunting game for their skins and fur, which were in such great demand in Europe. The decade of the 1760s saw many such parties enter the Valley through the Cumberland Gap, including, in 1769, that of Daniel Boone and John Finley. Their hunting trip lasted almost two years and imbued Boone with a passion for the land west of the Gap.

Boone's was one of the first attempts to actually settle the land that would be Kentucky. When he returned to his home in the Yadkin Valley of North Carolina, he told fantastic tales of the land over which he had hunted. Soon he had a number of families interested in moving to the rich wilderness. In September of 1773 he ventured out with some forty like-minded souls. Their effort stopped just short of the Cumberland Gap, however, when one of his sons and several other members of the party were slaughtered by hostile Indians. The pioneers realized that to attempt a settlement at that time was not wise, so they returned to the established outposts of the frontier.

Nevertheless, the stories and reports of the wilderness paradise that awaited on the other side of the mountains inflamed the imaginations of land speculators in the eastern colonies. Richard Henderson of North Carolina had the added advantage of being a lawyer and judge who had dealt extensively with the conflicting claims of the colonies, the English crown, and the Cherokee Nation. It was his opinion that the Cherokees had ownership by treaty to the land that would become Kentucky and that they had the right to sell that land to private individuals. Although his view was not shared by the colonial authorities or by the Crown, he was able to interest other investors in his idea. He formed the Transylvania Company to exploit his vision of a wilderness empire.

Henderson met with councils of the Cherokee Nation at Sycamore Shoals in March of 1775. He was able to purchase for his company all the land lying south of the Ohio River between the Cumberland and Kentucky Rivers, an area of some 20,000,000 acres. Of course, what he actually bought was the claim of the Cherokees to that land. Not only did other Indian nations claim the same territory but various land grants had already been awarded for some of the same area. In addition, the officials of both Virginia and North Carolina were vehemently opposed, declared his actions illegal, and called him a land pirate and worse.

For the gamble to pay off, the Transylvania Company had to encourage settlement, and to do that they needed a well marked road into the wilderness. Henderson contracted with Daniel Boone to blaze the route. Boone and his party of thirty woodsmen began at once. In general, their job was to clear out and mark the already established trails that the Indians had long trodden, and they moved along rapidly. In the Powell Valley they found that Joseph Martin was rebuilding the settlement from which he had been driven by the Indians in 1769. From Martin's Station (present location of Rose Hill, Virginia), the band could see the seemingly impenetrable wall of the Cumberland Mountains. Only twenty-five miles to the west, however, was the Cumberland Gap. The road at this point was so well traveled that they hardly needed to do more than clear a few fallen logs as they walked past.

Passing over the Gap, they descended into the flat valley described by Walker. The road probably passed behind where the Cumberland Gap National Historical Park Visitors Center is now located and crossed a small hill to level land at about what is now Middlesboro's 17th Street. It then followed the Creek until the waterway turned eastward toward its rendezvous with the Cumberland River. By this date it was called Yellow Creek, so named because of the color it took on as it flowed over the sulfa-laden deposits of soft coal. (Actually the path differed somewhat according to the season and rainfall, as the most direct and easiest way in dry weather was almost impassable when the streams were running full and the marshy land was saturated.) The road led north to the Narrows, that second gap in the mountains where the Cumberland River cuts its way through Pine Mountain to flow westward. The passage was very restricted at this point, with steep mountains rising on both sides and the river flowing swiftly through the gorge. The gorge being so narrow, the sun was late in penetrating the river mists and dispelling the shadows. This was to gain a reputation as one of the most dangerous parts of the Wilderness Road, as it was known to be frequented by Indians intent on ambushing would-be settlers; in fact, early travelers often referred to the Narrows as "Shades of Death."[3] It was then necessary to ford the Cumberland River, as passage was restricted on the southwest bank. Without the Narrows and the Cumberland Ford, the Cumberland Gap would have had little value, since it would then have led only to another almost impenetrable wall of mountains.

Boone and his men pressed on, leaving the main Indian trail at about the present day Flat Lick and hacking their way northwest toward the Bluegrass. Thus, when one is today traveling Highway 25E from Middlesboro to Pineville, he is generally not only following in the footsteps of Boone and all the westward-bound frontiersmen and settlers who followed the Wilderness Road, but is also taking the same path as did the many Indians who traveled the Warriors' Path long before the coming of the white man.[4]

Henderson set out only a few weeks behind Boone with a pack train carrying food and ammunition as well as seeds, farming implements, and other necessities for the settlement he envisioned. He stopped at Martin's Station in the Powell Valley. There he sold the first parcel of land for the Transylvania Company. On April 3, 1775, he recorded that Bryce Martin had purchased 500 acres of land on the first creek after crossing the Cumberland Gap going northward. (This was part of the Transylvania Company's "purchase" because the treaty had included all the land drained by the Cumberland River.)

Martin now had claim to a part of the Yellow Creek Valley, but he did not settle there immediately. The danger from the Indians was too great. When Henderson's company was crossing the Cumberland Gap, they met a party of some forty frontiersmen who were fleeing Kentucky because of escalating attacks from the Indians. The next few years were extraordinarily dangerous ones, as the English, fighting the rebellious colonists in the east, encouraged their Indian allies to attack any white settlers who had ventured to the western borders. In fact, it was even learned that some British were paying for the scalps of white settlers.

It was 1779 before the Indian threat had abated sufficiently that settlement could reasonably be attempted. For the thousands of settlers who poured through the Gap in the 1780s and early 1790s, the road from the Gap to the Cumberland Ford was considered particularly dangerous. In 1783 James Smith wrote of the Gap in his journal, "This is a very noted place on account of the great number of people who have here unfortunately fallen a prey to savage cruelty or barbarity. The mountain in the gap is neither very steep nor high, but the almost inaccessible cliffs on either side the road render it a place peculiar for doing mischief."[5] A traveler passing through what was to be Bell County noted in his diary in 1784 that he found the bones of two adults and a child at the Gap and a number of human bones in the Valley, the bodies having been devoured by animals, probably wolves. Just north of the saddle of the Gap is a huge boulder that to this day is called Indian Rock, since it supposedly served a number of times as a hiding place for Indians bent on ambushing travelers.

The path along Yellow Creek also had a dangerous reputation. Tall canes, some almost as thick as a man's thigh, crowded next to the trail, so that lurking Indians could easily hide almost upon it without detection by forward scouts. It was necessary to ford the creek at least twice, which was always a time of vulnerability. Bogs and marshy areas also slowed a party, increasing the chances of attack and decreasing those of escape. Early travelers, therefore, did not tarry in the Valley of Yellow Creek but pushed on through the Narrows to the Cumberland Ford.

All told, it has been estimated that well over 200,000 people migrated through the Gap and down the Wilderness Road by the turn of the century, including many who would be important in Kentucky history. Abraham Lincoln's father walked through the Gap when he was eight years old; Nancy Hanks was a babe in arms when she was carried through a few years later. But few who passed through the Gap chose to settle in the Yellow Creek Valley, their eyes being fixed on the promised wonders of the Bluegrass. Those who did soon had reason to regret their decision.

From the time of independence, the newly formed nation, soon to be called the United States, had been plagued by problems with the Indians on the frontier, as well as with foreign powers, particularly Spain, which still had colonies and claims in the New World. Land speculators and intrepid settlers pushing ever westward further aggravated the situation. The administration of President George Washington tried to deal with these problems by entering into a series of treaties with the Indians. Although these treaties were honored mostly in the breach, one did have an unfortunate effect on the settlers in the Yellow Creek Valley.

In 1786 the United States Congress appointed a commission to treat with the Cherokees and other southern tribes. The idea was to draw enforceable boundary lines between the settlements and the lands confirmed to the Indians, thus removing the cause of Indian raids on the settlers. On July 2, 1791, representatives of "the Territory of the United States south of the river Ohio" entered into a treaty with forty-one chiefs of the Cherokee Nation, the Treaty of Holston, which drew a boundary line through what was to be Tennessee, with a small spearhead into what would be southeastern Kentucky, giving the U.S. claim to lands east and north of the line and ceding to the Indians exclusive rights to that south and west of the boundary. As affected the Yellow Creek Valley, Article 4 of the treaty stated that the boundary was to be drawn from "the top of the Cumberland Mountain; thence a direct line to the Cumberland River where the Kentucky Road crosses it; thence down the Cumberland River." The boundary was thus drawn due north from the Cumberland Gap to the ford on the Cumberland River at what is now Pineville, then west along the River, placing almost all of what is now Middlesboro in the Indian lands. Settlers occupying Indian lands were to be denied the protection of the United States. Certain misunderstandings were later dealt with in amended treaties (each of which also upped the amount of annuity that would be paid the Cherokees by the United States in consideration of their cession of territory). One of these, signed in 1798, guaranteed that the Kentucky (Wilderness) Road between Cumberland Mountain and the Cumberland River "should be open and free."

The boundary was surveyed during 1797 and 1798, and once the survey was completed, federal troops were dispatched to remove any settlers who were on the wrong side of the line. This included most of those who had chosen to make the Yellow Creek Valley their home. There were to be no exceptions, and if the settlers could not be persuaded to leave peacefully, then the troops forcibly removed them and, in some cases, destroyed their cabins and farms. The Yellow Creek settlers complained that a mistake had been made, that the top of Cumberland Mountain was not near the Gap but should be located further west, exempting the Valley. But federal officials were not to be swayed.

The troops had a large territory to cover, so it was not surprising that after they had moved on to clear out another part of the Indian territory, some of the original Yellow Creek settlers who had been forcibly removed from their farms during 1799 and 1800 returned to their Valley, and that other settlers took over the cabins of those who did not choose to return. In 1803 one of the settlers, William Robinson, wrote to the Cherokee Indian agent that "the residents of Yellow Creek who consider themselves entirely out of the Indian boundaries...are a poor distressed people at best. They are in a continual state of alarm and terror owing to the demonstration made by the Indians and soldiers wherever they have already been, and I fear if their property is destroyed the consequence may be bad as desperation and distress drives men to desperate essence. The poor people of Yellow Creek however rely much upon your humanity and goodness of heart, and hope you will condescend to allay their fears by letting them know the truth, whether the military have orders to destroy and burn their property or not."[6]

The agent of Indian Affairs, Col. Return J. Meigs, had to inform the Yellow Creek citizens that the Secretary of War had ordered that they be ejected from the Indian lands but had agreed that "Those persons who originally settled on Yellow Creek within the Indian boundary will probably receive some allowance for their improvements, or misfortunes, provided, they immediately remove from the Indian lands." Col. Meigs went on to state that this consideration was being given because there had been some confusion about the exact location of the boundary line and that this offer was not being made to settlers in other areas. In one of his many reports, he made the interesting observation that some of the Yellow Creek settlers were not really farmers, but that "the principal object of many of them was to keep poor houses of entertainment, of which there is no need there, for if those on the lands all go off there will be only six miles between two good houses of entertainment."

At least ten families accepted the government's offer and voluntarily moved out of the Valley. In the spring of 1804, one of these wrote Mr. Meigs, "Those who have moved off the Indian boundary hope that the obstinacy of those who remain here will not affect the just compensation offered in this case," thus indicating that at least some of the Yellow Creek settlers elected to stay on their farms in defiance of the government troops. "Slicky" Turner was probably one of the latter.

"Slicky" was born in Ireland in about 1777 and immigrated to America as a boy, landing in Newport News, Virginia. He later moved to Chadwell Station, a settlement on the frontier in southwestern Virginia that had been established by his brother-in-law David Chadwell. He married Bettie (also called Betsy) Marsee and, sometime around 1800, moved to the Yellow Creek Valley.

He did not move alone. With his party were his two brothers, Berry and Joe, and several members of the Marsee and Rains families. Henry Rains was the patriarch of the Rains (sometimes spelled Raines) family. The Marsee family was headed by Thomas and Joseph (originally the last name was often recorded as Massey). It is very likely that they were related to "Slicky's" wife, but the exact connection has been lost. These three surnames are still among the most common in the Valley.

In order to protect themselves from the Indians, they built a blockhouse in the area near what is now the Fern Lake dam, which may have put them just outside of the Indian territory. The Wilderness Road would have passed very close to their small fortress.

These first families had garden plots and planted corn, but they also depended on hunting. Game was still plentiful, but they had rivals in the

Indians who lived in what is now Tennessee, who would come over Baptist Gap (which is west of the Cumberland Gap) into the Yellow Creek Valley, as they had done for generations, in order to hunt. Although the Wilderness Road had been largely made secure from hostile Indians, that was not true of the Valley, where a lone hunter could still be in danger.

The Turner family has long told the story of one of its members—some say it was William and others say it was Joe—who had the misfortune to be out hunting alone when he ran into a band of seven Indians, who killed and scalped him. The body was soon found, and the white settlers planned their revenge. They hid near the trail the Indians would take to return over Baptist Gap after their hunting trip. The ambush was successful and all seven Indians met their death.

Another family legend is of "Fiddler John" Turner who "killed nine Indians before breakfast." Soon thereafter a band of twelve braves, bent on vengeance, came upon the Parker cabin and dragged off the only person they could find, an old man by the name of Henry Parker. He suddenly began to bleed profusely from his nose, which somehow alarmed his captors, who released him and resumed their pursuit of "Fiddler John," whom they were never able to capture.[7] Parker survived to be remembered as the patriarch of another of the long-time families in the Valley.

By 1810 the Valley was considered safe enough that the blockhouse was abandoned and the settlers moved out to establish small farms. The third Treaty of Tellico, signed five years earlier, had ceded to the U.S. about a third of the land that had previously lain within Indian boundaries, including all of that in the Yellow Creek Valley, so they no longer needed to worry about being run off their land by the federal troops. The Turners moved mostly to the western end of the Valley, as did some of the Marsees and the Rains, since that area was less marshy. By this time they had been joined by other families, those of Thomas Beard, Samuel Lane, the Greens, and the Jones family.

Cabins went up and land was cleared for cultivation. Hunting became less important as the big game gave way to human population. Instead, the settlers' hogs and cows roamed the woods, foraging where they could. The Yellow Creek Valley was becoming a farming community. William "Billy" Raines taught at the first school in the Valley, a rough log structure on the Stony Fork branch in the far western portion of the Valley. John Turner gave land for a church, and Old Yellow Creek Baptist church was built in 1842 with Thomas Marsee as the first minister. Soon thereafter a Methodist church and school were established in the eastern part of the Valley.

The Wilderness Road before development; date of photo unknown. Courtesy of the Bell County Historical Society.

Meanwhile, the nature of the Wilderness Road was also changing. No longer simply a way for settlers and supplies to reach the Bluegrass, it had also become a conduit for farm products headed for the eastern markets. By 1825 the eastbound traffic was equal to that going west. Cattle, horses, mules, hogs, and sheep were driven down the Road and through the Gap on their way to markets in Maryland, Virginia, and the Carolinas. At times when the Powell River was at what the settlers called "high tide," produce was taken through the Gap and floated down the river to Chattanooga. Some fairly exotic stock passed both ways through the Valley. The famous statesman Henry Clay used this route to import blooded Herefords and Merino sheep from England as well as jacks from Spain to improve his own breeds. Numerous noted stallions were brought through the Gap to breed with Bluegrass thoroughbreds, then their offspring were taken back through—one of the more noted exports of early Kentucky. Representatives of foreign countries traveled the Road to buy blooded Kentucky stock. Some of the Yellow Creek settlers undoubtedly profited from trade with the trail drivers. Certainly, the Yellow Creek Valley was less isolated than most of the other hollows and coves of the Appalachians during the first decades of the nineteenth century.

The Overland Mail stage en route from Yellow Creek Valley to the village of Cumberland Gap, Tennessee, ca. 1880. Courtesy of Cumberland Gap National Historical Park.

The old Wilderness Road or, as it was then called, the State Road or Wilderness Turnpike, rapidly deteriorated under the strain of the commerce it was bearing. The dirt path was pocked with deep ruts and chuckholes that became mud sinks in rainy weather. Log bridges over the bogs crumbled under the incessant traffic of hundreds of livestock hoofs. If the riches of the booming Kentucky Bluegrass were to reach eastern markets, something had to be done.

In 1835 the Kentucky legislature established a Bureau of Internal Improvements charged with improving Kentucky's commercial network of roads and waterways. Various plans were discussed, including an ambitious network of waterways that would include a canal in the bed of Yellow Creek with a tunnel and canal through Cumberland Mountain in the area of the Gap. A more practical proposal was a railroad from Cincinnati to Lexington extending to the Cumberland Gap and southward to Knoxville. A company was formed and a charter secured to pursue this project. The future looked bright for the Yellow Creek Valley. Alas, as would happen almost fifty years later, financial panic engulfed the country, and these ambitious schemes fell victim. The Wilderness Road was soon overshadowed by commerce on the Ohio River and the railroad lines in central and western Kentucky.

The Valley of Yellow Creek would slumber for the next twenty-five years. A few more families—the Bledsoes, Morrisons, Tacketts, and Colsons—would settle on patches of land, but the Wilderness Road had lost much of its importance, and few outsiders would venture into the Valley until the Civil War again propelled the Gap to prominence.

FOOTNOTE SIX

Arthur Campbell

In 1889 workmen constructing streets for the new town of Middlesborough through what appeared to be open farmland unearthed large slabs of iron with something written on them. Like a huge jigsaw puzzle, they put together the dozen or so pieces and were able to decipher the message. It read:

> Sacred to the memory of Arthur Campbell who was born in Augusta County, Va., on Thursday, November 3rd, Old style, 1743, and a wellspent life, as his last moments did and well could approve, of sixty-seven years, eight months and twenty-six days, ere a constitution preserved by rigid temperance and otherwise moral and healthy, could but with reluctance consent, the lamp was blown out by the devouring effects of a cancer on the 8th day of August, 1811, A.D., leaving a widow, six sons and six daughters to mourn his loss and emulate his virtues.
>
> Here lies entombed a Revolutionary sage,
> An ardent patriot of the age,
> In erudition great, and useful knowledge to scan
> In philanthropy hospitable, the friend of man,
> As a soldier brave, virtue his morality;
> As a commander prudent, his religion charity
> He practiced temperance to preserve his health,
> He used industry to acquire wealth,
> He studied physic to avoid disease
> He studied address likewise to please.

For his greatest study was to study man.
His stature tall, his person portly
His features handsome, his manner courtly,
Sleep honored Sire in realms of rest,
In doing justice to thy memory a son is blest,
A son inheriting in full thy name,
One who aspires to all thy fame.
COLONEL ARTHUR CAMPBELL

Who was this man, so eulogized, who chose what was then an obscure valley in the wilderness as his final resting place?

Arthur Campbell was the son of David Campbell, whose family had come from near Argyll in Scotland. The Virginia of his youth was still frontier that had to be protected from Indian raids. At the age of fifteen young Arthur joined the militia and was stationed at Dickerson's Fort, an outpost on the Cowpasture River. As luck would have it, he was outside the fort with a group of his fellow Rangers, gathering wild plums, when they were suddenly surprised by a raiding party of Wyandotte Indians. He was caught up in a plum tree and could not escape; slightly wounded, he was captured by the Indians. He remained their captive from 1758 through 1762.

Certainly captivity was not a fate to be desired, but Campbell made the most of the experience. As the tribe traveled throughout what is now Indiana, Illinois, Ohio, and Michigan, he studied the lay of the land and the nature of his captors. He learned much of the woodsmanship of the Indians, undoubtedly planning for his eventual escape.

Accounts of Indian captivity during that period run the gamut from unspeakable torture to true kindness. Campbell's experience was more in the latter spectrum after an old chief took an interest in the young man. James Smith, who was captured at about the same time,[1] later gave this account:

> Wyndot Indian warriors had divided into different parties, and all struck at different places in Augusta (Va.) County. They brought in with them a considerable number of scalps, prisoners, horses and other plunder. One of the parties brought in with them one Arthur Campbell....As the Wyandots at Sunyendeand and those at Detroit were connected, Mr. Campbell was taken to Detroit, but he remained some time in the town of Sunyendeand. His company was very agreeable and I was sorry when he left me. During his stay at Sunyendeand he borrowed my

> Bible and made some very pertinent remarks on what he had read. One passage was where it is said, "it is good for a man that he bear the yoke in his youth." He said that we ought to be resigned to the will of Providence, as we are now bearing the yoke in our youth. Mr. Campbell then appeared to be about sixteen or seventeen years of age.

His yoke did prove very valuable. In addition to gaining knowledge of the western lands and of Indian ways, neither well understood by most colonists of his day, he was also started on the way to a liberal education, which he might otherwise have missed. The French Jesuits had a mission at Detroit, and the fathers took an interest in the young captive, giving him instruction in liberal arts and inspiring a love of knowledge and learning that would serve him the rest of his days.

After almost four years of living with the Indians, Campbell made his escape. Alone, aided only by his own wits and courage, he traversed two hundred miles of wilderness. Toward the end of his return trip, he met a detachment of British soldiers from western Pennsylvania who had received news of an impending Indian raid. Campbell was able to give them valuable information and serve as a guide before resuming his journey home. For this service the Virginia governor later rewarded him with a large grant of land in what was to become Kentucky.

What a joyful homecoming it was when Campbell greeted his family, who had long given him up for dead. He was quite different, however, from the carefree red-haired youth they remembered. Now taciturn and given to long silences, he must almost have seemed to have been replaced by an Indian. Even as years went by, he remained a difficult person for many, including those who professed love and admiration, and was often described as irascible, overbearing, and fractious.

The spark lit by the Jesuit priests led Campbell to enroll in Liberty Hall Academy (later to become Washington and Lee University) in Lexington, Virginia, where he gained an education superior to that of most men of his day.

In 1766 he left the established settlements and moved over the Blue Ridge to the middle fork of the Holston River (near present day Marion, Virginia). The plantation he developed, which he called Royal Oak, was on the frontier, at the outskirts of civilization, and still subject to Indian attack. Within two years his father and other members of the family joined him, perhaps providing some safety in numbers. Arthur married his second cousin, Margaret Campbell, and they eventually had twelve children. Soon he had quite a large establishment. Campbell tried to maintain good

relations with the Indians, but it became more and more difficult as the pioneers kept moving further into Indian lands. Raids in 1774 by Mingo Indians from the north resulted in a number of deaths along the Holston.

It was early 1775 when Colonel Richard Henderson met with the Cherokees at Sycamore Shoals and secured from them a claim on all the land south of the Ohio River between the Cumberland and Kentucky Rivers, along with land for a road from the settlements in Virginia to the newly purchased territory. That same year Daniel Boone and his men began cutting a trail for the pioneers who would be making their way to Henderson's lands. Soon Royal Oak would no longer be the last outpost but a stopover on the road west.

Campbell was interested in civic affairs and became embroiled in the ongoing disputes between the colonists and the colonial authorities. In 1775 he served on the committee that drafted a letter, called "The Address of Freeholders of Fincastle," that protested in strong, inflammatory terms restrictions placed on the colonists by these authorities. He was then chosen to represent Fincastle County in the Fifth Virginia Convention of 1776. This was the body that recommended the dissolution of the relationship between Virginia and the British Crown, which led directly to the Declaration of Independence.

Campbell was also a member of the first House of Delegates under the new Virginia Constitution of 1776 and served as a commissioner to review land claims of the promoters of the Transylvania Company. It was he who suggested to the then-governor of Virginia, Patrick Henry, that one of the new counties being formed out of Fincastle County be named for the recently chosen commander-in-chief of the colonial army, making it the first to so honor George Washington. In January of 1777, Campbell was named commander-in-chief of the militia of Washington County. He also served as presiding judge of the county court for many years.

With the Revolutionary War came further threats from both the English and their Indian allies. In 1780 Campbell led 150 militia to quell an uprising of Tories in North Carolina. He then joined with John Sevier to attack the Indians in their home villages. On this expedition fourteen Indian towns were razed, 50,000 bushels of corn were destroyed, and the Indians were temporarily pacified. Arthur also helped his cousin William Campbell plan the strategy and raise the troops for the Battle of King's Mountain, which is considered to be one of the turning points of the Revolutionary War. In 1781 he was appointed, along with others, to negotiate treaties with the Cherokee and Chickasaw Indians.

With the war over, Campbell devoted himself to improving his plantation. He increased his land holdings and, after the death of his cousin William Campbell, took over management of the latter's extensive saltworks at Saltville, Virginia. He continued his interest in civic affairs, corresponding frequently with the leaders of the fledgling country—George Washington, Thomas Jefferson, James Madison, John Marshall, Isaac Shelby, and others, many of whom were personal friends. Campbell served as a general clearinghouse for information about the Indians and about events in the western settlements. His penchant for conversation earned him the nickname "Long Jaw." He also entertained lavishly, even hosting the Duke of Orleans, who was later to become King Philip of France. And he watched as growing streams of pioneers passed his home on their way to the promised land of Kentucky.

That Kentucky became a state in 1792 was due in large part to Campbell's efforts. He served in the Virginia General Assembly during much of the 1780s and while there he was a leading advocate of independence and statehood for Kentucky.

In 1796 Campbell had his lands in Kentucky surveyed, including 600 acres on Flat Creek (now called Yellow Creek), two miles northwest of the Cumberland Gap, which would incorporate a good portion of present-day Middlesboro. Although he had entered his claim under Virginia law in 1780, he did the same under Kentucky law as soon as his survey was completed.

Campbell joined the tail end of the massive stream that had traveled the Wilderness Trail; in 1805 he moved to his land on Yellow Creek. Was it in order to protect his claims during a time when many of the old land grants were being challenged?[2] Or was it a long-suppressed desire to once again follow the road of adventure? Perhaps Virginia had become too settled a land. At any rate, he built a home on a small prominence from which he had a sweeping view of the wide, lush basin, with its winding streams and canebrakes and its high mountains rising like protective sentinels around this special valley.

He spent his last years writing many long letters to friends, relatives, and political leaders. He wrote most often to his nephew, David Campbell, who was to become governor of Virginia, but he neglected few of the new country's political leaders, most of whom he had known over the years. He had an opinion on most of the issues of the day, and everyone would know what it was. His temperament had not improved over the years; he continued to be a difficult, irascible man, but one who could not be ignored.

He also became passionately interested in writing a history of the Battle of King's Mountain and began amassing letters, reports, and other data related to that important battle. Campbell was particularly anxious that his cousin, William Campbell, be given credit for his pivotal role. The data he collected were to become the basis of Dr. Lyman Draper's acclaimed work *King's Mountain and Its Heroes.*

Campbell died of cancer in 1811, only five years after making his home in the Valley. He left an impressive estate. His will listed more than 12,500 acres of land and mentioned property that he had already conveyed to his children. His land in the Yellow Creek Valley he divided between two daughters, Mary Baird and Ann Augustee Campbell. Other possessions, including his slaves, were also divided among his children. In his will he directed that he be buried "in my garden....westwardly of Cumberland Gap, and that a handsome but not costly tombstone may tell where I lie."

Soon thereafter, his wife, Margaret, and his daughter Mary were laid to rest beside him. The graveyard, however, was neglected. Two of his sons were killed during the War of 1812. Several of his children moved to Louisville and were buried there. No one was left in the Valley to tend the graves, and they were gradually forgotten, covered over by vegetation. When the workmen uncovered the burial site, they found only the marker for Campbell but no gravestones for his wife or daughter. The broken iron slab was moved to a small building that was serving the city as a museum. The pieces were lost during the Great Fire in 1890.

In June of 1890, the local newspaper reported that a letter had been received from W.W. Anderson of Midway, Kentucky, a great-grandson of Arthur Campbell, who confirmed that his ancestor had indeed been buried in the Yellow Creek Valley. Campbell County, Tennessee, was later named in his honor.

There is some indication that Campbell's Tennessee relatives may later on have had the body moved,[3] but it is popularly believed, and so recognized by the Kentucky Historical Commission, that the body of Arthur Campbell still lies in the long-lost cemetery on the eastern side of 24th Street, between Dorchester and Gloucester Streets. A historical marker has been erected in the general vicinity.

Former occupants of the house on the northeastern corner, which was supposedly built over his grave, claim that Campbell can be heard some nights, still as irascible as ever. More rational minds may say it is only the sounds of the old coal furnace and hot water pipes, but those who have actually lived there say they always knew when "Old Arthur" was "at it again."

Footnote Seven

The Patriarch of the Valley

John Calvin Colson Sr. was widely known as the Patriarch of the Yellow Creek Valley. He was a man of many talents—preacher, teacher, doctor, merchant, miller, farmer, shoemaker, lawyer, judge, colonel in the local militia, and the leader of the people of the Valley in all things.

His father, James Madison Coulston, came to Kentucky in about 1802. (The spelling of the name changed around 1830.) The family tradition is that James was born in North Carolina, though others in the family identify Fauquier County, Virginia, as his birthplace. He first moved to Lee County, Virginia, before finally settling in Kentucky. The date of his birth was between 1770 and 1775.

James pushed west with an older brother, John Coulston. They settled on the banks of Clear Fork, a tributary of Yellow Creek that is northeast of the Valley itself (the area now called Colmar). John had brought with him one black slave and a horse. According to the tax records, James and John were the only adult male Coulstons in the area from 1802 through 1822. Both men served in the 54th Knox County Regiment during the War of 1812.

John was first taxed for land in 1814, when he was listed as having 100 acres on Yellow Creek. On the same tax records it was noted that he had already sold the four slaves he had previously owned. In 1816 he was taxed for a billiard table, an indication that he was operating a tavern or way station. John, with his wife Elizabeth and their children, moved back to Lee County in 1822 and eleven years later sold his land on Clear Fork to William Tinsley Jr.

James stayed in Kentucky. His first wife died prior to 1814. They had four children, the eldest of whom had been born in 1802, very close to the

John Calvin Colson Sr. Courtesy of the Bell County Historical Society.

time they moved to Kentucky. James later married Amelia Tinsley, the daughter of William and Mary (Molly) Tinsley. They moved from Clear Fork to Cannon Creek, a short distance to the northwest, onto land he later purchased from his father-in-law. There is some evidence that he too conducted a way station for the stagecoach, his property being adjacent to the old Wilderness Road. He and Amelia had seven sons and four daughters. In 1845 James and Amelia died of yellow fever within eight hours of each other. They were buried in the same grave on the banks of Cannon Creek.[1]

John Calvin Colson, their third child, was born on October 22, 1822. Little is known of his early life. How did he become such an accomplished man? There is no indication that schools were available to him as a youth. Did he learn from travelers who passed on the Wilderness Road and stopped at their home? Did he teach himself the many skills he was later known to possess? He must have been an extraordinary young man.

On Christmas Day 1843 John married Mary Catherine Smith of Lee County, Virginia. She was the granddaughter of John Ball, a Revolutionary War soldier who could trace his lineage back to colonial days and was distantly related to George Washington. She had been born in 1820, the daughter of Mary and Redden Taylor Smith of Lee County.

The couple began life together in a log cabin on Cannon Creek, probably on land owned by his father. They started, according to local legend, with nothing. Farming was little more than subsistence living, and John wanted better for his family. He began by selling whiskey. First he bought a jug and was able to resell it by the drink at a good profit. From the proceeds of that sale he bought a barrel of the same for resale. With that income he stocked a corner of his small home with thread, needles, coffee, and a few other staples that locals could not provide for themselves. Thus he began his career as a merchant. Gradually he increased his business, trading with the many teamsters who herded their stock down the old trail through the Gap and then returned home via the same route.

When they had accumulated sufficient capital, John and Mary Katherine moved to a two-story brick home on a small hill in the Yellow Creek Valley. The house had been built by slave labor in about 1800, the bricks being made from local clay, and was located directly beside the Wilderness Road. They purchased the house from Clark Hunter during the late 1850s.[2]

This was a good location for John's stock of staple goods. Soon he could afford to build a small store across the road from his home. He then enlarged his business operations by building a horse-powered mill behind his house. His house was also a recognized stage stop on the old road. Some

Catherine Smith Colson. Courtesy of the Bell County Historical Society.

have referred to him as operating a tavern there, but it is more likely that he simply provided bed and board for travelers who happened by.

Across the hill, less than a mile from his home (in the vicinity of the present-day city park, Ford's Woods) was the Green Meeting House, also known as Bethlehem Methodist Church. Used as both a church and a school, the building was constructed of logs with a puncheon floor and a large fireplace. There was but a single window, and the seats were split chestnut logs. John Colson became the first regular preacher at the church, which was built about 1845. He was also the first teacher at the school, and later several of his children also taught there.

While Colson labored in his isolated valley in the mountains, elsewhere momentous events were occurring that culminated in the secession of the southern states from the union and the plunge into civil war. Kentucky declared its neutrality but was soon invaded from North and South. Colson was, among all other things, the head of the Home Guard and strongly Union in sentiment. No mind that he had only a few mountaineers armed with hog rifles and shotguns. He marched his guards out to defend their valley from the Southern invasion. They were quickly overcome in one of the first Civil War skirmishes to be fought on the soil of Kentucky. Colonel Colson was taken into custody and imprisoned briefly.

Possession of the Gap changed sides several times during the course of the war, but Colson was able to avoid further overt conflicts and to continue to minister to the people of the Valley, who were plundered by foraging parties of both sides. According to family tradition, when the war was over Mary Catherine painted a huge American flag on a bed sheet and had it hung off the Pinnacle in tribute to the Union victory.

The end of the War did not bring complete peace to the Valley, but it did bring prosperity to the Colsons. Their store was well patronized and their mill busy. There were only two other stores in the entire area. John Myers had a very small place on Bennetts Fork, better than five miles to the west, where he sold mostly coffee, sugar, and calico. At the saddle of the Gap, Samuel C. Jones had an establishment that made a specialty of buying homemade products—beeswax, bacon, hams—which he had transported north to be traded for the merchandise carried at his store. He also sold liquor and hosted card games. Both Jones and Colson profited by trade with the teamsters who still used the old Wilderness Road to drive stock to eastern markets. Colson's store was also, from 1871 on, the post office for the entire Valley. His son John Calvin Jr. was the first postmaster.

His gristmill was the only one in the area. It was located under a large shed and had two sweep poles, one powered by a yoke of oxen and the other by a team of horses. One of Colson's tenants would stand nearby with a whip to keep the animals encouraged. Because of the difficulty of travel in the Valley, it was not uncommon for families to camp overnight near the Colson establishment while they did their trading and had their grain ground.

Colson also gained a reputation for being able to diagnose and cure diseases and was often called on to serve as a doctor to the population, which had no physician. He was by this time (1870) in his late forties, a tall, thin man with piercing black eyes and black hair. Some insight into this amazing man may be gained from the reminiscences of Wilburn Robbins:

> While on his way to preach at the head of Cane Run in 1880, he stopped at our house and treated my father and brother John, who were ill with typhoid fever. Some time thereafter my father sent me to

> his store to pay for his services. "How much do we owe you?" I asked. "Oh, two dollars and a half will be all right, I guess," he said half apologetically, and then, thinking he had perhaps charged too much, gave me a fine Bible with my change.[3]

Colson was considered so fair minded that the local citizenry often took their disagreements to him for arbitration rather than travel to the distant courthouse. Marriage records for the area at this time show the Rev. Colson was also officiating at many of the weddings in the Valley.

In addition to all of his other enterprises, Colson was accumulating land in the Valley, and was soon one of its biggest landowners.

John Calvin Colson Sr. died on August 30, 1882, soon after being elected county judge. He was almost sixty and had been the acknowledged leader, "the Patriarch," of the Yellow Creek Valley for almost half of those years. Mary Catherine continued on until August 13, 1914, when she died at the age of ninety-five.

Colson had come to the end of his days just as momentous changes were about to occur as a result of Alexander Arthur's vision for the Valley. His family, as the largest landholders in what was to become Middlesborough, was pivotal to that enterprise. John and Mary Catherine had five daughters and eight sons. Sadly, two of their sons died in infancy and the remaining six sons were all involved in some tragic violence and/or suffered a premature death.

Their oldest son, James Madison, was born on December 2, 1844. He was the first Circuit Court clerk of Josh Bell County, which was carved out of Knox and Harlan Counties in 1867. While performing his duties, he became involved in a dispute with James Lee, the County Court clerk. During the heated argument, the two men drew their pistols and fired at the same time. Both bullets met their mark and both men died as a result. It was 1870, and James was not quite twenty-six years old.

Their next surviving child was Redden Taylor, born on June 6, 1847. He was somewhat of a "wildhair" as a young man and, though he became a civil engineer, did not mellow with age. Or perhaps he was continuing his father's tradition of trying to keep order in the Valley. At any rate, about 1879 he became involved in an unfortunate affair when the store of Samuel Jones was robbed of a barrel of whiskey.

Jones related the event to Redden, who undertook to solve the crime. Red and his friend Alfred McTee found the missing barrel, which the thieves had rolled out of the store and hidden. They staked it out until the miscreants, brothers Bob and Joe Pearce, came back to claim their loot. Surprised, the Pearces nonetheless managed to escape into the woods. A few days later, however, one of the brothers was shot and killed while standing at the front door of his house with his mother. The same fate met the other as he ran out the back door. It was said that Colson and McTee had "done the deed." Bell County Circuit Court records for May of 1880 record the indictment of Rt. Colson, Alfred McTee, and John Thectin for murder. Red fled the county, spending most of his remaining years in Texas. When the will of John Sr. was probated in 1882, there was a separate provision made for Red's wife Thelma (Marthene nee Moss) and his children, but no mention of Redden ("who is now in the state of Texas") except that he was to receive $100. Red returned to Middlesborough only a few months before his death from asthma in 1896.

Red had two children. Houston was a physician who practiced in Middlesborough during the "boom" and was also postmaster for a short time. After three years of practice in the city, he was stricken with consumption and moved to Texas, where he died in 1900. Red's daughter married J.T. Neal of Pineville.

The Colsons' first daughter, Margaret Amelia, was born on August 11, 1853. She was twice married (to Mac Howard and to Jacob Slusher) and had two daughters and a son, Dr. John Howard. She lived most of her life in Pineville.

John Calvin Jr. was born on September 25, 1854. At the age of eighteen he married Susan Cottrell, and they moved to a farm at the base of the Gap. When the British arrived, John Jr. owned the pivotal property, located where the railroad tunnel would have to come through. In addition, he and his siblings controlled a good part of the best land in the Valley. Early American Association memoranda indicate that the developers considered it most important that John Jr. be a part of their plan. As one noted, "A hostile interest controlling either of these properties [referring to that owned by him and also those owned by others in his family] would seriously affect, and might greatly impair, if not destroy, the value of the whole enterprise."[4]

J. C. not only sold part of his own land to the American Association but also worked with them in acquiring other real estate. He was in a good position to do so since he not only knew the Valley and its people well but had qualified as a lawyer in 1878. In some cases he bought property at sheriff's sales; in others he obtained options from neighbors. These he later sold to the British company for a profit.[5]

As the new town of Middlesborough developed, J.C. followed in his father's footsteps and became a merchant. He built other properties to lease,

John Calvin Colson Jr. Courtesy of
the Bell County Historical Society.

including the Colson Saloon. He was also a politician and was soon on the City Council, serving with his brother David, who was the mayor. He was sheriff of Bell County in the mid-1890s and was running for county judge on the Republican ticket (a sure thing given the political sentiment of the county) at the time of his death. He had weathered the worst years of the "bust," and things were just looking up when tragedy struck.

On June 1, 1897, at about 5:00 p.m., pistol shots were heard on Cumberland Avenue between 19th and 20th. The paper described the scene: "Colson emerged from the darkness in the alley alongside the east wall of the Colson block, bleeding profusely, and ascended the stairs of the Cumberland Avenue entrance. At the top of the stairs he died from loss of blood caused by the pistol shot....the shot entered his breast near the neck and severed an artery." It was agreed by most that John Dougan (also spelled Dugan) had fired the fatal bullet. He was also said to have fired at William Miller but missed him. His motive was reported to have been a business dispute, though it was also later suggested that J.C. had been trying to break up a fight. It was even surmised by some that the fight had been a "setup" in order to lure him out for an ambush.

The Colson Saloon, ca. 1895. Courtesy of H.D. Sowders.

Dougan was considered to be a quiet man except when drunk. That day in June he was very drunk, and angry over a business deal that had gone sour. Miller had rented a saloon and fixtures in the Colson Block from J.C., but Dougan claimed that Miller had already contracted to buy his saloon and fixtures on the opposite side of Cumberland Avenue. Dougan was spoiling for a fight, and Colson had already had to disarm him earlier that afternoon.

Dougan went home, secured another pistol and, singing "Boys, your time has come," returned to face Colson, who was about to get on his horse when the shot was fired. No one saw the actual shooting, and Dougan always afterward proclaimed his innocence. He was convicted of manslaughter and sentenced to twenty-one years in prison. The local newspaper opined that the verdict was "the result of a compromise of personal or political feelings." In May of 1900 Dougan was pardoned by the governor.

That there may have been more to the Colson death than originally reported was the fact, brought out at trial, that Dougan had been "talking against" Colson for some months prior to the shooting. The *Weekly Herald* in reporting the trial, which was being held in Barbourville, stated that it "took no stock in the sensational stories" that the "White faction" was sustaining Dougan while "the Colsons have Winchesters for the purpose of intimidation."

In perhaps a strange coincidence, the other man involved in the dispute, W.M. Miller, met his own death soon afterward. He was said to have been intoxicated at the time and was attempting to gain admission to a traveling tent show without paying. There was an altercation, and one of those associated with the troupe shot Miller. Will Horr of Middlesborough, who had only joined the show a few days before, helped the killer flee safely into the mountains. The *Middlesborough News* stated:

> The fact that Miller was the main witness in the Dugan case for the killing of Colson and that his life has been attempted at least once since it was known how important his testimony was, coupled with the fact that his killer finds such ready assistance in getting away, has led to ugly rumors. Just or unjust as these inferential accusations may be, Horr would do remarkably well in a foreign country.

John Calvin Jr. left behind a widow and nine children. His sons would see their own share of tragedy and violence (see Footnote Twenty-six). The newspaper lamented his passing: "Colson...had a whole lot of friends in Middlesboro and Bell County. He was a man of great influence and considerable wealth. As a local politician he was invincible...true to his friends, brave as Caesar, and in former days had come out unscathed from many trying ordeals."

The next child of John Colvin Sr. was William Gillis Colson, born on February 6, 1857. He was the only son to livè out his allotted years, al-

William Gillus Colson. Courtesy of Bell County Historical Society.

though he did not entirely escape tragedy—he played an important part in the Quarterhouse Battle (see Footnote Twenty-two).

W.G., also called "Gil," was a lawyer and also had large land holdings in Kentucky and Virginia. He was the first popularly elected superintendent of schools in Bell County, serving from 1880 through 1890. His first wife was Margaret Wheeler, with whom he had five children before her death from complications of childbirth. She is remembered for the night that she, with several of her friends, tarred and feathered the residents of a house of ill repute that Gil had been rumored to favor.

His three daughters from that marriage remained spinsters and lived their lives out on their Lee County, Virginia, farm. The eldest, Nora, was said to have frequently ridden behind her father when he was traveling by horseback to prevent anyone from shooting him in the back. The sisters lived until the early 1960s, still favoring the long skirts of an earlier time and all carrying pistols. Nora was known to be the toughest. When the federal government started buying up land for the Cumberland Gap National Historical Park, she ran the federal agents off, swearing, "Like hell you will" when they threatened expropriation. She would sit in the yard cradling a shotgun and dare anyone to set a foot on Colson property without her permission. She underlined her determination by walking around at night, randomly firing her weapons.

Gil's second wife was Cora Sawyer. They had five children, one of whom died in infancy. One of their sons, Jack, was to gain fame as an aviation pioneer. Cora died in 1913 when the carriage in which she was riding overturned. The family story is that she and her cousin were chasing after Gil and his mistress when their horse bolted at a snake. The cousin was only injured, but Cora was killed instantly.[6]

John Colson Sr.'s second daughter, Mary Katherine, was born on February 15, 1859. She married William Ball Moss and moved to Lancaster, Kentucky. They had two daughters and two sons.

David Grant, born on April Fool's Day, 1861, was the most famous of all the children. He deserves a "footnote" all his own (see Footnote Nineteen).

Next in line was George Sherman, born on April 13, 1864. He is somewhat of a mystery as there are two very different stories about him. Both agree that he never married and that he died in another state at age twenty-two. Most family historians state that he was a physician who went to Georgia to help during a yellow fever epidemic and contracted the disease, dying of it while working there. Another source explains that because he came of age at a time when the family was not only prosperous but had gained political influence, he was able to aspire to the U.S. Naval Academy at Annapolis. Unfortunately, while he was taking the examination for a cadetship, he was accused of cheating by another student. He demanded an apology, and when that was not forthcoming, he is said to have shot and killed his accuser. According to this story, there was no trial, but he had to leave the area and went to Texas, where he was embroiled in some undefined trouble that resulted in his death.[7]

Laura Belle, the next of the April babies, made her appearance in 1866. She married Dr. James S. Bingham of Pineville and had five sons and four daughters.

Cordelia Violet, usually called "Cordie," arrived on April 19, 1868. She taught school at the old Green Meeting House before marrying John Glasgow Fitzpatrick, one of the "boomers." He was a lawyer from Madison County, Kentucky, who at one time was in partnership with her brother David. One of a close-knit group of young businessmen who still had faith in the opportunities offered by the proven coal resources of the area, he stayed on after the "bust." For thirty years he was connected with the mining industry and was also active in civic affairs. He was the mayor of Middlesborough from 1898 through 1900. Cordelia and John had two children, Thaddeus and Frances.

The youngest child, Eudoxia Olivia, was born on May 31, 1870. She was just twelve years old when her father died. In 1890 she married William Dempsey Hurst, who had built one of the first business houses in the boom city. After his store was completely destroyed by the great fire of May 1890, he became cashier at the bank owned by his brother-in-law David and then was assistant postmaster of Middlesborough for many years. For a short time he had a print shop and put out a news sheet called *The Record*. Eudoxia had inherited a good deal of property, including that just across from the old family home on the Wilderness Road. This he developed as a cemetery.

Eudoxia was very gifted in music and attended the Cincinnati Conservatory of Music. She is well remembered as a long-time organist for the Methodist Church and a mentor of musically talented youth. In her later years, as her mind failed her, she dressed in the manner she had as a young matron, favoring long flowing dresses and old-fashioned hats, and still assumed the manner of the favored youngest daughter of the family that led the Valley in all things. In 1943 she expired near the old homestead where she had been born, the last of John and Mary Catherine's children to join them in death.

Eudoxie Colson Hurst with her sons Ernest (seated on the left), John (standing), and William. Courtesy of David Hurst.

Eudoxia and Demps had three sons, one of whom died as a teenager. Their other sons, John and William, were active participants in the Ball-Colson Feud (see Footnote Twenty-six).

John Colson Sr. was not only the Patriarch of the Valley but also the patriarch of a large family that would continue to play an important role in the history of the Yellow Creek Valley for many years to come.

FOOTNOTE EIGHT

War Comes to the Yellow Creek Valley

On September 9, 1963, George H. McEntire Jr. stood at the site of Fort Pitt just below the Pinnacle, looked north over the Yellow Creek Valley, and cursed the "DamnYankees" for five full minutes.

The Texan was fulfilling a solemn promise made to his grandfather some forty-six years earlier. William R. McEntire, a member of Company A of the 9th Georgia Artillery Battalion, was in command of a cannon at Fort Pitt on September 9, 1863, when the Confederates were tricked into surrendering their fortified position to the surrounding Union forces. He spent eighteen months in a hellish prison camp. When he finally made his way back to his home in Georgia, he found that not only had his house been burned to the ground and his farm destroyed in Sherman's march to the sea, but his wife and children had also lost their lives. With nothing left, he migrated to Texas to start a new life, in which he was successful. But he never lost his hatred of the DamnYankees (always one word for him), and made his grandson promise to return one hundred years from the date of his capture to once again curse them.

McEntire was but one of the many profoundly affected by the military actions that swirled around the Gap during this most horrific of wars.

When Civil War came to the country, Kentucky declared its neutrality and called upon its citizens to form Home Guard units to protect the Commonwealth from invasion by either side. John Colson issued a call to the men of the Yellow Creek Valley. Almost the entire male population of the Valley, from fresh faced boys barely out of "aprons" to tottering grandfathers—close to one hundred in all—joined him, including his own eldest sons, sixteen-year-old James and fourteen-year-old Redden. They brought their squirrel guns and old-time one-shot muskets, which had last seen hostile action against the Indians, and a determination to protect their valley from invasion.[1] These men knew full well that a Confederate force had already massed in northeastern Tennessee under the command of General Felix Zollicoffer and that the Gap offered an excellent gateway for an invasion of the north. Soon they spotted Confederate soldiers on the Pinnacle. Most of Colson's men leaned toward the Union, but many had divided loyalties. Colson himself had a kinsman at the Gap who was fighting for the South.[2]

No matter the size of his force, Colson defiantly drilled his men in a level field near his home in full view of the Confederate troops. Throughout the summer of 1861 they met regularly, though in varying numbers as most of the men had farms to tend and families to feed, and some lived almost a day's ride from Colson's place over the rough trails that crisscrossed the Valley and its surrounding hollows.

On September 5, 1861, Kentucky's neutrality was breached in the west by Confederate General Leonidas Polk and his Union counterpart, Ulysses S. Grant. Immediately plans were put in motion to invade Kentucky from the east through the Gap, and on September 9 General Zollicoffer ordered the three regiments stationed at the Gap to advance. Colson's Home Guards, though hopelessly outnumbered, marched out to meet them. They had sworn to each other that they would not let anyone "come in on them" without a fight. What resulted was barely a skirmish for the Confederate Army, but one Valley man, John Rains, lost his life, and John Colson was made a prisoner.

Zollicoffer established a base at the Cumberland River ford (now Pineville), which he called Camp Buckner after the Confederate general Simon Bolivar Buckner. There Colson was imprisoned briefly. The Confederate Army pushed forward on the Wilderness Road until they met an advancing Union Army. The Confederates then drew in their forces and set about fortifying the Gap. They erected long hut-type barracks and brought in heavy guns. Seven forts, mostly built of dirt and rock, were constructed, and the Confederates settled in to guard the road through the Gap, a route that would be most tempting to the North in their strategy of dividing the Confederacy east from west. A secondary goal was to contain and neutralize Union sympathizers in the mountains of northeastern Tennessee and southeastern Kentucky.

All was quiet during the winter of 1861-1862 for the soldiers at the

Gap. Their most pressing problem was supplies, and they began to live off the land, much to the distress of the Yellow Creekers. Already by February of 1862 it was reported to the Union high command that the mountain area had been stripped of forage and could not support an invading army.

Nonetheless, in the spring of 1862 Union forces under Major General George W. Morgan were ordered to take the Gap. After considering the strength of the Confederates who had had all winter to dig in and fortify their position, Morgan decided that a frontal attack would be suicidal. Therefore he determined to march his army into Powell Valley south of the Cumberland Gap by way of two minor passes west of the Gap, in order to attack the Confederates' relatively unprotected rear.

Joe "Pet" Marsee was a young boy at the time, but he would always remember the brave show the Yankees made as they marched up Fonde Mountain, their uniforms bright against the June green of the mountains and their guns glinting in the sun. For the soldiers, despite their smart appearance, it was protracted, exhausting labor to climb the steep, narrow trails hauling their artillery and all their gear. As they advanced, their foraging officers appropriated all the provisions for miles around. Marsee recalled that his father, though a Unionist at heart, fled into the hills when he heard of their approach. He was concerned that he might be forcibly conscripted, leaving his family with no one to provide for them after the army had stripped them.[3]

On June 14, 1862, the Union troops finally rendezvoused at the base of Rogers Gap in the Powell Valley of Tennessee, ready to march on Cumberland Gap. The outnumbered Confederates, knowing they would soon be surrounded, decided to abandon their stronghold. They destroyed all the stores they had accumulated, split their tents to make them unusable, and spiked the large guns they could not take with them. One huge cannon, which would later be called "Long Tom," they managed to pitch off the Pinnacle. Then they stole away into the mountains of Tennessee. Morgan was left to take the Gap without a fight.

The Union troops immediately set about repairing the fortifications and building nine new batteries, these facing south. They repaired the Wilderness Road and began to bring in supplies from central Kentucky to feed the 10,000 men now stationed at the Gap. "Long Tom" was hauled up the mountain by a hundred or more men using rollers or skids, and was located so as to address an attack from the south.[4] Trees were felled to provide clear lines of fire. In fact, according to one local, the Union Army so completely denuded the mountain that a person "couldn't find even a riding switch."[5]

Union tenure was to be short. Slipping through the same passes that Morgan had utilized, Confederate forces infiltrated behind his lines and on August 10, 1862, captured the Cumberland Ford, thus cutting Morgan's supply lines and surrounding his forces. The Federal position was soon desperate. They had only enough food for three weeks even at half rations, and there was little to be foraged from nearby areas. By early September, rations had again been cut, and there was no alternative for Morgan other than to evacuate or surrender. Since the Confederates had temporarily turned their attention to Central Kentucky and had left the Cumberland Ford essentially unguarded, he decided on the former course, settling on a desperate retreat up the old Warriors' Path leading to Ohio.

Morgan was as determined as the Confederates had been to leave nothing of use behind. He ordered that all buildings and munitions be mined with explosives, as well as the roads the soldiers had built and even the mountain itself. The guns were spiked and "Long Tom" again pitched off the mountain. Everything that could not be carried with them the men piled up for burning. When all was in readiness and night had fallen, the Union army began quietly moving out and down the road that followed Yellow Creek. They left behind a small detachment to ignite the explosives.

It was an overcast night with a light drizzle falling on the almost deserted Gap. At 2:00 a.m. the order was given to light the fuses. The buildings started burning, then the mines fired. It was a night no one in the Valley would ever forget. "The mountain was afire all over" was how Sill Turner described that night years later.[6] Explosion followed explosion. Huge rocks and other debris thrown in the air landed a mile or more away, to the terror of the locals. The acrid smoke shot through with flames looked like the bowels of hell itself. Destruction was so extensive that it took the Confederate troops, stationed just to the south and bent on pursuing Morgan, several days to work their way through the Gap, which gave the Union soldiers time to make good their escape.

The Confederate forces in Kentucky were having their own problems. On October 8, 1862, they were defeated at the Battle of Perryville. They retreated along the Wilderness Road, through the Yellow Creek Valley, and into Tennessee. By the end of October the main body of the Confederates was through the Gap with again only a relatively small force left to guard the pass. Throughout the winter of 1862 and into the summer of 1863 there was not much action. There is one story that the Southerners tried to use "Long Tom" but without the labor of again hauling the cannon up the mountain. On its second flight down the mountain it had landed just above the old mill (the general location of the Iron Furnace) in what is now the

The evacuation of the Cumberland Gap by Union forces under General George W. Morgan, September 17, 1862. Engraving by Rufus M. Fry after a daguerreotype made by an attache of General Morgan. Courtesy of Bell County Historical Society.

town of Cumberland Gap, Tennessee. The soldiers put wheels on it so it was more maneuverable, since it was no longer certain from which direction attack might come. One day the men thought they saw some Yankees trying to reach the Pinnacle. They hauled the gun around and fired, but the ball struck far below their target. They raised the sights and fired again. This time the ball flew over the mountain and landed in the Yellow Creek Valley, killing a mule.[7]

It was probably about this time that Rebels ran crossways of "Fiddlin John" Turner. He was a Union man but heretofore had not joined the fray. He had enough of a problem just keeping his family fed, what with the young men gone off to war and one army after another stripping his farm of everything they could find. One day the foraging Rebels swept down on his place while he was gone. When he came back, he found that his brother (or according to some accounts his son) had been tied to a chair and killed, presumably in an effort to force from him the hiding place of some provisions. Witnesses reported that sixteen Confederate soldiers "had done the deed." Apparently the guilty ones were known to the family—perhaps they regularly foraged in the area. "Fiddlin John" got his old musket loader, the only firearm not already confiscated by one side or the other, and headed out. He hunted down one Rebel after another. Limited by his weapon, he would have to fire once, then run and reload before he could fire again. One time he shot, then ran and climbed into a big hollow tree trunk. His little feist dog followed him into the trunk. The Rebs were after him, and, afraid the animal would make a noise and give him away, he choked his dog to death. He later said he thought the Rebs could hear his heart beating. According to his family, he was finally able to kill all sixteen of the Confederates responsible for his brother's (or son's) death.[8]

Brigadier General John W. Frazer took command in the summer of 1863. He found the 2,500 men stationed at the Gap ill disciplined and the camp in poor shape, the wreckage of Morgan's retreat still quite evident. His efforts to further fortify his position were given urgency by the knowledge that Union forces were massing in Kentucky for a push to invade Tennessee. Among the assignments Frazer made was to put a young lieutenant of the Georgia Artillery Battalion, William R. McEntire, in command of one of the three six-pound field cannons at Fort Pitt, an earthen fortification overlooking the Yellow Creek Valley.

Frazer was right to be concerned. Although the main body of the Union troops under General Ambrose Burnside planned to invade Tennessee across the Jellico Mountains, the order had been given to clear the Wilderness Road through the Gap to serve as a supply line. Colonel John DeCourcy, who had been stationed at the Gap with Morgan the previous year, was charged with taking that pass. Unaccountably he was given only 1,700 green troops, poorly provisioned, ill equipped, and with only six light cannon. DeCourcy knew the topography of the area and immediately realized that any type of assault, particularly considering the forces under his command, would fail. He was a career military man, grandson of an Irish nobleman, and he had had to ignominiously abandon the Gap once. This time it would be his, by guile if not by force.

He knew that if the Confederates realized how pitifully small was his command, they would easily defeat him. Therefore he planned a clever deception. First he had his men change the regimental numbers on their caps to make various combinations, so that any spies—and there were always those, locals in camp selling provisions, etc.—would think he had sixteen different regiments, four times the actual number, and would report that strength to the Rebels at the Gap.

By the time DeCourcy reached Cumberland Ford, his command was in even worse shape, since many of his men had fallen ill on the march and had to be left behind. In addition, expected supplies had not reached him. His men had little or no food and only thirty rounds of ammunition. The situation looked hopeless, but Irishmen are used to facing the seemingly impossible. He moved his men forward to the base of the third Log Mountain, five miles north of the Cumberland Gap. From there they would be easily visible through the field glasses of the Confederates.

Then came the second part of his grand deception. He separated his men into groups and marched them at intervals around the bottom of the mountain, then into the forests that blanketed its slopes, where they could not be seen, across the mountain to the same spot from which they had started and from which they again, with great show, marched around its base. Four times each soldier, probably swearing at his commander under his breath the whole time, did this, so that it appeared to be a huge force that was deploying itself throughout the woods. DeCourcy then had what cavalry he possessed charge up the dry road to raise as much dust as possible. Under cover of the dust he moved his six cannons into their first position. Once sure they were observed, he made a great show of covering them with bushes, then surreptitiously withdrew them to another location, and again conspicuously camouflaged them. He did this over and over until the Confederates must have thought fifty or sixty cannons were trained on them.

From his post at Fort Pitt, Lieut. William McEntire watched as what appeared to be an overwhelming Federal force massed for attack. As he awaited the anticipated battle, he carved his name and rank onto a rock. If on this mountaintop he gave his life for the cause, someone would at least know he had been there.

Meanwhile, Frazer, while observing the Union forces in front of him, was brought intelligence that Union General James Shackelford had come up from the south with a brigade of 2,000 men, and that General Burnside had taken Knoxville with no opposition and could be expected to immediately reinforce Shackelford. The Gap was again surrounded, this time by Yankees.

As Frazer contemplated what seemed to be his untenable position on the morning of September 8, he received Colonel DeCourcy's demand that he surrender immediately. Frazer had already summarily rejected the same ultimatum from Shackelford the day before, but in view of what seemed to be insurmountable odds, he agreed to parley.

Messages were passed back and forth, and the emissaries for the two sides became friendly, even to the point that the Union officer offered his Confederate counterpart a drink. With much appreciation, the latter asked if there was any more where that had come from, as the Confederate officers were mighty dry. DeCourcy, understanding how well a little liquor will oil the machinery of negotiation, sent Frazer two gallons of good whiskey. (The fact that he had the whiskey was perhaps a good indication of priorities, since DeCourcy was entirely out of bread for his troops.)

Thus fortified, Frazer contemplated his alternatives. To his north, DeCourcy's troops were moving to forward positions. (Little did he know that DeCourcy had ordered their rifles unloaded so that no trigger-happy trooper would accidentally start a general battle that would reveal his weakness.) To Frazer's south, General Burnside was approaching with reinforcements and had also sent him a note demanding surrender. At 3:00 p.m. on September 9, Frazer ordered the white flags to be raised. When DeCourcy reached Frazer's tent to receive his surrender, he found Frazer "off poise" with snuff smeared on his face, and he remarked to the orderly, "The whiskey worked."

From most accounts, it appears that no shots were fired. But the McEntire family history has it that William refused to obey the command to surrender and ordered his men to continue firing their cannons. Other rebels, also reluctant to surrender without a fight, applauded him, but his entire company of the 9th Georgia Artillery was placed under armed guard for insubordination. Members of the same company, according to the same source, were able to sneak away and tear down the recently raised United States flag from the Pinnacle before they were marched off to prison.[9]

DeCourcy's triumphant march into the Gap had been precipitous; he should have waited for Burnside to arrive. As a result of his action, 400 of the Confederates stationed at outposts were able to slip away into the mountains and make their way South. Burnside was furious at DeCourcy and, rather than congratulate him, put him under arrest for insubordination. Although he was cleared of the charges, DeCourcy resigned from service and returned to Great Britain, where he later became Lord Kingsale the 31st. Frazer, too, was roundly criticized for his actions, and it was even suggested that he was a traitor. Thus two officers had their careers ruined that day at the Gap.

One persistent story that has floated around the Yellow Creek Valley for years and has fueled many an exploration of the mountains is that of the missing Confederate gold. According to this tale, the southerners had in their possession at the time of DeCourcy's coup a shipment of gold that was to be used as pay. (This in itself is unlikely, given the economic condition of the Confederacy.) Rather than surrender it to the Union, one or more officers buried it. It is said that whoever had knowledge of the exact location was killed before he told anyone and that the gold still lies hidden somewhere on the mountain. There is no proof of any kernel of truth in this story, but at least one Middlesboro man devoted his life to the unsuccessful search.[10]

The Union forces were now in firm command of the Gap and would be so until the end of the war. It was not an easy time, however. The forage supply was exhausted and the men were often on meager rations. In October of 1863 there was a smallpox epidemic that killed off hundreds of men.

It was an extremely difficult time also for the people of the Yellow Creek Valley. Both the Confederates and the Federal forces had confiscated everything they could find. It was a lucky family that had been able to hide away a few chickens or a milk cow. Even the crops in the fields were stripped before they could mature, and the Valley children grew gaunt with hunger. One story is told by the Marsee family of how, when the Federal foragers were gathering everything eatable on the place, Kate Marsee, with her family of stair-step children gathered around her, pleaded, "Aren't you going to leave us anything?" The Federal officer threw her a few used army blankets. Unfortunately, they had last wrapped soldiers who were sick with "the flux." One by one, the whole family fell ill. Four of her children died, two within minutes of each other. A few weeks later, Mrs. Marsee herself succumbed. Two other members of the family were also gravely ill but managed to survive after John Colson, who also served as doctor for the Valley, successfully treated them with grease from old fat-back skins.

In January of 1864, General Ulysses S. Grant came through the Gap on an inspection tour to see if the Wilderness Road could be used as a main invasion route. He found that the incessant march of armies back and forth had reduced the road to a ruin. He counted 258 dead animals in the fourteen miles between the Gap and the Cumberland Ford, along with numerous broken and abandoned wagons. To the relief, undoubtedly, of the Yellow Creek people, if they knew why he was there, Grant decided the Wilderness Road was unusable. The Valley would from then on be in the backwaters of the great conflict.

In April of 1865 arms were stacked and the war was over. Soldiers from both sides made their way home. William McEntire got to Georgia and found he had lost his family and everything else. Two Union soldiers returning home through the Gap stopped at the home of Betsy Howard and asked if they could stay overnight. She refused, and they insisted. Green Turner happened to be in the Howard house at the time, and he became involved in the argument. Green had somehow managed to hang onto his pistol throughout the conflict and was, as usual, wearing it. The Union men seemed to back down in their demands and become more friendly. One casually asked to see Green's gun. As soon as he got his hands on it, he turned and shot Green through the neck, killing him.[11] He was the last known casualty of the Civil War in the Valley.

Gradually enmities faded. During the 1890s, there were reunions at the Gap of soldiers from both sides who had been stationed there. These were quite festive occasions with speeches, music, and fireworks. There was even a strong movement to erect a Lincoln and Lee memorial on the Pinnacle. This was envisioned as a huge statue of the two leaders shaking hands. The plan had to be abandoned during a period of financial panic.

One can still see the remains of Civil War forts at the Gap. And still quite legibly carved on a large rock is the inscription "W.R. McEntire Lieut. Co. A9 Ga. Bat. Arty. Sept. 9, 1863."

Footnote Nine

The Turner-Sowders Feud

When Alexander Arthur first looked down on the valley of Yellow Creek that day in 1886, it appeared to be the picture of peace and tranquillity—a few cabins and cleared fields scattered over a wide natural bowl surrounded by majestic mountains. There was no evidence of the war that was raging in the Valley: the Turner-Sowders Feud, described by a contemporary metropolitan newspaper as a "reign of terror, lawlessness and rifle rule" that would eventually claim as many as twenty-seven victims.

The thirty-year period from 1870 through 1900 is notable in Appalachian history as the time of large-scale family feuds. Almost all of these were in some way connected with Kentucky. Why this should be true has been the focus of much research and discussion. The nature of the people, their Scotch-Irish origin with a tradition of violence and clannishness, has been advanced as one explanation. Another theory looks to scars left from the Civil War, which was particularly bitter and divisive in the mountains, and the fact that during the war it became more acceptable to settle disagreements with guns. Another culprit was Kentucky's antiquated legal system, which was ineffective and not generally seen as capable of securing legal redress. This fostered a vigilantism, much like that fostered by similar situations in other areas of the country. But in Appalachia the the vigilantes, rather than being an association of unrelated men, were usually an extended family.

To see the feuds as family vigilantism or a small war is to better understand why there are so few readily identifiable heroes. As in any war, the objective came before the means. Therefore we often see in a feud ambushes and men shot in the back; there are few "honorable" duels at high noon.

The study of any of the Kentucky feuds is difficult because of the lack of unbiased sources. Court records have often been lost. The newspapers of the day generally sensationalized the feuds they covered and ignored the others. Family records and personal recollections tend to be from a very definite point of view and are generally diametrically opposed to those from the other camp. Anyone examining the Turner-Sowders Feud encounters all of these difficulties. In addition, the arrival of the American Association and all the newcomers so overshadowed the conflict that the feud lost importance in the collective memory of the Valley.

By 1880 the Yellow Creek Valley had recovered from the worst deprivations of the Civil War. Herds of livestock had been rebuilt, and the produce of the fields and gardens once again nourished growing families. In 1867 a new county, Josh Bell County (later shortened to Bell County), had been formed from portions of Knox and Harlan Counties. The new county, an area of 361 square miles, encompassed the Valley and had as its county seat Pineville, the only town within its limits, which was twelve miles and almost a day's ride from the Valley. According to the Census of 1880, the population of Bell County was 6,049, with just 83 persons living in Pineville itself. The remainder lived on small farms. Though no exact population for

An early view of the Yellow Creek Valley. Courtesy of Cumberland Gap National Historical Park.

the Valley is given,[1] most contemporary writers and historians agree that there were approximately fifty cabins located in and around the Yellow Creek basin at the time.

The Turners were one of the oldest and largest families in the Valley. Because they were so numerous and tended to use the same first names over and over, many of the Turners had nicknames. Joe "Pussyfoot" Turner was one such. Also called "Hanc," Joe was the son of John ("Slicky") Turner. His brothers were Benjamin, Green, Robert, and Jackson "Jack" Turner. Sisters married into the Henderson, King, and Pierce families. Joe's farm was in the western portion of the Valley, in the area of present-day 34th Street. One of his closest neighbors was Jake "Squire" Sowders, who was a relative newcomer to the Valley. The Sowders farm lay on Yellow Creek between Stony Fork and Bennetts Fork. The two men were friends and often farmed together, helping each other, as was the custom. Both fathered good-sized families, each with several quick-tempered sons.

As might be expected, the origins of the feud are in dispute, with quite different versions handed down through the two families. Most likely the first incident happened at a social gathering. One of the boys in the crowd had constructed a type of crossbow for hunting, and everyone was anxious to try it out, including Jake's son General and one of the Turner boys. According to an eye witness, "one shot the other on the shin, but the arrow had no spike in it so the one that got hit got mad and wanted to fight...just fist and skull. It turned out that General being a quick and strong man soon knocked Turner out. But Turner swore vengeance on General."[2]

Though one of the Turner boys now "felt hard against" him, General was courting Hanc's daughter Elizabeth, who was called Lizzie. General was by all accounts a handsome young man with a devil-may-care air about him that she found attractive. He, in turn, was enamored of his beautiful young neighbor, and before long the match was made. Undoubtedly the community helped the young couple erect a cabin on a plot of Sowders land. There are two distinctly different versions of what happened next.

According to the Sowders family history, the bride's father gave the couple a calf as a wedding present. Her brother Tom resented the gift, feeling his father had been much too generous, and he stole the calf back.[3] General, justifiably aggrieved, tracked the thief to the Turner farm. Tom, now both angry and alarmed, tried to trap General in the Turner house, but General was too quick for him and killed Tom before the latter could get off a shot. Elizabeth's other brothers, Levi ("Lee"), Harvey, and Gordon, swore revenge.[4]

The Turners have a totally different story. Their family tradition is that

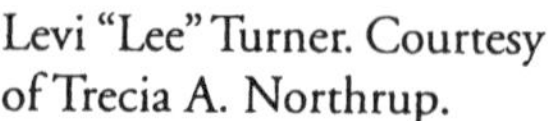
Levi "Lee" Turner. Courtesy of Trecia A. Northrup.

General was abusing Lizzie, and when her brothers learned of it they sent word that if he did not stop, they would stop him with a bullet.[5] An independent source gave a slightly different spin: "General and Elizabeth seemed devoted to one another. No one ever heard of any trouble between them, but somehow, during a playful scuffle, one of Elizabeth's thumbs was broken. Tongues began to waggin' and someone told Elizabeth's brothers...that General was mistreating their sister. Lee immediately sent word to General that he intended to kill him on sight."[6]

Still another version of the genesis of the feud was given in a contemporary newspaper. According to this account, a member of the Sowders family had committed some legal offense and was being hunted by a posse, one of whom was Marsh Turner. There was a gun battle in which Marsh was killed. It was said that General Sowders had been the triggerman. Marsh was a cousin to Lizzie, and her brother Tom tried to avenge his death, but it was he himself who was killed.[7]

However it started, by 1885 the war was well under way. The Turner family was much larger than the Sowders family, but not as unified, so that some of the Turners ended up fighting on the Sowders side. In fact, there had been so much intermarriage in the Valley that many could claim equal kinship with both sides. Other adherents came as the result of the theory that the enemy of my enemy is my friend. In addition, there was already one long-standing animosity in the Valley. Jack Turner, Lizzie's uncle, who became the leader of the Turner faction, had already made several enemies in the valley because of his violent ways. In 1871 he had killed his father-in-law, Samuel Lane, in a family dispute. Jack escaped punishment but left long-smoldering resentment in the hearts of the Lane family and their friends.

In 1885 Samuel's son William got into a timber dispute with Gordon Turner, brother to Lizzie and a nephew of Jack. Guns were drawn, volleys were exchanged, and Gordon lay dead. William was tracked by Gordon's brothers, Lee and Harvey, who, when they finally caught up with him, shot him down just as he reached the cabin of a friend.

On Christmas Day 1885, General killed two men in what was either a tragic case of mistaken identity or a drunken brawl. According to one version, General was at a Christmas dance on Tackett Creek (just over the state line in Tennessee) when he became involved in an argument with Chad Marsee and Reuben Carroll, two "Turner men," both of whom had been celebrating with liberal amounts of moonshine, as had General. The argument escalated, guns flashed, and both men were dead.[8] The Carroll family has passed down the story that Reuben and Chad were flirting with General's wife Lizzie and that this led to the fatal fight.[9]

A very different version has General, following the warning that Lee would kill him on sight, hiding out with a friend on Tackett Creek. Awakened late at night by a banging on the door, he leapt from bed, grabbed his rifle, and faced the door, sure the Turners had found him. As the door swung open, he blazed away, instantly killing the intruders. Too late he discovered he had killed two of his best friends.[10]

General was able to escape legal retribution by fleeing across the state line into Kentucky, where the Tennessee authorities would not pursue. But the Turners, anxious to avenge the deaths of Marsee and Carroll, hunted for him relentlessly. In the summer of 1886 General was ambushed and wounded slightly. He recognized his brother-in-law, Lee Turner, as the shooter.

Lee Turner met his maker in the spring of 1887. Again, there are two very different stories. According to one, Lizzie had managed to arrange a truce and there was an uneasy peace between the families. One day Lee and General happened to meet by accident, and Lee mentioned that he needed a haircut and shave. He asked if he could drop by later and have General do the job. In the days when there were no barbershops, this was not an uncommon thing to ask of a neighbor. But while General waited at home, he had a few sips of moonshine. As the liquor took effect, General began to brood on Lee's impending arrival, and he soon became convinced that Lee was actually planning to kill him. When the latter walked in the door, General reached for his gun, which was on the mantle, and, while Lee turned away to close the door, General shot him.[11]

A completely different version has General working in his front yard when he is shot and wounded by Lee. The wound is minor and General is soon able to confront Lee. They fight only with words, but as he stalks homeward, General becomes aware that Lee is following him. Convinced that Lee is planning to ambush him again, General wheels around and shoots Lee through the heart.[12]

There could be no peace after the death of Lee. Hardly had they buried him than the Turner clan assaulted the house of Squire Sowders (General's father) and almost demolished it. Incredibily, no one was injured, but Sowders realized that the Yellow Creek Valley was no longer safe for his family. He moved them to the only town in the area, Pineville. James Rains helped them make the move. In retribution, a gang led by Harvey Turner, brother to Lee, waylaid Rains and killed him.

General himself did not move to Pineville but roamed the mountains, never staying too long in any one place. Lizzie, adhering to the promise of forsaking all others, frequently accompanied him, camping out in "rock houses," as cliff overhangs were called, and staying with friends. Other times she contented herself with carrying supplies to General at one of his hideouts. It was during this difficult period, in 1887, that their only child, a son named Hubert, was born. One can scarcely imagine how torn Lizzie must have been. It has been said that for the rest of her life the Turners "felt hard" toward her because she had supported her husband instead of her blood kin.[13]

General was also helped by his extended family. One man told how his father used to fill an eight-pound lard can with food and leave it in a special spot in the woods. He would give a certain whistle, and soon General would emerge from the mountains to claim the provisions.[14]

At this time, the Sowders forces consisted primarily of their immediate family and that of the Renfros. Sam Renfro had been killed by cousins of the Turners, so his family allied themselves with the Turners' enemies. The Turner side could claim Joe's family (though two of his sons had already been killed), Joe's brother Jack and his son Alvis, and a number of other Turners. Three nephews, Jeff and Jim Henderson and Jeff King, also took an active part in the hostilities. Conspicuous by their absence were Ben Turner, a brother to Joe, and his sons, Marshall, John, and Green, who chose to remain neutral. (Some said Ben's refusal to support his brother arose from his bitterness because their father, when he divided his land, gave the largest parcel to Jack.)

Jack Turner had become the acknowledged leader of the Turner faction, and he did not believe in neutrality. He was particularly suspicious because Marshall Turner was married to General's sister. In June of 1887 a gang of Turners attacked Marshall's house. No one was injured, and Marshall was not even home at the time. It may be that Jack only wanted to show his brother's family that they should get off the fence and into his camp, but the attack had the opposite effect. Marshall asked for the law to protect him.

At the same time a group of engineers and railroad workers who were surveying for the planned railroad extension to Pineville complained to the county judge of the general lawlessness and of raids on their camp by a gang of outlaws they identified as Turners. The circuit judge was finally forced into action. He called out the militia to keep order. But out of the fifty men called, only fifteen reported for duty. The others declined to get involved, preferring whatever penalty would attach itself to their refusal to answer the judge's order to the fire of the Turner rifles.

The small group of men, more of a posse than a militia, set out to capture the "outlaws" who had attacked Marshall's house and the railroad camp. The group assembled at the home of Marshall and were guided by him and his brother John, who was a deputy sheriff, toward the house of one of the Turners. But a young boy playing in the woods saw them and ran ahead to warn the Turners, who slipped away. The disappointed posse returned to the Marshall house.

Lacking the element of surprise, the posse decided theirs was a lost cause and they should return to Pineville. Marshall knew that neither he nor his family would be safe from the wrath of his uncle, and felt it was imperative that his family be moved to the relative security of Pineville. Half of the posse volunteered to stay behind and guard the family while they gathered their possessions for the move. Among those who stayed were John Turner, Marshall's brother; Joshua Sowders, who was the brother of General; and the latter's cousin, Pen Sowders. George Thomas, a Pineville town marshal, and Charles Mutzenberg, the deputy Circuit Court clerk, also remained behind.

The next morning Marshall's family set out with a small escort. The balance of the men stayed with Marshall to help him transport their possessions. Suddenly Jack Turner rode up to the front gate and, bold as could be, dismounted and strode into the house. Undaunted by the armed men who surrounded him, he ranted and raved at Marshall for helping Turner enemies, and cursed the others. Just as suddenly as he arrived, he wheeled around and left.

As the startled men discussed the bizarre confrontation, they concluded that Jack was up to something and that Marshall's house was not a safe place. They decided to make a run for the nearby cabin of Tom Renfro, which was constructed of heavy logs and could more easily be defended. They could also depend on the Renfros to help in the event of a fight. What they did not know was that Jack's men had already surrounded Marshall's house and were lying in wait. As the men left the house, they were greeted by a barrage of rifle fire. George Thomas fell dead. The others dropped behind whatever shelter they could find and returned fire. They were, however, outnumbered and in a more vulnerable position, as the Turners remained hidden. John and Marshall Turner and Pen Sowders were all wounded, but somehow they were able to escape. Only one of Jack's band suffered any injury, and it was minor.

As a result of this encounter, the Sowders family found their ranks swelled by the addition of the dead man's brothers, Lee and John Thomas. The entire family of Ben Turner abandoned neutrality to side with the Sowders family, and Charles Mutzenberg also became an active combatant.[15]

The Circuit Court met in August of 1887 with Judge Robert Byrd presiding. On the docket was the case of Jack Turner and Harvey Turner, who were accused of the murder of George Thomas. Jack had earlier surrendered and was out on bail, while Harvey was in jail. Also in Pineville was Marshall Turner, who was living at the Monroe Hotel while recuperating from his wounds.

Jack had secured the services of Col. John Dishman of Barbourville to represent him when his case came to trial. On September 2, 1887, Jack was walking down the street with his attorney. Accompanying them were the commonwealth's attorney, A.H. Clark, and Jack's nephew, Jeff King. Suddenly Jeff wheeled around and headed toward the Monroe Hotel. At almost the same time, shots rang out and Jack fell to the ground. Sixteen bullets had found their target, killing him instantly. No one else was injured.

A grand jury was convened that same day and indicted General Sowders and Marshall Turner for the murder of Jack Turner. But the suspects had already fled. The next day it was discovered that John S. Turner and Charles Mutzenberg, fearing assassination by the Turner faction, had also disappeared.

With Jack's death, leadership of the Turners fell to his son Alvis, who was only twenty but already had a reputation for violence that rivaled that of his father. The killings continued, each in retaliation for another.

General was still hiding out in the mountains, but his thirst for some liquid corn almost did him in. As the *Cumberland Gap Progress* explained on July 25, 1888, he crossed the state line "to try the strength and character of the bug dust manufactured south of the old Cumberland." The whiskey evidently met with his approval, and he imbibed so deeply that he passed out on the road. Some passersby were able to hog-tie him and haul him to town, where he was turned over to the law in exchange for a reward that had been posted after the Christmas killings. While still under the influence of alcohol, he bragged that he had killed eight men and one woman, a statement that, when he was at last sober, he strongly denied.

General was jailed at Tazewell, Tennessee, but his family was soon able to free him with a clever ruse. They tied up one of their own men as if he were a prisoner and walked boldly into the jail as if to turn him over to the authorities. Once inside, they found it easy to release General, and all made the dash across the border into Kentucky, where they would be safe from Tennessee law.

In March of 1889, Alvis learned that Jim Burch, who lived on Log Mountain, had been giving General shelter. Alvis gathered some men to finally capture his hated foe. His "posse" delivered General to the Bell County jail, where he was held for the murder of Jack. But this did not satisfy Alvis. By giving aid to his enemy, Burch had also become his adversary, even though he was known as a peaceable man who had been on the verge of selling his property to the British so he could move away from the violence. (There was, however, some evidence that Burch was about to provide a witness to testify in one of the cases against a Turner.) Alvis, accompanied by his cousin Jeff King, returned to Burch's house, determined to punish him. To Alvis' consternation, when he drew his pistol on Burch, Burch pointed at him the rifle he was cradling. Jeff King then aimed his shotgun at Burch. All three weapons cracked almost simultaneously, and both Alvis Turner and Jim Burch fell dead. King fled but was soon tracked down by a posse led by John and Marshall Turner (Ben's sons, who were by this time allied with the Sowders clan). At about the same time, several other combatants were arrested.

By the end of 1888 most of the feud leaders were either dead or in jail, yet the vendetta dragged on. In June of 1890, John Rains, age eighteen, took revenge on Harvey Turner, who had killed his brother Jim some four years earlier. Marshal Turner met his maker that same year, but his death was probably not related to the feud. He was killed by W.J. Wyrick of Knox County.

General came to trial for the murder of Jack Turner in 1891. Jeff King struck a deal with him—he would testify for Sowders if the latter would do the same for him in his upcoming trial for the killing of Jim Burch. Both cases, he argued, could certainly be considered self-defense. The result was that King testified to the fact (whether true or not will never be known) that the Turners had hatched a plot to assassinate the Sowders clan leaders, who were known to be holed up in the Monroe Hotel. Jack and Jeff were the bait. He swore that Jack had died only because the Sowders men beat them to the punch. General was acquitted. The favor was returned and Jeff King also escaped punishment.

By this time, things in the Valley had changed completely. Middlesborough had been established, and the American Association, along with the Town Company, had acquired much of the land that had once belonged to the Turner and Sowders clans. Squire and Birdie Sowders, General's parents, sold their farm to Alexander Arthur in 1888, and Squire became the Justice of the Peace for the young city. On the wall of his office he kept a framed list of the twenty-seven victims of the feud. The Turners sold much of their land that lay in the west end of town to the Belt Railroad Company and other British interests, and the land to the southeast, which would be the site of Fern Lake, to the Water Company. Several of the Turners entered politics and/or joined the police force of Middlesborough.

In the late 1890s three of the Turner clan met their deaths, though probably not as part of the feud. "Wild Bill" Turner killed John Crook Turner in revenge, according to some of the Turners, for abuse the latter had heaped on him when he was a child. Bill himself was killed in 1898 while trying to break up a fight at the Quarterhouse, a saloon he operated in Mingo Hollow. In March of 1899, word reached the newspaper that Bill's brother Lee had been killed in Tennessee. The paper noted that "he was a member of the famous Turner family, of which so many have met death as he had—with their boots on." The report of his death was an exaggeration, and Lee went on to do in "Popeye" John Turner.[16]

In September of 1899, General Sowders had an urge to have a drink at the Quarterhouse. General Turner was tending bar. Turner had his back to Sowders, pouring his drink, when someone in the bar shouted out, "He's got a gun." Thinking he was about to be shot in the back, Turner whipped around, pistol in hand, and fired at Sowders, who had jumped up and was running for the door. The bullet got him in the hip. Sowders, though bleeding profusely, hid all night in a culvert, afraid even to take a deep breath lest he be discovered by the Turners, who were out searching for him. Sowders nursed his grievance until 1902, when he joined with the Balls and Colsons to march on the Quarterhouse.

General lived on until 1914. It was widely accepted that he had shot fourteen men over his lifetime. For years local children were made to behave by warning them, "General Sowders will get you if you don't watch out."

Footnote Ten

Alexander Arthur and His Lady

Nellie Maud Goodwin, tall and graceful, entered the East Boston drawing room that fateful day in late 1880 with the air of assurance given to one of that particular stratum of American society, the well-to-do merchant class. Her abundant dark hair was piled in soft waves to make the most of her high forehead, fine features, and graceful neck, and her gown emphasized her narrow waist and queenly carriage.

Nellie's family could trace its American roots through the Osgoods and Peabodys back to the earliest days of the colonies, and they were distantly related to Daniel Webster. Her father, George Goodwin, was a trader in silks, fine dress goods, shawls, and table linens in the town of Lowell, just outside Boston. He was able to provide his family with a comfortable living and an established place in society. Nellie's brother Charles, foreshadowing the adventuresome spirit of his sister, had earlier emigrated to Australia, where he was already doing well for himself. At eighteen, Nellie was a gracious, unassuming young lady, popular with both the younger set and the matrons of society.

Did she know as she entered the room that she was about to meet her destiny? Were her eyes immediately drawn to the well dressed man who bore a striking resemblance to his distant kinsman, President Chester Arthur? In her later years she was to tell her granddaughters that she knew at once that he was "the one."

Alexander Arthur was thirty-four at the time she met him, a sturdy, well-set man with reddish brown hair extending into sideburns, an ample mustache, sparkling blue eyes, and a ruddy complexion. It was his charismatic personality, however, that made him the center of every gathering. He was a born leader, with such an optimistic attitude that it was difficult to believe the blows life had already dealt him.

Alexander Alan Arthur was the eldest son of Alexander and Catherine Arthur. His paternal grandfather, who was born in London of Scottish parents, was the minister of a Congregational church in Dalkeith, Scotland, and was also the private tutor to the family of the Duke of Buecleuch. His paternal grandmother was Bethiah Flemming of Glasgow. Alex's father was their fourth child. He became a prosperous merchant-trader with business ties in both Scotland and Canada, and part owner of a merchant ship that plied the sea between Europe and the New World. He married Catherine Allan in 1845, and Alex was born to them in Montreal on August 30, 1846.

While Alex was still very young, the family returned to Scotland. Their first daughter, Bethiah ("Bertie"), was born to them in 1848 while they were living back in Glasgow. The family crossed the ocean again, and Macaulay made his appearance in 1850 in Lachine, Canada. Mary, James, and Alan were all born in Montreal in the years from 1852 to 1856. The family moved back to Scotland soon after Alan's birth. George was born in Glasgow in 1858 and the twins, William and Kathleen, arrived in 1860. Meanwhile, Alex attended Larchfield Academy in Helensburgh, Scotland.

In 1862 the family moved back to Canada. The American Civil War was raging, making the merchant shipping business uncertain, and Alex's father needed to be near this base of operations. The Arthurs took possession of a large home at Lachine, near Montreal, on the banks of the St. Lawrence River. The river was wide enough for steamers to travel it at this point, and the children could watch the ships go back and forth as they played on the grassy lawn. It was a comfortable, carefree life for the young ones, but Alex was almost eighteen and well aware of how precarious were the family fortunes. He was attending McGill's College in Montreal and laying plans to make his own mark in the world of business.

Another son was born to the Arthurs in 1863 but lived only two weeks. A daughter, Frances, made her appearance in 1864, and then, on September 22, 1866, the last of the children, Jean, entered the world. Already their father was in poor health. He had been diagnosed with diabetes a year or so earlier and was suffering from a large, festering carbuncle. Catherine, worn down from nursing her husband and worried about providing for their large family, never recovered from that last childbirth. She succumbed to pneumonia on February 4, 1867. Her husband did not tarry long thereafter, meeting his death less than a month later.

Alex was left, at the age of twenty, as head of the household, responsible for ten younger siblings, ranging in age from eighteen to a baby less than six months old. To complicate matters, there was no money. The American Civil War had caused disruptions in trade and made business difficult. There had also been problems in Scotland, of such a nature that Alex later spoke of his father's "involuntary ruin of himself" in order to help out Catherine's family. Then, during the last two years of his life, as his health was failing, Alex's father had neglected business, so that upon his death the family was left virtually penniless.

The Arthurs had many close friends in Canada but no immediate family. It was determined that Alex should take the girls and young William back to Scotland under his care, where they could be reared in the households of family members. The other children found jobs or places with friends. Macaulay and George went to work on farms, while James obtained a position at a photography studio. Alan was taken in by the Shewan family, and the baby, Jean, was adopted by the Sharpe family.

Alex later recalled how he felt at the time about so much responsibility being thrust upon him:

> I need not tell you what a world of care fell upon me with my father's death—how hopeless loomed the future—how dreary the parting with the nestlings who went abroad into the cold world alone and so young....I saw my brave little brothers brace themselves up to fight the battle by themselves....The determination to send my sisters and Will—then a little fellow of six years—to Scotland, under my charge, was a terrible blow. I knew it was best for them, but dreaded the stop for myself, as the prospects of succeeding in the old country were very dim as compared with those of Canada.[1]

William, young as he was when they had to leave Canada, also had vivid memories of the leave taking, which occurred just two months after his father's death:

> These were hard days and the parting was heartbreaking. Our party...went to Shewans for the final parting and there were my fourth brother, and my twin sister, and I remember sobbing and hanging on to the leg of the dining room table, until at last I had to be carried away by force to the train leaving for Quebec.[2]

Will recalled that it was a very rough passage, and the younger children were seasick almost the entire two weeks it took to make the crossing. How difficult it must have been for young Alex.

The reception in Scotland was not quite what they had expected. Their maternal grandmother, Margaret Macaulay Allen, was still living, but Alex felt they were "coldly met" by her and complained, "My mother's family...appeared to look upon our advent in Scotland as a hardship—a thing we could have helped—and because of their neglect of my poor brother and sisters...I shall never be able to bear them in the same affectionate remembrance as others."[3]

Alex's paternal grandparents were already deceased, but there was a large extended family on that side as well, so that his sisters were able to find hospitable homes. Unfortunately, his youngest charge, Frances, died at the age of eight, just two years after the demise of her parents.

Alex found employment in Glasgow with a Mr. Morrison who dealt in iron and steel. He was later to say that he acquired a valuable knowledge of trade while in Morrison's employ, though he enjoyed the travel the job entailed more than the office work. He was able to see much of Scotland and make many valuable contacts while working for Morrison. His free time he spent visiting his many relatives and keeping a watch over the siblings left in his care.

In the early 1870s, Alex met and married Mary Forrest of Birkenhead. They set up housekeeping in the suburbs of Glasgow and, soon after their marriage, also provided a home for William, who was then fourteen and had left school. The household grew with the arrival of their first child, James Alan, born in 1875. He was soon followed by a daughter, Winifred.

In 1877 Alex decided to leave his job in Glasgow, and he set up his own agency to trade in iron and steel in Gothenburg, Sweden. He also became interested in the timber industry in Sweden and acquired valuable knowledge and contacts during his time there. But after almost two years of work and no great success, he decided to try his luck elsewhere. He wrote to Mary, who had remained behind in Scotland with the children, that as he began this new business venture, he felt there was "surely some providence that directs all," and that as he looked back to past years when "plan after plan fell through and as hope following hope dropped away unripened," he had faith that his affairs were about to improve. This did little to ease the misgivings of Mary, who was not happy about his next proposal: a move across the ocean to Boston, Massachusetts, where he would represent a Sheffield steel company that made springs for carriages and railroad cars.

Alexander Arthur in Sweden, 1878. Courtesy of Abraham Lincoln Museum, Lincoln Memorial University.

Nellie Goodwin Arthur, ca. 1885. Courtesy of Maggie Pickett.

Alex's hopes for his new business were realized. He had some initial success, and his wife and children were soon able to join him in Boston. But bad luck continued to stalk him. While he was in England on business, Mary and the children became ill. James and Winifred recovered, but his wife succumbed in mid-1880. Alex was again left alone with the care of young dependent children.

It was soon after this that Alex first met Nellie Goodwin at the home of one of her East Boston relatives. In August of 1881 the two became engaged.

During 1882 Alex, while promoting his company's steel products, spent time in Asheville, North Carolina, which was a beehive of activity. The railroad had recently reached the town, turning it into a Mecca for tourists and those who valued the purported health benefits of the unspoiled mountain air, as well as for those who saw the economic opportunities that rail transportation would bring. All sorts of businessmen, industrialists, engineers, lumbermen, railroad men, and the like congregated in Asheville to work and play. It was a breeding ground for many business ventures, an atmosphere that just fit with Alex's personality and modus operandi.

Alex was impressed with the timber resources of the area and began to promote the possibilities to potential investors. Soon he was able to help establish the Scottish Carolina Timber and Land Company, with headquarters in Glasgow, which entered the burgeoning logging business in the foothills of the Great Smoky Mountains. The company acquired 120,000 acres of woodland in western North Carolina and East Tennessee, and Alex was named the company's general manager for America with responsibility for developing this resource.

The area chosen to begin operations was a virgin stand of hardwoods on the upper reaches of the Pigeon River. The potential in timber was exceptional, but there was a logistical problem in getting the logs to market, since the terrain was too steep and rugged for normal hauling methods.

For years the mountain people in the area had supplemented their income by cutting trees during the winter months, "snaking" the logs down the mountainside by means of oxen and the force of gravity, stockpiling them beside small waterways, and then when the spring "tide" came—that time when every creek and rivulet swelled with melting snow and spring rains—floating the logs to market. Alex, with his characteristic vision and optimism, had a grander vision of the same principle. He proposed building booms across the Pigeon River that would serve essentially as large holding pens for logs as they were harvested upstream. The booms would be constructed by chaining heavy logs together at an angle across the river and would catch the logs as they floated downstream. He would build his sawmill at Newport, Tennessee, a town of only a few hundred people but one that had a railhead. The lumber could be transported from there by train. There was also the opportunity to do as the mountaineers had done for years and float some of the logs on down to Knoxville for processing.

Alex's enthusiasm carried the day in the Scottish home offices, where tales of fortunes being made in the "New South" abounded and where there was excess capital just waiting for investment opportunities. He was given the go-ahead to begin the development immediately. No one seemingly paid much attention to the residents of the area around Newport, who would have told Arthur and his associates that the Pigeon River, so calm as he surveyed it, could on occasion become a rampaging torrent, far in excess of the normal springtime "tide," against which he wrote in one of his reports, "great care must be taken not to overload our booms, or have them weak, as the consequences might be disastrous"[4]—a truly prophetic warning.

Nellie and Alex were wed on November 1, 1882, at the High Street Church in Lowell, Massachusetts. It was undoubtedly with some trepidation that her family surrendered her to this adventurer some sixteen years her senior who was proposing to take her off to the wilds of the southern highlands.

The newlyweds visited Newport, Tennessee, that first year, and Nellie was somewhat disconcerted to find that her grand adventure with her dashing new husband would mean living in a place that lacked all the finer accoutrements of the society to which she was accustomed. That concern, however, was quickly pushed aside as her pregnancy became evident. On September 17, 1883, Percy Macaulay, to be known as P.M., was born in Arlington, Massachusetts. It was a bittersweet time, as Nellie's father had died just eight days before the birth of his grandson.

The move to Newport was accomplished the next year. For Nellie, it was difficult to be in such a strange place, with people so different from any she had known, and with a new baby besides. She was later to recall that even the servants seemed alien, with disparate standards and unable to cook the simple New England style meals she craved.[5] It was a lot for the young mother to overcome, and she found herself growing discouraged and depressed.

But yielding to depression was not Nellie's style. She invited her recently widowed mother to make her home with them, and she sent back to Boston for two of the Irish women who had worked as domestics for her family to come and help her. Soon her household was running more in the manner she had always known. She and Alex were able to make frequent trips into Knoxville, which was readily accessible by railroad and, while not in a league with Boston, did offer some cultural advantages.

Then too, Alex's enterprise was attracting all manner of newcomers. There were those from London and Edinburgh who brought a certain European sophistication to the changing town. A large number of Canadians had come to work the logging operations, mostly rough lumberjacks but also some more congenial supervisors. Other adventurers who had lived in Africa and the Near East added to the flavor of social evenings. They evolved their own entertainment, which included tournaments in the mode of the knights of old, with various contestants taking fanciful noble names and jousting from the backs of their reincarnated workaday horses.

The lumbering operation was proceeding as planned, with Alex in the saddle most days supervising and encouraging. Preparatory work took two years. Logging camps had to be established, timbering sites readied, the booms built, and in the town of Newport a sawmill, lumberyard, and related processing facilities had to be constructed, as well as offices and a commissary. The first hundred experienced lumberjacks arrived from Canada in 1882 and immediately set to work. They began cutting and trimming the huge trees and snaking them down to the river, while other workmen built the booms and readied the lumberyard. As the first board feet of fine poplar came through the huge band saw and were stacked by the railroad bed, it seemed that nothing could stop Arthur.

And Alex had grand plans for the town of Newport. He did not limit himself to the lumberyard and commissary his company was building. Where others might see only mud-mired streets, a few poorly stocked shops and overused saloons, and a stretch of cornfields, he envisioned paved boulevards and fine business houses. Alex drew up a map of the future Newport, with the streets already named and areas set aside for parks, various factories, and even a college, and another for a grand hotel on the river.

The Arthurs spent the summer of 1884 vacationing in Asheville, enjoying parties and gatherings at various fine hotels and private homes. Both Nellie and Alex enjoyed people and liked to entertain. They were sought-after guests for all the social functions, and for a time Nellie could forget the bleakness of Newport as it existed. Coincidentally, they made contacts with various influential people that would prove invaluable when Alex embarked on his project at the Cumberland Gap.

In early 1885, Alex and Nellie began building their own house in Newport. They called the huge Victorian structure the Arthur House, but future generations of Newport residents would refer to it as the Scottish Mansion.[6] Arthur planned it as a showcase for the various native timbers, so each room was finished in a different wood—oak, cherry, walnut, poplar, willow. Canadian craftsmen fashioned the elaborate interior woodwork.

The house was nearing completion when Nellie went into confinement at a residential hotel in Knoxville. Their daughter Marion was born on February 1, 1886. When Nellie returned to Newport with the baby, they were able to move into the mansion. Nellie was finally living somewhat the life she had been brought up to expect.

Early spring rains were unusually heavy in 1886. Each little rivulet and stream that fed into the Pigeon River was already full-running when there came a virtual cloudburst on the river's upper watershed. The rapid fall from the mountains added to the ferocity of the flooding river as it raced toward the Scottish company's booms, behind which floated a fortune in logs waiting to be cut into lumber. With the rain still pouring down, every man turned out to attempt to reinforce the booms. All night they worked, with Alex at their forefront, knowing that the future of the enterprise depended on the boom chains holding against the wrath of the river. Nellie and the other women spent the night listening to the rising river against the background of the still falling rain and worrying about the safety of their men.

It was almost daybreak when, with a horrendous scream, the chains broke, and thousands of huge logs went crashing downstream, destroying everything in their path. The force of the flood was so great that the logs were scattered down the length of the French Broad River and reached the Tennessee River. Even the invincible, optimistic Alex must have returned home depressed and needful of his young wife's strength and support. The lost logs represented four years of Alex's life and almost the entire investment of the Scottish company. Furthermore, the representative sent over from Scotland to assess the situation felt that the flood should have been anticipated and precautions taken by their general manager. The company lacked confidence in Arthur's leadership and would make no further investment.

Alex and Nellie were not defeated. Almost immediately he took on a mission for the Richmond & Danville Railroad Company to investigate the advisability of extending a rail line from Morristown, Tennessee, to southeastern Kentucky, where there were reported to be large untapped coal and iron ore resources as well as a wealth of virgin timber.

It was in the summer of 1886 that Arthur rode up to the home of Dr. James Harbison, who lived just south of the Cumberland Gap. Because of the nature of his profession, which entailed making calls over much of the area in which Arthur was interested, Dr. Harbison was an excellent source of practical information. Arthur spent several days exploring the area around the Gap, talking to mountaineers about land values, assessing the timber potential, and collecting samples of coal and iron ore. As he did so, his enthusiasm grew. He was later to recall his first view of the Yellow Creek Valley thus:

> The first glimpse of the magnificent amphitheater was bewildering for I had not imagined or in all my travels ever seen any place so clearly designed for man's enjoyment and use. So I studied it in every way, crossed and recrossed its spreading plain, searching in its encircling mountains and found there vast quantities of the boasted coal in easily worked beds of rare good quality and economic value....here lay resources of almost inestimable worth and a sufficiency of them to justify building and peopling of a great city with all varied utilities, modern needs and splendid opportunities. Foreseeing all that I said to myself, here I will induce my people when the time comes to build their town.[7]

Arthur returned to Morristown full of enthusiasm only to find that the railroad had merged with another during his absence and the new company was not interested in the project, at least in the near future.

No matter. Arthur could see the vast possibilities that this undeveloped region offered. He betook himself, coal and ore specimens in hand, to Asheville, where many well-to-do young men were passing the summer in the healthy mountain air. Alex was well acquainted with a number of these gentlemen from previous sojourns in Asheville and was soon able to infect several with his enthusiasm for the lands around the Cumberland Gap. Most were "up" for an adventure after weeks of socializing and decided to accompany Alex back to have a look for themselves.

An adventure it was. On August 31, 1886, the group camped at the saddle of the Gap with the Pinnacle looming overhead. Just as they were settling in for the night, the ground beneath them began to quiver and shake. The earthquake lasted only a few minutes, and its epicenter was far to the east, but it certainly seemed an omen of great things to come.

After several days of exploring the area, the men were so convinced that they had, with Arthur's guidance, stumbled upon a potential bonanza that they took options on 20,000 acres of land. They then headed back to the comforts of Asheville to plot how they could best exploit their find. The grand plans and designs that Arthur was weaving would take capital, and lots of it. It was finally decided that the company they had formed, the

Gap Associates, should use its somewhat limited funds to send Arthur off to Britain, which was at the height of its empire with excess capital to invest, to find backers for their enterprise.

The task was easier than even the optimistic Arthur could have imagined. Potential investors examined his samples, listened to his stories of cheap land covered by stands of virgin forest and bursting with high-grade coal and iron ore, and, thinking of the fantastic profits that were flowing in from other developments in the post-Reconstruction South, could hardly wait to join Arthur in his venture. In January of 1887 they formed the American Association, Ltd. and hired Sir Jacob Higson, a widely recognized geologist and engineer, to investigate Arthur's claims.

Higson arrived with a small group of Englishmen in the spring of 1887. Arthur and his Gap Associates shepherded the party, many of whom had never before traveled in rough countryside where there were few trails and no amenities. Arthur later recalled:

> There were many pathetic, ludicrous and unusual experiences which space will not permit me to detail; suffice it that my "Associates" made merry over the scares and discomforts of the Englishmen and "bantered" them to the limit, as was the native custom at that time. But they were grit all through. They made a thorough investigation of everything and when we emerged...after ten days of hard work, the leading expert of the party and solicitor representing the buyers, cabled London to the effect that they were more than pleased with the properties and the prospects and to go ahead with the deal. To say that I was pleased at the outcome is to put it mildly, as one Scotchman in the party said to me, "Mr. Arthur, you maun feel a prood mon th' day."[8]

The British investors made Arthur the general manager and chief American representative of the American Association. He and other members of the Gap Associates were able to trade their land options for shares in the company, making a nice profit on the transaction. Arthur arranged for these options to be exercised and further lands purchased, so that within a short time the American Association held title to more than 80,000 acres in the vicinity of the Gap.

Meanwhile, in the latter part of 1886, Arthur and Nellie had moved their family from Newport to a large home on West Hill Avenue in Knoxville. Besides caring for her own two young children, Nellie also had the responsibility of her step-children. James and Winifred were away at boarding school part of the year, but the rest of the time they were members of the bustling household that Nellie supervised. Luckily she had an able second-in-command in her mother, Rhoda Goodwin.

It was a busy time. The naturally gregarious Arthur immediately became the center of Knoxville's business community and was named president of the city's newly fledged Chamber of Commerce. Nellie, with her natural social graces, was soon entertaining Knoxville's most influential businessmen and politicians as well as society leaders. Visitors from England came in a steady stream, some of them minor nobility. It was a lot to expect of a twenty-four-year-old, but Nellie managed all with style and a graciousness that added much to Alex's image.

Alex moved rapidly ahead with his plans, shuttling back and forth between the Cumberland Gap area and Knoxville, negotiating land deals, laying out plans, talking to industries about relocating. On his back porch were bags of coal and piles of ore that were regularly the center of attention as he expounded on the area's possibilities. It was a huge boost to his credibility when in late 1887 the Watts Steel and Iron Syndicate, Ltd. of England announced plans to build two large blast furnaces in the Yellow Creek Valley.

The most immediate need was for transportation. Arthur tapped his Knoxville contacts for local capital, using imaginative promotions to sell stock in a new railroad company, the Knoxville, Cumberland Gap & Louisville Railroad, which would provide easy access to the developing coal and iron center. The American Association also subscribed to stock, and construction was soon under way, including implementation of an ambitious plan to dig a tunnel almost a mile long under Cumberland Mountain. He was also, with the promise of the Watts Syndicate in his pocket, able to induce the L&N to turn their tracks southward toward his planned city. This would give Middlesborough access to markets all over the country.

Alex set up an office on Gay Street in Knoxville. The city's mayor and other dignitaries attended the ceremonial laying of the rail for the train track. Everyone seemed anxious to jump aboard the bandwagon, and almost daily there was some announcement of a business or industry that had expressed interest in locating in the industrial Mecca that Arthur envisioned. He organized the Middlesborough Town Company to build a model city with broad, straight streets and all the modern conveniences. On July 16, 1888, a crew began laying out the town, and the first lot was sold in September of that year.

Did Nellie have a sense of *deja vu* as she listened to Alex's plans for his new city of Middlesborough? Was she excited when she heard him recount his vision of industries, hotels, great avenues, etc., or did it remind her too much of his plans for Newport?

Alex sent for his younger brothers to join him. Macaulay, George, and William had all gone to the Dakotas in 1880 to serve as the nucleus of a community of Scotsmen who took up claims for homesteads in the territory. The colony had prospered for a time, but then the price of wheat dropped precipitously, so that they could no longer meet their obligations. Consequently they were happy to join in Alex's new venture. Several others from the colony also moved to Middlesborough. They arrived, often in covered wagons with all their possessions, reversing the normal east-to-west odyssey, in the latter part of 1888 and early 1889. Alex's oldest sister and her family came from the East, so that for the first time in their marriage Nellie and Alex were surrounded by an extended family.

Meanwhile, in the summer of 1888, Nellie and Alex left the children at home with her mother while they traveled to England, where they spent more than five months. Alex met daily with potential investors, promoting his grand plans. Together they socialized with all the most important people of the day. It must have been a heady experience for young Nellie to be presented in Queen Victoria's Court. Even for one accustomed to the best that Boston society had to offer, London was something special, the center of power for the British Empire. There was surplus capital looking for a place to be invested, and Alex could certainly supply that need. They returned home with a sense of a mission accomplished—there would be sufficient resources to build his dream city.

The year 1889 was grand. Businesses and people were piling into the Yellow Creek Valley. There were daily announcements of new industries that would be locating in his city, and contracts were signed to establish the basic services for a large metropolis. Railroad lines were racing toward Middlesborough; the Knoxville, Cumberland Gap & Louisville Railroad was laying track north from Knoxville, while the L&N was heading south from Pineville. On August 8, 1889, the tunnel was cut through and there was wild celebration on both sides of the Gap.

August 22 was set as the date for the first train to travel from Knoxville to Middlesborough. The mayor of Knoxville and other city officials, as well as many prominent businessmen, investors, and newspapermen, were invited to make the initial run. It was a festive group, already celebrating the culmination of a project sure to bring huge profits and increased business to both cities, that boarded the cars and set off on this historic run. Hundreds of people gathered to witness the departure of the first train, and a number of young ladies gaily waved their handkerchiefs as the engine pulled out. The men cheerfully returned their waves, then settled down to enjoy the ride.

The gala company was about twenty-five miles north of Knoxville when disaster struck. As the train came around a sharp curve and onto the wooden trestle over Big Flat Creek, the rear coach, in which most of the passengers were riding, unaccountably left the track, then detached from the train and plunged over the trestle, landing upside down across the narrow creek some twenty-five feet below.

Men from the other cars rushed down to pull their comrades from the wreck. The scene they encountered was terrible:

> Those who were more or less seriously injured had pulled themselves out and were lying on the east bank of the little stream, groaning and writhing in pain. Inside the car...was a scene too horrible to describe. The wounded people, the seats, the stove, the chandeliers, all piled up together in a frightful mass! Clots and pools of blood were standing in the center of the car. Gaping wounds met the eye everywhere.[9]

Three men died immediately and four others soon succumbed to the wounds they had sustained. The injured numbered better than twenty, including Alex, who had internal injuries and damage to his leg. The paper reported, "Mr. Alex A. Arthur...although pinioned to the floor and suffering the most intense pain, refused to be removed or treated until all the others had been cared for."

News of the wreck reached the city before the wounded, and Nellie, who had seen her Alex off with such high spirits, now waited with dread. An ambulance brought him to the house, where medical care was given, and he was found to be less seriously injured, at least physically, than originally thought. Within two days, he was able to sit up enough to sign his name to several important documents, and it was felt that he was out of danger, though, as the paper reported, "the mental strain on his system is simply terrible."

Knoxville was devastated by the news of the wreck. All of the dead and injured were prominent citizens—"The Flower of Our Citizenry," as the papers put it. One of the deceased was the mayor of Knoxville. When the town learned of the tragedy, all of the stores, business houses, and offices closed in respect for the departed. All over the city small groups gathered in the gray, drizzling rain, which had come up in the afternoon, to lament the passing of so many. An inquiry was made into the cause of the wreck, but no defect could be found in the track or the train. The K,CG&L Railroad was absolved of all fault, but Alex could not dismiss the wreck so readily. As Nellie was to write after his death, "He was never the same, physically or mentally, after that Rail Road accident....The M.D.'s said he would not live over six yrs—He lived over twenty—but it was a *struggle,* in every way."[10]

The accident could not have happened at a worse time. The heavily advertised auction of lots for the Middlesborough Town Company was scheduled for October 14, 1889. Alex had to be present.

He moved into a small portable house on a hill overlooking the planned downtown area just east of where a large hotel was being constructed. Nellie traveled with him to Middlesborough and nursed him as he supervised the final arrangements for the grand sale. It was not easy, as the accommodations were very primitive. Meals were available only in the commissary tent, and the streets were so muddy that one traveled even short distances only by horseback.

On the day of the auction, Alex was still essentially bedridden, so Nellie attended the sale as his eyes and ears. She rode a large, pure white horse so that Alex, watching from the hill above, could easily identify her from a distance. The sale was eminently successful.

Nellie's mother brought the children from Knoxville for Thanksgiving. They stayed at the yet-unfinished Cumberland Hotel, where they had to hang blankets over bare headers to have any privacy. For the children, eating in the mess tent was quite an adventure.[11]

By December of 1889 Arthur was sufficiently recovered that Nellie could return to their Knoxville home. In early 1890 they traveled once again to Europe, visiting both England and France. While Alex was concentrating on business, Nellie was able to do some shopping. She bought a handsome emerald and diamond ring in London and a black net dress of the latest style in Paris.[12] Middlesborough might be located in a heretofore backwater area, but it would not be lacking in fashion.

A large, elegant hotel, the Middlesborough, opened in Alex's city in April of 1890. Thereafter Nellie and Alex maintained a suite of rooms in the hotel and entertained important visitors, potential investors, and publicists there. At a typical affair hosted by the Arthurs, they served a fourteen-course dinner followed by dancing that lasted most of the evening. A light "lunch" was served their guests at midnight.

The weeks leading up to the second land auction at the end of May were particularly heady ones. Almost daily new enterprises announced their intention to open in Middlesborough, and new residents poured into the city. The sale of town lots on the first day of the auction exceeded anything even the optimistic Arthur had predicted. That night there was a dance at the Middlesborough Hotel. Nellie wore a dress of canary silk with a white lace overdress and her diamonds. Her height, presence, and stately manner proclaimed her the First Lady of Middlesborough.

Just as everything seemed to be going well, disaster again struck, this time in the form of fire. Two relatively small fires, one in April and the other in early May had already destroyed several businesses and a number of homes, demonstrating the vulnerability of the frame and tent structures. The morning after the sales closed, Alexander Arthur was in his office working when his secretary suddenly called to him. The town was on fire! Already flames and pillars of dense black smoke were pouring from one of the buildings, and a strong breeze was spreading the conflagration. Alex, along with all available men, fought the fire valiantly, but to no avail. By mid-afternoon the nascent business district was no more.

The Middlesborough, built on a hill overlooking the town, escaped the general destruction. There Nellie and the other ladies gave aid to those injured fighting the fire and began the task of providing for those left homeless by it. The paper anointed them that "kindly band of ladies."

Even before the flames had been totally doused, Arthur issued a proclamation that the Town Company would extend aid to the victims of the fire in the form of food, temporary housing, and financial assistance. Probably aid has never been more quickly available to victims of a disaster. The papers reported that Arthur was "here, there and everywhere." He then turned his energies to obtaining capital and backing to rebuild. This time brick business houses would replace those of timber and the tent stores. He was successful, and the town rose "Phoenix-like" from its ashes. People continued to flow in and lot sales were brisk. In June, exhausted by his efforts, Alex retired to the seashore on orders of his physician.

By the fall of 1890, the population of Middlesborough was estimated to be approaching 7,000. Industries continued to announce plans to locate in the city, and several, including the largest tannery in the country, were under construction. It seemed nothing could interfere with Arthur's grand plans. Yet when one of the investors, the Duke of Marlborough, visited the new town as a guest of the Arthurs, he returned to England with misgivings. So much had been spent to develop the city and then spent again to rebuild, but there had been no real industrial production yet and no return on investment other than through the sale of town lots, mostly on speculation. His voiced reservations infected other investors.

The Arthurs would have been nonplused by such a harsh, albeit shrewd, assessment, as they had gone to great lengths to make the duke and his duchess welcome and to impress them. They had vacated their own suite at the Middlesborough so the royal couple could have the best of accommodations. Nellie sent to Knoxville for her fine silver and her own butler in order to assure proper service. For all that, Nellie later confided to her grandchildren that the duke (who was the uncle of Winston Churchill) was a "rather dull" dinner companion who seemed more interested in rolling his bread into tiny pills and creating pyramids with the resulting balls than in making conversation.

The land auction in November of 1890 was the most successful of all. Nellie, mounted this time on a coal black horse, watched from the sidelines. As reported by the *Middlesborough News,* bidding was especially brisk for the corner lot at 20th and Cumberland. Beginning at $250 a front foot, "bids started popping like firecrackers" and soon reached $400. Suddenly, "in a state of a little excitement the fair rider raised in her saddle and cried $410. A murmur of approbation ran through the large crowd." No one topped this bid, and Nellie rode away "a smile of satisfaction overshadowing her features." According to family tradition, Alex was not completely happy about her purchase—she had just paid more than a comparable lot was bringing in downtown Manhattan at the time.[13]

Meanwhile Alex and Nellie were busy constructing an estate, which they called Craig Neuk, across the mountain in the Powell Valley. In his grand scheme of things, Alex envisioned country estates on the Tennessee side of the Gap to which wealthier residents could retire to escape the industrial center that was to be Middlesborough. For his own home he chose a ten-acre plot in the area he called Harrogate, after the English suburb of the same name outside of industrial Leeds.

Work on the home began in the spring of 1890. It was a large, substantial Victorian structure, patterned after the English country houses of the time, and was rumored to have cost $65,000 (roughly equivalent to $1.25 million in today's currency). The stained-glass window on the stair landing proudly displayed the Arthur family crest. The furniture came from one of the best known firms of its kind in London. There was an excellent library with row upon row of books, along with fine etchings, original paintings, and deep leather chairs. The dining room boasted a massive silver service, numerous cut-glass pieces, and a Chippendale cabinet filled with fine china adorned with the Arthur crest. An elegant central stairway led to multiple bedroom suites on the second and third floors.

Arthur also purchased blooded stock—horses and dogs—and had an elaborate stable, pigeon house, and kennels constructed for his animals at a cost of $9,000. The grounds were carefully landscaped with fruit trees and many unusual flowers, including a rose that had green blooms. Seventeen

Alex and Nellie Arthur in front of Craig Neuk. Courtesy of Mary Stonecipher.

servants were employed to run the house, tend the animals, and groom the grounds.

It would be June of 1891 before Alex could finally move his family into their grand new home. They lived there only seven years, but they always recalled those as the happiest times of their lives, despite the financial hardships that arose. In her later years, their daughter Marion often reminisced about the golden days spent with her cousins exploring the area, picnicking by the creek near the old iron furnace, and playing with their dogs. She did not realize then what lay ahead.

The difficulties foreshadowed by the spring fires multiplied when there was a financial crisis in England in the late fall of 1890. Baring Brothers Bank, which had supplied much of the capital for the development of Middlesborough, failed. It was with this bad news in hand that Arthur and his secretary, Charles Roberts, sailed for England in December of 1890. There he met with the stockholders of the American Association, Ltd., who expressed dissatisfaction with his stewardship and discharged him from his post as general manager of the Association. (For the time being, he retained his position with the other related companies.)

Arthur returned to a hero's welcome in Middlesborough. No one believed events in far-away England would have much effect on their booming town. Alex had just announced that the Town Company, of which he was still president, would be paying a 10 percent dividend, resulting in a total return to investors of 30 percent over eighteen months. Furthermore, he promised new sources of capital to continue the development of his city. A mass meeting was held at the new Opera House in March of 1891 to endorse his leadership.

Alex made another trip to England that summer and returned in August with E.F. Powers, who was to be the new general manager of the American Association. Powers went over the books and reported back to investors that the investment was generally sound but that there had been too much "booming" and that Arthur, though he had personally taken nothing more than his salary, "had been lavish and wasteful in the handling of the money sent out."

The London investors were feeling the pinch of a depression in England, and they turned on Arthur. The London *Financial Times* for October 12, 1891, called Alex "as arrant a financial braggart as even New England ever produced" and professed themselves ashamed that "a professional Yankee boomer of his impudence...should ever have been able to swagger about in the City of London as a great financier. No serious man of business could ever have been taken in by him unless he had been more than half willing to be deceived....A single inquiry addressed to certain people in Glasgow whom he had victimized in lumber would have proved him a very good man to let alone."

In October of 1891, the entire management of the Middlesborough Town Company resigned under pressure. Bankrupt, the company reorganized itself in November as the Middlesborough Town and Lands Company. Alex retired to Craig Neuk to contemplate his future.

He and Nellie still held their heads high and continued to lead the sort of life they had expected. They dressed every night for dinner, even if they were having no guests. In February they made a trip to New Orleans for Mardi Gras. Alex began to investigate new business ventures. Nellie must have called on all her reserves of character to support her husband and run her household during this difficult time. In later years people recalled that she was always the gracious lady, no different when their fortunes failed than when she ruled as the First Lady of Middlesborough.

The Arthurs were supported in large part by townspeople who could not believe the boom was over or that Alex was anything less than the consummate businessman. When the *Sunday Critic* learned that Arthur

The Arthur family on the grounds of Craig Neuk, 1894. Alexander Arthur stands at right admiring his family. Left to right, Kathleen Behenna (Alex's sister), Winifred (his daughter by his first wife), Nellie, Alan (Alex's brother), Ruby (Alan's wife), James (Alex's son by his first wife), Georgie (James's wife), Marion (Alex and Nellie's daughter), Percy (their son), and Bertie Railton (Alex's sister). Courtesy of Mary Stonecipher.

was contemplating a move, its editor solicited comments from the citizenry. The response was overwhelmingly positive. Typical was one from F.L. Howe, a photographer: "There are a few chin-whiskered polecats in every man's path but that don't prove that Alexander A. Arthur is not a man of great ability."[14]

Bad luck continued to hound them. In April of 1892 the stables, kennels, and pigeon house at the home in Harrogate were all destroyed by fire. In July the first of many law suits related to the development of Middlesborough was filed. In this one, a lot buyer claimed that the Town Company had induced purchase by "falsely and fraudulently advertising business." At the same time, Arthur's new venture in town and land development, the South Watauga Company, was not going well.

Arthur decided to apply his talents in another locale. Leaving his family in Harrogate, he moved to Alexandria, Indiana (the town was named for him), where he was to manage a large land and gas company. One of his brothers and several of his other associates went with him. But the financial crisis of 1893 was already on the horizon, and almost any new venture would have been doomed.

The people of Middlesborough were belatedly awakening to the fact that their paper profits were just that. Businesses were failing, and some found it easy to blame Arthur. In January of 1893 Arthur, writing from Alexandria, was threatening to sue the editor of the *Middlesborough News* for criminal libel because of an editorial casting "unsavory reflections" on him.

The Arthurs themselves were not immune to the financial crisis. When he retired from active management of the Middlesborough companies, Alex was still a wealthy man on paper, but he had believed in his own dream and invested all of his own money in the development, and Nellie had done the same with the assets she had brought into the marriage, even selling various properties she had inherited in order to raise the capital to support Alex. Now they were caught in the downward whirlpool. The lots they had purchased on speculation were suddenly worthless and the companies in which they had invested were bankrupt. To make matters worse, there were numerous lawsuits. In February of 1893, the American Association sued the Cumberland Company over a timber lease granted the Middlesborough Lumber Company with A.A. Arthur as director. The court's judgment was that the shares held by Arthur had been fraudulently issued. Then in April of that year the American Association filed suit against Alex, Nellie, and their son James, claiming they had hyped the value of land and timber options they had originally bought in their own names when the options were transferred to the company. Alex brought a countersuit for monies he said the American Association still owed him. An out-of-court settlement was reached, so that many of the particulars were never aired in open court.

Alex continued to pursue his fortune in Alexandria, but it was impossible. His brother Alan, who had gone into the real estate business in Boston, wrote to another brother, Macaulay, in May of 1893: "I spent about four months in N.Y. trying to work up scheme for Alex—it didn't work out." He went on to say that he had heard from his brother George that the Alexandria enterprise was a failure, and that "Alec appears to be very blue."[15]

On October 28, 1893, the American Association went into receivership (bankruptcy). Many of the other companies associated with the development of the town had already done so or were to follow. So many independent businesses were going under during the crisis that businessmen of the town, with gallows humor, organized the Receivers Club for all those going bankrupt. In desperation a mass meeting was held at the Opera House in February of 1894, and those attending adopted a resolution favoring the return of Arthur to town management. Alex was present and must have been very gratified. He spoke to the group, reminding them, "If I come back to you, I will come without money, but instead I will give your affairs unceasing and intelligent direction." Nothing came of this, however, and Alex's affairs continued their decline. The company at Alexandria, and several other land development schemes that he tried to start all succumbed to the nationwide financial crisis.

Nellie was still keeping the home at Craig Neuk together for the children, but it was getting daily more difficult as she had had to let most of the servants go. Alex was back and forth from his various business ventures, making it a lonely time for the family. The Knoxville papers reported that he was "well nigh or quite at the bottom of the worldly ladder."

In October of 1895 the Middlesboro newspaper reported that Alex was back in town with a big mining scheme he was trying to float in London. The columnist opined that "many think he needs a bigger balance wheel." Alex was undeterred. He was by that time the secretary-treasurer of the British North American Trading and Exploration Company, which had purchased properties in Klondike gold fields. A number of his Middlesboro friends invested in his new venture.

In 1897 the Arthurs bowed to the inevitable. Craig Neuk had to be sold to settle debts.[16] In the economic depression it brought much less than its true value. The following year all of the fine furnishings were sold at auction. An indication of the amazing strength and fortitude of the family in the face of such reverses is the letter Nellie's mother Rhoda wrote to Marion the day of the sale:

> We are really having a circus....All rooms are full of people...a number came from Knoxville before I was dressed and some came in my room....All the natives are here too—I hope they will have lots of money for dear Mama—She is well and in fine spirits so do not worry about us dearest one bit....While I write Mr. Gee is shouting as loud as he can in the dining room selling things.[17]

The family moved to a cottage on Arthur Heights in Middlesboro, but Alex stayed there only briefly. Much of his extended family had already left town. His brother George had followed him to Alexandria and then moved on to New York. Alan and William went to Boston. Sister Bethiah and her family moved to Norfolk, Virginia. Only his brother Macaulay, who as a physician felt his services were still needed, stayed on. Alex was constantly on the move, working, but his business ventures were not going well. On May 27, 1899, the *Middlesborough News* reported, "We have an inquiry of what became of Alex A. Arthur's Klondike scheme. Our inquiry is to the tune of $200 or more and there are many others." How difficult it must have been for Nellie to live with these questions.

It was undoubtedly with some relief that she undertook the next move, back to upstate New York. In 1901 the family settled in New Rochelle, which was nearer her hometown and her family and old friends. Nellie was by now almost forty. P.M. at eighteen had completed his formal education and was already working away from home as an engineer. Marion was fifteen and somewhat frail, so that she did not attend public school but studied at home. Winifred, who had not yet married, was still living with them, as was Nellie's mother.

In 1903 Alex and P.M. both took jobs as construction engineers for the Midway and Vernon Railroad in British Columbia. The rest of the family remained in New Rochelle. When the railroad failed to meet its goal of being the first to tie in with the Canadian Pacific and thus win the mail contract, Alex returned to New York. In 1904 the Middlesboro papers excitedly reported that he might be coming back with sufficient capital to breathe new life into the town. Sadly he was in no position to do so.

It was during this difficult time that Nellie was drawn to the Christian Scientist Church, which had a strong nucleus in the Boston area. While in Middlesboro, she and Alex had attended the Episcopalian Church, as had most of those in management positions. But in January of 1905 she, along

Nellie Arthur in Boston, 1905. Courtesy of Alexander Arthur II.

with Alex and Winifred, joined the Christian Scientist Church. She was to be very active in this church for the rest of her life.

In the summer of 1907 Macaulay's wife Ruby made a vacation trip to New England and visited with her in-laws. When apprised of the impending visit, Nellie wrote her, "We have anticipated so much seeing you—and I hope you can stop off....We are having an awfully hard time just now—and Alec thought I should tell you although I *know* God is with us and will provide—Perhaps under the circumstances you would not feel comfortable for more than a night or two dear and I am awfully disappointed that we cannot offer you more. You will understand when you come and we will give you lots of love."[18]

Ruby did understand when she saw how they were living. She wrote to her husband from New Rochelle:

> We arrived here at last, found them fairly comfortable. They have rented this house furnished....it is a very small flat, only two bedrooms. So we had to sleep on the parlor floor last night. This 6:30 a.m., we had to get up early so as to have room cleared for breakfast. They are only two blocks from the trains....it is awfully noisy....Nellie is very pleasant and took us to the park last night....They are doing their own housework now, Winifred seems to be the chief cook. Alec says that everything is at a standstill out west, and no prospects at present. They seem to be blue, but are trying to make the best of it. Alex is particularly nice.[19]

Even more difficult for Alex might have been the necessity of obtaining a loan from his erstwhile young secretary, who had gone with him to the Yellow Creek Valley when he was just sixteen and had served him throughout the early years. Charles Roberts had moved to New York City and was a clerk in a law office. In a note dated August 10, 1907, and scribbled on the legal firm's stationery, Arthur wrote, "Dear Charlie—I am not able to wait in any longer today so may miss you when you come down as you said you would. May I count on you tomorrow, then?" Another note, dated September 7, explained the nature of Arthur's visit: "I am disappointed that I cannot return your helpful loan this week as I expected to do. My remittances have again been delayed, but they are bound to come soon when I will at once repay you."[20]

Nellie needed all her strength of character to encourage her family and manage her household in their reduced circumstances, so different from what she had known as a young lady growing up in the same area. Their son P.M. was still working out west. After his stint in British Columbia he had gone to the state of Washington, where he worked at construction companies and on a ranch. Marion was working at a fashionable millinery shop in New Rochelle, creating the wonderfully elaborate hats of the day. Winifred continued to live with them until 1909, when she married Nelson Baker. Rounding out the household was Nellie's mother, who was affectionately referred to by one and all as "Gram."

In 1909 Alex traveled to Germany and England in an effort to interest European investors in a new enterprise, the Hudson Counties Company, which proposed to build railroads in order to open new timber and mineral properties. Alex was in London in December, trying to keep everyone's spirits up by writing home, "I have just been thinking of how much we have to be thankful for, although we are still poor in worldly goods, and I am absent from home. Yet I know and am sure that comfort and ease will come to us soon and we will have many happy and merry Christmas celebrations in the years to come. God is good and his promises are sure!"[21]

He was hard put, however, to keep his spirits up when Christmas Day arrived. He wrote, "I am setting all alone in my gloomy room in front of a crackling fire, if it weren't for this wee bit of comfort I don't know what I should do for I feel ill used by my associates in New York and very solitary and friendless....I don't believe that I have ever had such a fierce longing to be home with my darlings as I do now....How I am going to stand tomorrow, I don't know. I did hope and plan to go up to Scotland and visit the Forrests, but again, an empty purse barred the way."

It takes little imagination to know the holidays were not easy for Nellie either, with Alex so far away and admitting discouragement, and with finances so tight. She did, however, have the comfort of friends and relatives nearby, and she and Marion went on many "outings."

In January of 1910 Alex was able to write, "I'm getting over my Xmas loneliness, dear, for now I'm busy, being out calling and negotiating all day, and writing up my notes and reports often til 12 of a night." He had two rooms at his London hotel, one a bedroom and the other a sitting room he used as an office, "to receive my business callers—I have no others." He went on to say, somewhat sadly considering his natural gregarious nature, "I never go out, and simply devote every moment to my work." The only bright spot he could report was that his rooms were very near Covent Garden Flower Market, and his waiter kept him well supplied with fresh flowers.

In May, with the traditional time for holidays approaching, Alex wrote, "If I can manage funds I'll go up to Birkenhead—if Kate will have me. But the question of funds is the rub." Alex was sixty-three and no longer in good health. The leg that had been injured in the train wreck so many years before was giving him problems and, like his father before him, he had developed diabetes. He longed to be home with his family. Even the pleasures of business came to pale. In his last letter to his daughter from London, in early July of 1910, he spoke of the monotony of his days spent working, the frustrations of dealing with the English, who were "not systematic, dawdle too much," of the "wretched" weather, of it being too cold to sit in his room even though it was July, and the fact that the only parlor in the hotel was crowded and noisy, so that there was nothing to do in the evening after dinner but drink port and gossip. Though his letters to Nellie are not available, he was undoubtedly even more candid with her. How her heart must have ached for him.

Then, in July of 1910, while still in London, Alex had a stroke. Though he recovered sufficiently after six weeks of treatment to return home, he was still almost completely incapacitated. After caring for him a short while in New Rochelle, Nellie determined to take him back to Middlesboro, where his brother still practiced medicine. She was quite close to both her brother-in-law and his wife, Ruby, and felt she needed their support. Perhaps she also felt Alex's spirits might be lifted by returning to the scene of his greatest triumphs.

They arrived in Middlesboro in the fall of 1910, and rented a small cottage. The town welcomed him home. The newspaper reported that he had suffered many vicissitudes since leaving Middlesboro and that "his dream of rehabilitating his fortune is no more," but assured him that he had "come back to the friends who honored him in his palmy days with the knowledge that he need not make the effort again to stem the tide."

The return to Middlesboro did seem to invigorate him. Within a few months, he could tell his daughter:

> Spring has come and I am very happy that I get better everyday....The garden is going well, and the birds and blossoms and the mountains are just everything you would want to see!
>
> Mother and Doctor took me to the Elk's reception. A lot of ladies and gentlemen were delighted to see me, and it was like old times to see them all. It was very swell, like old times when I was boss of the magic city.

He tried to involve himself once again with the life of the city. In March he wrote to Andrew Carnegie requesting his help with the construction of a public library in Middlesboro. In May of 1911 he was one of the featured speakers when the Louisville boosters visited the town. His health continued to deteriorate, however. Finally all he could do was sit on his porch and look out over his beloved valley. Marion and P.M. both moved back to help with his care. In his last days Alex was a totally helpless invalid. Gangrene and blood poisoning set up in his leg. On March 4, 1912, he had a fatal stroke.

The entire town mourned his passing. The schools and all the business houses closed in respect for the man who had been the founding father of their city.

Nellie buried him on a hill overlooking the Pinnacle and his Magic City. Among the many letters of condolence that the family received was one that must have given Nellie particular satisfaction. His former secretary, C.B. Roberts, wrote, "Knowing what a wilderness the region of southeastern Kentucky was when he came upon the scene, I have often thought of him as not only its good genius but as a type of Cecil Rhodes; and as the great empire builder's dust lies amongst the Matappa Hills of South Africa, so it is meet that the remains of Arthur, the instrument which opened to man another of the waste places of the world, should rest amid the theatre of his achievement."[22] Nellie replied, "I feel you truly understand and appreciate my dear husband. He *was* a great man! and the generation to come will realize it better than this generation."[23]

Nellie elected to stay on in Middlesboro after Alex's death, participating actively in the life of the community. She continued Alex's interest in the library and was one of those most responsible for finally getting a Carnegie library for the city. She also helped reorganize the Women's Club and was one of its early presidents. With the help of several adherents, she established the first Christian Scientist Society in Middlesboro, which met in the Masonic Building. She taught the older children in Sunday School and was a practitioner who was called upon when someone was sick. One resident, who recalled Nellie coming to sit with her when she was ill, remembered her as a very beautiful woman with almost pure white hair piled up on her head, "a very lovable person."[24]

Nellie's mother continued to make her home with her until her death in 1919. Toward the end she became confused and believed herself back at Craig Neuk, the home everyone in the family recalled with such pleasure.

Marion also continued to live mostly in Middlesboro with her mother, occasionally teaching kindergarten classes. They lived in the old Middlesborough Hotel, by then renamed the Booneway Inn and somewhat down at the heels, catering mostly to traveling salesmen, though it still billed itself as a resort hotel and was still the scene of some grand parties and dances. One of those who met Nellie during this time recalled,

> During my first stay of two weeks at the Booneway in 1921, a regal appearing lady with a abundance of white hair and a black velvet band around her neck (the fashion of the late 1800's) attracted my attention not only because of her regal appearance but because she was always alone in the dining room....I learned that this regal looking lady was Mrs. Arthur....she invited me to her room which was on the first floor immediately beyond the Reception Desk. From her windows, she could

> look across the mountains to the east and down at Middlesboro below....On one of these visits to her room, she showed me professional-size photographs of the Arthurs and their friends on horseback....On another occasion, she told me about the home Mr. Arthur had built for them at the Gap....Only once in a later visit did Mrs. Arthur allude to their having experienced a great financial loss.[25]

She concluded her reminiscences by saying, "Mrs. Arthur remains in my memory a beautiful regal...lady who accepted most difficult experiences and losses...with dignity and without complaint."

In mid-1926 Nellie and Marion moved to an apartment in a large home on Brentwood Circle, just a block away from the Booneway. Ever one to put the best face on things, Nellie wrote to her step-daughter Winifred that she would be glad to have a kitchen as she had gotten tired of eating out. The kitchen, however, could be reached only by way of an outside stairway, and to reach her apartment Nellie had to enter through the front hall of the apartment of another family. It was certainly different from the days at Craig Neuk, yet she did not complain. The City Directory for 1926 listed Nellie's occupation as Christian Science Practitioner.

P.M. had moved to Mascot, Tennessee, after the death of his father to work for the American Zinc Company. His visits back to Middlesboro to see his mother and sister were also an opportunity to court. In 1915 he married his cousin Cathie, who was the daughter of Macaulay Arthur and his first wife, Mary Elizabeth Sikes Arthur.

In 1930, P.M. asked Nellie and Marion to move to Knoxville, which was much nearer to Mascot. They found an apartment directly across from the Christian Science Church, and Nellie was soon a leader of that society and a recognized healer. The apartment was within walking distance of downtown and had a good view of the river. The two women seemed content there, and they enjoyed the proximity of P.M. and his family. Marion loved children and always kept a stack of puzzles and games for her nieces, Mary and Maggie, and her nephew, Alex II. Her nieces recall that she was very talented at making paper flowers and would make "tons" of them for the girls. Marion also loved animals and always had pet turtles and a canary. P.M.'s children grew up with a family tradition of going into Knoxville on Friday night for shopping and a visit with their grandmother and aunt. On Sundays after church they usually visited again, often taking Nellie and Marion for a ride. When the girls were in high school they took a Greyhound bus into Knoxville to attend school there. Usually they went to their grandmother's house after school, and their parents would pick them up there in the evening. They recall that it was "a joy" growing up around their grandmother. She and Marion always seemed to have lots of friends and enjoyed visiting with them.[26]

In 1946, when she was eighty-four years old, Nellie went to Louisville for the annual convention of the Christian Scientists. While there she fell down some concrete steps, fracturing her hip, though no one realized at the time that it was broken. As dictated by her faith, she declined medical care, but she did decide to cut her trip short and go home that night. The friend she was with wired P.M. explaining what had happened. Nellie was put on a sleeper by herself, with only the porter to help her. He removed her shoes, then left. By the time she got to Knoxville, an overnight trip, she was suffering from severe edema. P.M. met the train with a neighbor, who was both a family friend and a doctor, in tow. As a Christian Scientist, Nellie did not have much to do with doctors, but she did know and respect "Little Doc," as they familiarly called this neighbor. When he saw her, the physician immediately knew the hip was broken. She had so much edema that there was no way to remove her from the sleeping car other than to remove the window and take her out that way. She was immediately transported to the hospital and surgery performed to pin the hip. She was told she would never walk again unassisted.

At home, with the grit and determination she had demonstrated all her life, Nellie practiced walking, using a chair as a walker, until she could get around the apartment. She then abandoned the chair and was soon able to do almost everything she could before the accident. But the surgery had been a severe emotional blow, since she felt she had to give up being a practitioner/healer after having resorted herself to medical care via a physician. She continued, nonetheless, to be active in her church and a joyful participant in all life offered until the time of her death on April 26, 1955.

The *Middlesboro Daily News* mourned her passing with the following tribute:

> The passing of Mrs. Alex A. Arthur brings a special sadness to friends in Middlesboro and Harrogate who remember her so affectionately.... This gracious lady, beloved by all who knew her, had experiences of great triumphs and tragic misfortunes which would have broken the spirit of anyone with less courage and philosophic acceptance of fate....She maintained a quiet dignity, sweet spirit and wholesome philosophy of life which endeared her to everyone. She was a kindly, generous, devoted neighbor and friend, never complaining or despondent, and always smiling and cheerful. She was never heard to express a single

word of despondency or disappointment over the cruel reverses which denied the realization of her husband's dreams in the building of Middlesboro.

Striking in her queenly beauty and stately dignity, Mrs. Arthur was always the perfect hostess and considerate friend. In the happy and hopeful days when Middlesboro was so rapidly rising from the old fields of Yellow Creek Valley, she was the leader and arbiter of all social affairs. In her retirement she was no less gracious and kindly, and her humility and beautiful spirit touched and inspired all who knew her.

Nellie was laid to rest next to her Alex in the Middlesborough Cemetery. From their hill one can look over the Yellow Creek Valley and the town of Middlesboro to the Pinnacle that guards the ancient pass. Their indomitable spirits serve as an inspiration to the Magic City over which they keep watch.

Footnote Eleven

Boom and Bust

James Lane Allen, Kentucky's first important novelist, made a trip through the Cumberland Gap in 1885. Of that first journey he wrote, "I took my course over the ancient Wilderness Road through the valley of the Yellow Creek. Many a time since the memory of that ride has come back to me—the forests of magnificent timbers, open spaces of cleared land showing the amphitheater of hills in the purple distance, the winding of a shadowy green-banked stream, the tranquil loneliness, the purity of primeval solitude."[1]

Alexander Arthur first saw the Valley of Yellow Creek a year later. He too marveled at the lovely, lonely vista and the wealth of natural resources. In contrast to Allen, however, as he looked at the valley he exclaimed aloud, "Here is where I will build my city!" What audacious optimism! Yet, with unbridled enthusiasm and enormous energy and force of character, he accomplished just that, and did it in less than four short years.

When Allen revisited the area in 1890, he marveled "that the shadowy valley of my remembrance had been incredibly transformed." He went on to exclaim:

> These Englishmen...are at work developing their city to the intent that it shall bring as great a change in the steel market of the United States as a few years ago was made in the iron market by the manufacture of Southern iron....the working out of their plan it is the same—no stint, no drawing back or swerving aside, no abatement of the greatest intentions....The mountain is in their way—that mighty wall of the Cumberland Mountain which has been in the way of the whole United States for over a hundred years...they dig through it....Less than a year

> ago there were three buildings and a population of twenty-five; there are now over six thousand people, with their electric lights and street cars, and seven churches, and eight hotels, and banks, and telegraphs, and telephone, and what not.[2]

How did Arthur accomplish such a feat?

He first touted his vision of a bonanza in the wilderness on the basis of the untapped natural resources. Investors could immediately grasp that in order to exploit these, there needed to be laborers, and to insure the latter, housing would need to be provided. But Arthur did not want just another mining town. He envisioned a city with industries that would process the raw materials and would attract all types of other businesses and provide the amenities of city living to its inhabitants. As one of his associates explained, it was not enough for workers to make a living, or even their fortunes; it was imperative that "their lives shall be worth living while they are doing this."[3]

Such a city would need a good transportation system that would link it with markets in every part of the country. Using all his considerable powers of salesmanship, Arthur convinced the Louisville & Nashville Railroad, which was laying tracks from Corbin to Pineville and planned to continue on to Harlan, to instead turn southward toward the rich coal fields surrounding the Yellow Creek Valley. He then sold the Knoxville business community on the idea of the railroad line from there to the Cumberland Gap and a tunnel through the mountain to hook up with the L&N line. Most of his business acquaintances subscribed to stock in the Knoxville, Cumberland Gap and Louisville Railroad, as he called it. The city of Knoxville agreed to issue $225,000 (equivalent to well over $4 million today) in bonds to underwrite the project. Thus he insured transportation lines to all parts of the country.

To demonstrate the viability of his grand scheme, Arthur needed at least one industrial giant to commit early on to building in his city (much like an anchor store for a proposed mall today). He had the advantage of long-time contacts in the steel industry from his early years in the business, and was able to make the Watts Steel and Iron Syndicate, Ltd. in England an offer they could hardly refuse. Not only would they have the first crack at the huge cache of untapped minerals that he and his associates had already optioned, but they would be provided with free land on which to build their furnaces, free railroad spurs, $100,000 of paid-up stock in the American Association, Ltd., and a large cash bonus when they actually went into production.

When the Watts Syndicate announced in late 1887 plans to build a large steel-processing plant in the Yellow Creek Valley, Arthur was on his way. He had already formed the Middlesborough Town Company, with a majority of the stock being held by the American Association, Ltd. (in return for a grant of land in the Valley) and by individual stockholders of the American Association. Arthur now set about establishing various subsidiary companies to provide services for his city. The Middlesborough Electric Light, Heat & Power Company would not only supply homes and businesses with the new incandescent lamps but also light his city streets with arc lights, an almost unheard-of modern convenience for the mountains. The Middlesborough Water Company was charged with building the first masonry core dam in the country in order to impound a large lake capable of supplying water to a city of 100,000 or more. Transportation within the city in that time before automobiles would be provided by the first electric streetcar west of Washington, D.C., which would be operated by the Middlesborough Street Railroad Company and would run down the center of the main thoroughfare, Cumberland Avenue. Encircling the city would be a rail line built by the Middlesborough Belt Railroad Company. This would cross the streetcar lines and would connect with the L&N and the K,CG&L tracks so that all parts of the city would be readily accessible. Spurs from the Belt Railroad would go into the hollows where coal mines were to be located so that raw materials could be readily transported to the city's foundries, coke ovens, and steel mills.

Other needs were addressed. The Middlesborough Hotel Company began planning a large luxury hotel, while the Manchester Building Company and the Ousiotto Building Company organized to build rental houses for common laborers and other accommodations, such as the four-story boarding house constructed on Arthur Heights. There was even the Middlesborough Cemetery Company to provide for the inevitable. The Cumberland Gap Park Company and the Harrogate Land Company would develop properties just over the Gap in Tennessee, where Arthur envisioned an exclusive residential area and resort. Stockholders in the American Association, Ltd. were given the right to purchase a specified number of shares, as determined by the number of shares they owned in the parent company, in the subsidiary companies at par value. The offering was then opened to other investors.

Even as he was organizing these companies, Arthur began the work of building his city in the wilderness. One "native" who came in the spring of 1888 to work at clearing the brush for the surveyors recalled, "The standing wage was $1 per day and you had to furnish your own bunk and food.

Many lived in tents and some slept outside on the ground. All kinds of old cans were brought into use for cooking utensils. We used to boil sostingears [*sic*] in old powder cans, then we would roast them. Many people through the summer lived mostly on green corn."[4] (This may in part account for the fact that in the fall of 1888 the *Cumberland Gap Progress* reported that the company was having difficulty filling its labor needs with "regular workers.") Another of the early residents recalled that he was paid seventy-five cents a day for a twelve-hour day grading the right-of-way for the railroad.[5]

On July 16, 1888, the first survey stake was pounded in at what is now 30th and Cumberland, which was the approximate center of the Valley. Arthur planned for the future, a time when he envisioned there would be a major city in the Yellow Creek Valley. Thus the main street was 100 feet wide and laid out along the Valley's greatest axis. North-south streets were numbered while those running east-west were given traditional British names—Gloucester, Cirencester, Dorchester, etc. At noon on that first day, the surveying crew was treated to a fried chicken dinner to celebrate the tangible beginning of Arthur's city.

That same month, Arthur sold his first town lot. A.D. Campbell purchased the southwest corner of 21st & Cumberland and began construction of a general merchandise store. Most of the building supplies had to be hauled by wagon from Knoxville or from Ewing, Virginia, over very difficult roads. It took eight months to build that first frame structure.

Meanwhile a vanguard of investors and businessmen descended on the area. The Watts Syndicate sent out two brothers, Frank and Edgar Watts, to supervise their project. Arthur's brother William arrived from out West to oversee road construction, and several managers were brought in for the timbering operations and the three sawmills that were to provide raw materials for the railroad, tunnel, and other construction. And already there were visitors who had heard rumors of the bonanza in the wilderness and wanted to see for themselves. There was an immediate need for housing, so one of the first projects was the building of a large boarding house, usually called the English Hotel, just south of the Gap. The first guests arrived in the spring of 1888, and already by that fall an addition was needed to accommodate the overflow.

The Watts brothers, who were described by their contemporaries as "elegant young gentlemen," bought a farm not far from the hotel and began construction of a "bungalow," which to local eyes was more of a mansion. There they entertained visitors from England with hunting and shooting expeditions, gallops through the woods, and other sports enjoyed

Alexander Arthur (far right) with potential investors, 1888. The English Hotel is in the background. Courtesy of the Bell County Historical Society.

by young English bloods of the day. Their devotion to business was, unfortunately, less evident.

Arthur was operating out of an office in Knoxville. His energy and imagination were astonishing. In addition to overseeing the American Association, the Town Company, and the multiple subsidiary companies, he was also engaged in publicizing and selling his vision to investors, industrialists, and businessmen, and to the general public. So successful were his efforts that people began flocking to the city even before there was a city.

One problem, of course, was that the railroad had not yet arrived, and building supplies were hard to obtain. The Town Company had managed to erect a few portable houses, one of which was used by Arthur when he was in residence, but almost everyone else was relegated to a tent. As people piled in, the Valley came to look, according to Arthur's young secretary, Charles Roberts, as if "it were occupied by an army." Businesses set up in tents. There was a bath tent, a barber tent, and even a billiard tent. Some did not even have a tent. Jake Goodfriend, who would found the store that was the progenitor of the present day Goody's chain of clothing stores, started with just a goods box on which he displayed his merchandise during the day and in which he packed it away at night.

Arthur's secretary later described early living arrangements thus:

> The establishment where we ate and lodged was called the "Hotel Encampment." The mess-house, of pine timbers with the bark on, which stood between double rows of tents, was manned by darky cooks and waiters from Knoxville, the chief of the latter of whom was "Laughing John," a jolly negro...who proudly wore in his shirt bosom a faceted glass "diamond" as big as a black walnut. The meals in this rude victualing-place would not, ordinarily, have gladdened a gastronome, but now and then we sat down to some especially toothsome viand. Once this was provided through the occurrence of an unusual incident: a deer wounded by hunters in the mountains had fled, baffled and desperate, into the valley and was swimming Yellow Creek, then in flood, when a man plunged in to his armpits and dispatched it with a knife. We had venison for several days.[6]

The nascent city's population was almost entirely male. As Roberts put it, conditions were like those of a gold rush town, with men dressed in "slouch hats," boots and "negligee" (open necked) shirts, most openly carrying pistols, "while the native, according to immemorial habit, seldom went abroad unaccompanied by his rifle." Like the Wild West, "Killings were common, and not infrequently several men would fall in a single fight." Another of the city's early settlers, who came in the fall of 1889, said, "You could hear pistol shots at short intervals during the day and night. The natives used to shoot through a tent just to see a lamp chimney break, or shoot a man in the foot to see him jump. It was not an uncommon thing for a man to be killed for every day in the week."[7] Women were at first so scarce that "the sight of a lady stilled the hatchets and saws on the buildings, while workmen gazed in admiration at the passing figure."[8]

One woman who visited the Valley prior to the arrival of the railroad recalled that although the carpenters were hard at work and there were a few places being rented in as-yet-unfinished buildings, no one would rent to a couple when he could rent the same room to fifteen men instead. She and her husband had to return to Cumberland Gap, where they were able to find a place in a primitive boarding house, which was so infested with bedbugs that they were unable to sleep. Instead, they passed the night "catching these animals and burning them by throwing them down the lamp chimney."[9]

Meanwhile Arthur was busy securing industries for his city. Almost any enterprise willing to locate in Middlesborough was given free land as well as other concessions. Within two years the Town Company had donated 163 acres of prime land to various companies. In addition, Arthur, either personally or through one of the companies he controlled, often invested in the new industry and/or loaned it money. For example, to entice Overbeck Brewery to build in Middlesborough, Arthur himself subscribed to $100,000 of the total $300,000 capitalization, agreeing to pay seventy-five cents on the dollar. He actually put up only $61,000 in cash; the balance was to be paid by the Southern Investment Corporation, which he controlled. This scenario was played over and over again, with the announcement of each new industry and business creating excitement and the certainty that here was a fertile place to invest and to make one's fortune.

Most of the new industries, even those secured "on the come," were established on the firm basis of the availability of raw materials, labor, and markets. Timber, for example, was readily available and there was a demonstrated need for building supplies, so a number of wood product enterprises started up. Besides four sawmills, five planing mills, and several lumber yards, there opened a sash and window company, two furniture factories, a novelty wood company, and even a casket supplier.

From the beginning the Town Company addressed the need for proper sanitation and drainage, which would entail an extensive and expensive channeling of Yellow Creek. This was only prudent, as had been pointed out early on: "A few cases of illness might destroy the entire prospects of the place."[10] Besides, as the same source explained, if the creek were straightened and made into a drainage canal for the city, then a good deal of land could be reclaimed from the swamps and made into buildable, and salable, lots. In fact, it was first thought that the sixty or so lots that would be thus created would be sufficient to pay for the canal.

As it turned out, early efforts to construct a canal were poorly conceived. The first flooding of Yellow Creek washed away several months of work. The Town Company then hired George Waring, a well known engineer who had worked on the sewer system in Memphis, Tennessee, and was later to design a system for Havana, Cuba, to take over the project. He imported a large number of Italian contract laborers who pitched their own tent city along the banks of the canal in the area of 24th Street. They began the work of digging the canal, almost entirely by hand, and lining it with heavy timbers. In order to drive large piles in the center of the canal to anchor the timbers, a heavy weight was pulled six feet in the air by ten men tugging on a rope, then allowed to fall on the pile. This was repeated every five feet along the length of the lined canal. It was a monumental task, and one that cost far more than originally anticipated.

An even larger undertaking was the railroad tunnel through Cumberland Mountain, a distance of approximately 4,000 feet. With pick and shovel, black powder, hard muscles, and strong determination, men started on the two sides of the mountain in the spring of 1888. They laid track as they went, and on August 8, 1889, met in the center of the mountain. (Compare this with the more than six years it took to complete the present, albeit larger and much more elaborate, tunnel using modern equipment.) There was wild excitement and celebration on both sides of the mountain when the work parties met. Although a wreck caused a slight delay, the first train was able to travel through the tunnel on September 1.

Everything was now in place for the first big lot sales in October of 1889. Arthur blanketed the country with flyers proclaiming the wonders of his city-to-be. He arranged for round-trip excursions from many major cities and announced accommodations for an expected 1,500 bidders. Included were tents, each sleeping four persons, at $2.50 a day, and rooms in yet-unfinished hotels and boarding houses. The auction was more than successful, netting in three days well over $300,000 (equivalent to almost $6 million today[11]). Even better for many buyers was the fact that they were able to resell their lots within a few months for more than double what they had paid.

The "boom" fed on itself, with new enterprises announced almost every day, and each train bringing carloads of new residents. By the spring of 1890 it was estimated that 5,000 had already arrived. As one person who came that year recalled,

> It was all plowed up, a lot of little paths and gullies with plenty of mud all around....People were coming here so fast and so unexpectedly that a newly-built livery stable was turned into a hotel or boarding house. Boards were used for a table hastily put up in the center of the stable and horse stalls were converted into bunks for people to sleep in, and at that, some of the stalls were used double shift—someone sleeping in them during the day and someone at night.[12]

The Town Company, true to its credo, tried to provide for the amenities. It not only donated lots to any denomination that wanted to build a church but also provided most of the building supplies. Four lots were set aside for schools. Arthur hired a director of entertainment and sports and provided sporting fields. An opera house opened in the fall of 1889. Soon hotels, restaurants, and saloons offered a varied social life.

The grandest of the hotels was the Middlesborough, which opened in

The Yellow Creek Valley in early 1889, before the “boom.” Courtesy of the Bell County Historical Society.

The same view of the Yellow Creek Valley in late 1889. Courtesy of the Bell County Historical Society.

April of 1890. Set on a hill overlooking Cumberland Avenue, it was initially built to accommodate eighty guests. A Victorian marvel of native stone and wood, four stories high with wide verandas on two sides, it would serve as the center of social life for the new city. Its large public rooms were lit with the new incandescent lamps, so that at night it seemed magically ablaze with light.

For the Middlesborough's opening ball, invitations were sent to people in Louisville and Cincinnati, accompanied by free tickets for a special train to be run just for the event. It had rained for much of the day and night preceding the ball, and the streets were a sea of mud, but the guests were not to be inconvenienced. When their train arrived at 5:30 p.m., all the whistles of the new factories in town were blown to welcome them. They were then transferred to the new dummy train that carried them in style to the grounds of the hotel, where they were greeted by a crowd of revelers. The doors of the banquet room were thrown open at six o'clock to reveal a huge, beautifully paneled and furnished hall. The large and varied menu, each course accompanied by fine wines, took four hours to serve. After dinner, the dining room and parlors were cleared for the ball. A fine orchestra from Lexington provided the music for dancing, which continued until three in the morning, with a brief interval at one o'clock, when a "dainty luncheon" was served.

Hardly had the hotel opened when it found itself overwhelmed by the influx of guests, with cots being placed in the halls. Soon an addition was built on the north end, bringing its capacity to 120 (though it was known to accommodate 250 if need be). An annex called the Occonita Club was built across from the Middlesborough and connected to it by a bridge over the street. According to the newspaper, it was modeled on a London gentlemen's club, "a veritable heaven to tired businessmen, indolent swells, to all male creatures, in fact, who love to take a royal meal, with wines and afterwards a cigar at leisure." It offered billiard, card, and reading rooms in addition to the reception and dining areas, and twenty-four bedchambers. A third building for the hotel complex was soon under construction to the east of the Middlesborough. Referred to as the Casino, it featured a huge round ballroom under a massive rotunda. (It was destroyed by fire before completion; building was never resumed because of the "bust.")

Other hotels and rooming houses were rapidly constructed and expanded. The Cumberland on 18th was designed for 60 but was known to serve 150 "in a pinch." The Phoenix, Tyler, Delmonico, Park Place, Exeter, Bellevue, and Ashbury hotels all scrambled to accommodate the flood of visitors. Even so, one man recalled paying a dollar for the privilege of sleeping in a chair at one of the small hotels, that being the only spot available.[13]

Excitement, and the speculation frenzy, were increased by Arthur's next publicity venture, the outfitting of a special train to showcase his wilderness empire. The Exhibition Car, as he called it, was supplied with specimens of all the natural resources—ores, minerals, and types of wood—found in the area. There were also stereopticon views of Middlesborough and the surrounding area and a lecturer on board to explain everything. The train left in March of 1890 for a six-week trip to Connecticut, Massachusetts, Maine, New Hampshire, Vermont, and New York. It returned before the land sales in May so that the exhibits could be viewed by prospective bidders.

The weeks leading up to the second land auction, held in late May, were particularly heady ones. Almost daily new enterprises announced their intention to locate in the Magic City. The Belt Railroad was officially inaugurated on May 18. A few days prior to the sale, Arthur was able to announce a grand coup—the South Boston Iron Works, one of the largest suppliers of armaments to the U.S. government, had announced plans to move its entire operation to Middlesborough, and the same day contracts were signed for a huge sanatorium to be built across the Gap in Tennessee. Trains coming into town were loaded with visitors, so that by the first day of sales it was estimated that there were 1,500 to 2,000 would-be investors, and the Town Company was utilizing every public building, church, and tent to lodge them. The first day exceeded anything heretofore seen in the New South, with sales of over $350,000 (roughly equivalent to $6.5 million today) in less than four hours.

A series of three fires in the spring of 1890 destroyed most of the frame buildings that had been hastily constructed along Cumberland Avenue. Rebuilding was delayed somewhat by a dispute between the two railroad lines serving the city but was well under way by mid-summer. This time construction was of brick and stone. By early 1891 the tents would be largely a thing of the past.

In the fall of 1890, a publicity pamphlet entitled "Middlesborough Catechism" avowed that $23 million had already been spent to develop the town, and estimated almost 7,000 residents. Ten hotels and two hundred residences were either completed or under construction. Seven churches were being built. Eighty-three business houses had already been erected, with another seventy-two going up. There were three banks, a steam laundry, an electric plant, fifteen miles of belt railroad, and a streetcar line. Besides all the wood-related industries, there were two fire brick yards and four red brick yards, three hundred coke ovens, a foundry, and a machine shop. Hall and Vaughn Tannery, with a capitalization of $400,000, would be one of the largest tanneries in the world when completed. The South Boston Iron Works had committed to moving its entire operation to Middlesborough. A large brewery was under construction, and the Watts Syndicate had plans for a major steel mill. Workers were promised excellent salaries, with bricklayers making $5.50 to $6.00 a day, carpenters earning $1.75 to $3.50, and common laborers able to command $1.50 to $2.00 daily.[14] Coal mines were opening in the nearby hollows. It was reported that the L&N Railroad was doing a larger business at Middlesborough than they were anywhere on the line except for Louisville, Nashville, and Birmingham. It seemed that nothing could stop Middlesborough from becoming "the new Birmingham."

To further publicize his town, Arthur hosted a meeting of the Kentucky Press Association in September of 1890. They arrived by special train in the morning and were given an extravagant breakfast at the Middlesborough, then taken on an all-day tour of the area with excursions to the Pinnacle and to King Solomon's Cave (now Cudjo's Caverns). The day ended with "one of the most elaborate banquets ever spread in Kentucky...[a] dozen or more tempting courses, washed down by sherry, claret and champagne of the finest vintage." Special waiters had been imported from Louisville to serve the 150 diners. No wonder Middlesborough got such good press!

In October the Exhibition train headed out again, this time bound for Albany, Buffalo, Chicago, St. Paul, Kansas City, and St. Louis. These publicity efforts were almost too successful. Mayor Brooks complained that he got 500 letters of inquiry in one day alone, half of them without stamps for a response. At that rate, he opined, the treasury would be in trouble just from the cost of answering letters.

That same month the British Iron and Steel Institute arrived on tour. The 310 men and their wives were met by Alexander Arthur, Mayor Brooks, and other dignitaries. They toured the area, rode the Belt Railroad, and then repaired to the new Exhibition Hall, where they examined samples of minerals and ores and heard lectures by geologists and others detailing the American Association's plans and prospects. The president of the Institute, Sir James Kitson, responded, "I think we all, as Englishmen, rejoiced to see a town which was being developed with so much sagacity and so much judgment and energy; that it was being developed under English auspices and with English capital."[15]

Two other parties from England arrived soon after the Iron and Steel

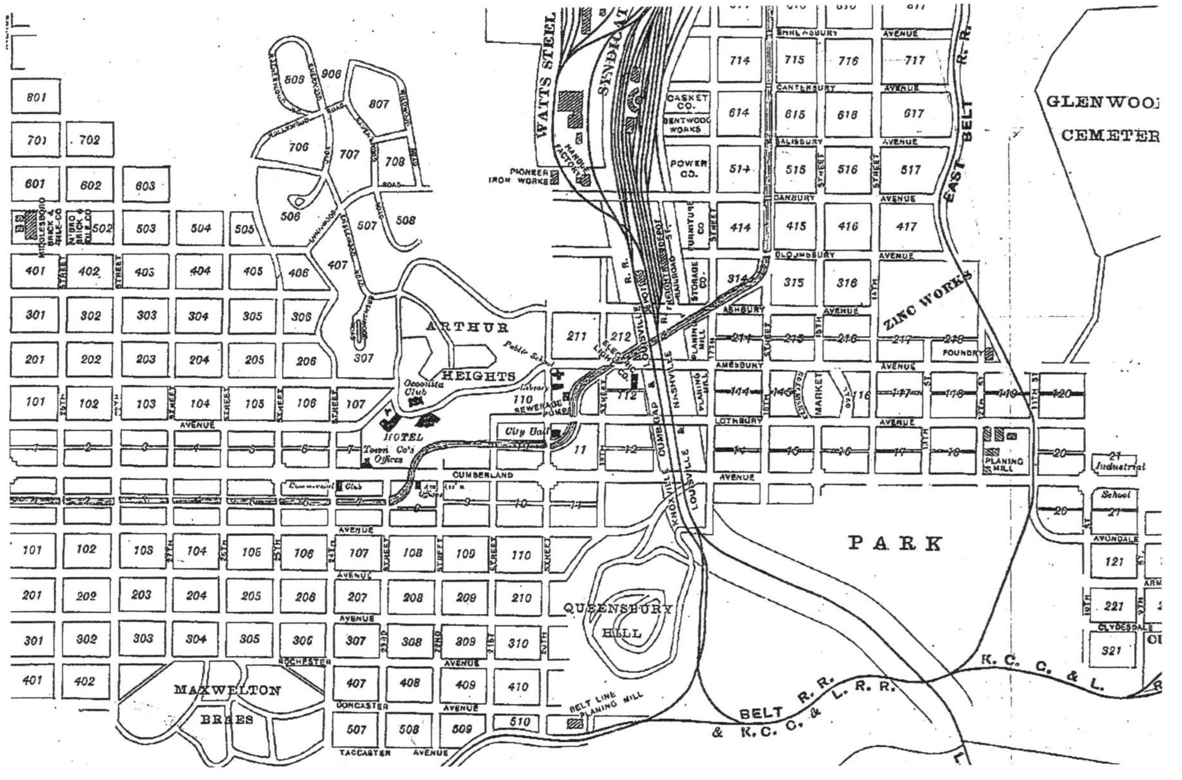

Plan for downtown Middlesborough, 1890. Courtesy of the Middlesboro-Bell County Public Library.

Institute but were less impressed. The first of these was the patriarch of the Watts Syndicate, who came out himself to see how his sons were progressing with the steel mill. His wife, two daughters, and a younger son accompanied him. Edgar and Frank were able to offer them fine entertainment but not much in the way of solid achievement. Even the former paled when their younger brother went bird hunting and, as the papers reported, was "shot down in cold blood, by one of the natives of the Tennessee side of the mountain." A special train was sent to Knoxville for a well known surgeon who, with three other physicians in attendance, was able to remove the bullet, which had entered the groin and had lodged near the spine.

As it developed, the case was not quite as simple as the paper implied. Young Henry had been near the Johnson Saloon when he flushed a covey of quail. This establishment had an unsavory reputation. It was built directly on the Tennessee-Virginia line, and indiscretions committed there often went unpunished because of questions as to which state had jurisdiction. When Watts fired at the quail, a couple of pellets of birdshot hit one of the men lounging outside the saloon. This man denied that he had responded in any way, but apparently someone did. The police explored several leads and even went as far as Louisville to pick up two suspects but were never able to "run to earth the would be assassin," as the Watts family demanded. When Henry was able to travel, they returned to England. It is safe to say that the patriarch of the Watts Syndicate left with a somewhat less than favorable impression of the area and its prospects.

The Duke and Duchess of Marlborough arrived in November of 1890 in their private railroad car. They were given a royal welcome by everyone. The duke was cordial, but when he got home he advised his friends to delay any further investment until the steel mill was actually in production.

These visitors had hardly boarded the train for home when the first rumors filtered in of a financial crisis in England. At first the Americans could not see why their town should be affected. True, the Baring Brothers Bank, which had furnished much of the British capital, had failed, mostly because of poor investments in South America. But as the famed writer John Fox Jr., who was a frequent visitor to the Magic City, put it, "Nobody saw why a hurt to the Lion should make the Eagle sore." The land sales held in mid-November brought in $431,186, which was in addition to the $180,000 worth of lots that had been sold since the May sales.

In January of 1891, the Middlesborough Town Company moved into an elaborate three-story building on Cumberland Avenue near 24th Street, directly below the Middlesborough Hotel. The first floor boasted a lobby with fine carved oak panels, marble cash counters, and brass wickers. Off the lobby was the private office of C.M. Woodbury, the resident manager. The second floor hosted administrative offices along with a Directors' Room and the private office of A.A. Arthur. The latter was furnished with "quartered oak in the antique style," large fireplaces with high mantles, and inlaid hardwood floors. On the third floor was the engineering department.

Arthur sailed to England with his secretary for stockholders' meetings held in early 1891. With the crisis deepening in Britain, investors were nervous, so much so that they discharged Arthur as general manager of the American Association, choosing to replace him with one of their own, E.F. Powers. Arthur was later to put his own spin on their action: "When the Baring troubles came upon our stockholders in England...they began to recklessly sacrifice our good and sound securities...all the more galling and stupid because of the unreason and fear of the panic stricken mob abroad that would not listen to good counsel, but rushed like sheep to 'cut their losses' and to run to cover."[16]

The stockholders of the Middlesborough Town Company, however, of which Arthur was still president, were somewhat mollified when he expounded on the results of the past year's sales and recommended a 10 percent dividend. Capital stock was increased by $1 million in order to complete improvements and secure new industries. By securing this additional capital, Arthur was able to return to his Magic City in triumph. He was met at the railroad station by a huge welcoming crowd. Two days later a mass meeting was held at the Opera House to endorse his leadership. He had with him several company men from London, but the newspaper proclaimed, "Middlesborough fears no investigation, no matter how searching."

One man who was visiting during this time recalled:

> My third and last trip was made after the Baring Brothers had failed....The town was absolutely "busted." Arthur was discredited... and the remittance men left were wholly concerned with getting away. No one had any money, it seems, and everyone would say, "Now if I can just get to Baltimore, Philadelphia or New York City, I can get a cattle boat to England"....despondency reigned....But while I was there, word came through that 50,000 pounds of new English capital had been secured. The news completely electrified the despondent remittance men and the others who were hanging on. As if by magic, a few dollars, which each apparently had hidden away were brought out, and wine and liquor flowed freely in the celebration which got under way.

> Everybody was happy. Bonfires were built. Guns were shot off. Impromptu speeches were made. Great rejoicing replaced the previous gloom.[17]

Certainly to the casual observer things could not be better. Construction was proceeding at breakneck speed, with new businesses seeming to spring up daily and established businesses moving into more elaborate quarters. For example, in January of 1891, the Lowe & Hugerly Drug Store moved into a handsome new building on Cumberland. The newspaper waxed eloquent over the extravagant carving and scrolling on the woodwork, the fancy French mirrors, and the cut-glass bottles and druggist sundries. Their highest praise, however, was reserved for the "giant soda apparatus," which was twelve feet tall and eight feet square and contained seven different types of marble. There were twenty-four syrup cups, three soda jets, and places to draw thirteen kinds of mineral waters. To top it off, the gas jets used to light the soda fountain were encircled by different colored globes.

For those who indulged in stronger drink, L. Coon & Co. enlarged their Crescent Saloon. The papers reported that they had purchased fixtures produced by Rothschild at a cost of $15,000.

> The back bar consists of 168 French plate mirrors, bevel edged, 2½" deep of various shapes, and mounted in silver and marble. The bar consists of innumerable slabs of foreign marbles whose beautifully harmonizing and contrasting grains and colors are joined much as a cabinet maker puts together pieces of wood. The rail is a solid shaft of Italian marble and in the bar top and mammoth cooler, marble takes the places usually given to wood.

The paper went on to explain that the bar with its fixtures had not been expected to sell in one piece because of the cost, but that Middlesborough, "which has the best and biggest of the world," saw it and price was no barrier.

A few months later business was so good that a new building was constructed next to the Crescent, doubling its size. The addition offered a card room "at which an innumerable crowd pass away their leisure time in the various ancient, historical and modern enjoyable games that are played with 52 pieces of pasteboard." The cigar case displayed all types of cigars and tobacco. The barroom was considered "not gaudy and flashy" but "clean, substantial and correct," with imported artificial flowers in hanging baskets and vases of ivy twining about the pillars. The ceiling was "plain and of dark blue and gilt." The archway leading into the addition was curtained in dark green and "at the left stands Eve in snowy whiteness." To the rear there were tables of food, an elaborate "free lunch."

And the Crescent was but one of an estimated forty saloons and barrooms ranging from other elegant establishments such as the Saratoga and the Palace to the watering holes over the Rhine (that area in the northeastern section of the city known for its "blind tigers," which sold cheap, and often illegal, whiskey).

Despite all this apparent prosperity, when the new American Association general manager, E.F. Powers, arrived from England, he proclaimed that there had been too much "booming" and that a more solid foundation of industry and exploitation of natural resources was needed. The tannery had started operations, but the Watts Syndicate seemed to be dragging its feet. Some of the other industries, such as the Davis Charcoal Company, were delaying plans until Watts started up, since they had based their own venture on the prospects of that company. It was also evident that Arthur had made some one-sided contracts to the detriment of the American Association in order to secure certain industries.

There was no longer to be the "blank check" that Arthur had drawn on to create his Magic City. Businessmen began to examine the underpinnings of Middlesborough's "boom" and to draw back. If the large industries did not materialize, there would not be sufficient well paid laborers to consume their products and services. Property owners realized that the value of their holdings depended upon demand by a rapidly growing populace backed by the promised industries, and this demand seemed to be evaporating. Powers was able to convince stockholders that certain promises had been made by the Town Company that had to be honored, and on this basis he obtained additional funds to complete developments already well under way. But the handwriting was on the wall.

As the price for another infusion of capital, current managers and officers of the Town Company and its subsidiary companies were asked to resign. Most of these men held positions in a number of the companies as well as in some of the "manufacturies." Many of the latter had been partially capitalized by stock in other companies. Without the prospect of further funds from Britain, the entire structure began to come apart like a house of cards. On November 21, 1891, the bankrupt Middlesborough Town Company reorganized as the Middlesborough Town and Lands Company with new officers.

Nonetheless, the final act had not played out, as the most ambitious project of all was even then nearing completion across the Gap in Harrogate, near where Arthur had built his own home: the Four Seasons resort and sanatorium.

Back in the heady days of 1888-1889, Arthur had sold several prominent New York physicians, including the brother of one of the original Gap Associates, on the idea of a resort hotel and spa in the healthful mountains near his dream city, where the air was clear, the water pure, and scenery beautiful, just as in Asheville, where Vanderbilt had recently built his Biltmore Estate. In addition, there were various mineral springs reputed to have the curative powers of the famous watering places of Europe.

Even in Arthur's most grandiose dreams, he could hardly have conceived of the design of the Four Seasons, a 700-room hotel supplied with the finest furnishings, decorative arts, linens, silverware, and china. Its wine cellar was renowned even before it opened. Riding trails, lawn tennis courts, a polo field, hiking paths, and the like encouraged healthful pursuits, while wide verandas furnished with comfortable lounges provided for relaxation and rest. A 200-bed sanatorium with lavish Turkish baths, which replicated the famous baths of the Rue de L'Etat Major in Algiers, offered further benefits for those seeking good health. Plans were made for special railroad cars, equipped with hospital beds and doctors, to make weekly trips from the Northeast to transport sick patients, while other special trains would make regular runs for the majority who would come just to enjoy the resort.

In April of 1892 the Four Seasons had its grand opening. A special train conveyed many members of New York's high society to the festivities, which lasted for over a week with excursions, picnics, and sports during the day and dinner and dancing at night. For the grand banquet, the tables were decorated with rare plants and colored candles and the Cincinnati Grand Orchestra provided the music while the guests were served a ten-course feast accompanied by rare wines and fine liqueurs.

Then the guests went home, and few others came. Like the town of Middlesborough, the hotel stumbled along on hope and optimism for a time, then finally gave up. In 1895 it was dismantled and the furnishings sold for a fraction of their value. All that remains today is a remnant of the sanatorium which is part of a dormitory, Grant-Lee Hall, at Lincoln Memorial University.

Meanwhile, Powers tried mightily to put the American Association on a sound basis by concentrating on completing improvements, such as the railroad spurs, that would facilitate mining and industrial development. But the financial crisis in Europe had crossed the ocean. He would have had a difficult job had times been good, but with the country spiraling into a panic, it was impossible. Businesses began to fail, lot holders defaulted on payments, buildings were vacated, banks closed. One thing led to another until finally the American Association, Ltd. was forced into receivership in October of 1893. A new company, made up primarily of stockholders from the old company, organized as the American Association, Inc. and took over all the assets of the bankrupt company.[18]

One man recalled that from 1892 to 1895, "everything went dead....most all dwelling and business houses were empty and in the summer time the chief sport up and down Cumberland Avenue was baseball and a marble game all along the avenue and there was not enough traffic to disturb what few boys, young and old men left that passed most of their time playing marbles."[19] There was so little money in circulation that bartering was a common way to carry on commerce, and those who could no longer pay rent simply "squatted" in the tenant houses the English had so optimistically built. A reporter for the *Lexington Morning Herald* wrote, "Middlesborough shows scarcely any signs of life." He noted that business houses were boarded up and that Cumberland Avenue had weeds four feet tall growing in the middle of the street where the streetcar tracks were located. There were so many fires, sometimes five or six a night, rumored to be the result of arson, that insurance companies had canceled all policies. The Middlesborough Hotel, which the reporter remembered as "crowded from cellar to garret," was deserted. "In fact," he went on, "over the whole town there seems to be a pall of despair, and its citizens who are trying to eke out an existence here scarcely ever smile."

One has to doubt that last observation. People might have to barter, but they continued their lawn tennis parties and literary clubs, their picnics at Fern Lake, and excursions to the Pinnacle. They also organized a soup kitchen and a Welfare Association to give aid in cases of hardship, and people pulled together to help each other survive. The tannery operated throughout the panic and prospered. Coal was mined. The railroads continued to run. Even in the depth of the depression, there remained more than 3,000 residents, a drop from the 7,000 or more at its zenith, but still a large increase over the few families in the Yellow Creek Valley only ten years earlier.

And those who stayed on had been strengthened in the crucible of hardship. They had, as the poet wrote, "met with triumph and disaster." When prosperity returned, they would build their city on a stronger foundation.

Footnote Twelve

The Melting Pot

Middlesborough at its inception was a true American melting pot. In fact, considering the Valley's shape and the small area into which everyone was crammed, it was more of a mixing bowl. From every part of the country and abroad, and from every level of the socioeconomic strata, fortune seekers rushed into the Valley. Because the enumerator reports for the census of 1890 in Bell County were lost, detailed information about the exact makeup of the new city is not available, and it is necessary to draw inferences from other sources. Fortunately the local newspapers were diligent in reporting the social scene and local events. It is certain that the majority of those pouring into the Yellow Creek Valley were from Kentucky, Tennessee, and Virginia, but they were joined by representatives from almost every state of the Union and most European counties, and by diverse religious, ethnic, and racial groups.

The English

A unique feature of early Middlesborough was the number of those born in the British Isles who were involved in the founding and early development of the city.

In 1880 there was but one foreign-born resident in all of Bell County. That was to change dramatically with the coming of Alexander Arthur. Several Englishmen were with him in Knoxville during the earliest days of planning: Otway Cuffe, who was to become Sir Otway, the Third Baronet of Lyrath Kilkenny; Arthur C. Chester Master ("Cocky"), who was said to be another heir to a baronetcy and a large estate; and Captain Claude E.

Prescott. Later, Arthur's own Scottish and Canadian family gathered in to join him.

As English investment in the Yellow Creek Valley grew, so did the influx of Englishmen. Some came to lend their expertise, others came as investors, or representatives of investors, and/or to start up new businesses. Not a few were "remittance men," young bloods who had an income from home and were mostly out for adventure. Alexander Arthur's secretary later described two of these "young chaps of wealthy upper middle-class derivation," nephews of one of the investors, whom he first met while on a business trip to London with Arthur:

> [When] I first met the young men...they were in silk hats, spats, morning coats, not to mention monocles and walking-sticks. They made known their intention of going out to his development in "the States" to engage in dairying for an uncertain period. One brother arrived in Middlesborough some weeks ahead of the other and bought a farm about a mile from town....They did their own milking, or assisted employees in doing so, and one drove the milkwagon, making deliveries to customers. The spectacle of these young fellows, fashionables at home, here milking cows, and one of them ringing his bell before houses, drawing the creamy liquid and pouring it into housewives' pitchers, was amusing.[1]

They certainly added color to the population mix of the new city. Many expatriates brought with them their dinner jackets, riding clothes, and golf outfits, which stood out exotically against the mountaineers' coarse open-necked shirts and slouch hats. Their British accents were a source of merriment. The newspaper, noting the different ways residents were reacting to a bar that had been placed across a driveway, quoted one: "I say, why cawn't they leave the beastly beam down. I cawn't see the necessity of having it there, don't you know." One visitor reported that the British gathered at the annex attached to The Middlesborough (hotel), where the "favorite words around the club were a 'peg of brandy,' ' Scotch and soda' or 'lemon squash'"[2] He also recalled that this group wore evening clothes to dinner each night, which was held at the fashionable hour of eight or nine o'clock, past bedtime for many of "the natives." Of course, the Englishmen had fortified themselves with tea and crumpets at four o'clock, an amenity not offered in other mountain towns.

Their talk around dinner often ran to polo and fox hunting. The expatriates formed cricket clubs, and the team from Cumberland Gap would play the one from Middlesborough. In the grand scheme of his city, Arthur

English investors visiting Sterling Coal Mine; date of photo unknown. Courtesy of Clyde Mayes.

had included a racetrack and playing field in the area called the Commons, which was just north of Cumberland Avenue and west of 25th. There the Englishmen met to play golf, a game new to the States and unheard of in the mountains. Concerts and shows were held at the newly constructed Opera House, also quite a change from anything the Yellow Creekers had known. Dances and other "entertainments" were held at The Middlesborough, and a lending library society organized. Although their numbers were relatively small, the English and Scotsmen greatly influenced the culture of the area.

One of the most famous of the English property owners never actually came to Middlesborough. Lillie Langtry, "the Jersey Lilly," had an international reputation as an actress, though she was renowned as much for her intimate friendship with the Prince of Wales, later to be King Edward VII, as for her beauty and talent. It has been claimed that she came for the opening of one of the large hotels; some say it was The Middlesborough and others that it was the Four Seasons. But she is not mentioned in any of the contemporary accounts of those events, and she is someone who would not have been overlooked.

She was, however, an investor. In 1889 she bought stock in the American Association, Ltd. As the *Manufacturers Record* in London reported, "The Lily is credited with the perception to know a good thing when she sees it, the justice of which attribution is attested by the fact that she has secured an interest in this great enterprise of her countrymen." She later bought a lot on the south side of Cumberland Avenue between 25th and 26th and had a two-story brick townhouse-style dwelling constructed. Though she never lived in it, nor even saw it, the structure was known for years as the Langtry House.

Middlesborough was, of course, very gratified when she chose to build in the Valley, but why did this English actress decide to build a house for herself in Middlesborough? Her investment lawyer in New York, Herbert Satterlee, explained that while performing in this country she became a patient of Dr. Holbrook Curtis, a brother to Randolph Curtis, one of the original Gap Associates. Dr. Curtis was planning to make a large investment in the Cumberland Gap area, which was said to have a particularly healthy climate (he was one of the major backers of the ill-fated Four Seasons resort), and he shared his enthusiasm for the area with his famous patient.[3]

Middlesborough did not lose hope that the Jersey Lily would grace the city. The newspaper quoted the English papers:

> The English beauty is determined to visit Middlesborough as soon as she can escape the clutches of the double demon gout and rheumatism, who, like the hideous giants of fairy stories, hold her in enforced embrace, unmoved by tears, wails and piteous pleas. She would do wisely not to defer her visit but go now even if accompanied by the heartless brute. Under the benign influences of the climate and mineral waters of the Cumberland Gap his power would soon begin to wane; her dear little tootseywootseys would be reduced to their normal size and cuteness and her lithe and shapely form regain its active suppleness and vigor.

The Lily never came, and most of her compatriots left when the "bust" hit. In 1899 under the headline "Still They Go," the newspaper bid farewell to one of the Englishmen with the rather brutal comment, "He was not at all Americanized and consequently not well liked." The 1900 census takers found but twenty-four Englishmen and just six who named as their place of birth Scotland. By the 1910 census their number had been reduced even further, to six persons born in England and one from Scotland.

They left as their heritage many fine buildings, a tradition of culture, and Fountain Square, the intersection of 20th and Cumberland, where the English community built a three-tiered fountain in commemoration of Queen Victoria's Jubilee.

They also left their dead. Arthur's plans included a cemetery in the far northeastern section of his city. He named it Glenwood, but later generations have called it Lynch Cemetery. Unfortunately, when the "remittance men" and the others departed, no provision was made for the upkeep of the graves, and the few identifiable gravestones remaining from that period are in deplorable condition.

One grave is that of "Cocky" Masters, a close confidant of Alexander Arthur. When the other boomers departed, he stayed on. He was a sociable, much loved character who had served as a colonel in the Egyptian campaign. Perhaps the tour in the desert started a thirst that could not easily be satisfied; at any rate, his drinking led to some unfortunate accidents. In 1895 it was reported that he simply walked out of a second story window and fell fifteen feet to the pavement, smashing himself up and breaking an arm. Several other falls and a bad burn finally culminated in his death from blood poisoning in 1900.

C.B. Roberts, the erstwhile secretary to Alexander Arthur in the boom days, returned to Middlesborough in 1914 and visited the grave of his friend Cocky. He had difficulty finding the site because of all the underbrush. Near it he located the resting place of one of the "remittance men" who had succumbed to cholera in 1889. Roberts wrote to the family at Menlough Castle in Ireland:

> [The grave is] overgrown, most densely overgrown, by wild rose plants of the creeper kind. Through the tangled vines I just could discern at the head a stout wooden cross—of hickory, I fancy rising from the ground a foot and a half perhaps....On the transverse piece...is an inscription which apparently was made with a hot iron, for it was a crude country in those days, with slender facilities. One line, some sentiment or quotation, I think, is hopelessly indecipherable, but I was able to make out all the rest:
>
> Valentine Joseph Blake
Dearly Beloved Son of
Sir Valentine Blake
Born March 22nd, 1871
[Here follows the indecipherable line]
Died Sept. 6th, 1889

> Even that which is still legible, however, will not now long remain so—some of the characters have almost faded—with the consequence that the identity of the grave will probably be lost.[4]

Mr. Roberts was able to find only a few other graves of "boomers," and today little remains other than some fallen gravestones and an iron fence enclosing the graves of Masters, Blake, and one other Englishman, with a large tree growing in the middle of the small plot.

The African-Americans

The Yellow Creek Valley had no African-American residents prior to the arrival of Alexander Arthur. (There was, however, a community of persons of color in and around Pineville; of the 6,049 residents of Bell County counted in the 1880 census, 94 were designated black and 75 mulatto.) It was only the developers' grand plans that attracted a large black workforce to the planned city. They came mainly from the southeastern states, often arriving with a "gang" of workers recruited for a specific job.

When Middlesboro was granted its city charter in March of 1890, it had approximately 4,068 residents. Of these, 447 were African-Americans, and they were overwhelmingly male contract laborers. As the town grew, more African-Americans came and brought their families. In November of 1891 the newspaper counted a total of 726 families within the city limits, 30 percent of whom were persons of color. The newspaper also noted that of the 1,060 registered voters in the city, 353 were African-American.

In general, early Middlesborough seems to have been a congenial place for its African-American residents. There were many social events--dances, cakewalks, dinners, socials, and musicals. The newspaper reported that the Colored Odd Fellows had a good lodge and that the Colored Masons were "in a very flourishing condition." Churches were organized and there were camp meetings and church picnics. There were a number of black-owned businesses and businessmen. An African-American doctor, Dr. John Branham, came in 1889 and remained until his death in 1926.

There was less segregation of the races in early Middlesborough than there was in most of the country at the time. Several of the bars, saloons, and dance halls catered to both races. This was mostly in places like the Barrel House, which was in a working-class neighborhood, rather than in uptown establishments. There was also social interaction on what could be considered a more family-oriented basis. For example, the newspaper, reporting on a dance for the town's young people in August of 1892, noted,

"The building was filled with people, many colored and a few whites, all of whom seemed to be enjoying themselves." A notice in the paper the next month issued the invitation, "Come one, come all, white and colored, let us have a good time. The Mount Moriah Baptist Church will give an ice cream entertainment." Besides refreshments of all kinds there was also to be a croquet yard. Religious services were also sometimes held together. A notice in the paper from one of the pastors (no indication as to his race) invited, "Come white and colored, for I want a word with each of you."

Also indicative of early race relations was an editorial published in the *Daily Herald* in 1894 under the title "A Public Outrage." It referred to an act that had been committed by a white man, a city policeman, who had assaulted a black man by cursing him, "using vile and filthy language and threatening to kill him." The man's only offense, apparently, had been that he had "talked back" to a white man. The editorial opined, "This is the first time that colored men have been abused in this city by city officials. This action...is an outrage upon the public....In the eyes of city government there should be no color line."

When one of the African-American citizens filed for election to city council in 1893, the newspaper gave him a ringing endorsement: "Frank L. Cowan is the only colored man among the candidates. He works for A.C. Titus & Co...is steady, hardworking, and reliable, and has the confidence of all who know him....if elected we believe he will make a good councilman." There was a later note that he had withdrawn his candidacy after meeting "with people of his race." In 1897 the papers again supported a black candidate: "Thomas Jones...is one of the leading colored citizens of this town. He is a contractor and in his business relations is recognized as a substantial man. He is upright and industrious." He was, however, defeated in the election.

This is not to imply that racism was unknown. There was a general idea among the white residents, unfortunately held in common with most of the country at the time, that persons of color had a certain "place" in society that was different from that of their white neighbors. In 1891 there were reports of trouble at Mingo Mine over the hiring of black miners. That same year white teachers complained when they were scheduled to go to a training session with their black counterparts. The 1893 Order Book for the grand jury has a notation of a fine levied on several people who were "party to marriage between Negro and white person."

The most fortunate event for the African-American community in Middlesborough was the arrival in 1891 of Professor George Bell, a black educator who was a product of Berea College. He, along with his wife

Professor George W. Bell (left) and Elgetha Brand Bell (right). Both courtesy of Lincoln School Alumni Association.

Elgetha, inspired a tradition of academic effort and achievement in the black community.

George Bell had been born a slave in Marion County, Kentucky, in 1858. He knew the value of striving toward a goal. Professor Bell had worked long and hard to save enough to start at Berea College in 1881. He was already almost twenty-three and old to be embarking on an academic career, especially as he had had very little formal education before entering Berea. In addition, because he had to work for most of the college year, he could attend classes only a short time each year. It was not until 1892, after eleven long years of work, that he actually received his B.A. degree. At that time he was one of fewer than 1,800 African-Americans to have earned a B.A. degree in the United States.[5]

When Prof. Bell arrived in Middlesborough in 1891, the city did not yet have a public school system, but one was in the planning stages. The city fathers had written to Berea asking that the college send one of its graduates to teach "the colored school we need in this region." Bell had ninety students in his first school, which was held in a former grocery store. After two years the Colored School, as it was then called, was moved to a regular schoolhouse, a two-room building on Danbury Avenue.

In December of 1892, Prof. Bell married Elgetha Brand, a teacher who had also received her education at Berea. Immediately after the wedding in her hometown of Winchester, the couple boarded a train for Middlesborough. The new Mrs. Bell was impressed with the size and apparent wealth of the city, but somewhat dismayed by the Wild West atmosphere, with saloons on every corner and frequent brawls and shootings. From all accounts she was a woman who saw this not as a determent but as a challenge—it was a town that needed taming. She did not teach regularly but plunged into the job of civilizing the town, just as did many of the other early female residents, white and black. She helped her husband to organize a church, worked on various committees to put on benefits and social events, and was in the forefront of most efforts of the black community.

The first commencement exercises for the Colored School were held in 1899 for three graduates. That same year the black community initiated an effort to enlarge their school, raising half of the cost of an addition themselves. This gave the school three large rooms. Already there was one teacher in addition to Prof. Bell, and in the fall of 1899 an assistant teacher was added for the primary grades. Bell then instituted a high school course that included classes in algebra and Latin. A hundred and fifty students were enrolled for the 1899-1900 term.

With the addition of the high school course, Prof. Bell was able to amplify his effect in that he was producing teachers for other schools, since a high school graduate was considered ready to be a teacher. In 1903 the newspaper announced that Prof. Bell expected to be able to send out five teachers that year, and that the year before he had sent ten teachers to schools in Tennessee, Virginia, and Kentucky.

By 1907 the enrollment of the colored school had grown to better than four hundred students, and it was evident that a larger building was needed. Again the black community worked with the School Board to raise the necessary funds. It took more than a year of work, but the resulting building was worth the effort. It was a two-story brick structure costing about $12,000 and able to accommodate as many as six hundred students. This was Lincoln School, to be the hub of the African-American community for the next sixty years.

In 1909 there was a terrible reaction when a black teenager was accused of assaulting and raping an eight-year-old white girl. Feelings ran high and the paper reported that only prompt action in getting the boy out of town prevented "a roping." At the first trial the accused pleaded guilty and the jury voted eleven to one for the death sentence. There were two retrials and a hearing before the Court of Appeals, which upheld the death sentence. The sentence was carried out in 1911, the man being the last person to die on the gallows in Bell County.

The African-American population of Middlesboro decreased rather significantly after 1915. The coal mines, which employed many black miners, were notorious for their boom-and-bust cycles. During times when the job market was poor, the African-Americans, often the first to lose their jobs, left town in increasing numbers. Those who stayed on found the town a little less accommodating. Facilities were more segregated. The new movie theater had a separate entrance and balcony for the black audience. Although African-American residents were scattered over the city, they had coalesced into several neighborhoods that were primarily black. One skating rink was black only. In the few bars that served both races, "vertical integration" was the rule; that is, only standing drinkers mingled. But when Middlesboro's black youth marched off to war in 1918, the newspaper proclaimed, "The day has forever passed when a black skin can disqualify a man for preferment and advancement."

During the early twenties, the Ku Klux Klan was active in Middlesboro and held a number of rather large rallies. In response, the city fathers passed an ordinance making it a punishable offense "to speak in public in a manner that will bring ridicule to any person or race or incite hatred between classes or races." They also voted to outlaw masked persons in the city. According to contemporary newspaper stories and the memories of those who actually belonged, the local KKK directed its ire toward immoral persons and certain types of immigrants rather than any particular race.

African-American residents who grew up in Middlesboro during the thirties and forties have mixed memories of interaction between the races. Generally they remember some incidents of unpleasantness and some not so subtle indignities and say there were certain limitations, but they also have many good memories of their place in the community. In common with many southern towns, the children played together and were good friends. One man who grew up in the generally more prosperous west end of town, where his family sharecropped and did other work for one of the wealthy white families, explained, "We sat at each other's tables....we were raised up together."[6] In times when coal was booming and jobs were plentiful, the African-Americans were valued workers in the coal mines and other businesses around town. They were welcomed as customers in all the stores, though the finer shops did not allow them to try on clothes in the fitting rooms. Schools were segregated, but they came out to cheer each other's athletic teams. Though there was more segregation than in the early days, and certainly African-Americans made up a much smaller percentage of the population, the atmosphere could still be described as relatively positive, especially when compared to that elsewhere. As a lifelong resident put it, "Race was never a problem—there was no place that I didn't feel comfortable."[7] In the early fifties Middlesboro had the only integrated Little League teams south of Cincinnati. Integration of the schools was accomplished in 1965 with little fanfare.

The Jews

Early Middlesborough boasted a relatively large Jewish community, many of whom were immigrants from Russia, Romania, Lithuania, Austria, and Poland. Most were merchants; a few had restaurants or hotels.

Typical were the Weinstein brothers. The Weinstein family had immigrated from Russia in 1888. When they arrived in New York, the family was practically penniless, so two of the brothers decided to strike out on their own. Sam, the elder, worked as a carpenter and Herman as a peddler. They headed south, working in Tennessee and Georgia, before hearing of Middlesborough.

They arrived in the Magic City in 1890, and Herman talked his brother into joining him in a mercantile venture. They had no capital but Herman's peddler's pack; but it was a time when many merchants were still operating out of tents and makeshift shelters, so they were not at much of a disadvantage. By dint of hard and continuous work they were able to move into a small store by 1893. Their timing was bad; the city was reeling from "the bust" and many were reduced to barter. The brothers did not lose faith, though, and gradually increased their inventory, moving into larger quarters. When the economy improved, they were ready to expand. In 1906 they were able to construct a three-story building on the southeast corner of 20th and Cumberland and open a department store. By this time Herman had six children and Sam four.

The Weinsteins were active in the rather large Jewish community, which included the Eusters, Horrs, Goodfriends, Ginsbergs, Friedmans, Abrams, and Effons. The Horrs had a hotel and restaurant; all the others had stores of various kinds. Early on there was also Simon Hesse, who sold jewelry; J. Rothschild of the Golden Rule Store; Joe Rosenfield, who worked as a jeweler at Callison's; and the Spiros. There were several branches of most families, so that when Bnai Brith held a meeting in Middlesboro in 1926, more than a hundred people attended. For a time the Jewish merchants had such a large percentage of the mercantile houses that the town closed down for Jewish high holidays.

The southeast corner of Fountain Square (20th and Cumberland), ca. 1910. The building to the right was built by the Weinstein brothers. In the center, next to the street, is the fountain given by the English expatriates in honor of Queen Victoria's Jubilee. Courtesy of the Bell County Historical Society.

In 1904 the Jewish community purchased property on Maxwellian Brae, in the western part of town, and established their own cemetery. Prior to that time they had buried their dead in Knoxville. They talked of building a synagogue; meanwhile, they met at the Masonic Lodge. Sam Weinstein served as their leader and was identified by gentile neighbors as a rabbi, though he was not trained as such.[8] For special occasions—the consecration of a marriage, the circumcision of a baby—a rabbi would usually come from Knoxville. The Society of the Daughters of Zionist met regularly during the first two decades of the century.

Gradually the Jewish community diminished as first one and then another moved away. The Goodfriends were one of the first to go. They had a large store on the southwest corner of 19th and Cumberland. When it was completely destroyed by fire in 1904, the insurance covered only a small portion of their losses. Most of the family moved off to try their luck elsewhere. One of the Goodfriends eventually founded Goody's, a chain of clothing stores now numbering almost a hundred in ten states, one of which is located in Middlesboro today.

Herman Weinstein left in 1916, reputedly after a dispute with his brother, and their store was sold. Sam stayed on to work at his trade as a carpenter. He built his own home, which still stands just behind the Middlesboro Public Library, facing Chester. He also had a large garden on his farm in the western part of the city and used to enjoy providing his friends with fresh vegetables. He was active in city government, served on the City Council, and was involved in many philanthropic endeavors. Sam particularly valued the water in Middlesboro; each evening he would take his young son David by the hand and they would walk down to the artesian well behind the old city hall building for a drink of water.

Sam fell ill in 1932. One of his sons had become a physician and was practicing in Nashville, so the family moved there. David eventually went into the jewelry business, got his own store, expanded, and at the time of his retirement owned a chain of jewelry stores in Tennessee and Virginia.

Several families stayed on. The Eusters had the Fair Store well into the seventies. Jack Friedman operated Royal Jewelers, also into the seventies. The Ginsbergs were influential in politics as well as in the economic life of the city and had a restaurant, Colonel's, that attracted patrons from a wide area. John Abram ran John's Store until the building was destroyed by fire in the eighties.

Today the most visible remainder of Middlesboro's Jewish community is the Hebrew Cemetery, still maintained by the now far-flung Jewish Cemetery Association.

The Italians

The single largest group of foreign-born residents of the Yellow Creek Valley in 1890 was the Italians. The newspaper reported in July of that year that two hundred Italians had arrived in the city. They were contract laborers, brought in to construct drainage and sewerage systems for the new city. It was common at the time for agents to go to Europe and recruit workers. Often the contracts were very one-sided, with the laborer having to pay off a large debt incurred for his transportation and other costs, so that he became almost indentured to the contract agent.

The Italians were housed in tents strung out along the creek bank. It was their job to turn meandering Yellow Creek, which crossed what was to be Cumberland Avenue ten times, into a canal that would drain the marshy lowlands. It was not easy work, but one old-time resident recalled, "Twelve hours daily they labored and at nightfall were never too tired to sing in chorus the songs of their native land."[9]

Some of the local workmen strongly resented this contract gang. An editorial in the newspaper complained that the Town Company was pay-

Italian laborers working on the canal, ca. 1889. Courtesy of Clyde Mayes.

ing the Italians $1.65 a day to the dig the canal when it could have gotten local laborers for $1.50. The paper went on state, "Besides, these Italians will be of no permanent good to our city....They are a shiftless, quarrelsome, slovenly class of people....there is a very strong feeling against these Italians and they are justly looked upon as intruders."

Part of the problem, undoubtedly, was that the Italians kept to themselves and spoke a different language. They were more alien to the mountaineers than the African-Americans, and as such were subject to more prejudice. When the papers reported a fight in the "Italian camp" in which a man was killed, it explained, "Like all other quarrels among themselves, the dagoes tried to keep the matter quiet." In July of 1891, the paper reported on a knife fight and editorialized, "The Italian question could be easily solved by letting the Dagoes carve each other up were it not for the influence that such a course would have on the community."

The perceived problem solved itself, as when the city took over canal work a portion of the contract laborers moved on. Already by the summer of 1891, half of the Italians had left. In addition to the remaining Italians, there were fifty white laborers and forty African-Americans working on the canal. Most of the rest departed within the next couple of years. The 1900 census takers found only eight residents who had been born in Italy, and by 1910 that number was down to three.

As the demand for coal grew, however, so did the need for miners, and the labor bosses again looked to southern and eastern Europe. A large number of Italians moved into the mine camps of Bell County. Few lived in Middlesboro, but they did come to town to spend their paychecks. There is an enduring story of six (or some say eight) Italian miners who had just been paid and were known to be on their way to Middlesboro, heading for the Melody Club. They simply disappeared and no one ever saw or heard from then again. It is said that a farmer, plowing his field one spring several years later, turned up evidence that they had all met a violent end on the road to town.

Two of the families who came to Middlesboro after the turn of the century and stayed on to disprove the newspaper's predictions were the Bisceglias and the Constanzos. Pascal Constanzo immigrated from Italy in 1907 at the age of sixteen. He was immediately attracted to the area because its mountains reminded him of home. He married Mary Bisceglia and, with his brother-in-law "Little Tony," opened a barber shop in downtown Middlesboro. Soon his brother, "Big Tony" Constanzo, came over to join them. Their shop became a favorite meeting place where one could always hear the best jokes and the town's latest news. The Constanzo and Bisceglia families have since been in the forefront of many business and civic endeavors.

The Germans and Others

The manager of the New South Brewing Company, William Wallbrecht Sr., was originally from Germany, though he came to Middlesborough in 1893 from Cincinnati. His brewmaster was a massive German who weighed better than 300 pounds. Rather than burden a carriage horse, the brewer always had the brewery wagon with its powerful draft animals drive him around town. Another of the Germans was Fred Huber, who had been one of Bismark's soldiers when he marched into Paris in 1870. He had a restaurant on Cumberland Avenue and then built the Huber Hotel (later known as the Empire Hotel and then the Marboro) on 19th.

One of the young city's most colorful residents was Austrian. He called himself Baron Anton von Stauffenhausen. He was "a little stout man, with hair a la Pompadour and mustaches bristling like badger-hair shaving-brushes, who ran a small stationery store and who let it be known, confidentially to a few that he had fallen on financial misfortune in his native Austria. He wore tight-fitting doeskin trousers disappearing into knee-high glistening patent-leather boots."[10] One day authorities from Ohio turned up to arrest him—he was an international swindler.

A sprinkling of other nationalities added to the Valley's melting pot.

When the town was new there was even a Chinese Hand Laundry run by an oriental gentleman. He left, however, with the "bust." After the turn of the century two new ingredients were added to the melting pot, the Greeks and the Lebanese.

The Greeks

Greek immigrants originally came to the area to work in the coal mines, then migrated to the city. Nick Hill's story is typical:

> He immigrated to this country in 1901, with his brawny muscles and his willingness to tackle any kind of hard work as his only capital. In 1910 we find him near Middlesboro working in the mines, and turning out carloads of coal a day—the best miner in the section. "I used to eat five or six meals a day," he told us, "and was always hungry; but, believe me, few miners could beat me in turning out and loading the darn black diamond." One year after such arduous mining, Mr. Hill turned his attention to business. He came to Middlesboro and opened a small poolroom.[11]

Nick later had the Nineteenth Street Cafe, where he employed a compatriot, Theo Nakis.

Another Greek, Bill Hill, built the Wabash Hotel at the corner of Lothbury and 18th Street, just across from the railroad depot. He was a big man, deep-voiced and friendly, proud of his establishment. The Wabash had three stories, with the downstairs given over to a bar and restaurant, as well as the Tropical Gardens, a dance hall graced by tropical plants in polished containers, elegant golden columns, and a long bar with brass railing. At a time when most visitors arrived by train, it was a prosperous business. In the mid-thirties Hill decided to cash in his chips. He sold the Wabash to Alvey and Floyd Ball and, fulfilling the dream of many immigrants, returned to his hometown in Greece a rich man.

Hill bought a hotel in Tripolis and enjoyed the life he had envisioned, living, he told his friends in Middlesboro, like a millionaire. Then in 1940 the Germans invaded Greece. They commandeered his hotel as a headquarters and appropriated everything of value that he had, throwing him out on the streets to get along as best he could. He was reduced to stealing green corn from the fields in order to eat. After the war was over his friends learned that he had regained the title to his hotel, but not his pre-war life style.[12]

Other Greek businesses, primarily eateries, flourished in Middlesboro

Lothbury Avenue between 18th and 19th Streets, 1920s. The Wabash Hotel is in the center; the edge of the railroad depot is visible at the far right. Courtesy of the Bell County Historical Society.

in the twenties, thirties, and forties. George Zaharias had the New York Confectionery; Pete Bendas, the Sanitary Lunch; Roufas Nazarias, the Three States Cafe; George Nazarias, along with Tom Psathas and Nick Leventis, the Lunetta Cafe; Louis Kalfas, the Coffee Pot Lunch; and Pete Calages, the Palace of Sweets. Older residents remember not only the wonderful Greek food and drink but also the extravagant Greek parties and weddings. Gradually, however, as the business climate changed, most of the Greek families moved off.

The Lebanese

In contrast to the Greeks, the Lebanese who came to the Yellow Creek Valley in the first decades of the century—the Tamers, the Latiffs, the Jacobses, and the Wakins—have remained an integral part of the town. They were all from the same area in Lebanon and always said that Middlesboro reminded them of their home in Zahle.

One of the first to come was Joseph Tamer, who immigrated from Lebanon in 1905, settling first in Boston. Over the next few years he was able to sponsor two of his brothers and a sister. The boys had been farmers in Lebanon, but in this new country they decided to be merchants. They moved to Middlesboro because they had heard good money was being made in the coal mines, and that meant customers.

Joseph first worked as a peddler. He would load up four suitcases and a backpack with the kind of merchandise coveted by the miners' wives. He would take the mine train to the end of one of the railroad spurs and then, with the pack on his back, a suitcase in each hand, and another under each arm, would walk back toward town, calling at each house along the way. At the time, mine camps and miners' homes were strung out all along the tracks, so the potential was good. Soon he was able to open a dry goods store in town, and by 1915 the papers were calling him "Middlesboro's most successful merchant."

His brother Mike also tried peddling, but he was at heart a farmer. In 1920 he returned to Lebanon to care for their mother and their farm, which allowed another brother, Herbert, to immigrate to Middlesboro. Herbert also started out as a peddler. He used to tell his son that when he wasn't selling much, the pack and suitcases seemed to get heavier and heavier as did his spirit, but when he was selling a lot, not only did the cases get lighter but his spirit also. Soon he had saved enough to open his own clothing store in town in partnership with his brother Joe.

Meanwhile, their brother Fred Tamer operated a fruit stand and confectionery in town, and their sister Minnie married Sam Latiff. The Latiffs had moved to Middlesboro in 1918 and were in the grocery business.

John and Anna Jacobs opened a restaurant in Middlesboro in 1907. Herbert Tamer married their daughter Fannie, and Joe married John's daughter by a previous marriage, Daisy. While Herbert and Joe got along well, the half-sisters did not, so Joe sold out his part of the business and moved to Harlan, Kentucky, where he established another successful mercantile business. He and Daisy retained an interest in Middlesboro and in 1929 built a hotel on 19th Street which they called the Majestic. In 1936, Joe closed out his business in Harlan and opened a store on the ground floor of the Majestic. The hotel itself did not do well until Daisy took over its management, operating it as a house of prostitution during Middlesboro's "wide-open" era in the forties and fifties.

Anna Jacobs opened a grocery store after the death of her husband. Her sons, known as "Smoky" and "Big Dog," had restaurants and quick food stands and were also known to provide liquor, even after the town went dry. Fifty years later people still talk of Big Dog's fried bologna sandwiches with peppers and onions, and how he was always quick to provide a free meal to anyone down on his luck.

Ramsey Tamer, also from Zahle, had married Assad Wakin, and they had gone into the grocery business in Texarkana. After Assad's death, Anna Jacobs and her four sons, Boston, Joe, Ernie, and Shaffee, joined their compatriots in Middlesboro, where they opened a grocery store. When she remarried, it was to one of the extended family of Tamers. Two of her sons did the same. The Wakins also operated a hardware store near their grocery.

Thus, within a two-block area, the Lebanese community could provide for almost every need. It was into the eighties, after business had mostly moved from downtown to the malls, that the town lost the wonderful tradition of the Lebanese merchant epitomized in the devotion of Joe and Herbert to their customers.

Footnote Thirteen

The Ball Boys

Among those from the nearby hills and valleys who answered the seductive siren call of the boom town were the sons of Philip and Emeline Ball, who lived just over the Cumberland Gap in Lee County, Virginia.

The Balls were an old Virginia family, able to trace their ancestry back to fifteenth-century England and to claim as a distant kinsman George Washington. The name Ball is of Saxon derivation and came from bal, meaning bold, quick, or swift. The Balls immigrated to the colonies prior to 1650 and settled in coastal Virginia. William Ball was the grandfather of George Washington. His brother Richard was the sire of John Ball, great-great-great-grandfather of Philip. It was John's son George who first moved from Stafford County to Lee County, then the far frontier. Several families made the trip together about 1785. As they neared the area that is now Abington, Virginia, a band of Indians attacked the travelers, killing several in the party. George lost his wife Kezziah and his son William in the massacre.

George's son John Ball, born in 1756, was already a grown man when the family moved to Lee County. The first mention of John in official records is in 1774, when he was listed as part of a party of surveyors that needed to be warned of an impending Indian attack. His party suffered several losses before they were able to return to safety. Soon thereafter he was listed on a roster of Revolutionary War soldiers. The next official notation was in the Lee County records for August 23, 1791, which stated: "Ordered that David Chadwell, Joshua Ewing, John Ball, and Joseph Johnson, being first sworn for that purpose, to view a road from Martin's Old Station to Cumberland Gap, and make a report to next Court of the nearest and best way for said proposed road."

Gradually John and his brother Moses began to buy up land in the area of the present town of Ewing, becoming large landholders. The county records show that they, along with their kinsmen the Yearys, who had traveled with them to Lee County, also owned slaves.[1] Soon they were established as one of the well-to-do families in what had become a settled area. When John died in 1809 he was buried in a shallow cave, really more like a rock overhang, on one of his farms.[2] He had said that in his early years in Lee County he frequently evaded Indians by hiding in the cave, and that was where he wanted to be buried.

John and his wife Mary "Polly" Yeary Ball had eleven children, one of whom was George W. Ball, born about 1787 in Lee County. George's son Arthur was the father of Philip McNally Ball, who was born in 1837 and grew up on the family farm. Described as being tall, blond, and looking like a Viking in his youth, he married the short, dark-haired, pleasingly plump Emeline Rebecca Noe in 1860, and their first child was born a year later. When the country exploded in civil war, he sided with the Confederacy. Philip served with Captain Shelby Gibson's Cavalry, and was part of the Southern force at the Cumberland Gap, where he was wounded during a skirmish. After the war he returned to his farm and became a leader in his community. He and Emeline had sixteen children, two of whom died in infancy. Their sons were to play a central role in the history of Middlesborough.

At the time of the first exciting stirrings in the Valley of Yellow Creek in 1888, their oldest son, Charles Dudley (C.D. or Charley) was twenty-seven, married, and with four young children. George Shelby was twenty-six and had three children. Their next son, Rufus, was twenty-five. Then came Sillus Arthur (S.A.) who was twenty-one, married, but with no children. John Randolph was nineteen years old; Joseph Franklin (Frank), eighteen; Timothy Tyler, sixteen; and Houston Edward (H.E.) was fifteen. Emeline's great-granddaughter recalled her as an old woman lamenting, "Middlesboro ruined my boys." To which the girl's mother retorted, "No, your boys ruined Middlesboro."[3] There is some truth in both statements. It is also true that the Ball Boys contributed greatly to the growth and development of Middlesboro.

Except for Rufus, who stayed on the family farm, and Timothy, who died in 1890, all the boys were drawn to the brawling, booming Wild West town with its excitement, opportunities, and the promise of easy money. C.D. started in construction, working first on the road at the Narrows near Pineville, and then on Middlesborough streets. S.A. took a job as a clerk in a store owned by John C. Colson Jr. Frank first found work as a stone mason. Houston worked on the crew that was surveying roads for the new town, then took a job at the brick factory. Soon, however, they all gravitated to the liquor business, law enforcement, and politics. Although different in temperament and disposition, the Ball Boys always stuck together and helped each other, even when they were on opposite sides of the law.

The Balls early on saw that money was to be made in satisfying the town's thirst. By 1896 C.D. was already running a saloon on 19th Street, and H.E. had been granted a liquor license. Over the next six years all the brothers except S.A. operated one or more saloons: the Keg House, the Palace, the Log Cabin Saloon, the Mecca, the Shady Grove, the Elk, and the Little Gem Saloon. The Ball Boys soon controlled the majority of the watering holes being supported by the town after the "bust."

The Boys were also active in law enforcement and politics. Both C.D. and Frank served as Bell County deputy sheriffs. In 1892 S.A. became the deputy chief of police of Middlesboro; when he died in 1902, John took his place. H.E. Ball joined the police force at age seventeen and later became chief of police. In 1903 Frank was serving as a special policeman and Shelby was listed as assistant chief. Over in Lee County that same year their father, Philip Ball, was elected high sheriff by the largest vote ever given to a candidate for that office.

The Balls' forays into politics reflected more attention to expediency than to party loyalty. As sons of a Confederate soldier, the Balls had all been Democrats. When they arrived in Middlesboro, however, they found the prevailing sentiment was for the Republicans, and they immediately changed their allegiance. In the election of 1896 C.D. used the gambling rooms over his saloon to register illegal voters. The Democrats alleged he was part of a "ring" that rounded up African-Americans the night before the election and registered them to vote the next day. C.D.'s partner, Harrison Ausmus, acted as doorkeeper because of the large crowd waiting to be registered. One man later testified that he had been rousted out of bed at eleven the night before the election and informed, "C.D. wants you to register."[4] With this service C.D. advanced in the political hierarchy and in 1903 was a delegate to the Republican District Convention. He was also elected to the Middlesboro City Council.

Nonetheless the Ball Boys often found themselves on the wrong side of the law. Part of the problem was that the law and community standards kept changing so that what was a legal or acceptable business practice one day might be illegal the next. But the Balls also showed a certain disregard for the niceties of the law. For example, a cursory look at court records for January of 1901, to take only one month, reveals John and C.D. indicted for selling liquor to minors, and C.D. and Shelby Ball charged with selling liquor on Sundays. In addition, C.D. was indicted for running a gambling house. With Frank the problem went even further. As his nephew explained, "Uncle Frank Ball was a man that feared no man. The best thing for all concerned was to refrain from offending him."[5]

On May 9, 1894, Frank was offended by a certain J.D. Davis. At the time, Frank was serving as a special patrolman, and he had a warrant for Davis' arrest. As Ball tried to put the "nippers" on his prisoner, who was unarmed, Davis either hit Frank or spit on him. In an apparent fit of rage, Ball shot Davis in the neck and through the heart, despite the fact that a regular policeman was on the scene—so close that the policeman was splattered with blood—and there was no danger of Davis escaping.

Frank was arrested but managed to escape while in the custody of his two brothers, Deputy Chief of Police S.A. Ball and Patrolman H.E. Ball. The *Middlesborough News* reported:

> Never in the history of Middlesborough have people been aroused as they are today. That an unarmed man in the possession of the police should be shot down like a dog in broad daylight and in the heart of the city is beyond comprehension....Public opinion holds the police department responsible for Ball's escape....a storm of indignation has been aroused that is now demanding a clean sweep of the police department.

A mass meeting was held at the Opera House to call for a thorough investigation of the matter. Seven hundred attended. As a result, Mayor David Colson appointed a commission to investigate the matter. Meanwhile, S.A. Ball tendered his resignation, and H.E. was indicted as an accomplice in the escape. Indignation ran high, and the *Louisville Courier Journal* of May 11 even suggested that if Frank Ball was recaptured he would be lynched. Governor J.Y. Brown offered a $500 reward for his capture. Frank, however, came back of his own volition.

The Commission reported its findings in July of 1894, exonerating the police of the most serious charges while castigating them for carelessness and neglect of proper procedures. The Bell Circuit Court indicted Frank for murder on July 11, 1894. Charged along with him was the regular policeman who was on the scene, Frank Cecil.[6] The case was continued from one term of court to another throughout 1894, 1895, and 1896. Potential witnesses for the prosecution were fewer with each passing session, while witnesses for the defense grew more numerous and came to include some of the leading citizens of Middlesboro: David G. Colson,

J.C. Colson Jr., J.G. Fitzpatrick, and W.H. Turner. Finally, on July 8, 1897, Frank was found not guilty.[7]

In 1901 Frank was involved in another shooting. Patrolman John Turner was attempting to arrest a man when the latter grabbed Turner's gun and bolted. Frank and Zack Steele, who happened to be standing nearby, joined Turner in the chase. They shouted for the man to surrender. He answered with a shot, and his pursuers returned fire. He fell with four bullets in him, three of his wounds being mortal.

February of 1902 found the Ball Boys technically on the right side of the law as they marched on the Quarterhouse, a saloon and bawdy house located in Mingo Hollow (see Footnote Twenty-two). At that time C.D. was a deputy sheriff and led the posse. Frank and H.E. were both part of the posse, as was their cousin Charley Cecil, who was the first to die in the battle. (S.A. had by this time been ill for several months; he died on February 28, 1902, of "an affection of the brain.") To this day, the descendants of Lee Turner, who owned the Quarterhouse, claim that the entire affair was simply a way for the Balls to rid themselves of competition, as Turner's Quarterhouse had become so popular that it was siphoning off their business.

When time came for the next county elections, Frank announced his intention to seek the Republican nomination for sheriff of Bell County. His advertisement in July of 1905 covered the entire front page of the newspaper and featured a large picture of himself. It noted that he was "one of the men to whom 'ready money' is no unaccustomed thing." By this time Frank had three sons: Ira, who was eleven, William Floyd, age six, and James Alva, who was almost two years old. His only daughter had died in 1900 at the age of six months.

His candidacy came at a difficult time for Middlesboro. The "bust" had left the town essentially bankrupt, meaning that city employees could not be paid regularly, if at all, which resulted in a lack of adequate fire and police protection. Into the void had stepped the lawless element, and respectable citizens were frustrated. Frank Ball was the lightning rod—his reaction the next time he was offended enraged the town.

Jack Bolen was one of Frank's closest friends prior to the Republican primary, and Frank had expected his support in his bid for office. Instead, Bolen came out for Frank's opponent. Frank did not take kindly to such opposition, especially in one on whose loyalty he had counted. To make matters worse, he was defeated. When he vented his spleen on Bolen, his target went to the grand jury in Pineville and had Frank indicted for intimidation and placed under a $1,000 peace bond. Bolen also brought a $10,000 suit against him for slander. Certainly Frank was "offended."

Frank Ball campaign flyer. Courtesy of W.W. Hoskins.

On October 2, 1905, Jack Bolen was sitting in one of the chairs of his barber shop on 19th Street when someone stepped to the door and pumped three shots into him, one of which went through his forehead, causing instant death. Eyewitnesses identified Frank Ball as the killer.

The killing brought to a head the public's outrage at the general lawlessness in Middlesboro. The funeral for Bolen had to be held at the Princess Theatre because no church was large enough to accommodate the estimated one thousand mourners. Three hundred members of the Odd Fellows came from all over the state for the funeral, Bolen having been a member of that organization. Business houses and saloons in the city were closed during the ceremony. It was reported that feelings ran so deep that at one point in the service, the congregation "forgot itself and broke into applause." The public schools were closed, and more than 600 children marched in the funeral procession.

On October 6 a mass meeting was held at the Princess Theatre to address the general lack of respect for the law in the city. Frank Ball had been allowed to simply walk away from the shooting and leave the city, and a lack of confidence in the police force was evident at the gathering. The outcome was the formation of a Law and Order League. One hundred and fifty men signed up as members of this vigilante organization.

At the same time, Bell County Sheriff Tyrus Howard wired Governor John W. Beckham that he could not "cope with the condition of affairs in Middlesboro" and asked him to send in state troops to keep order. The governor responded by ordering the mustering in of a company of local men. The *Middlesborough Record* reported on October 12 that "Col. Roger D. Williams of the Second Kentucky will arrive tonight accompanied by Adjutant Montgomery and will muster in the company here. Guns, ammunition and uniforms have been sent from Frankfort and will arrive most any day. The mustering in...will take place at the Odd Fellows Lodge."

For the next several months the troops camped on a hill overlooking Middlesboro, while Frank remained at large. His family intermittently gave out bulletins: he would be surrendering any time, he had left the country, etc. The big city newspapers were fascinated with the story, though there was often more fiction than fact in their reports. For example, the *Knoxville Journal,* in an article that was reprinted in papers from New York to Florida, reported:

> The Middlesboro militia company spent Sunday afternoon in the mountains after a lawless gang, said to be headed by Frank Ball....Ball is reported to have with him a crowd of at least 40 men, who intend to resist his arrest to the last....Tonight the town is comparatively quiet, but all the telegraph wires have been cut, and the news can get out of there only by telephone. Governor Beckham has been asked to send more soldiers, and another company is expected tomorrow.[8]

A special to the *New York Times* carried another version:

> The recently organized company of State Guards was defeated this afternoon four miles south of here by Frank Ball and his band of outlaws. At least two soldiers are dangerously wounded, two are missing, and Shelby Ball, a brother of the outlaw leader, is perhaps fatally wounded....It was planned by Capt. Albrecht to take the band by surprise, but that part of the scheme failed....firing was heard up the mountain side—first one shot and then a fusillade. For two hours this kept up, and then the soldiers...slowly retreated down the mountain. Dodg-

> ing from boulder to boulder, they backed away from the enemy, who followed, firing. Half way down the mountain side the soldiers made a stand, but Ball sent a flanking party out, and forced them to keep going. That more men were not killed is surprising. The fight was kept up to the outskirts of town.[9]

The next day a further "Special to *The New York Times*" reported that the above action had been led not by Frank but by his sixteen-year-old nephew Riley Ball, "who is now under indictment for murder." There was an assertion by the family that Frank would surrender in two weeks if the circuit judge would promise him a fair trial.

The question of a fair trail was foremost on the minds of the Ball faction, who circulated the story that Frank had shot in self-defense, that as he walked past Bolen's barber shop, Bolen made a move that Frank interpreted as going for his gun, so he shot first. Adding credence to this interpretation of events was the fact that Frank suffered from poor eyesight, and it was said that might have caused him to misinterpret a movement.

Rumors and newspaper stories to the contrary, the only known casualty during the three months Frank was at large was one of the men in the militia, who shot himself in the foot during target practice. His wound did not appear to be serious, but in those days before antibiotics, even relatively minor wounds could be fatal.

Finally on January 6, 1906, Frank surrendered. He traveled to Middlesboro from Virginia by train, escorted by four of his brothers. He was met at the station by a large and none too friendly crowd, but there was no threat of mob violence. The militia was disbanded, and the town took on a more normal aspect.

A change of venue was granted, and the trial was held in Barbourville during April of 1906. Frank was convicted and sentenced to life in prison. The request for a new trial was overruled, and he was lodged in the Madison County Jail at Richmond, Kentucky, some hundred miles from Bell County.

In June of 1906 Frank escaped from jail. He made his way by foot, traveling along riverbanks and creek beds, to the Red Bird area of Bell County. There he met by chance with one of the Knuckles clan who was out fishing. He took Frank home to dinner, provided him with clean, dry clothes, gave him a bed for the night, and the next day lent him a horse so he could escape to Lee County, Virginia. This deed led to a firm friendship between the Knuckles family, which was one of the leading powers in the northern part of Bell County, and the Balls. Forty or fifty years later a

Knuckles had only to ask to receive any favor from the Balls that they were capable of granting.[10]

The news of Frank's escape set the entire area in a frenzy. A total of $500 in reward money was offered for the recapture of Ball. Governor Beckham offered $300, the Madison County jailer $50, and each of two Middlesboro fraternal lodges posted $75. But for two months Frank remained at large, eluding capture despite the reward and the fact that "Middlesboro detectives" were unleashed to shadow him. For a time he was reportedly at the home of his father, who was the high sheriff of Lee County. Then he moved to the house of his brother Rufus, on a farm some four miles outside of Rose Hill, Virginia.

When it was determined that he might be extracted from this redoubt, Bell County Sheriff Rice W. Johnson gathered a posse. Evidently the Middlesboro police, whose loyalties could not entirely be trusted, were not informed of the sheriff's intentions. Neither were the law enforcement authorities in Lee County notified, since Frank was known to be under the protection of his father. In a comment on the transportation system of the day, it was necessary for the posse to ride the night train to Rose Hill, some twenty miles across the Gap, then hike the distance to the farmhouse. They arrived about 5:30 a.m. and stationed themselves on the hills surrounding the two-story log house belonging to Rufus.

Sheriff Johnson then demanded Frank's surrender. Frank was asleep at the time but, awakened by all the commotion, suggested the posse return to Kentucky as he was not giving up. Since it was generally believed that Frank had with him "several desperadoes" in the heavy log building, a stalemate developed. Sheriff Johnson hiked back to Ewing and telegraphed the Middlesboro Civic Union (a group organized by the Law and Order League): "Have man in house surrounded. Get special and all men you can quick. Come to Rose Hill." Thirty Middlesboro men immediately stepped forward, and by noon they were on a special train bound for Virginia, determined, according to the newspaper, to "arrest Ball at all hazards...as it will put an end to further trouble in Middlesboro."

They arrived too late for the battle, however. The sheriff's posse, commanding the heights overlooking Rufus's house and undoubtedly tired, hungry, and impatient after spending most of the night getting there and all morning watching the house, began to fire at about one o'clock in the afternoon. Their shots were answered from within the house and the battle was engaged. The firing was furious for an hour, with volley after volley of bullets exchanged. The interior of the house, along with its furniture, was later found to have been riddled with shots.[11] But there was no sign of

Frank and Sallie Ball with sons Alva (3), Floyd (4), and Ira (5), ca. 1907. Courtesy of W.W. Hoskins.

surrender until one of the inmates of the house, a friend of Frank's by the name of John Lee, was killed. Soon thereafter, Frank Ball surrendered.

Meanwhile the special train from Middlesboro arrived in Rose Hill about 2:00 p.m., and the paramilitary force immediately set out for Rufus' farm. Of course, by the time they arrived all that was left for them to do was to escort Frank back to Middlesboro. Evidently no effort was made to arrest anyone else at the Ball home; in fact, some of Frank's friends were allowed to accompany him back to Kentucky and even stay with him until he was delivered to jail. Sheriff Johnson, along with his posse and the vigilante group, carefully guarded him, some staying on the job until he was securely jailed in Louisville. This time he stayed in jail a while.[12]

In late 1906 there was an effort by Lee County, Virginia, to try Sheriff Johnson and his posse for the "murder" of John Lee, since his death had occurred during an unauthorized action taken by persons from out of state. Some felt this was a ploy by the Ball clan to obtain leniency for Frank in return for dropping the extradition orders for the Bell County officials. There was an exchange of communications between Kentucky's governor, J.W. Beckham, and the governor of Virginia, Claude A. Swanson, in which Beckham explained:

During the seven years that I have been Governor, I have had a great

> deal of trouble with lawlessness and crime in that little mountain city, and the head and front of the lawless element there was this Frank Ball, some of his family and his associates....After our courts had succeeded in bringing him to justice...he made his escape to Lee county, Virginia...placed himself under the protection of his father, who was Sheriff of Lee county....it was complete evidence to the Bell County authorities that they would never have an opportunity to recapture Frank Ball through requisition papers....I want you, my dear Governor, to carefully consider this point and see if you do not think that it, at least morally, exonerates these officers for any technical violation of the law in crossing over the Virginia line.[13]

Governor Swanson did reconsider and dropped the extradition order.

In April of 1911 the governor rejected a plea for Frank's pardon, which had been signed by a number of Bell County officials and all the city officials of Middlesboro. In doing so, however, he did complain of the "gross impropriety" of the petitions against the pardon which had come from more than sixty fraternal lodges in the state of Kentucky and which included warnings of the political penalty that they would exact should he decide to grant the pardon. In June of 1912 it appeared that a petition for Frank's parole was going to be approved thanks to the good services of State Senator Joe Bosworth. But at the last minute the parole was revoked because Ball had not served the minimum sentence required by law.

Frank managed to gain his freedom by 1920. He played a part in the Ball-Colson Feud, and was again sentenced to jail in 1923 for involvement in the Bell County Courthouse shoot-out (see Footnote Twenty-six). But if he served any actual time, it was short. During the twenties he operated a livery stable behind his home on Cumberland Avenue at 15th, a grocery store, and then a wholesale and retail grain and feed business. He was also involved in the liquor business, which was, at that time, illegal. In 1929 he ran for jailer but was badly defeated. That was his last hurrah in politics as a candidate.

By the early thirties, Frank's sons were coming into power in Middlesboro, but his own health was failing, and he was almost blind. Frank died in February of 1942 at a time when his sons Floyd and Alvey, whom he adored, were at the height of their political power and wealth. Upon his death, "A Friend" eulogized him, writing that "at the end of the trail of kindness and good deeds, he has gone away to a golden paradise, of which he will still be a credit. Although he is gone, his good deeds will linger in the minds and hearts of his kindred and friends for ever."[14] Though

C.D. Ball and his second wife, Evelyn. Courtesy of the Bell County Historical Society.

this description does not seem to fit the quick-tempered roughneck of earlier days, it was apparently more accurate for the man Frank became in later years. Longtime residents remember him as being humorous and good-hearted, often providing groceries for poor families and going out of his way to help the less fortunate in town. His wife Sally survived him by three years. She is also remembered as being generous, though sharp-tongued, and quick to help those in need. Both were devoted to their family.

Meanwhile the other Ball Boys, though less colorful than Frank, were making their own contributions to the history of Middlesboro.

C.D. had married Martha Yeary about 1881, and they had nine children together. Their last child was born in 1901, and soon thereafter he and Martha were divorced. In 1905 he eloped with Evelyn Moore, who was a second cousin. He ran saloons, was involved in politics, and did hauling and street work for the city. In 1906 C.D. and his eldest son Patton, who was then twenty-four, were indicted for the murder of Meade Cottrell, which had occurred four years earlier. The case was dismissed when Judge

M.J. Moss rendered an opinion that he had no jurisdiction since, although the shooting had occurred in Bell County, Cottrell had crossed the line into Tennessee before he actually died, so no murder had been committed in Kentucky. This novel reasoning was later challenged, but by that time Patton and his wife had relocated to St. Louis, and then on to Oregon. The charge against C.D. was dropped. When Moss was chided about his decision he replied, "What is the Constitution among friends?"[15]

C.D. was able to return to construction work, working for the railroad and the Highway Department, and was involved in various mercantile businesses. As time went on, he dealt in real estate and had a large farm in Tennessee but continued to reside in Middlesboro near his brothers.[16] He lived to be ninety-five. In his later years the newspaper described "Uncle Charlie" thus: "He gradually became guide, philosopher, and friend to the widow, the orphan and the lowly, and by his conciliatory temperament and the trust reported in him by opposing factions in the city, became known as 'the Peacemaker'." At the time of his death in 1956, he had twenty-three grandchildren, thirty-one great-grandchildren, and nine great-great-grandchildren.

Philip Ball's second son died on June 16, 1911. The newspaper notice of his passing was brief: "Shelby Ball, a well known citizen of Middlesboro, died suddenly at his home in East End. He was one of the early settlers in Middlesboro and had a wide acquaintance in the county....He leaves a wife and seven children. He was the brother of Frank Ball." Shelby's second son, Edgar, spent the better part of his life in prison, having been convicted of murder in 1903. His third son, Riley, lost his life during the Ball-Colson Feud. A daughter, Rosa, married George Whited. Their son Muriel was a hero in World War II. Ernie Pyle described his deeds in his book *Brave Men,* reporting that Whited "used to run his uncle's bar in Middlesboro and he said when the war was over he was going to drink the bar dry, and then just settle down behind it for the rest of his life."[17]

Rufus lived out his life as a prominent farmer in Virginia. His four children remained in Lee County.

John Randoph Ball continued in the liquor business and also branched out into real estate. He built a number of cottages between 19th Street and the railroad, using material salvaged from the old electric plant, which he had purchased for scrap. He died in November of 1913 at the age of forty-four of kidney disease. He left four children. His youngest son, Harry, was the Bell County jailer from 1935 through 1957.

The youngest son of Philip and Emeline, Houston Edward, had come to the Yellow Creek Valley as a teenager. He helped clear the land for the new city. Although he left for short periods during his early years to work out west, he lived most of his adult life in Middlesboro and served the city in official capacities for more than fifty of those years. Early on he worked as a special patrolman, then as night chief of police. He held that position for sixteen years, then took over as the chief of police. In 1926 he lost the job when a political opponent became mayor. He worked for two years as a salesman for General Mills before being elected city police court judge in 1928. Judge Houston held that office until 1952, being known by one and all as "The Grand Old Man" at City Hall. He had a total of eight children and lived to see ninety-two years.

Middlesboro had not ruined the Ball Boys as their mother had lamented, nor had they ruined it. But they had left an indelible imprint on the city's history. From the earliest boom-and-bust days to the Ball-Colson Feud of the early 1920s (see Footnote Twenty-six), and through the thirty-year period from the mid-twenties to the mid-fifties, when Floyd and Alvey Ball ran the city (see Footnote Twenty-nine), the Ball family was one of the most significant forces in the saga of Middlesboro.

Footnote Fourteen

Fire! Fire!

Dateline Middlesboro, December 5, 1997: "A piece of Middlesboro's past went up in flames Thursday night, as the American Association building fell prey to what city officials say was arson." Tragic, but only another in a series of fires that has left Middlesboro's downtown resembling, in the words of one resident, a snaggle-toothed old woman. Arson has often been suspected. In September of 1986 even the old city hall with its attached fire station fell victim to a fire.

A legacy of the past? Within the first months of its existence Middlesborough suffered three major fires that threatened to doom the city before it could get properly started. An incendiary was blamed. Although the city managed to rebuild, the financial drain was a major factor in its "bust."

Even prior to the city receiving its charter in March of 1890, the Middlesborough Town Company had built a structure on the east side of 20th Street between Cumberland Avenue and Lothbury that was to serve as a fire house as well as a city hall, and they installed a fire engine and hose truck.

On April 21, 1890, fire broke out in the frame building occupied by H.G. Pigg's drugstore. The cause was initially thought to have been an explosion in the stove. The fire spread quickly to the billiard parlor and saloon next door and then engulfed the other buildings on the north side of Cumberland between 20th and 21st. The fire station was less than a block away, but when the recently organized fire department tried to operate the new engine, it poured water for only a few minutes, then the large steamer "gave out" and the pumps would not work. The delay was fatal as the fire spread rapidly through the timber and fabric structures that lined

Cumberland Avenue in early May 1890. Courtesy of the Bell County Historical Society.

the street and burned all the way to the creek behind and to the roadways in front and on the sides. One of the buildings in the path of the flames was the city jail, and all incarcerated lawbreakers were turned out to fight the fire. According to the newspaper, "In less than two hours, the most thickly populated portion of Middlesborough was utterly effaced." Only a brick building that housed the post office at the time was saved.

Residents immediately began rebuilding. The volunteer fire department started drilling, and an experienced engineer was put in charge of the fire engine. They were put to the test a week later when the livery stable of C.E. Clay burned to the ground. The fire was contained, and twenty-two of the forty-five horses stabled there were saved; however, the paper reported that the origin of the fire was a complete mystery, and stated, "The only reasonable conclusion is that it was the work of an incendiary." This brought into question the cause of the first fire, especially after a third conflagration nearly destroyed the city.

May of 1890 was a hot, dry month--dangerous weather for a town constructed almost entirely of frame buildings and tents. The first city council and mayor were elected May 14, 1890. One of their initial actions was to appoint the chief of police to act as a fire inspector. They also started negotiations with the Middlesboro Town Company to purchase their fire apparatus. Before they could proceed, disaster struck again.

At about ten o'clock on the morning of May 31, fire was discovered in the rear of Hoyland's grocery on the north side of Cumberland Avenue between 20th and 21st, very close to where the first fire had occurred. The alarm was sounded immediately, but with the wind blowing strongly from the northeast, the flames spread rapidly, leaping from flimsy building to tent with abandon. Sparks flew across the wide avenue and torched buildings on the south side of that heretofore barrier. The second stories of many buildings were used as residences, and frantic people began throwing their furniture, trunks, and other possessions out of windows into the street. Equally frenzied merchants yanked whatever they could out of their establishments and carried them onto the wide avenue. Everyone pitched in to help. The paper reported that all was "in the wildest confusion. Men worked like beavers and women and children ran hither and thither WEEPING AND SCREAMING in the wildest manner, and only adding to the din and confusion." As the flames shot ever higher on both sides of the avenue, there was an arch of fire and smoke over the frantic scene.

The fire apparatus arrived but was of little use. According to the paper

> The engine was at the 20th street bridge making a frantic endeavor to do some sum effectual work, but without avail. The machine worked for a litle wile and then was compelled to stop owing to giving out water of in the boiler, and the failure of the pump to work. Engineer Jones struggled manfully with it and did all in his power to get it into successful operation, but failed; finally after a delay of perhaps an hour the TERRIBLE DISCOVERY WAS MADE that sum one had bin tampering with the engine and in the valv check of the pump was found a larg piece of waste wound in and out and around the thng so that it was impossibl to force water thru it at all.
>
> This dammabl act was evidently the work of sum fiend who cherishes a terribl animosity for Engineer Jones and is doutless an aspirant for his position. The thing was seen by a number of the bystanders and indignation ran high for it was evident that such a thing coud never hav happened sav by design.[1]

Alexander Arthur and his secretary were working in the Town Company offices just a few blocks from where the fire started. Seeing the commotion, black smoke, and flames, Arthur rushed to the scene. The situation was desperate. Men lined up to form a bucket brigade stretching from the canal, but the flames were racing ahead of them. Merchants redoubled their efforts to empty their businesses as the fire advanced toward them. Bars and saloons disgorged their barrels of whiskey and bottles of liquid corn onto the pile in the center of the avenue. Arthur, concerned that the

The Davis and Hurst store before the Great Fire of May 31, 1890. Courtesy of David Hurst.

The Great Fire, May 31, 1890. Courtesy of the Bell County Historical Society.

easy availability of so much "strong drink" would prove too much of a temptation for many and might lead to drunken riots, gave the order to take ax and hammer to the bottles and barrels. The gutters ran with liquor, and many a man abandoned his work fighting the fire to fall to his knees and swill the precious whiskey from the puddles.

The fire leapfrogged to the next block, where stood a building with empty lots on both sides. Arthur ordered the building dynamited to create a fire break. That and the constant stream of water from the fire engine, which was finally in operation, stopped the fire on one side of the avenue, while the lack of further buildings controlled its progress on the other. It was mid-afternoon, but the conflagration was finally under control.

Even as the fire still burned, Arthur cabled London of the disaster and by afternoon was able to issue the following circular:

TO THE SUFFERERS!

The Town Company desires to inform the sufferers by this morning's fire, that it wil hav prepared before night accommodations for all who have bin burnd out of their hmes, and that an appropriation of $5,000

> has bin made to provide food and clothing for the needy. All persons desiring accomodations, will apply to Mr. John R. Rodgers and Mr. Dorsey Williams, who wil see their needs supplied on the part of the company by order of
>
> Jno. B. Cary, Secretary

Fortunately, the Town Company had on hand a supply of large tents and bedding that had been utilized during the land sales and had escaped the fire. These were pressed into service for housing. The mess tent served meals. Extra food and supplies were immediately brought in by train from Louisville. Seldom have the needs of those suffering from a disaster been so promptly met. One misfortune, however, was that the city was forced to draw all its drinking water from a spring south of Exeter Avenue. Cattle and horses were also watered there, and the spring became contaminated. A number of people died from typhoid.[2]

The better part of Middlesborough had been leveled with all the buildings destroyed in a swath from the canal to Exeter and from 19th through 23rd. The cause of the fire was of immediate concern. At first the most likely explanation seemed to be children playing with matches in the shack at the back of Hoyland's store. Mr. Hoyland reported that he had on more than one occasion discovered children with matches and had warned them of the danger. The rumor swept the town, however, that this was yet another act of an incendiary. The paper elaborated:

> Harry Price, a carpenter of Louisville, states that about five minutes previus to hearing the alarm of fire he observed a man, apparently a laborer, leaving the shack. Mr. Price describes him as being a man about 40 years of age wearing blue pants and a blue and white striped shirt with the sleeves rolled to the elbows. This part that Mr. Price describes may have bin the firebug that caused Middlesborough's disastrus fire.

The rumor gained such wide circulation that at their meeting on June 6, 1890, the City Council passed a motion "to employ detective to ferret out origin of recent fire."[3]

The cause of the fire was never discovered. The city fell to work rebuilding itself. Merchants had fire sales in tents and immediately contracted for new buildings. The City Council passed an ordinance mandating brick or masonry buildings in the downtown area and prohibiting the storage ofhay, straw, and other such highly flammable material that was for sale in anything other than a fireproof building. They also went ahead with their plan to obtain the Town Company's fire apparatus in exchange for city bonds. The police chief, in his fire inspector hat, was to inspect all buildings yet standing to see that they were safe.

One of the merchants who immediately fell to rebuilding was A.D. Campbell. He had been one of the first to buy a lot in the proposed town, purchasing it in Knoxville while Arthur's city was yet just a dream. It had taken him eight months to get his building up since there was no train service at the time and no tunnel, so all the building materials had to be brought over the Gap by wagon. Yet, speaking of A.D. Campbell & Co., the paper could report that "the energetic merchants, not withstanding the heavy loss they sustained by fire , still continue to carry smiling faces....They are good men and cannot be kept down." They reopened two weeks after the fire in a temporary building, and were able to rebuild in 1891, this time with a brick building that still stands and is still proudly operated as A.D. Campbell Company.

Although new capital flowed into the Magic City for rebuilding, many plans had to be delayed because of the "railroad war." This war involved the right-of-way at the north portal of the Cumberland Mountain tunnel, which

Cumberland Avenue after the Great Fire. Courtesy of the Bell County Historical Society.

both the L&N and the K,CG&L (Knoxville, Cumberland Gap and Louisville) railroad lines claimed. The L&N lost the first round in court, and so on the premise that possession is nine-tenths of the law, purposefully wrecked a flatcar at the disputed spot. The K,CG&L railroad sent fifty armed men to clear away the wreckage, tear up the L&N's track, and lay their own. Ten men with Winchesters were left to guard the area. Few building supplies reached Middlesborough until the dispute was settled in mid-July of 1890. Then there was an avalanche of materials. By October of 1890 it was noted that Middlesborough was the fourth busiest place on the L&N line, right behind Louisville, Birmingham, and Nashville. So many building supplies poured into the city that there was difficulty getting them unloaded. Two hundred and fifty freight cars were waiting in the railroad yard to be unloaded while others weresidelined along the track, unable to get into the yard. A hundred additional men were brought in just to unload the freight.

Within a year of the disastrous fires, not only had all the establishments destroyed in the fire been rebuilt, but this time of more durable materials. They had been joined by many other buildings. Yet the Magic City's "rising like a Phoenix" from the ashes of the fire had a dark side. The capital that should have gone to underpin industrial growth had been largely used for rebuilding. When the economy contracted, there was no safety margin to help the city ride out the crisis.

FOOTNOTE FIFTEEN

The Magic City

"The Magic City"! It was an appellation of admiration, denoting a bustling, vibrant city that had sprung up, as if by magic, from the wilderness. The term was also used to describe the city's "phoenix-like" recovery from the ashes of devastating fires in the spring of 1890, and was used again after the "bust" to celebrate economic recovery. But magic has another connotation: the creation of illusions by sleight of hand. There is evidence that the latter definition should also be used when speaking of Middlesborough as "The Magic City."

In 1949 the *Knoxville Tennesseean Magazine* interviewed Hugh Allen, a successful Middlesboro businessman. Allen recalled how in 1889, at the age of twenty, he was manager of the Western Union Telegraph for the nascent city. At the time, he was operating out of a half finished building, using a packing crate for a table and a candle box as a chair. He described how Alexander Arthur would dictate long cables to London, a single one costing over $350 (approximately $6,500 in today's currency). At the time, Middlesborough, though mostly just a collection of tents, was second statewide only to Louisville in the volume of business handled on its wires. Allen added, "I sent hundreds of words over that wire that were nothing but lies."

Many accusations were flung about after the "bust." When the newly appointed general manager of the American Association, Ltd., E.F. Powers, reported to the English stockholders' meeting in October of 1891, he defended the honesty of the American managers. Yet when he stated, "We have been told that the enterprise is a swindle," the response was shouts of "Hear! hear!" The London *Financial Times* in April of 1891 called Middlesborough "a paradise of jerrybuilding, mud lashing and land

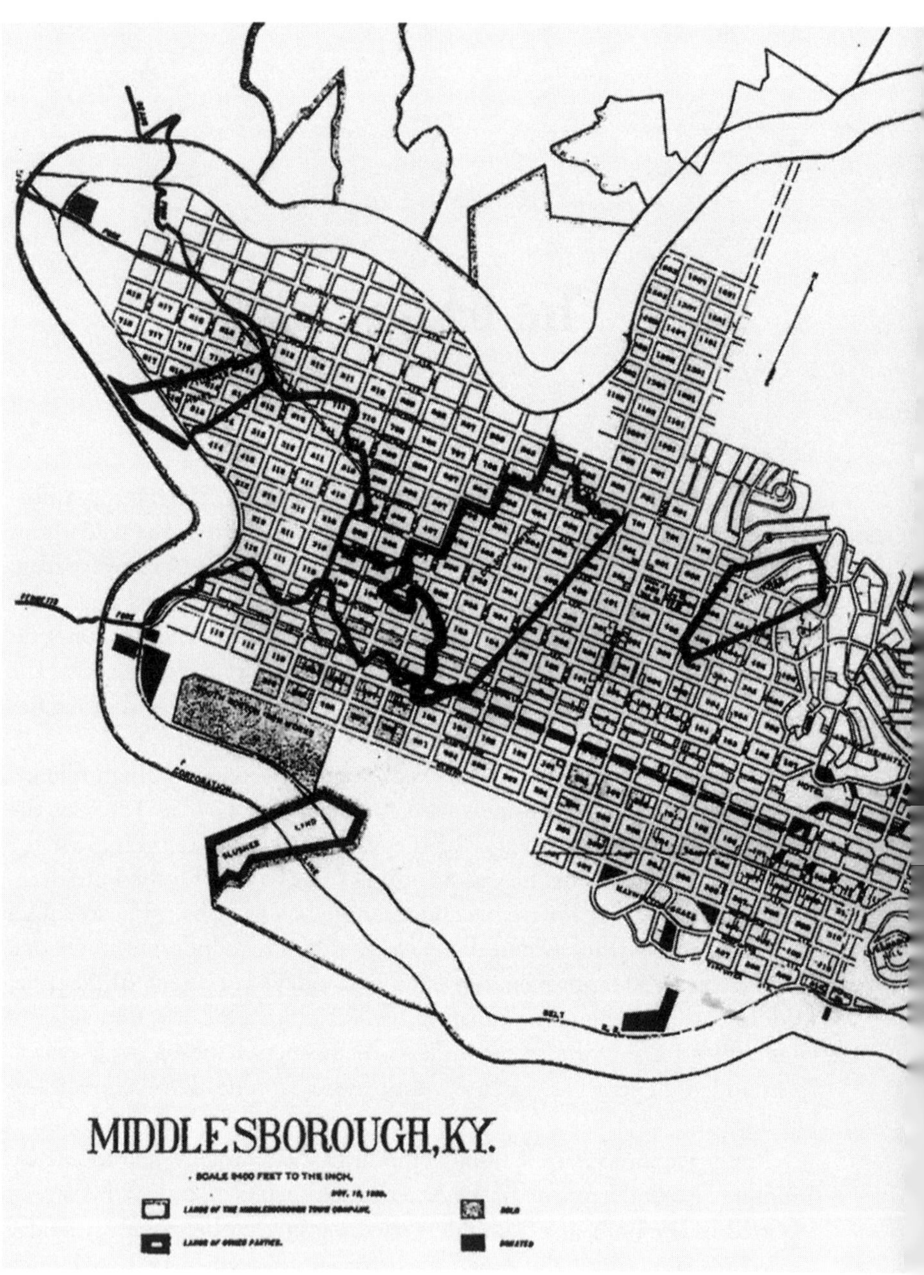

An 1890 map of Middlesborough. Areas shown in solid black had been donated to various enterprises. Areas enclosed by a dark outline were still under private ownership, the largest portion by members of the Colson family. All remaining property

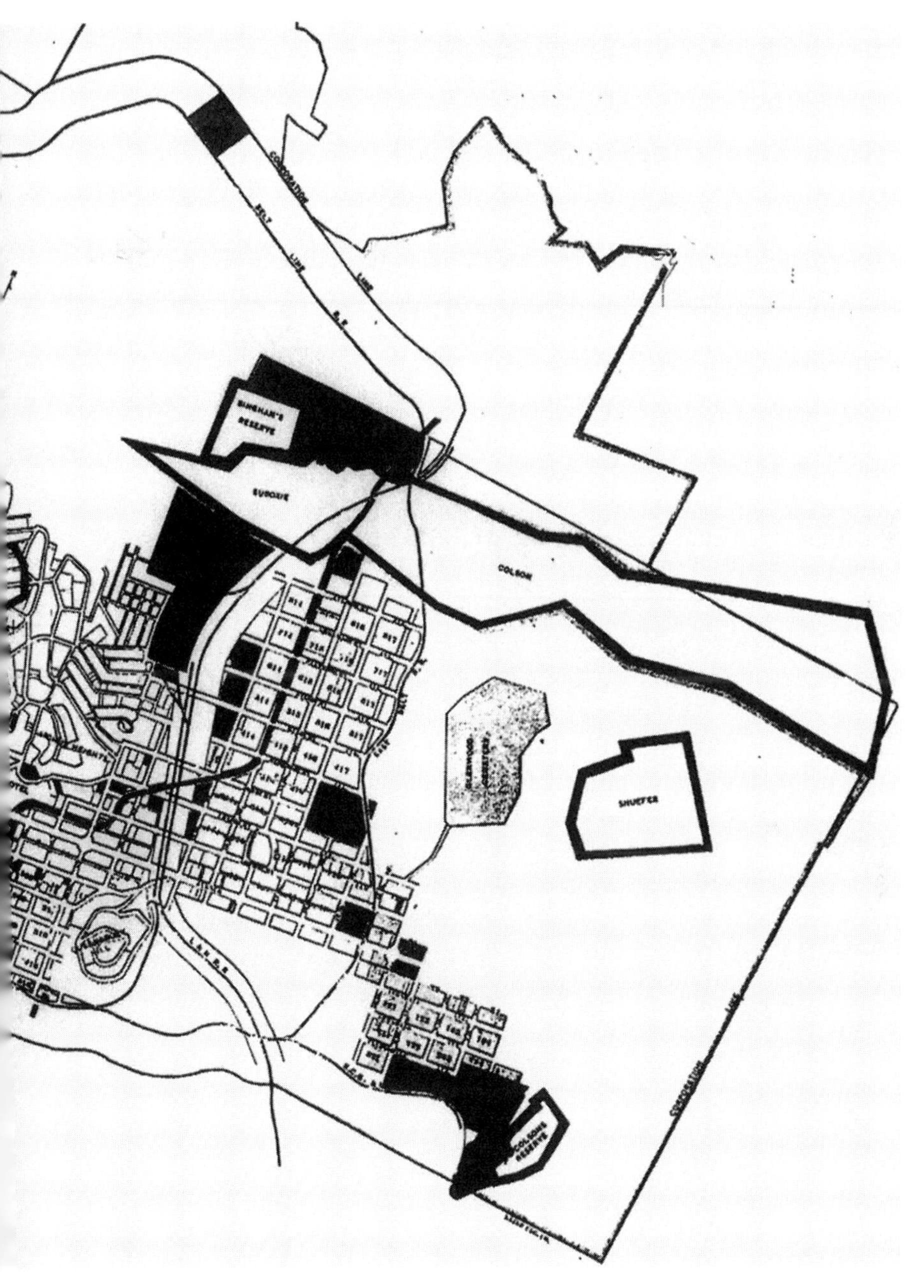

belonged to the Middlesborough Town Company except for those shaded in gray, which had been sold by the Town Company. Courtesy of Clyde Mayes.

jobbing...a funny example of a City made while you wait" with many speculative schemes and "not a single honest dollar" being earned except by the hotels and the day laborers. It described the railroad between Knoxville and the city as being "poorly built and maintained" and the expenditure of capital in the city as "foolish and useless in the last degree." As the "boom" turned to "bust" there were more allegations, legal suits, and countersuits, more journalistic outcry. How much was due to the failure of the unrealistic expectations of speculators, and how much to sleight of hand magic and the desire on the part of those being misled to believe the magic? Was there actual fraud?

There are at least two directions in which deception could have been practiced—on the native population and on investors, both those who risked financial assets and those who ventured their future.

It does not take a very liberal definition of fraud to suspect that such was perhaps perpetrated upon those who lived in the Cumberland Gap area when the English first became interested. The "natives," many of whom had lived in the mountains for generations, were mostly poor and uneducated, lacking in the sophistication to know the value of their land and its resources, or to deal with would-be buyers on an equal basis.[1] Those few men among them who were educated usually allied themselves with the outside investors, often helping them to convince neighbors to sell their land at much less than its potential value. Though ethically questionable, this would not be considered actually illegal.

When someone did not agree to sell land the Association coveted, however, several methods were alleged to have been used that were definitely fraudulent. There were reported incidents when those who would not sell were burned out.[2] Also deeds were supposedly signed in legible script by owners who were known to be illiterate and who always signed with their special mark.[3] Such actions were almost certainly not sanctioned by the American Association itself but may have been carried out by intermediaries.

Not illegal, but still reprehensible, was the method, apparently used a number of times, whereby the Association acquired the rights of a single heir to an estate that had been left in common to many heirs. If the other heirs refused to sell, the Association would then go to court and ask for a judgment as to whether the property could be fairly split or divided. When the court ruled there was no way to equitably partition it, as the court almost invariably did, the land would be put up for public auction. Since none of the heirs would have the resources to buy the entire property, the American Association could get it even cheaper than if the family had originally all agreed to sell. For example, at one such auction in 1889, 2,000 acres of land that had been in a family for fifty years were sold to the Association, as the highest bidder, for just $200.[4] Of course, the proceeding could be tricky. As a company official described in one case, "The ores right was owned by the heirs of Wm. Kincaide, and a partition suit was filed by some of the heirs to have the ore right sold and proceeds divided. At the sale decreed by the Court, the Association became the purchaser." It was then discovered that there were other outstanding interests rendering the rights purchased to have little value.[5]

There are families still living in the Yellow Creek basin who are bitter toward the English company that they believe stole their ancestral lands. In the late 1980s an elderly Middlesboro lady went about town wielding a spray paint can to mark out the "ugh" any time a business or governmental body used the English spelling of Middlesborough in its name. She explained that the English had stolen her family's land, and she wanted no trace of them in her city. Although her identity was widely known, she was never prosecuted.

What about investors and "boomers"? Were they dealt with fairly? Certainly after the "bust" many were bitter and believed themselves to have been conned by a magical illusion created by Alexander Arthur and his cohorts. The *Middlesborough News* presented this view when it editorialized in November of 1893: "It has been developed that the secret operations of the directors of the old Middlesborough Town Company were the most corrupt and far reaching...swindling scheme yet planned and executed. The shareholders of the Company have been duped and robbed to an extent inconceivable."

But one must understand that the Middlesborough "boom" followed a pattern already pioneered, often with spectacular success, by other towns of the New South, and one not too different from the incentives provided today to induce new industries to invest in a particular area. Industries that agreed to come to Middlesborough were given free land on which to build and provided services, such as rail connections and/or utilities, at a reduced rate. In many cases the Town Company or Arthur himself would invest in the business or would make guarantees of loans. There was a very aggressive courting of new industries for Middlesborough, and sometimes large bonuses were paid to an industry when it announced its intention of relocating to the new city.

A case in point was that of the Watts Steel and Iron Syndicate, a well known English concern and perhaps the single most important industry to give credence to Arthur's claims for his Magic City. The Town Company originally contracted with George Reiss to organize a company to build blast furnaces in Middlesborough, for which he was to receive a total of $100,000. He assigned the contracts to Frank and Roger Watts of the Watts Syndicate, who were promised a $75,000 bonus. The contracts included forty-eight acres of free land, a free rail spur, reduced water and rail rates, and $100,000 worth of Town Company stock. (This stock the Watts family sold at its height, receiving $300,000, roughly the equivalent of $5,500,000 today). The Watts brothers received $35,000 of the bonus in 1890, but the balance was to be paid only when the blast furnaces were completed and in operation. There were many delays in construction, and in late 1892 E.F. Powers, who had by then taken over from Alexander Arthur, threatened to withhold the final payment of $40,000 unless the furnaces were put into operation within the next few months. In February of 1893 the first furnace began production, and the next month the second followed. Soon thereafter both furnaces were banked when the seventy-five iron workers the Watts Syndicate had imported from Birmingham went on strike. Within a few days all the strikers left town without explanation, leaving the people of Middlesborough, according to the newspaper, "with the strong impression that somehow they had been made the victims of a huge joke." There were sporadic efforts over the next few years to put the furnaces back into operation, but none lasted long, and in 1926 the equipment was finally dismantled to be moved out of state.

It is not at all certain who was the villain in this tale. Certainly the townspeople could say that the Watts Syndicate had not fulfilled its promises, thus causing a huge drop in property values. But the steel producers themselves probably felt "duped." They had been assured that a great quantity of high-grade iron ore, located in close proximity to coking coal, was available for their enterprise. Yet they came to find, according to later reports, that the ore was of inferior quality and lay only in thin deposits on the opposite side of the mountain from the coal.

Why this was discovered so far into the venture has never been adequately explained. As early as 1875 Dr. Nathaniel Shaler of Harvard University and his geology students had spent time in the area and mapped outcroppings of iron ore. They returned for five summers and continued to be impressed by the ore. Alexander Arthur's claims for the ore were investigated by a noted geologist and engineer, Sir Jacob Higson, who gave a glowing report. In early 1887, Arthur obtained a number of references, all laudatory, on E.J. Bird as a practical furnace manager who had developed and run plants in Pittsburgh and also in England, Spain, and India. Bird came down in the spring of 1887 to survey the American Association properties and give a realistic view of the commercial prospects for producing iron. His estimate was that iron could be produced for $10 a ton, "even figuring in the strikes, accidents, insurance," and sold in Cincinnati or Chicago for $19 a ton. After allowing for freight costs, he estimated a profit of more than 40 percent, enough to whet the appetite of any investor.[6] Kentucky state geologist Dr. John Proctor also testified to the abundance of good quality iron ore. Samples of the ore were studied by a lab and assay office in London and certified as being of top quality. Why were so many experts mistaken?

Perhaps it was simply a matter of timing and the fact that most things are relative. The Mesabi Range near Lake Superior, which was uncovered in 1892, had superior ore that lay in flat, thick seams close to the surface so that it could be easily and cheaply extracted, giving it a competitive advantage that neither Arthur nor Bird could have foreseen. Also the Panic of 1893 hit in England earlier than in the U.S., and this would certainly have affected decisions of the Watts Syndicate.[7]

Many of those who purchased property in the new city did so with the express assurance that numerous industries were locating there and, most important, that the town would, like Birmingham, be a major iron and steel production center. They felt "duped" when these promises were not realized. But unbridled greed certainly played a part in their losses. Speculation fever had run rampant, with property values increasing daily. In 1888, when the project had barely started, land prices in the Valley had already increased by 400 percent. By mid-1889 people were piling into Middlesborough intent on cashing in on the bonanza. Street corners and hotel lobbies often served as trading floors. The newspaper reported that frequently $20,000 (more than $350,000 today) changed hands in the Cumberland Hotel in just twenty minutes. In January of 1890 two corner lots sold for $200 a front foot when only six months before the price had been $10. The reporter went on to opine that "property is increasing in value every hour."

In that atmosphere it was no wonder that many men bought with no idea of doing anything other than selling when the price increased. Because the property was offered by the Town Company on the installment plan, one needed little capital to get into the game. When the bubble burst, those who had bought on speculation, with only a small down payment, walked away from their losses, causing multiple foreclosures and deepening the problem.

For the investors back in Britain, there may also have been elements of what would later be called a Ponzi scheme in which phantom profits are paid as dividends or returns, thus encouraging further investment. In 1890-1891 the Town Company paid two 10 percent dividends, a total of £40,000 on what appeared to be a £156,000 profit, which made it look like a very good investment indeed. It was largely paper profit, however, the result of showing the total sales figures for lots rather than the cash actually taken in. The cash came from new investors. In some creative bookkeeping, the Town Company "treated heavy obligations as contingent and postponed to the future while assuming all monies due the company would be paid."[8] As payments came due on the lots and speculation fever waned, many obligations were not met.

It then became obvious that Alexander Arthur and his associates had been taking a bold gamble. In order to "boom the town" they were betting on being able to simultaneously provide the city with services, businesses and industries, and workers. The industries would not come without a labor pool. The workers would be slow to come if there were few jobs and no place to live. Arthur did not want just another mining camp, he wanted a grand city. Instead of building slowly, he tried to do it all at once. According to a later report, "They did not exactly put the cart before the horse, but they bought the cart and harness and prepared to start before the horse was foaled."[9]

In the final analysis E.F. Powers was probably closest to the truth when he reported to the shareholders in October of 1891 that there had been no fraud but rather an extravagance born of "overexuberant animal spirits."

Footnote Sixteen

"Judge Lynch"

At 3:00 a.m. on July 17, 1891, two masked men entered the electric light plant in Middlesborough and demanded that the engineer turn off the generator. He refused. Immediately he was faced with fourteen men, all masked and armed, with the same demand. He did as they bid and plunged the city into darkness.[1] When the sun came up that morning, a man was found hanging from the west side of the 20th Street Bridge in the center of town, the victim of "Judge Lynch."

How had the Magic City come to such an act?

Early Middlesborough resembled in some ways the brawling boom towns of the Wild West, where lawlessness caused men to take justice into their own hands and "necktie parties" were not uncommon. In March of 1891 there had been a lynching just over the Gap in Tennessee, and the *Middlesborough Daily News* had editorialized, "We must say a fervent amen to the lynching...at Cumberland Gap yesterday. There are extreme harsh cases which demand extreme measures."

In Middlesborough itself, the police were having difficulties, what with so many unattached males with ready cash, far from the restraints of home and family, brought together in a constricted valley by the "boom." Although there were never quite as many killings as later histories would have us believe, the police did do a steady business in shootings, knifings, drunkenness, burglaries, and the occasional murder. One early resident later described the general atmosphere with an example: "Some mountaineer came to town, was offended at something, pulled his .45 and shot through a drug store window. The shot was a signal for everyone who had a gun to pull it and shoot at someone."[2]

As if the "blind tigers" and dives in the northeastern portion of the city known as the Rhine were not enough (see Footnote Twenty-Three), there was a particularly unsavory saloon just outside the city limits, to the southeast, near where the L&N Railroad lines were crossed by those of the Beltline Railroad. Run by Gillus Johnson, it was sometimes referred to as Johnson's Saloon but usually was simply called Gum Springs after the commonly used name of the locale. Outside of city police jurisdiction and ignored by county authorities, it was said to be a favorite resort for "tough characters," both black and white. The newspaper described it as "that hotbed of villainy....gamblers congregate there, murderers resort there; it is the headquarters for rogues, scoundrels and villains of all kinds."

The Middlesborough City Council called on the county attorney and the sheriff to do something about Gum Springs, but no action was forthcoming. Throughout the first half of 1891 the newspapers were reporting on "the usual program" of gambling, drinking, fighting, shooting, and more than one murder at "that foul resort of the scum of creation." The place was a thorn in the side of city officials. The *Daily Herald* asked, "Isn't it about time this sink of corruption was wiped out?...It is a curse to the community and a blot on the fair name of the city."

On July 16 at about three in the afternoon, shooting was heard in the east end of town. Two police officers went to investigate. That is the last event in the whole affair that is not open to question.

The version that first circulated in Middlesboro was that the shooting was a plot to lure the city police outside the city limits, then ambush them. The perpetrators of the plot were identified as Gillus Johnson and a man named Frank Rasmussen (sometimes spelled Rasmussin). Supposedly when the policemen, who had been joined by others on the force, followed these two, they were lured toward Gum Springs. As they approached the saloon, according to this first report, a gang of "Yellow Creekers" rose up out of the bushes and fired on the police, shooting one officer in the calf, another in both knees, and putting several bullet holes through a third policeman's clothing. Over a hundred shots were said to have been fired before the police fell back.

A posse was quickly organized to aid the policemen. They searched the hills and captured Rasmussen, it was said, just as he was about to shoot another policeman. According to the story, the "would be assassin" was kneeling behind a bush, with his Winchester pointed at a patrolman, when others in the posse came up behind him. He was taken to the Middlesborough jail, even though the whole affair had happened in the county. Meanwhile, Johnson had circled back to the city and surrendered on the condition that he immediately be transported to the county jail in Pineville.

All of this was immediately reported in a "Special" by the *Daily Herald* under the headline "Villaneous! Plot to Murder Police—Gum Springs Gang Shows Their Hand," with the assurance that the *Herald* reporter had been an eyewitness to all the action.

Later reports suggested that by the time the city patrolmen reached Gum Springs to investigate those first shots, nothing was going on other than several men lounging about with their Winchesters, as was the custom, at their sides. The police nevertheless decided to arrest the proprietor of the saloon for reasons never made clear. According to one account, Johnson was at that point in time bareheaded and in his stocking feet. He at first refused to go with the policemen since they were clearly out of their jurisdiction and had no warrant. But he finally agreed to go quietly without insisting on a warrant if they would permit him to go back inside to complete his wardrobe. As he headed toward the saloon, he passed Rasmussen, who was carrying two rifles. Johnson suddenly grabbed one, wheeled around, and ordered the police off his property. They refused. He and Rasmussen then leveled their Winchesters at the police contingent, which by then numbered at least seven patrolmen and Chief of Police Douglas Maples. When the police still would not move off, they opened fire. At the same time, according to later accounts by the police, shots were fired from several places in the bushes. Two patrolmen were wounded, and the police force withdrew for reinforcements. (Given the accuracy of Winchesters and the proximity of the antagonists, it strains credibility to think that there was any attempt to actually kill anyone.)

Word went out, and fifteen members of the Alford Light Infantry (the local unit of the Kentucky State Guard) answered the call and were sworn in by the deputy sheriff. It was 6:00 p.m. by the time this posse was organized and was able to start its search of the area around Gum Springs. Twenty minutes later they found Rasmussen. He was manacled and taken into town. Johnson had already shrewdly made his way into town and surrendered. The posse arrested one other man, Jack Rains, whose only crime seems to have been that he was seen running in the area and was in possession of a Winchester.

The city was in turmoil. All that was known of Rasmussen was that he was a stonecutter who had come to the city several months before to work on the dam for the Water Works. He was described as being six feet tall, weighing 160 pounds, and having sandy hair. He was twenty-five years old at the time and was said to have fallen in with the group that frequented

Gum Springs. The *Herald* reported with authority that he was from Cincinnati (actually he was from Athens, Ohio) and had

> allied himself with a band of gamblers and toughs who have long been a disgrace to the community; he joined with this gang and took an active part in the ambuscade which had been prepared for the police; he fired upon officers of the law when they attempted to arrest him, and it was not his fault, but an intervention of providence that he was not a murderer. When he was captured he had a Winchester rifle which he was about to discharge at a policeman.

According to the same article, at the time of his arrest Rasmussen had a full magazine in his Winchester, an ammunition belt with thirty-one additional cartridges wrapped around his body, a pocketful of cartridges, and a holster holding a revolver with every chamber loaded and more bullets in his pockets.

Rasmussen was lodged in the city jail. Johnson had been taken to a point outside the city and put on a train to Pineville—a good move since a loud and rowdy mob had gathered at the depot downtown where it was assumed he would be boarded. But the mob's disappointment at being denied the chance to revile Johnson may well have caused even more anger to center on Rasmussen.

One can well imagine the excitement and agitation in Middlesborough that evening. From refined homes to cottages and tents, from the elegant saloons to the bars over the Rhine, the talk must have centered on the supposed plot to ambush and annihilate the entire police force of Middlesborough. It was known that Rasmussen claimed complete innocence, disclaiming all knowledge of the shooting. Given the county officials' past history of looking the other way, there must have been concern that he would escape punishment, especially since the city police had clearly been outside their jurisdiction during the entire affair.

In the early hours of the morning, with the city plunged into darkness, fourteen masked men entered the city jail with drawn revolvers, supposedly surprising the sleeping jailer. They took Rasmussen, who was already handcuffed, out of the jail, tied a half-inch rope around his neck, stuffed another section of rope in his mouth as a gag, and dragged him the short distance to the 20th Street bridge. According to one newspaper account, the gag was not effective and Rasmussen uttered "a series of horrible screams." The same account went on:

The municipal building, jail, and 20th Street bridge are seen in the background of this photo of a lot auction, 1890. Courtesy of the Bell County Historical Society.

> Here the rope that was around his neck evidently slipped, coming over his chin and tightening in his mouth. He evidently reached up with his manacled hands and endeavored to climb back up on the bridge, as when cut down his right leg was swung up and over the rope where it caught with his foot near his head. In this position it is thought that fearing he would succeed in regaining the bridge some of the vigilantes struck him as several severe wounds were found on his head from which the blood flowed freely.

The body was discovered at five that morning. Attached to the railing where the rope was tied was a manila envelope on which was written in lead pencil: "Warning! The fate of all would be assassins." It was signed simply "Vigilants."

A crowd had gathered by the time the police cut the body down at 6:00 a.m. They conveyed the corpse to the jailer's office and telegraphed the coroner at Pineville to come immediately for an inquest. All day there was great excitement in town, with "specials" issuing every few hours from the newspaper office and people gathering downtown to hear the latest. One store even used the event in their ad that day: "Some businesses have nothing to do but talk about Judge Lynch. But Bosworth, Kinnaird and Hodges have been opening goods and have a fine line to show."

When the coroner had not responded by mid-afternoon, the city attorney convened a jury of twelve. They heard testimony from Engineer Dupont of the Fire Department, who slept in the fire station that was located between the jail and the bridge. He testified that he had heard the noise and seen the vigilantes on the bridge but recognized no one. There was little other testimony, and the jury quickly reached the verdict that Rasmussen had come to his death "by hands of parties unknown to the jury." Immediately after the inquest, the body was prepared for burial that same day at Glenwood Cemetery.

By the next day the rhythm of life in Middlesborough began returning to normal, but rumors abounded. It was reported that Johnson's wife had gone to the jail to collect the Winchester that had been captured with Rasmussen, claiming it belonged to her husband. There was a rumor that on the day of the supposed ambush, Johnson had left his rifle at Conway Brothers Grocery in the east end of town, as was his habit when going into town. (Two days later Conway Grocery mysteriously burned to the ground.) Some people now claimed that there were only two "Yellow Creekers" doing the shooting. The story was also repeated that Rasmussen had finally been killed by having large rocks dropped on his head. Another rumor was that relatives of the dead man were on their way to the city to investigate the lynching and that the Stonecutters Union, to which he had belonged, was planning to hire a detective for the same purpose.

Johnson was given a hearing in Pineville, and the judge found there was sufficient evidence to bind him over to court, with bond set at $300. In announcing his decision, the judge stated, "Johnson is known to be the leader and most likely fired the first shot which caused the trouble last week between the police and the opposition party near Gum Springs."

Papers across the state reacted to the lynching with condemnation. Although their comments were reported in the local paper, the only one that was felt by locals to show true understanding of the situation was the editorial in the *Lexington Transcript,* which stated, "Lynch law, alone, was able to free the Western towns of murderers and God defying toughs." Local opinion seemed to agree with the *Herald* that, "while the action taken by the people is to be deplored, it is to be hoped that this occurrence will serve as a warning to others of his ilk to stop their nefarious practices....The people are aroused....the state of affairs which has hitherto existed needed a strong remedy and the remedy has been applied."

Things were quiet for a time. The city fathers voted to hire four additional policemen and to buy several more Winchesters and additional ammunition, but no official discussion of the lynching was recorded in the City Council's minutes.

In late August 1891 the grand jury convened in Pineville for an inquiry into the lynching. They returned indictments for murder against the city jailer, the chief of police, four patrolmen, the city attorney, and a number of others, including several members of the Alford Light Infantry. Sheriff Slusher and his deputies came to town on the train to arrest the suspects, taking them to Pineville for arraignment. Members of the Infantry were served warrants in Frankfort, where they were at a state encampment. The newspapers reported that "great excitement prevails here on account of the prominence of the citizens arrested. The universal opinion here is that the parties arrested are perfectly innocent." It was suspected that detectives hired by the Stonecutters Union had a good deal to do with the indictments. Bail was set at $5,000 each. Bond was posted by no less than Alexander A. Arthur himself, along with Mayor John Brooks and a number of leading citizens. Trial was set for February 1892.

The first case to come to trial was that of Riley Douglas, one of the patrolmen. It took a full day and a half to impanel a jury. Testimony began in the afternoon of the second day of the trial, a Thursday, and continued all the next day. The prosecution called at least twenty witnesses, and the defense answered with ten of its own. It was noted by the defense that all of the evidence was circumstantial. At 4:00 p.m. on Friday, the jury retired to consider their verdict. They returned after only three minutes of deliberation to pronounce Douglas "not guilty."

The case against J.C. Hutchinson was then considered and dismissed. The judge ruled that the defendant had been indicted on the testimony of a prisoner who was in jail that night, "a felon and lawbreaker," whom Hutchinson had earlier prosecuted in his official capacity as city attorney. The judge decided that the witness was motivated by a desire for revenge and could not be believed.

The cases against the remaining men indicted in the lynching were continued until the next session of court, and then continued again until, on July 8, 1893, all the rest of the cases were dismissed. Gillus Johnson was sentenced to one year in the State Penitentiary for "rioting" on the day before the lynching.

By this time the city was mired in a nationwide financial panic. Well over half of its former residents had abandoned it, including many who had been involved in the affair, and the lynching faded from the town's collective memory. Middlesboro would have several periods of extreme civil unrest ahead, and there would even be a time when a vigilante group would form (see Footnote Thirteen), but never again would the Magic City resort to such a violent reaction as a lynching.

Footnote Seventeen

The Father of Ragtime

Benjamin Robertson Harney was one of the "boomers." He came to Middlesborough as a young man, drawn by the excitement and the promise of the boom town. While playing piano in the Wild West atmosphere of the honkytonks, he developed an entirely new style of music, one that would be called ragtime. Harney, like many others, left town in the aftermath of the "bust." He returned to Louisville, and there he played his new tunes for appreciative audiences, which led to his publishing the world's first ragtime song in 1895. He then took his syncopated music to New York in 1896, where his sensational performances catapulted ragtime into a nationwide mania that soon spread to Europe.

Biographies of Harney state that he was born in Middlesborough on March 6, 1871. That cannot be—there was no town in 1871 and very few families in the entire Yellow Creek Valley, none of whom had the surname Harney. It is more likely that when Harney claimed Middlesborough as his birthplace, he was speaking of his music and his persona as the originator of ragtime.

Was there something about the boom town of Middlesborough that made it a particularly fertile field in which the seeds of ragtime would flower? Why in an isolated town in the mountains of Kentucky rather than in New York, New Orleans, St. Louis, or some other sophisticated urban center?

Ragtime, which swept the country in the late 1890s, was a totally new music. Music historians have long debated its antecedents. Some hear primarily the Negro plantation songs and cakewalks, an African-American tempo. They detect the special effects elicited by these blacks from the banjo and the echoes of the minstrel show "coon shouts." Others look to a

Latin origin, to Spanish and Mexican folk music or that of the Hungarian gypsies. There are musicians for whom the sound of old English folk cadences that were part of the Appalachian tradition is evident. Some even believe there are "ancestral influences" in the "syncopations of the classical masters."[1] Most music historians settle on some combination of these elements. All agree that it was a music radically different from the ballads and waltzes of the day, and that it appeared suddenly and completely on its own rather than evolving gradually from an already popular musical style, as jazz would later evolve from ragtime.

The Middlesborough to which Harney came in 1890 actually contained all of these postulated components. At least a fourth of the new town's population were black, many from the deep South. The African-American population enjoyed an active social life with weekly dances, cakewalks, socials, and church affairs, and, contrary to the custom of the day, many of the saloons and other public facilities in early Middlesborough were integrated. There was a veritable army of contract laborers, mostly Italians, but also Hungarians and others from southern and eastern Europe. Jews newly immigrated from Poland and Russia came as peddlers and stayed on as merchants. People from all over the country crowded into the new city. Most were businessmen and laborers, but there were also many gamblers, whores, and con artists who had intimate acquaintance with the saloons and dance halls of every big city. The single largest contingent was from the surrounding mountains, those sturdy mountaineers who brought with them their Appalachian traditions and music. And of course there were the educated and cultured Englishmen who, as one of their first acts, built a theater.

All of these diverse people were thrown together in a relatively small valley, most of them living in tents and other close quarters, and all united in the belief that they could grasp the quick riches offered by Alexander Arthur's vision. Like the "primeval soup" from which life is said to have sprung, all the postulated elements of ragtime were combined in one place, and it took only the right spark of musical genius to give life to ragtime.

Ben Harney was probably born in or near Louisville, Kentucky. His paternal grandfather, John Hopkins Harney (1806-1868), was one of eleven children. John's parents died when he was still quite young, and he was reared by his uncle, Judge Benjamin Mills, a distinguished jurist of the Appellate Court. John had graduated from Oxford College in Ohio and became a professor of mathematics at Indiana University. In 1827 he married Martha Rankin Wallace. He was appointed president of Hanover College and then, in 1839, president of Louisville College. He went on to become a publisher, editor, and joint owner of the *Louisville Democrat*. He had a daughter, Elizabeth, and three sons, Shelby, William Wallace, and Benjamin Mills. Shelby became a lawyer, and William gained a national reputation as a writer and poet. William was particularly interested in Appalachia, and it was he who in an article first coined the phrase "a strange and peculiar people."[2]

Benjamin Mills Harney followed in his father's footsteps. He became a professor of mathematics at Louisville High School for Boys, and later at the Louisville Presbyterian College. He enlisted as a private in the armed forces during the Mexican War and later served as a captain in Company A, Regiment Cavalry, in the Union Army during the Civil War. In May of 1864 he married Margaret (Maggie) Draffen.

Maggie was the daughter of John Draffen, a lawyer in Anderson County. He served as county attorney and also represented his area in the state legislature three different times between 1839 and 1867. A veteran of the Mexican War, he enlisted in the Union Army in 1862. Maggie herself performed a valuable service to the Federal cause. In the records of Harney's unit there is a note dated October 8, 1862, reporting, "We got some news from a Miss Draffin [*sic*] of Anderson County, that [Confederate] General Kirby Smith was lying in wait for us with 30,000 men and 64 pieces of artillery."[3] Was the army warned of the planned ambush because of what Maggie had seen while on her way to a tryst with Ben, or did she meet him at the time she delivered her warning? Perhaps neither, but the romantic cannot help but imagine one or the other.

Ben and Maggie were married at her parents' home in Anderson County. They moved to Louisville, where they set up housekeeping on Guthrie Street. Ben at first worked as a bookkeeper for a publishing company owned by his father and his uncle. Within a few years he became a partner in the firm of Harney and Randolph Civil Engineers. Benjamin Robertson Harney was born to Ben and Maggie in 1871. There may also have been a daughter, as some sources mention that Ben R. had a sister Lizzie. The reference, however, may have been to his aunt Elizabeth, as some of the same sources identify his uncle Shelby as a brother.

There were evidently problems in the marriage. By 1875 Ben M. was living in a boarding house on Gray Street. Neither Maggie nor Ben R. was listed at that address in the Louisville *City Directory* for that year, but a Maggie Harney was a teacher at the Episcopal Orphan's School. By 1880 the Harneys had divorced and she had moved back to Anderson County. The census in 1880 found the Draffen household to include a daughter Margaret, divorced, and a grandson, Ben, age nine.

Young Ben probably spent some of his time with his father and other relatives in Louisville, since his friend and first publisher, Bruner Greenup, later related that he was raised on Madison Street in "a neighborhood of good families."[4] The same source stated that he had a sister, Lizzie, who married a Louisville surgeon, Dr. Louis Frank. His uncle Shelby had married into the prominent Long family. There is a tradition that Ben attended a military school while a teenager, but no record of such has been found. There has never been any suggestion of a formal music education. The assumption has been that Harney was "a natural." He is thought to have married young, possibly when he was only seventeen or eighteen, though to date no record of the marriage has been found. His bride was Jessie Boyce. Her antecedents are a mystery.

Harney probably arrived in the boom town of Middlesborough in the spring of 1890. On July 1 of that year he enlisted in the Alford Light Infantry, a unit of the Kentucky State Guard, which was as much a social club for the young bloods in town as a military unit. The guard frequently gave dances, musicals, and minstrel shows.

When Harney joined the guard, he gave "reporter" as his occupation, but there was no indication as to which newspaper was his employer. The Magic City was literally crawling with reporters from all corners of the country and even from Europe. It will be remembered that Harney's grandfather was part owner, editor, and publisher of the *Louisville Democrat*. His uncle William was one of its editors during the mid-1860s. That paper merged with the *Louisville Courier* and *Louisville Journal*, but the family may have continued its ties with the Louisville newspapers.

Harney liked what he saw in the new town and elected to stay on. He worked by day at the post office as a clerk and later as assistant postmaster. He evidently spent his evenings playing the piano in the saloons that abounded in the booming town. An interview that he granted in 1916 contained the following description of those performances:

> He was first heard of as a local celebrity in his own mountain home because of his ability to extemporro songs, the airs of which were catchy and easy to whistle and remember....they (the mountaineers) would cluster around to Harney in some popular place and listen to his rather musical selections. As these songs were just being created by Harney, they made a tremendous hit with the natives, and when ever he would start the piano, a thumping out of one his go-band songs, business in the immediate vicinity would be suspended and Harney would own the place until he got tired.[5]

One can imagine how it might have begun—out on the town with his young friends, taking a turn at the piano, first playing songs he knew, then imitating some that he had heard in other saloons, showing his natural talent. Soon he would be playing regularly, with first one patron, then another yelling out requests for different types of music, so that he became well versed in many different styles of musical interpretation and began to combine them into his own special sound.

In the fall of 1890 Ben's father joined him in Middlesborough, setting up an office to offer his services as a land surveyor and civil engineer. During the winter of 1890-1891 his father wrote several letters to the newspaper suggesting solutions to the city's drainage and sewer problems. In one he suggested that a dam be constructed on Stony Fork, one of the tributaries of Yellow Creek, which would impound sufficient water that at regular intervals it could be let loose to flush out the sewer system, much like a giant water closet (toilet). The city fathers, however, did not adopt his suggestions. In April of 1891 the *Daily News* did note that "Mr. Harney...comes here well recommended." Perhaps emboldened by this praise, he wrote the papers again in May, this time suggesting that a plant be constructed to produce gas.

Young Ben also made the papers in May of 1891. The *Daily Herald* reported:

> Bricks and cobblestones filled the air on Cumberland Avenue about 5 o'clock yesterday. They did not injure anyone, luckily, but they made Andrews, the peanut man's tent, look ever more dilapidated than before. The occasion was a little fight between Ben Harney, Jr. and Chas. Schuck. Harney was doing the rock throwing and just proving to an appreciative audience that he was a poor marksman when Officer Bundrum arrived on the scene and took both men to headquarters. They were released on bond to appear this morning to explain matters.

According to *The Cumberland Republican,* the rock throwing had been preceded by a dispute that same morning during which Schuck had slapped Harney in the face. The result was a $10 fine for each man for disturbing the peace.

On June 6, 1891, under the heading "A Pleasant Affair," the *Daily Herald* reported a "gathering of young people" with an excursion to Bennetts Fork for an outing and picnic and then a return to Middlesborough for supper at the Exeter, one of the early hotels, followed by "amusements." Among those attending were Ben Harney and his wife.

The next time Ben made the papers, it was not nearly so pleasant an affair. The Alford Light Infantry had been involved in the incident at Gum Springs in July of 1891 (see Footnote Sixteen), which led directly to the lynching of one of those who had been arrested. Although the coroner's jury had found the lynching committed by "parties unknown," in late August the grand jury in Pineville returned indictments for murder against several city officials and a number of well-known citizens, including some members of the Alford Light Infantry.

At the time, the Infantry was at Camp Buckner in Frankfort for a state encampment and the inauguration of Governor John Young Brown. The newspaper reported that "Our company had the honor of color sergeant for the regiment....The company has been highly complimented on appearance, neatness and familiarity with soldiers' duty." But the article, which was datelined Frankfort, continued:

> Sheriff Colson arrived here yesterday with warrants for the arrest of some of the privates. Ben Harney was turned over to him last night by Col. Gaither, but this morning Col. Gaither found that he had no authority to do so and reclaimed him. Harney is now under guard....Nearly everyone from commandant down signed a petition to the governor to hold Harney until his own company could escort him home. Harney claims an alibi, and Bullock [one of the others indicted] denies that he has turned state's evidence.

The company was in Frankfort for nine days. The paper, in reporting their homecoming, stated that the "appearance of Sheriff Colson disturbed them but slightly." Their mood on the way home might be judged by the fact that the company almost got into trouble "owing to some innocent amusement they were indulging in while waiting for the train." Their horseplay so angered the locals that the latter "drew their revolvers on the boys," and it was only the intervention of their officers that prevented tragic consequences.

The trial date for those accused in the lynching was set for January 1892. After the first two defendants were judged not guilty, the trial for the rest of those implicated in the lynching, including Harney, was put off from one court session to the next until, in July of 1893, the charges were dropped. On July 18, 1893, Ben Harney was mustered out of the Alford Light Infantry. He left Middlesborough and, as far as is known, never returned.

The Columbian Exposition and World's Fair in 1893 drew many from

Middlesborough to Chicago. Besides all the exhibitions and events at the fair, much was going on in the city. Numbers of unknown itinerant musicians came to play in the saloons that catered to the fair crowds. Though no evidence is known to exist, some sources have suggested that Harney was one of those who was drawn to the city, and that he probably introduced his new music while there to some of his fellow musicians.

Harney went back to Louisville to play the piano in a saloon and dance hall on the southeast corner of 8th and Liberty. It is not clear how much of his own music he was able to work into the program. One man who saw him perform in those early days, Bruner Greenup, related how Ben would sit at the piano with a cane in one hand or the other and would do a sort of tap dance with one or both feet and the cane while playing.

Greenup was a prosperous Louisville merchant when he met Harney. He was taken by the young man's musical style and agreed to publish one of Harney's songs, "You've Been a Good Old Wagon, but You've Done Broke Down." There was difficulty, however, in getting the song down on paper, since Harney was primarily a performer rather than a composer. In an interview in 1899, the publisher recalled:

> Harney had no more idea than a monkey how to write ragtime, though he could play and sing it better, perhaps, than any one ever succeeded in doing....Finally we took the song to Mr. John Biller, then musical director for Macauley's Theater. Harney played and sung it, and Biller worked on notes. I guess we went over the thing five hundred times. At last by great patience and perseverance Biller succeeded in getting on paper the very first "rag" that the world ever saw. This was in 1893.[6]

Though it was committed to paper in 1893, the actual publication date for that first song was January of 1895. The title page gave credit to both Harney and Biller. There is no evidence, however, that Biller ever wrote any other tunes, while Harney went on to write almost a hundred.

"You've Been a Good Old Wagon" was not a financial success for the publishing house. In fact, according to Greenup, "It succeeded so poorly, that when Harney came around a year or so later with another composition, 'Mr. Johnson, Turn Me Loose,' we turned him down cold." The article continued:

> Harney carried "Mr. Johnson" in his pocket for many a day. The publisher, as he expressed it, "gave him a chill" whenever he attempted to get the song on the market. But he had unbounded faith in rag-time,

Sheet music for Ben Harney's first ragtime song. Harney is the man wearing the bow tie. Courtesy of William L. Ellison.

and stuck to his ideal with wonderful tenacity. In the early part of 1895, Harney joined a minstrel combination, doing his stick dance specialty and singing "Mr. Johnson." In Evansville, Ind., he encountered a turning point in his career. He attracted the attention of Harry Green, a former friend, by the singing of "Mr. Johnson," and the result was Green plagiarized the song, words and music, and published it under his own name. Its success was instantaneous.

By this time Harney had organized a minstrel troupe, which he called The South Before the War. He wrote the songs for the traveling extravaganza and played for every show. He and Jessie also performed as one of the earliest "Black and Hi Yaller" teams, doing a ragtime song-and-dance number to the accompaniment of a banjo. Working with them was Strap Hill, a young black entertainer from Memphis. Jessie later described their act:

> In the trio, Ben played for me to sing and dance and the name of the song was "I Love One Sweet Black Man"—Exit—Cartwheel. Ben opened the Act making his announcement, singing "Johnson" at the piano, Strap answering him from gallery, came down on stage and did his Hoss imitations, Ben doing his stick dance and playing at the piano made his exit for the finish. I blacking up, came back on stage, all three together singing "I Love My Little Honey" and did a two-step off.[7]

In early 1896 Ben took his act to New York. He had just turned twenty-five when, in April of that year, he was booked into Tony Pastor's Theatre. As a reporter later wrote,

> This was Harney's first appearance before a regular paid audience in a big city, and he thought millionaires had nothing on him when Pastor offered him the magnificent sum of $25 a week to do his turn. Harney went big with the theatre and the next day New Yorkers began whistling, "Mr. Johnson, Turn Me Loose." Before the week was over, everybody in the big town who was not actually nailed to their bed by sickness was either humming or whistling the catchy strains of Harney's ragtime.
>
> Before the week was over, Harney almost lost his breath when B.F. Keith made him an offer of $150 a week to put on his rag-time at his Boston Theatre. Harney jumped at the offer like a candidate does the grab act at a promised nomination....Boston awoke with a jump when Harney began his ta te ta stuff and rattle de bang playing on the piano at Keith's Theatre. After that the theater wasn't one-third big enough to hold the crowds who flocked to the theater to get an idea for themselves what the new line of music was that Harney was putting across. Harney made "hummers" of everybody in the staid old bean town in a couple of days, as they caught on to his ragtime songs.[8]

Harney's sensational success immediately attracted imitators, one of the first of whom was Mike Bernard, who was musical director at Pastor's

Theatre, and was present in the orchestra during that first electrifying performance. Soon Bernard was playing his own brand of ragtime, and others followed.

Ragtime had arrived at an opportune moment. During the 1890s every family that possibly could afford it had a square piano or an organ in the parlor. Tin Pan Alley was coming into its own, and sheet music was for the first time inexpensive enough for the common man to purchase. In addition, by the latter half of the nineties the country was pulling out of a long depression that had been marked by hunger marches and riots. People were ready for a happy music. As one writer put it, "It was all like a fresh start; no past associations, good or bad, clung to the new music."[9]

Immediately cashing in on the craze he had created, Harney went to the highly respected New York music publishers, the House of Witmark, with a book on how to play his music, which he entitled *The Ragtime Instructor*. As Mr. Witmark later explained, the company was not only interested in this work but also in his already published songs. But there was the question of authenticity, since Green had plagiarized and published "Mr. Johnson" first. Mr. Witmark recalled, "The matter was important, for this was something new under the musical sun. Isidore [Witmark], therefore, decided to conduct the investigation personally, and took the train to Louisville, proceeding from that city to Evansville, Indiana, to interview various musical folk and dealers. They all knew Ben Harney, and testified that he had written every note he had claimed as his own."[10]

The Ragtime Instructor was published in 1897. On its cover Harney was described as the "Original Instructor to the Stage of the Now Popular Rag Time in Ethiopian Song."

The origin of the term ragtime to describe the new music is open to question. Even when M. Witmark & Sons published Harney's "Mister Johnson, Turn Me Loose" in 1896, it was identified on the cover as "A Coon Melody." Some say the expression was first used by an unknown writer for a Chicago newspaper, though it is more likely that he simply repeated a name already in usage. The most commonly held theory is that the word came from the clog dancing of blacks that was sometimes called "ragging." Another explanation was given in the September 1901 issue of *Musician*. According to the magazine, Harney was at an African-American party and was at the piano, attempting to imitate the rhythm of two banjos being played. He was asked what kind of music he was playing, and he was said to have replied, "I don't know what it is myself....I suppose if I had a dress suit on....I might give it a nice fashionable name. But as it is, I can't think of any name in these rags and you will have to let it go at that." When

Ben Harney.
Courtesy of the
Bell County
Historical Society.

people requested the same music at another party, they were said to have asked for "that rag-time music," and the name stuck. This explanation has been rejected by most music historians.

During 1896 Harney capitalized on his successes. The 1897 *Clipper Annual,* which covered the events of the previous year, carried a "courtesy" advertisement, to wit:

> BEN R. HARNEY, author, musician and comedian.
> Originator of the only Absolute Novelty in this
> Season's Vaudevilles. Piano playing in
> cyncopated or "rag time," singing his own
> "Coon" melodies and doing his original dancing
> AN ABSOLUTE HIT EVERYWHERE

Soon there were other published ragtime pieces. One of the early important ones was W.H. Krell's "Mississippi Rag," brought out in January of 1897. The first African-American rag, Tom Turpin's "Harlem Rag," was also published in 1897. Scott Joplin's first ragtime composition, "Original

Rags," came out in March of 1899 and was followed that September by his famous "Maple Leaf Rag."

Meanwhile Ben Harney was playing vaudeville's top circuits, where he always led the bill as "The Inventor of Ragtime." He toured the Percy G. Williams, Keith, and Orpheum circuits and played with the A.T. Pearson Stock Company, the Old Soldier Company, the Howard Atheneum Star Specialty Show, and Ben Harney's All Colored Minstrels. In most cases, he not only performed but also wrote the music for the shows, eventually producing at least a hundred ragtime songs. Isidore Witmark, the music publisher who knew Harney well and was also familiar with all the other major performers of the era, had this to say:

> Ben Harney had the huskiest voice most people had ever heard in a human being and this quality made his voice just right for ragtime singing. It had queer breaks in it that affected the words as well as the music. Broadly speaking, he might even be called the first of the crooners. He would sustain certain notes, for special effect, to extravagant, breathtaking lengths; others he would break in a way that he alone could manage.[11]

It was his playing that others found most intriguing. His obituary in *Variety* asserted that his "nimble fingers...were the basis of his artistry."

In the town where it all began, people were reading that Harney was up North where "he has made a great success on the stage with his rag-time music, and is making money hand over fist." The article went on to state that "Harney will be remembered by many in this city, he having been one of the original boomers, and was, during the early days of the city, assistant postmaster."

The ragtime craze not only swept the country but crossed the Atlantic to Europe, where the music was just as popular, and Ben crossed with it. In 1916 a reporter for the *Evening News* of Lynn, Massachusetts, described his international career, which included three trips around the world. He reported that "Harney was a little bit doubtful at first just how some countries would take to his jig time music, but after he had given them one snatch of his raggy goods he found everybody calling for more." He went on to say that Harney was concerned about how his music would go over in conservative England, but he "had hardly opened his mouth...and let out the first rag bar of his music when he saw he had them coming. And he kept them coming during his tour thru the British domain." The reporter stated that he met with similar successes in such far-off places as China and the Fiji Islands. In Fiji, he said, "The natives there took to his ragtime songs and jig steps like a duck takes to water. The whole island went wild over Harney's songs and he was a little king while he remained there."

In 1915 Harney had a song-and-dance act with James P. Johnson, who later came to be known as "The Father of Stride Piano." Johnson subsequently referred to Harney as "one of the greatest pianists" he had known, and recalled how he used to play two pianos at once, using one hand for each. Meanwhile Jessie performed independently under the stage name Jessie J. Haynes. When they played together, Ben and his wife were billed as Harney and Haynes.

The year 1916 brought a challenge to Harney's claim that he was the originator of ragtime music. James McIntyre declared that a dance routine he had learned from southern blacks and had brought to Tony Pastor's in 1879 was the first ragtime. He claimed the music had come from an African chant. Harney replied that he would pay $100 to the person who could show him a piece of ragtime music that antedated his own. The bounty was never claimed. In the arguing back and forth, however, Harney did acknowledge his debt to black banjo players. He explained in an interview, as he had earlier stated in *The Ragtime Instructor*:

> On the banjo there is a short string that is not fretted and that consequently is played open with the thumb. It is frequently referred to as the thumb string. The colored performer, strumming in his own cajoling way, likes to throw in a note at random, and his thumb ranges over from this effect. When he takes up the piano, the desire for the same effect dominates him, being almost second nature, and he reaches for the open banjo-string note with his little finger. Meanwhile he is keeping mechanically perfect time with his left hand. The hurdle with the right-hand little finger throws the tune off its stride, resulting in syncopation.[12]

Although Harney won the battle over who could claim the title of originator of ragtime, he was losing the war, since the music world was changing, jazz was evolving from ragtime, and he was less in demand as a performer. By the early 1920s he was playing in small theaters, but still with large posters proclaiming "Ben Harney—World Famed Creator of Rag Time." In 1923 he suffered a heart attack and afterward was seldom able to perform.

His last tour was probably the one that started out in Chicago in the early summer of 1923 and was remembered thus by one of the musicians on that tour, a trumpet player by the name of George Orendorff:

> In 1923 I came to California with a piano player named Ben Harney....It was a show. It had five acts and he was the star....The first act maybe was a comedy act, and then a dance act, and then the last act of the five was him. He would come out and introduce himself. We were behind another curtain. We were dressed in overalls, and he would start playing this ragtime piano, then the other curtain would go up and then we were on stage. Then he had another fellow way up in the balcony who would come down the aisle playing the harmonica, and everybody would turn around....they didn't know what was happening!...He [Harney] was a very nice person, but he liked to drink a lot and his wife traveled with him. Sometimes he would try to have some of the boys go out and get something for him on the sly, so she watched us as well as she watched him.[13]

The troupe traveled by train from Chicago to Montana and on to Washington and California, ending up in Long Beach in September.

Middlesboro paused to remember Harney in 1925 when an old building on the northeast corner of 19th and Cumberland was being demolished. The paper recalled that it had been the town's first post office and that at the time Dr. Colson was postmaster and Ben Harney "was a clerk and later went to New York where he became a noted writer of song."

By 1930 Jessie and Ben had totally retired from show business and were living in an upstairs flat in a poor black ghetto area of Philadelphia.

That brings up one of the mysteries surrounding Harney—the question of his race. Was he white, black, or mulatto? The great Eubie Blake stated definitely that he was "a Negro," and that his fellow black entertainers knew he was only passing for white.[14] This "fact" has been repeated in several recent biographies and histories. But a study of his genealogy, as already given, makes this highly unlikely, despite the fact that in surviving photographs Harney could easily be taken for mulatto, especially as he is often seen with all-black groups of musicians.

The mystery predates Blake, since Harney was apparently assumed by some to be African-American even in the early years of his career. In 1901 when the chief of the Music Division of the Library of Congress sent out letters to musicians, music publishers, and other knowledgeable people asking for a list of "foreign and American negro composers of music," the name that was second in the number of times submitted as a Negro composer was that of Ben Harney.[15] Since he was at that time an active and famous performer, he could easily have corrected the assumption had he desired to do so.

Some recent historians have suggested that he was essentially "passing for black," that he was "genuinely affectionate toward the louche life of the good-time Charlies from the black tenderloin. Like a lot of other bordello professors, Harney may have absorbed black life and culture eagerly and preferred the unfettered existence of the demimonde to middle-class gentility."[16] Of course, there is always the cynic who points out that no matter how well researched the genealogy, until very recently only maternity was a matter of fact, paternity being a matter of supposition.

After retirement from the stage, the Harneys rented a flat from Ludwig Pfundmayr, who later described their last years. Fame and fortune had deserted them, and they managed on small relief checks from the Actors' Fund. They kept to themselves, usually staying up much of the night, as had been their habit when they were performing, and sleeping much of the day. They seemed to delight in each other's company and in reliving their stage triumphs.

But Ben was very ill. In February of 1938 he took a turn for the worse but refused to consult a doctor or go to the hospital. On March 1 he died in his wife's arms. He was buried in an unmarked grave in Fernwood Cemetery with only his grieving widow to accompany his body to the grave. Although Jessie in later years was often heard to allude to Harney's socially prominent family in Kentucky, there was no apparent contact with any of his relatives, nor did anyone from his family attend his funeral.

His passing was noted by a number of national publications, including *Variety,* the *New York Times,* and *Time.* The last publication asserted,"Nobody knows how old a story ragtime is to the Negroes of the South. But the first man to write ragtime down on paper was a slick haired Kentuckian, Ben Harney....last week Harney, forgotten in the era of swing, died of heart disease in a Philadelphia rooming house." The article went on to outline his career, noting that when Harney first played in New York,

> (his) violently syncopated pianism, which according to contemporaries 'could be heard for blocks around' was regarded as a passing fad. But it caught on so rapidly that...Harney...launched a nationwide school of composers active during the 1900's. Prominent followers included Lucky Roberts ("Pork and Beans"), Scott Joplin ("Maple Leaf Rag"), Northrup and Confore ("Cannon Ball"), George Botsford ("Texas Steer Rag") and Earl K. Smith ("Hot Ashes"). Oldtimers who heard Harney do his stuff, recall that his playing sounded very much like that of Zez Onfrey ("Kitten on the Keys"), a little like that of Fats Waller.[17]

Middlesboro did not note his passing.

Jessie was left with her loneliness and her grief over the fact that Harney's grave had no headstone. But admirers had not forgotten the great musician. Isidore Witmark, publisher of many of his hits, together with Roscoe Peacock and others, launched a campaign for a fund to provide a suitable marker.

A touching description of Jessie's last years is given by Rudi Blesh, who had access to the letters she wrote Peacock:

> While money was being raised, lonely Jessie took flowers by day and sat by the unmarked grave and between times wrote long letters...."I am on my way to get a bouquet," she wrote Peacock, "and I think I'll swing and sway out to Fernwood today." In another she wrote: "I should like to see you....I get the jumpin' jitters. I just hate to be alone." In another letter she would reminisce of Harney and the life they had together: "As you know, my Fancy Man, Ben, was a very sympathetic nature, and did certainly enjoy life as did I. Did we have thousands or a dollar, fifty-fifty at all time"....She dwelt, too, on the fact that Harney had died in obscurity. Her desire to obtain recognition for his life and accomplishments became almost obsessive. "Every music publisher that ever heard him play," she wrote, "tried to grab his ideas. But they said he never played anything twice alike, which was the truth. That was the reason it took so many years for them to get the swing of Ragged Rhythm Harneian."[18]

Jessie's passionate desire for a headstone was finally realized in 1941. It was granite with an inscription reading:

IN MEMORY OF MY BELOVED
HUSBAND
BEN R. HARNEY
CREATOR OF RAGTIME
BORN MAR. 6, 1871 - DIED MAR. 1, 1938

Jessie stayed on in her lonely flat only a short time after she ascertained that the final resting place of her Ben would not be forgotten. One morning her landlord found her seated in a chair next to an open gas jet. Although the official record reads "death accidental," it was assumed that she could wait no longer to be with her Fancy Man. She was laid to rest next to him in Philadelphia's Fernwood Cemetery.

Certainly Jessie would have been happy to know the music world's assessment of Ben Harney: "Some reports credit him a more spectacular jazz technique than that of any modern pianist....he put rag-time on the map and thus laid the foundations for all the later developments of the jazz age."[19]

Addendum to second edition:

Ben Harney was born on a steamboat near Memphis, Tennessee. He has been described as having olive skin, blue eyes and reddish hair.

There is an unresolved mystery about how many times he married. Bruno Greenup, his friend from his earliest days as a performer in Louisville, stated that he married a Kentucky girl named Jessie Boyce when he was very young; however, no record of the marriage has been found. There is an indication that he was already married in 1891 (see page 183), but the reporter might have been mistaken about the couple's marital status. It is well documented that in January of 1897, he married Edyth Murray, a Canadian born actress/singer who performed with him. Some sources state that she used the stage names Jessie Haynes, Jessie Boyce and Jessie Harney. Other sources state that they divorced and sometime in the early 1900s, he met and married Jessie Haynes. There appears to be no reliable documentation of this claim.

In the mid 1920s, Ben Harney granted an interview to an unidentified Indianapolis newspaper in which he gave the following account of how he came to develop his new music: "I procured a job in the post office in Middlesboro...it wasn't long until I was in good standing with all the inhabitants and was invited to attend their dances...It was at one of these dances that I first heard broken rhythm music which I later named 'ragtime.'

"Among the mountaineer musicians was a lanky chap called 'Chaw' George who played a long-necked fiddle tuned to a G chord like an old-fashioned banjo, and occasionally one of his fellows would embellish the tunes 'Chaw' played by rat-tatting the strings across the neck of the instrument with a piece of wire or sticks, thus breaking the musical rhythm in perfect syncopation. The effect was not only startling but also decidedly pleasing to the ear...I was so taken by the broken rhythm tunes played on the fiddle by 'Chaw' and his assistant that I immediately set to work to reproduce broken rhythm on the piano, and within a few weeks I had it perfected to such a degree that I was composing ragtime tunes."

Footnote Eighteen

The Athens of the Mountains

The tall, gaunt mountaineer, squirrel rifle under his arm, standing in the door of an isolated log cabin, behind him his shy wife in her homespun dress, and their stairstep children, uneducated and relegated to a hardscrabble life that left them ignorant of all but the basics of existence—this was the portrait of the Appalachian people drawn by popular writers in the late 1800s and early 1900s. Sometimes the highlander was portrayed as a romantic, noble savage, at other times as a backward barbarian, but always as a "peculiar" throwback to an earlier time, "our contemporary ancestor," as novelist John Fox Jr. put it, who was devoid of any knowledge of "the finer things of life"—art, literature, classical music.

The people of the Yellow Creek Valley probably avoided this stereotype since the area was never as isolated as most in the mountains. Though the Wilderness Road fell into disrepair, it still saw a steady stream of traders, livestock herdsmen, and the like. There was a regular stagecoach route between Knoxville and Lexington that traversed the valley, so outside influences were constantly filtering in. John Colson Sr. established a school in the 1850s at the Green Meeting House and served as its first teacher. It was still in operation, the work being carried on by Colson's children, when the English came. Billy Rains had a private subscription school in the western part of the Valley even earlier, so that there was at least some smattering of education available. Nonetheless, the valley that Alexander Arthur chose as the site of his city did not offer much in the way of refined culture.

The Middlesborough Town Company, however, was not long in addressing the cultural and recreational needs of the new city. The company hired a prominent actor and singer, James Barton Key, who was related to Francis Scott Key (composer of the "Star-Spangled Banner"), to plan ac-

Views of The Middlesborough, 1890s, from the hotel's stationery. Courtesy of Jane Brewer.

tivities and events to meet those needs. Key was well known for his performances in various Gilbert and Sullivan light operas but had developed a throat problem and needed to give his voice a rest. He was not only charged with arranging for various vaudeville companies and other types of shows to visit the city but was also responsible for staging benefits and concerts and planning for dances and parties. The Town Company donated instruments for a brass band that was organized by amateurs even before the city had its charter. A racetrack and a polo field were constructed on "The Commons," where other sports, such as golf and cricket, could also be played (see Footnote 24). In addition, Key maintained a stud of hunters and a kennel of hounds so the Englishmen could enjoy fox hunts.

One of the first buildings to be constructed in Middlesborough was the Opera House, built on the north side of Cumberland Avenue between 21st and 22nd Streets. It opened in October of 1889 with a comedy entitled *Culpepper*. This was followed by dramas, minstrel shows, lectures, and concerts. That some performances were of questionable cultural value is indicated by an editorial in the newspaper in May of 1890: "A law and order league would have been in order at the Opera House during the engagement of the leg opera....One of the most indecent shows that has ever disgraced the 'boards' of a Kentucky theatre has been appearing here nightly during the present week....The question arises of where the authorities have been."

Another of the earliest buildings was the Library and Exhibition Hall on 20th Street.[1] Although it was built primarily as another way to promote the city to potential investors, it did have a subscription library of more than a thousand volumes. Reading material also included three local newspapers.

Social life centered around The Middlesborough, the elegant hotel overlooking the city, and the various saloons and dance halls. As families established themselves in the city there was more home-centered entertainment and socializing. The papers soon featured social notes with reports of teas, card parties, "at homes," tennis parties, and picnics.

The "boom" was barely under way when educators arrived to provide city schools. Miss Maggie Chumley and Professor E.L. Grubbs were already operating small private schools toward the latter part of 1889. In March of 1890 they combined their efforts, stipulating that "only children of respectable parents need apply for admittance." Tuition ranged from $1.50 a month for the earliest grades to $3.00 for older students.

The need for public schools was evident. In August of 1890 the Town Company donated a school building at 20th and Edgewood (present site of the Board of Education), and on September 1 the first public school opened with Prof. Grubbs as its principal. He was assisted by two "competent lady teachers." By the next year there were two public schools for white children and one for African-Americans, and in October of 1891 a public school system was formally established.

At the same time, private schools still flourished. In 1891 there was a private school for young ladies on Arthur Heights and a French school, headed by a Prof. Berthel, that advertised a "natural" method of teaching. There was also the Middlesborough Commercial College and Normal School, which offered typing, stenography, and bookkeeping along with the usual math, English, and elocution. Four years later, in 1895, the Middlesborough University School opened under the auspices of Central University in Richmond, Kentucky. The school was located on Arthur Heights in what had been the Bellevue Hotel. Students wore uniforms, had regular military drill, and took a rigorous academic course.

Schools, a library, the theatre—Middlesborough was becoming "civilized." Businessmen, company managers, and investors began building substantial homes and moving their families to the new town. Their ladies interested themselves not only in various charitable causes but also in cultivating the arts. In February of 1891 several women, along with their husbands, joined together to form the Middlesborough Circle of Literature, Music and Art. They met regularly to discuss the great masters of the arts

Boating on Fern Lake, ca. 1900. Courtesy of the Bell County Historical Society.

and to hold readings and recitations. The younger set in town had their dances, hayrides, moonlight excursions to the Pinnacle, and picnics at Fern Lake. They also had their get-togethers at home, such as a Longfellow Party at which each guest had to recite a quotation from Longfellow. The best quotation got a bouquet as a prize and the worst got a jack-in-the-box.

Even as the cultural and social life of the new city flourished, the storm clouds of the "bust" were gathering on the horizon. The financial panic began in England toward the end of 1890 and in early 1891. By 1892 it had crossed the ocean, and many of the new residents abandoned the Yellow Creek Valley. Those that remained were much reduced in circumstances, many of them going bankrupt. It hardly seemed possible that they would continue their devotion to the arts and education, yet that is exactly what happened. This was in contrast to many of the Wild West boom towns that boasted their opera houses and concert halls but soon were nothing but dusty cow towns.

One of those who was instrumental in nurturing the cultural life of the town during the tough economic times was Alice Woodbury. Her husband, C.M. Woodbury, had played an important part in the founding of Middlesborough. He was with Alexander Arthur in London in 1888-1889 and induced many of his friends to invest in the American Association. He served as vice-president of the Town Company and was a manager-investor in the Water Works, Electric Light Company, and Street Railroad Company. His first wife had died in 1890, leaving him with four small children to rear.

Alice Gale was from Vermont. She had moved to Knoxville with her first husband, who died in 1880. The young widow supported herself and her young son by becoming the editor of the Home Department of *Gentleman Farmer,* a popular periodical of the day. She also contributed regularly to various magazines such as *Harper's* and *Scribner's* and wrote several well received dramas. According to the *Knoxville Sentinel,* she "stood high in the literary world."

The two married in June of 1892 and embarked on a honeymoon tour of the Continent. While they were away, the Ocoonita Club, which had been built across the road from the Middlesborough as an annex but was no longer in use as a part of the hotel because of the "bust," was "rearranged" as quarters for their large family.

Almost immediately upon moving into her new home, Alice Woodbury organized a literary club with the purpose of studying writers and musicians, their times and their works. The Wasiota Club began with twenty-five members meeting at the library. Alice was the first president, and a list of its programs is impressive. For example, in November of 1892, in recognition of the Columbian Exposition, papers were read on "The Norse Dies," "Columbus," and "Social Conditions in European Countries at the time of America's Discovery." In December they studied colonial life and the work of Washington Irving. Members were responsible for researching and presenting the papers. The newspaper reported that a tea the Wasiota Club held at the home of Mrs. Woodbury in June of 1893 attracted "the youth, beauty, fashion and intellect" of Middlesborough and that the music and the "fresh and clever" papers presented on Mozart, Beethoven, and Shumann caused the men, who were invited guests, "to express astonishment that a woman could do so well." Despite the hardness of the economic times, the guests could relax in the flower-bedecked reception hall of the huge house, listen to the piano selections, and enjoy the "dainty" refreshments served by the ladies.

One of Mrs. Woodbury's close friends was the renowned novelist John Fox Jr., who visited frequently in Middlesborough while writing *The Trail of the Lonesome Pine.*

The older women in town had their own Columbian Chatauqua Circle. Their group was somewhat smaller and more exclusive and tended to study a wider range of subjects. One meeting featured papers on Grecian law and law givers along with a discussion of Greek history; another, international relations; and still another, Mars and the solar system.

There was also a local amateur theatrical group, the Comedy Club. Both Mr. and Mrs. Woodbury served at one time or another as president of the club, and both acted as leads in many of the performances. Alice also wrote several original plays for the group. The stage manager was Owen Davis, whose father was in the iron and coal business. A few years after the "bust," Owen moved to New York, where he became well known as a prolific writer and playwright and won a Pulitzer Prize.

In 1893, with economic conditions deteriorating rapidly, C.M. Woodbury was forced to resign from the management of the various subsidiary companies of the American Association. But he was able to retain his large holdings in the Mingo Mountain Coal and Coke Company, which would soon be in the forefront of the resurrection of the coal industry in the area. Alice, however, would not live to enjoy their coming prosperity. A son was born to the couple in mid-December of 1897, and Alice succumbed to complications of childbirth on January 1, 1898.

Nevertheless, the literary club she founded lived on. In 1911 it became the Middlesboro Women's Club, which would sponsor many concerts, lectures, and literary benefits and would take as its special mission the obtaining of books and funds for the new Carnegie Library. The Woodbury home burned down in 1908, but another mansion, built on the same site, was later to be the home of an influential president of the Women's Club, Viola Flowers, who would have a lasting impact on the cultural life of the city.

During the late 1890s there was, for those less interested in the fine arts, equally engaging entertainment. The town hosted a constant stream of visiting circuses, vaudeville shows, and fairs. One such traveling show in 1899 offered a veritable international education—a Hindoo Theatre, Filipino Dancing Girls, Mexican Troubadours, Japanese jugglers, and an Oriental Theatre. The latter featured La Belle Rosa, the famed "coochee-cochee" dancer, and Babe Riel, who had been the "Queen of the Midway" at the World's Fair. The newspaper claimed it was "one of the greatest collections of artists....ten shows and everyone is worth going ten miles to see," though it did warn that "the supersensitive may avoid the Oriental Theatre."

The first decades of the twentieth century saw a continued interest in the arts and education. This, in turn, attracted educated residents to the city, as traveling salesmen and managers of larger concerns chose to locate their families in Middlesboro in preference to other towns within their territory because of the cultural advantages.

In the day of rail travel, the fact that the city had good train connections to all the larger cities and thus did not depend on the poor to nonexistent roads of Appalachia meant the accessibility of all types of entertainment. The Chautauqua, with its combination of concerts, lectures, dramas, light opera, and comedies made popular annual visits. The Middlesboro Civic Concert Series brought in classical musicians. Annie Oakly gave a shooting exhibition. The Great Blackstone confounded crowds with his magic. John Philip Souza and his band played to enthusiastic audiences. Carrie Nation berated the saloon keepers, while Henry Watterson spoke on international relations. William Jennings Bryan, who was three times a presidential candidate and was a principal figure in the Scopes "monkey trial," lectured the town. Middlesboro was regularly visited by Shakespearean companies and also by A.G. Field's Minstrels. Local people saw their first moving picture show in 1900. The town even hosted Billy Sunday, the famed evangelist, and Franklin D. Roosevelt, who would one day be president.

The trains also brought in vacationers. The erstwhile Middlesborough, which was now called the Booneway Inn, played host, as did several other hostelries. Guests came to enjoy the fresh mountain air and the supposed health benefits of the mineral spring at the Booneway. There were excursions in the surrounding hills, trips to the cave at the Gap, boating on Fern Lake, swimming in the hotel pool, and in the evening dancing in the hotel's three ballrooms to the music of orchestras from Louisville and other big cities.

In 1910 several Middlesboro matrons joined together to organize the Music Club in order to study musicians and their music. The members were all amateur musicians, and they liked to perform for each other. During World War I the Music Club diverted its attention to Red Cross work, and gradually meetings became less regular until they finally were no more. The club might have died had it not been for Mrs. Robert Maddox.

Sybil Sipher, who was a native of Washington, D.C., was one of those who visited Middlesboro as a performer. She toured with the Lyceum and Chautauqua circuits for ten years, playing the xylophone, marimbaphone, staff bells, sleigh bells, four-in-hand bells, violin, mandolin, banjo, and musical glasses. She used to say that Middlesboro was well known on the circuit as "a musical town." In the early twenties Judge R.L. Maddox fell in love with the beautiful musician and persuaded her to abandon the stage to become his bride. As Mrs. Maddox, Sybil continued her love of music, often giving impromptu performances on water glasses and collaborating with a former associate to write musical plays for children, which were produced professionally. She was known as a delightful hostess who took her adopted town to heart. Among her many projects, she spearheaded the effort to rejuvenate the Music Club. This organization has continued to be active to this day.

Middlesboro's reputation as a musical town was enhanced by the Hoe Brothers Quartet. Harry, Walter, William, and Edward Hoe were the sons of J.R. Hoe, who in 1909 bought the Pioneer Iron Works in Middlesboro and moved his large family from Pennsylvania to their new home in the Yellow Creek Valley. (The company that he founded, J.R. Hoe & Sons, is still operating today under the fourth generation of Hoes.) During the twenties the brothers gained a reputation for close harmony and versatility, singing ballads, religious works, and humorous songs at numerous live performances throughout the state and later on the radio.

Edward's daughter Louisa Hoe became even more famous. Old-timers said that she took after her grandmother, for whom she was named, who had a lovely soprano voice. When Louisa was four years old she was placed on the piano at the First Baptist Church in Middlesboro and sang for the congregation. Throughout her school years she took piano and violin lessons and sang. After completing Carson-Newman College, where she studied piano, violin, and dramatics, she went to the Chicago Musical College. In Chicago she performed with the Chicago City Opera Company. She then went to New York, where she was a professional soloist at the 5th Avenue Presbyterian Church and also performed in all types of shows, including work at the Radio City Music Hall. In 1937 Middlesboro could read with pride the headlines in their local paper: "Louisa Hoe Acclaimed by 100,000 in New Triumph of Musical Career." She had taken first place as a vocalist in a nationwide contest held at Soldiers' Field in Chicago. She went on to appear as guest artist on many national radio shows, such as the Bing Crosby Hour. Her career was sidelined when her mother passed away, and it was, as Louisa so graciously put it, "my joy to come back to take care of my father."[2] She nurtured another generation of Middlesboro musicians by becoming a professor at Lincoln Memorial University, just across the Gap in Harrogate, where she taught voice and played the organ and piano for all types of occasions at the college. Her voice students, whom she taught in the Music Conservatory, the building that had once been Alexander and Nellie Arthur's mansion, put on many difficult concerts over the years, including *Messiah* from the original score and various operas. She later married Dr. Charles Cawood, whose sister Viola Flowers was very interested in Little Theatre. Louisa directed the most ambitious effort of that group, a performance of *The King and I* that is still talked about today.

Middlesboro's African-American community made a large contribu-

Middlesboro High School, 1930s. Courtesy of the Bell County Historical Society.

tion to the musical heritage of the town. Frank Emery's Band was a staple of parades and political get-togethers in the early years. Churches presented cantatas and other music for the enjoyment of the entire town. During the Big Band Era, Cleveland Hall on 19th Street and the Silver Slipper just behind it on Ironwood, both black establishments, presented some now-legendary bands. Cab Calloway, Louis Armstrong, Count Basie, and the Sweethearts of Rhythm all appeared in Middlesboro. In those days of segregation there was usually one section of the hall roped off for the whites. Some remember that at the Silver Slipper it was an unspoken custom at certain times for the dance floor to be reserved for black dancers while white patrons remained spectators. Others recall bleachers being brought in for particularly popular performances.

Education was also high on the list of Middlesboro's priorities, another reason why the city attracted so many well-to-do and cultured residents. In 1922 a school bond issue carried 1,180 to 8, and in 1925 Middlesboro was one of only 45 schools, out of a total of 615 schools in the state, named to the State's Honor List. The city system was also one of a select group of 36 to be classed AA by the State High School Inspector. Students won top honors in debate and speech. In 1930 Phi Beta Kappa, the college honorary society, named Middlesboro High School as one of the 1,000 outstanding schools in the United States. Two brothers, Karl and

Don Price, were named Rhodes Scholars, and each thereafter carved out a distinguished career. A decade later, Charles Blakeman won a Fulbright Scholarship—not bad for a small town in the midst of the Appalachian Mountains.

Middlesboro entered the decade of the forties with a Music Club, Art Club, Book Club, and multiple civic groups—the Elks, Kiwanis, Masons, Women's Club, Garden Club, and the like. The town also began the decade with a new citizen who would be important to the cultural life of the city: Viola Cawood Flowers.

Viola was from Harlan County, where her father was a well-to-do shopkeeper, postmaster, and landowner. Her first husband was originally from Georgia, and soon after their marriage they moved to his home area. Her husband died young, and there were tough times as she worked to rear her two small children by herself. Viola had earned a teaching degree from Berea College, and she taught school for a number of years. She finally decided to return to Harlan and was living at home when her brother Charles brought a handsome friend home with him on vacation from the University of Louisville, where they both were attending medical school. There was an instant attraction. After graduation, Dr. Sam Flowers took a job as a doctor in a coal camp near Harlan and their love flourished. They married in 1932, and a couple of years later they moved to the mine town built by Sterns Coal Company. But Viola was a strong, ambitious woman, and she wanted more than the coal camps offered. She encouraged her husband to take a surgical residency, insisting that she would find a job and support the family while he did so—quite a bold thing to do in the thirties. Though the Great Depression was at its height, Viola soon secured a job with radio station WAVE in Louisville, where she wrote and presented a regular one-hour show. When Sam went on to take specialized training in Philadelphia, she was again immediately able to obtain a job.[3]

In 1939 the couple moved to Middlesboro. Most of Viola's family had already relocated to the town. Her brother Hobert, who was an undertaker, had purchased a funeral home in Middlesboro, and her parents had joined him to help run the business. Another brother, Pope, first came to work with Hobert but later joined with a friend, Perry Siler, to buy a drugstore. Viola's sister Faye had married an attorney, Hubert White. They moved to Middlesboro when, with the help of Hobert's friends, he was appointed city attorney. Her brother, Dr. Charles Cawood, had set up his practice in the city. So it was natural that Sam, Viola, and the children, who were almost grown, would also make their home in the Magic City.

Hardly had Dr. Flowers gotten established when war broke out, and he was very soon taken into the service. When he shipped out to North Africa, Viola, not willing to sit at home, joined the WACs. Her radio training landed her in public relations, and, as her abilities were recognized, she received a commission in the Air Force and was sent to Officers Candidate School. She was made a first lieutenant and was offered a captaincy if she would agree to stay in the service after the war ended. But as soon as Dr. Flowers was able to return to Middlesboro, she joined him.

A civilian again, she turned her considerable talents to encouraging the arts and improving life in her adopted town. Along with several others, she formed a stock company to develop a radio station, WMIK. She had a regular program, which she always introduced by saying that the station's call letters stood for "Wonderful Middlesboro in Kentucky." In addition, she wrote a syndicated newspaper column, "The Doctor's Wife," and she served on the state Board of Health. She was also very active in the Women's Club and became the president of the Kentucky Federation of Women's Clubs. During her first year in office she persuaded the members to purchase the building that is still used as state headquarters. Under her tutelage two of the local club's departments (committees) were spun off into successful organizations. One, the Garden Department, became the Cumberland Park Garden Club, which has, to the present time, played an important part in the beautification of the city.

Another was the Drama Department, the chair of which in 1947 was Juanita Smith. She, like Viola, was originally from Harlan. Juanita had majored in drama and English at the University of North Carolina, where she met her husband, Kirby. Her father was in the coal business and had a number of mines, including one at Garmeda, just outside Middlesboro. He convinced Kirby to join him in the business, and after a few years in Harlan the family moved to Middlesboro. It was a congenial place for the young couple, a prosperous town with people interested in culture and ideas. Juanita joined the Music Club, Art Club, and Women's Club. There were parties, bridge games, and every weekend a formal dance at the Country Club.

The Drama Department, under Juanita's direction, mounted a performance of a play written by a professor at the nearby college. At one of the rehearsals Viola turned to Juanita and said, "Do you know what we need? We need a Little Theatre."[4] As was her wont, Viola almost immediately turned this idea into action. At the intermission of the last performance of the play, she asked everyone who was interested in forming a Little Theatre company to stay behind. Fifty people did so, and the group was organized that night. Within two years the organization had 400 members. Participation was good throughout town, with sufficient ticket sales to sustain the productions and people willing to lend from their own homes whatever props were needed. Those who could not act helped with scenery, costumes, and other necessary details. The group was fortunate to have the use of the auditorium at the Middlesboro High School, which accommodated 900 and had great acoustics. They were soon doing five plays a year. Once a year Juanita Smith, who was dramatic director, went to New York, where she saw all the new productions she could. Then, as soon as a play she wanted was released, she would get it for the group.

Meanwhile, Dr. and Mrs. Flowers had moved into the huge house that had been built by Fred Hart in 1919 on the site of the old Ocoonita Club, where once had lived another patroness of the arts, Alice Woodbury. Viola's health, however, was compromised by emphysema and asthma, and she was less and less able to be out and about. For the last ten years of her life she was essentially bedridden, but she did not lose interest in promoting the arts. She cast *The King and I* from her bed.[5] Viola Flowers died in 1970 at the age of sixty-seven.

The King and I, which was staged in 1960, is recalled as the Little Theater's greatest success. The cast was huge, and it seemed almost everyone in town was involved in some way or other. The musical even attracted the governor of Kentucky and the drama critic from the *Louisville Courier-Journal.*

The group continued to produce plays through the mid-seventies. There was then a period of fifteen years or so when, although officially still in existence, it mounted no productions, part of the problem being the lack of an adequate stage after the old high school was replaced. There was a revival of Little Theatre in the mid-nineties, and today the amateur group regularly presents various types of theatricals.

Juanita Smith's four children remember the busy household as always seeming to include someone she was rehearsing for a part. Their father was frequently engaged in building scenery and creating props. The constant stream of playmates and later teenage friends who made their house a second home enjoyed the exciting atmosphere. One of the teenagers who "hung around" the Smith household during the fifties was Harvey Lee Yeary, who lived just up the hill. He was dating a girl who lived across the street from the Smiths, and they found the Smith home a congenial place to meet. Yeary showed no interest whatsoever in all the activity related to Little Theatre; his passion was football. He was a star player for Middlesboro and was named to the Kentucky High School All-State Team. Upon graduation he received a football scholarship to Indiana University, and he dreamed of an eventual career in professional sports. His two years at Indiana were disappointing, however, as the coaches deemed him "too light" at 160 pounds for Big Ten competition, and he did not get into the starting lineup. A suspension due to a fraternity brawl was the last straw. Anxious to actually play, he transferred to Eastern University in Richmond, Kentucky. Unfortunately during his junior year he suffered an injury while attempting to run back a kickoff. He was sidelined for the rest of the year, though he did remain with the team as an assistant coach. He returned to the lineup the next year, but his game was, he felt, not as good as it had been before the injury. He no longer considered a career in professional sports an option.

Meanwhile, he had developed other interests. For one, he had gotten married, and for another, he had become involved with a drama group. After being dared by his teammates to try out, he won a leading role in a college production of *The Crucible* by Arthur Miller. The football team went to the play en masse, thinking to get a good laugh, but came away moved by his performance. Harvey Lee had discovered he had a real talent for acting. That year he did summer stock at the Pioneer Playhouse in nearby Danville. During his last year in college he continued to participate in college performances but also earned a teaching certificate.

While at the Pioneer Playhouse, he met Rock Hudson, who was already a Hollywood star. Hudson encouraged him to try for a movie career and even helped by paying to have his teeth straightened and aiding in his move to California after graduation. It was quite a coup when Yeary brought the famous movie star to Middlesboro for a visit.

Like many aspiring actors before him, Harvey Lee was not immediately embraced by Hollywood. He found a job as an assistant playground director for the parks department and started taking acting classes at night with Estelle Harman, who had coached Rock Hudson and other Hollywood greats such as Tony Curtis and Charleton Heston. It was not an easy life, nor one his wife had envisioned, and she left him, returning to Kentucky with their young son. Finally, in 1964, he got a bit part in the Joan Crawford movie *Strait-Jacket,* in which his character was beheaded by Joan in the first scene.

It was at this time that he took his stage name. People in California seemed to have trouble spelling Yeary. Since his high school days, Harvey had idolized Johnny "Drum" Majors, who had been a star player for the University of Tennessee and had played professional football before becoming a well respected coach. Harvey decided to combine his middle name with his idol's last name and came up with Lee Majors.

Harvey Lee Yeary (later Lee Majors), back row right, while lifeguarding at the Middlesborough Country Club, with some of his young charges. Courtesy of the Bell County Historical Society.

Fortunately Lee had an excellent agent who had represented a number of acclaimed actors, including Jimmy Dean, and who was able to arrange for him to audition for a part in the Barbara Stanwyck TV western *The Big Valley*. Lee beat out several well known stars to win one of the leading roles. From 1965 through 1969, *The Big Valley* was one of the most popular shows on TV, and the Middlesboro boy was suddenly deluged by stacks of fan mail.

He went on to star in the NBC production *The Men from Shiloh* (1970-1971) and the ABC show *Owen Marshall, Counselor at Law*, which ran from 1971 through 1974. This was followed by the hit show *The Six Million Dollar Man*, in which he played a bionic superhero. In 1973 he married the beautiful Farrah Fawcett, whom he helped guide to stardom. Together they made television history in 1976 when both were starring in separate hour-long prime-time series that were in the Top Ten in the Nielsen ratings. Farrah's part in *Charlie's Angels* and her stunning smile made her an international icon, while Lee's *Six Million Dollar Man* was everywhere—as toys, in comic books, and on lunch boxes, notebooks, and all types of paraphernalia.

When he returned to Middlesboro to visit his parents, Lee had to travel incognito, and he slipped into town with no notice, seeing friends in the privacy of his parents' home and venturing out only for brief evening drives around town. In an interview he complained, "Nothing would please me more than to visit the old pool hall, or sit down and have a bowl of chili with some of the guys I used to know....But I can't do that." The show was so popular that when he wanted to leave it because of concern about being typecast, Universal Studios doubled his salary to $3 million and gave him a number of perks, including the right to produce his own movies, to induce him to stay on through 1978.

Lee starred in a number of movies, none very memorable, and then in 1981 he took on a new series on ABC, *The Fall Guy.* The *Knoxville News Sentinel* called it "one of the best new shows of season," and it soon catapulted into the Top Ten. His character was a stunt man who moonlighted as a bounty hunter. As he had done in his previous shows, he did many of the stunts himself.

The Fall Guy left prime time in 1986. Lee had been a big star for more than twenty years. He was in his mid-forties, a wealthy man, and he was ready for a rest. He accepted a few movie roles and did a couple of short TV series, *Tour of Duty* in 1990 and *The Raven* in 1992. By this time he had married for a third time and had three young children in addition to a grown son from his first marriage. After three decades in California he moved to Florida and, though still open for interesting roles, he no longer engaged in the Hollywood grind.

The local football stadium is named for Lee Majors. Some in the town also wanted to name a main street after him, but Lee demurred. He urged the town to retain all the original names given by the English as its unique heritage.

In 1994 the School Board, seeing a need in both the school system and the community for a place to hold various types of performances, built the Central Auditorium and Arts Center. It is hoped that this modern-day opera house will inspire in a new generation a love of the arts.

Footnote Nineteen

David Colson

David Grant Colson was born on April 1, 1861, the seventh child of Mary Katherine and John Calvin Colson Sr. Twelve days later Fort Sumter was fired upon and the country embarked on a tempestuous course of civil war. It was a fitting time for his birth, as the same adjective—tempestuous—could be used to describe his life.

At the time of his birth the family was living in the two-story house on the old Wilderness Road, and his father had already earned the title Patriarch of the Valley (see Footnote Seven). Although little is actually known of David's early life, much can be extrapolated from what is known of the family and the events of the day. Throughout the first four years of his life the country was engaged in civil war, and the Valley saw the constant movement of soldiers from both sides. David must have watched round-eyed as the armies marched by. Frequently his home served as a stopping place for soldiers of one side or the other. During his childhood and adolescence his home continued to be the hub of the Valley. His father's store and mill were a magnet for people of all kinds. Transportation was difficult, and people who came to trade often camped overnight before heading home. Additionally the Wilderness Road was still used by hog herders and other travelers, so that there was a constant stream of "outsiders." David was exposed to a far greater number of strangers than the average mountain youth of his day.

He was also very lucky to have for a father a man who believed in education. David went to school at the Green Meeting House, just over the hill from his home. He then attended academies at Tazewell and Mossy Creek, Tennessee, and later may also have studied at the University of Tennessee in Knoxville. When he returned home, he himself taught school for a short time while he read for the law. He then enrolled in the Junior Course of Law at Kentucky University (now Translyvania) and completed the requirements to become an attorney.

David obtained a position in the Department of Interior in Washington, D.C., in 1882, the same year his father died. After two years in Washington he was appointed Special Examiner of Pensions, with headquarters in Knoxville, Tennessee. But he had already been bitten by the political bug and in 1887, at the age of twenty-six, ran for and was elected to the Kentucky state legislature to represent Bell, Harlan, Perry, and Leslie Counties.

By all accounts he quickly made himself known in Frankfort—the handsome, intelligent, well educated young man from the mountains. His charismatic personality propelled him further into state politics, and in 1889 he was nominated by his party for the position of State Treasurer. Unfortunately this was the year of a huge Democratic majority, and he lost the race.

Meanwhile things were changing rapidly at home. The English had first come in 1886, buying up options on land in and around the Yellow Creek Valley. By 1889 the town they were establishing was a sea of tents, with new people arriving daily, and the land that David had inherited in the Valley was suddenly very valuable. He returned home from his political defeat to embrace the new order of things in the Valley by joining in the business boom as well as practicing law. In late 1889 he was cashier of the Peoples Bank and was spending time in Louisville and Cincinnati making arrangements for extensive improvements in his property, which was referred to as the Colson Addition. His brothers and sisters were also heirs to extensive tracts within the new city limits, and together they owned the majority of the property not already purchased by the Middlesborough Town Company. In March of 1890 the Bank of Middlesborough merged with Peoples Bank, with David as president. The newspapers referred to him as "a very shrewd businessman." His sale of a portion of his lands at the height of the "boom" made him a wealthy man by local standards.

Middlesborough was granted a city charter in March of 1890, with city elections scheduled in May. David was in the political thick of things, running unsuccessfully for mayor (see Footnote Twenty-One). At the same time, he built a beautiful house on his property in the western part of Middlesborough. The papers called it "one of the finest residences" in the new town.[1] His widowed mother came to make her home with him.

David was almost thirty, tall and dark-haired, with striking blue eyes. According to C.B. Roberts, secretary to Alexander Arthur, he was "a courteous, soft-spoken gentleman of cultivated tastes, with a natural, spontaneous charm that made him very attractive. To these amenities of personality were joined attributes of a stronger description, one of which was cool, unshrinking physical courage."[2] Roberts recalled that in negotiations between the American Association and the Colsons, David always served as the family spokesman. The *Louisville Post* could not help noting, however, that in addition to being an attractive "billionaire," the "young gentleman from the mountains" was a bachelor, and added, "They do say...that his semimonthly visits to Frankfort are not entirely of a business nature."

David continued his interest in politics and in 1891 was named temporary chairman of the Republican Convention in Lexington. In February of 1892 he announced his candidacy for the U.S. Congress. The mountains reacted with great enthusiasm, and the newspapers were full of glowing praise and pride in their native son. Despite this, he lost in the primary to Silas Adams. Ever the faithful party man, David immediately proposed that the Colson Club, which had been organized to support his candidacy and numbered more than three hundred members, change its name to the Adams Club, and Colson hit the campaign trail for Adams.

At the same time, the "bust" was underway in Middlesborough, and many of those looking to get rich quick were abandoning what appeared to be a sinking ship. The English company lost its control of the town when John Brooks was soundly defeated in his bid for a second term as mayor, as were all of the incumbent councilmen who had chosen to run. It was a new day. When the next mayoral election came around in the fall of 1893, there was no contest. David Colson announced his availability, and the papers jumped on the bandwagon, noting that he was the largest individual taxpayer in the city and "the tool of no man....a vote for him [is] a vote for good government and sound municipal finances." He was elected in a landslide.

His term as mayor was notable mostly for having to deal with the problems brought on by the "bust" and the huge financial obligations of the city. David had been in office only a short time when, in August of 1894, he again announced his candidacy for the U.S. Congress. He was officially declared the candidate of the Republican Party in October of that year, and the *Middlesborough News* gloated, "Middlesborough can rejoice in the fact that the 'Magic City' has for her citizen a magic man. Harrah for Colson!" When he carried the district by more than 4,000 votes, the papers proclaimed it was a "victory won without money and without whiskey." He remained on as mayor until the fall of 1895, so that he was holding two offices at the same time.

David's congressional career almost ended before it began. When he boarded the train to Washington for the opening of Congress, he was pleased to have a young belle from Middlesborough ask to sit next to him. Unbeknownst to him, she was actually eloping with her young man. They had decided to separate on the train to escape detection. Colson was conversing pleasantly with the young lady when her father suddenly appeared, bent on preventing the elopement. The father thought Colson was helping the young couple and began to abuse him, whereupon Colson attacked the father, and the latter drew his revolver. It was only quick action by other passengers that prevented a tragedy.

As a member of the Fifty-fourth Congress, Colson represented the Eleventh Congressional District, comprising seventeen counties: Adair, Bell, Casey, Clay, Clinton, Harlan, Knox, Laurel, Leslie, Letcher, Metcalfe, Owsley, Perry, Pulaski, Russell, Wayne, and Whitley. His constituents must have been satisfied with his performance, as they returned him to the Fifty-fifth Congress with a substantial majority: he received 22,404 votes against 12,518 for the Democratic candidate and 4,587 for the Independent.

David was to make his mark as a congressman for his vehement advocacy of intervention in the Cuban uprising that had begun in February of 1895. The administration was anxious to stay out of the conflict, but as the newspapers reported the news, true and invented, from Cuba, public opinion became excited. On the House floor Colson made impassioned speeches, which were reported all over the country, in support of the United States entering the fray. "I will," he stated, "endorse any methods, no matter how revolutionary, that will give the House expression of the question of Cuban belligerency." The *Cincinnati Post* proclaimed, "The bold defiance of Congressman Colson...met support in many bosoms."

War was actually declared in April of 1898, and David was one of only four congressmen to vacate his seat in order to take up arms in what was to be called the Spanish-American War. On April 23 the local papers reported that Representative Colson was coming home to lead his mountain boys into the fray. Already a full company of seventy-five men had enlisted from Bell County, and on May 5 a crowd of two thousand gave that group, "The Helburn Rifles," a grand send-off with speeches, bonfires, and martial music. David Colson was on hand to cheer the boys on and to present his own sword to their captain.

In June of 1898 Governor Bradley was directed by the War Department to enroll the Fourth Regiment of Kentucky Infantry. David Colson was named colonel, and Lexington was to be the point of mobilization. Hometown boys responded with enthusiasm.

Most of the recruits had never before been to a big city, and discipline

David Grant Colson, ca. 1897. Courtesy of David Hurst.

was a problem early on. Colson, like many of the politicians-turned-military officers at that time, had never had actual military training or experience. The responsibility of turning his raw recruits, most of whom were used to the complete independence of their mountain life, into well trained, disciplined soldiers was challenging. Throughout July and early August, the men marched and drilled while waiting for orders to leave for Cuba. This was to be a short war, however, and a peace protocol was already being drawn up by mid-August. Colson's regiment never got farther than Anniston, Alabama. A rumor was reported in the local papers on December 9, 1898, that the regiment would soon be mustered out, "giving Col. Colson free rein to make the race for governor." Unfortunately the mustering-out was delayed until February of 1899, allowing time for the seeds of tragedy to be sown.

One of the men who served directly under Col. Colson during this period described him and his style of command thus: "a man of marked peculiarities, one being a most exaggerated notion as to loyalty to his political friends and helpers, a notion which led to unwise political appointments and to his submitting to having foisted upon his regiment officers who should have been rejected....The lengths to which he would go for a political friend led to army imposition which increased insubordination, the demoralization of his regiment and culminating in a personal affray."[3]

The incident to which the writer referred was Colson's feud with Ethelbert Dudley Scott, which led to the deaths of three persons. Scott, a Lexington lawyer who was the nephew of Kentucky Governor William O. Bradley, was not only politically well connected but also popular socially, with many prominent friends. A strong Republican, he had supported Colson in his bids for public office, sufficient reason to be appointed an officer in the Fourth Kentucky. He, like Colson, had had no military experience, but he felt himself superior to the mountain man who was to be his commanding officer.

Discipline in the Fourth Kentucky Regiment was never very stringent under Colson, but Scott flouted his infractions. Scott liked to frequent the saloons around the base and seemed to revel in drinking with enlisted men while making fun of their commander and undermining his authority. Scott was warned about his infractions but ignored the warnings. Finally Colson preferred charges of incompetence, incapacity, and insubordination against him. A Board of Inquiry heard testimony and found Scott guilty of the charges, recommending that he be discharged from the Army. Scott went to Washington, D.C., and, with his connections, was able to get himself reinstated without prejudice. Colson was incensed at Scott's circumvention and immediately began preparing for a court martial. With the regiment about to be mustered out, he was persuaded to drop the charges. But the enmity burned on. Each had made public statements about the other that could not be ignored.

On the Saturday night following the mustering out of the troops, Scott was having dinner with friends at an Anniston restaurant when Colson walked in. The restaurant was crowded, and Colson swung into an empty place without noticing until too late that Scott was already seated directly across the table. Something was said that Colson interpreted as an insult, and he replied. Scott rose deliberately from his seat, carefully laid down his napkin, and stepped behind his chair. Suddenly he raised a pistol, and Colson did likewise. Both fired at about the same time, but Colson missed, while Scott's bullet found its mark in Colson's groin. Scott fled through the restaurant kitchen with Colson in pursuit. Provost guards intervened, one of them smashing Colson on the head with a heavy revolver, rendering him unconscious.

Colson was taken to the base hospital, but the bullet was difficult to excise because it had taken a circular route and had lodged close to his spine. The wound left Colson partially paralyzed, able to walk but with a pronounced limp. According to medical knowledge of the time, it was assumed that his condition would gradually worsen. He recovered from his head wound to a degree, though the beating seemed to have had a residual effect. On at least one occasion in subsequent months Colson suffered a seizure in public that was attributed to the beating he had sustained at the hands of the provost guard.

The David Colson who returned to Middlesborough in the spring of 1899 was markedly different from the man of a year before who had been a rising star on the national political scene. He had given up his congressional seat for active military service that had not materialized. (When he tried to reclaim his congressional seat, saying that he had never drawn a salary from the Army and had planned to retain his seat, the House Congressional Committee nonetheless declared it vacant.) He was crippled, with a prognosis of deteriorating health. To add insult to injury, his wounds had not been sustained on a field of glory but in an incident that he felt had besmirched his honor. Colson had recovered sufficiently to be able to return to his legal practice and his love of politics, but he was a bitter man, hungry for revenge.

Scott had escaped injury. He returned to his law practice and an active social life in Lexington. In July of 1899, both men were delegates to the Republican State Convention. It was well known that both were carrying pistols, and all present feared the worst. There came a time when they were facing each other, hands near their guns, a single breath away from some incident. Just then an old mountain acquaintance of Colson's came up, clapped him on the back, essentially turning him half way around, and talked to him in an animated fashion. The showdown had been averted for the time being.

The gubernatorial election of 1899 was a particularly bitter one. William Goebel, a Democrat, ran on a platform of cleaning up Frankfort and giving power back to the common man. Republican William S. Taylor was the announced winner, but the vote was close, and Goebel, alleging fraud, challenged the election results. The Democrats, who were in power in the state legislature, felt they could invalidate enough votes not only to put Goebel in office but also to capture other state offices. The Republicans, strong in the eastern mountain counties, were determined to prevent this outcome. A small army of mountaineers armed with rifles and pistols descended on the Capitol. At least a hundred Bell County men joined in, among them three—Berry Howard, Zack Steele, and Frank Cecil—who would later be under suspicion of complicity in a plot to assassinate Goebel.

Scott and Colson were also in Frankfort, both expecting to participate in the controversy, both being pro-Taylor. Tension was high throughout the city, and many men were armed with firearms and with liquor. (A legislative committee, in a very controversial decision, did later invalidate the election results and declare Goebel the winner. He was shot by an assassin on January 27, 1900, and died on February 3, just after being sworn in as governor.)

On January 16, 1900, Frankfort was even more crowded, as William Jennings Bryan was to deliver a speech that night. That morning, as Colson made his way along the congested sidewalk, still limping from his painful wound, he came face-to-face with Scott, who was walking with Ben Golden of Barbourville, another of those from the Fourth Kentucky Regiment with whom Colson had had problems.[4] They glared at each other but made no move. It was later brought out that each man felt, and had so stated to friends, that the other was pursuing him and that his life was in danger. Golden also testified that he had told Scott at the time of that first encounter that Colson's hatred of him had become a dangerous obsession.

Colson normally carried a .38 caliber Smith & Wesson. That morning he had borrowed a second weapon, a .44 caliber revolver, from Frank Cecil, a Bell County deputy sheriff, and stowed both guns so that they were concealed by his frock coat.[5] It was almost noon when he made his way toward

Frankfort's Capitol Hotel, one of the most popular spots in town, a gathering place for those with power and influence.

Colson had seated himself in the crowded rotunda of the hotel and was talking pleasantly with a business associate when his face was suddenly seen to change. Scott and Golden had walked into the room. Colson rose from his chair and, as he did so, a long revolver materialized in his hand. Scott had drawn his own weapon. Both fired almost simultaneously; bystanders dove under tables, scrambled behind chairs, or made a mad dash for the exits. Eighteen bullets were fired in less than a minute, thirteen of them hitting someone.

Colson took a bullet in the left arm, yet coolly and deliberately advanced on his foe, steadying his long .44 with his left hand as he shot. Scott backed away, firing as he retreated. When Colson's revolver was empty, he laid it down with quiet precision in a leather chair and drew out his .38.

Scott had also been hit, in the neck and abdomen. Badly injured, he lunged forward and caught a bystander, Luther Demaree, by the shoulder. It was never determined whether Scott intended to use him as a human shield or as a support. There was later testimony that Scott may have gotten off at least one shot from under Demaree's arm. Colson aimed his gun, but Demaree was now between him and his enemy. With his own life in peril, he shot anyway, one bullet going through Demaree's heart and killing him instantly, and another passing all the way through his body and lodging in Scott. Scott, feeling Demaree go limp, dropped the body and tried to escape down the steps to the hotel basement. Some said he got off one last shot as he fled. Colson pursued him and, taking careful aim, shot him in the back of the head. Colson fired again as the body fell.

A traveling salesman from Chicago, C.D. Redpath, had jumped over a stair railing when the gun fight broke out, the resulting fall causing him to break his leg. He was immobilized at the foot of the stairs, and the dead Scott fell on top of him. Some testified that Colson fired one more shot into the corpse as it lay across Redpath. He then calmly stepped over the bodies of the two men, walked out the basement door and up the street, the empty pistol still in his hand.

One other bystander was killed in the crossfire. Charles H. Julian was shot in the leg as he ran from the building. The wound did not seem to be serious, but then it was discovered that an artery had been severed, and he died suddenly. It was never certain who had shot him, since Scott was also firing a .38 caliber weapon. Because Julian and Colson had been sitting together at the outset of the battle, it was assumed that it had been one of Scott's bullets that ended his life.

Four people had been wounded. Ben Golden, the man who had accompanied Scott, suffered a rather serious injury. Colson later stated that Golden had also fired several shots at him. Golden claimed he was not even carrying a gun at the time. He did admit, however, that he had started forward to grab Colson but then thought better of it and started to run across the room. He was hit in the small of the back. Three bystanders suffered minor wounds.

Colson proceeded to the boarding house of a friend and there borrowed another pistol. He then went to the room of another friend and had a doctor summoned. The bullet was extracted from his elbow, but it had badly shattered the bone. The chief of police arrived and Colson was arrested, charged with the death of three men.

Word reached Middlesboro, and the papers responded: "The general opinion is that Colson's mind was unbalanced, and that in this insane state he was crazed with revenge at his old enemy as ordinarily Col. Colson was looked upon as being of a very cool and deliberate nature....nearly all believed he had grounds for killing Scott....Since the trouble at Anniston...he has never been himself. The recent stroke of paralysis added to his mental condition proved too much for him, and for some time the worst has been feared."

Colson was originally taken into the home of the jailer to recuperate from his injury. He was moved to King's Daughters Hospital when his condition proved more serious than originally thought. Dr. A. Morgan Vance was brought from Louisville in February to perform surgery on the arm, which was splintered at the elbow. The papers reported that Colson was receiving large doses of morphine to alleviate the pain. Meanwhile his trial for the killing of Scott was set for April 20,1900.

The case turned on the matter of who had fired first. Colson claimed self-defense. He stated that he had been warned Scott was threatening to kill him. He testified that he had been conversing with friends when, as he turned to expectorate into a cuspidor, he saw Scott advancing toward him. He explained that Scott was wearing a loose sack coat, and he saw the coat lift as Scott went for something under it. "He did not utter a word, but his eyes told me very plainly what his intentions were. I realized that I was in danger, that I must defend myself or die." Fifty-eight witnesses were summoned, but there was conflicting evidence as to who fired the first shot. One witness did report that he had seen Scott preparing his weapon prior to walking into the Capitol Hotel. Colson stated that he certainly regretted the death of Demaree and had tried to shoot around him but was limited in his choice of action, as Scott was firing at him from behind Demaree.

Character witnesses testified to Colson's service in both state and national legislatures and to his public and military service. Scott was painted as a "hotheaded young man, who, pursuing and insulting him...rushed upon his own destruction."

On April 21, the jury brought in a verdict of not guilty after just eighteen minutes of deliberation. They did not even go to the jury room but reached their verdict on the stairway. The decision was met with loud cheers from Colson's friends, who crowded the courtroom. In fact, such pandemonium broke out that order could not be restored, and the judge finally adjourned court. There was also great celebration in Colson's home town, which gloried in his vindication. On April 24, the commonwealth's attorney moved the court to dismiss the other cases against Colson—those charging him with the murder of Demaree and Julian and those related to carrying a concealed weapon. Both of his guns were returned to him.

The papers reported that Colson received hundreds of letters and telegrams congratulating him on his acquittal. Henry Watterson, the celebrated editor of the *Louisville Courier-Journal,* wrote, "I have rarely had occasion to sympathize with any man more than I sympathize with you. I had knowledge of the trouble from the beginning, and I know that you not only acted upon the defensive but that you displayed uncommon forbearance. I do not believe there is any Kentuckian, man or woman, whose opinion is worth having who entertains any other opinion. Let me hope that you are on the road to the complete recovery of your health and that there will be many years of happiness and usefulness for you in this world."[6]

Watterson's expressed hopes were not to be realized. David Colson never completely recovered from either of the wounds inflicted by Scott. He was thirty-nine years old and should have been in the prime of his life. Instead he was partially crippled and his left arm remained totally useless even after surgery. In June of 1900 he had a narrow escape while driving a carriage. The horse ran away, and he was unable to rein it in with one hand. He was able to jump out just as the buggy ran against a tree. Colson was not seriously hurt, but the buggy was "smashed to smitters."

He did attempt to return to his old life, which had centered around politics and the practice of the law. In May of 1900 he was elected chairman of the Bell County Republican Convention—somewhat of a comedown from previous posts but a vote of confidence, coming, as it did, so soon after his trial. In June he was admitted to practice law before the Interior Department. That same month he went to Louisville, where he had further surgery on his elbow. He attended the State Central Committee meeting in July of 1900, and the newspapers noted that he had done the state Republican Party a real service by securing uniform rules for holding ward and primary elections in Kentucky. In August he conferred with the Republican candidate for governor for whom he was planning to make a number of speeches in the mountains. By October of 1900 he was speaking to large crowds. The Knoxville papers, in reporting on the Kentucky campaign, described him at this time as being "straight as an arrow...a man of magnetism and his manner is that of culture. He is well proportioned in stature, his head is round, his face classic, and his black hair closely cropped. He was attired in black and wore a Prince Albert; he looked a true 'Colonel from Kentucky.'"

Colson resumed his legal career with a case that was not only followed closely within Kentucky but was of national interest. He represented Berry Howard, a Bell County man who was accused of complicity in the assassination of Governor Goebel. It was quite a triumph when Colson won Howard an acquittal, particularly since all but one of the other defendants were convicted, at least in their first trial.

There was already talk of Colson running for another public office. On November 24, 1900, the Middlesboro paper noted that Colson was being considered to succeed Senator Dehoe, and he was described as "one of the cleanest and ablest Republicans in the state." Letters came in urging him to run for other offices, and in 1901 he returned to the state legislature. The *Louisville Post* opined that "Col. Colson is far and away the most brilliant speaker of the present General Assembly. He is of distinguished appearance and magnetic personality, a good parliamentarian and a man in whose makeup there is as much public spirit as party spirit. His record in Congress was a good one, and in case he concludes to run again, there seems to be hardly a chance of his defeat." But when Colson made himself available in the 1902 primary for the Eleventh Congressional District seat, he was defeated by a small margin.

Perhaps his defeat was rendered less bitter by events in his personal life. Still a bachelor at age forty-one, he would undoubtedly have been considered a "catch," despite his health problems. He was both wealthy and handsome, with what is known in the mountains as "a good turn." On December 18, 1902, David married Ethel Elliott at her home in Paris, Kentucky. He had met Ethel during the summer of 1898 when she, then a newlywed, attended a band concert put on by the Fourth Kentucky Regiment while that unit was quartered in Lexington. The marriage notice in the Middlesboro paper revealed that "Miss Elliott was formerly the wife of Ernest W. Helm, a prominent newspaper man of Lexington, and is a young woman of charming manner and many accomplishments." There was evidently more to the story, since in an age when divorce was uncommon and difficult, she had only divorced Helm in August of that same year, hardly what would be considered a decent interval for courtship before marriage. Ethel had just turned twenty-nine at the time of her marriage to David.

The couple took up residence in Middlesboro. David devoted himself to his law practice, served on the Board of Education, and represented the city in various cases. Ethel hosted card parties—euchre and progressive Flinch—and generally lived the life of a young society matron.

Although it would appear that David was settling down to the peaceful life of a small town lawyer, all was not well. He was haunted by his memories of the tragedy in Frankfort and his fear of retribution.[7] Gradually, as his obituary later stated, "the failing of his mental powers became apparent to his friends through the persistency with which he recurred to life in nature, giving glorious, if sometimes tiresome, talks on farm subjects and life, on the beauties of the forests and the grandeur of storms." His obituary in another paper suggested that to the terrible beating over the head that he had received in Anniston could have caused the stroke of hemiplegia which came to him about four years ago, from which he was thought to have fully recovered, but which undoubtedly gradually sapped away the strength until the final crash came in a fury of dementia which for months had been gathering force."

One glorious fall day in late September 1904, David rode into the mountains alone, as had been his habit in recent months. He returned in a fury; his horse, frightened by something in the road, had bolted, and it was only with great difficulty that he had been able to rein it in. This so angered him that in a fit of "extreme excitement" he shot the horse, and then, barely reaching his house, collapsed.[8]

Colson did not die instantly but lingered unconscious for a day. His brother-in-law, Dr. J.S. Bingham, and several other local physicians were constantly by his side, and the whole city seemed to grieve. Crowds gathered outside his house all that day and night, praying for his recovery. But it was not to be. Death came to him on September 27.

The entire front page of the *Middlesboro News* was dominated by a picture of the deceased, captioned "A Native Oak, Storm Wrecked." The funeral was the largest ever seen in the area, with special trains bringing in mourners from out of town. David was buried next to his brother John in the cemetery just across from the house where he had been born. In a fitting tribute, the *Middlesboro Record* opined, "Fewer men had a greater facility for making friends and keeping them....a man of firm, honest principle....let charity incline us to throw a veil over his foibles, whatever they may have been, and not withhold from his memory the praise that virtue may have claimed."

There was an epilogue. As is often the case when money is involved, there was some question about the estate. David had been a very wealthy man at one time, but it was said that much of his money had been dissipated, a good deal of it in seeking political influence and office. On October 15, 1904, the newspapers reported that no administrator had been appointed for the estate, as there was "some opposition to the appointment of the widow who otherwise has the right." By mid-November the widow's father and uncle had arrived from Texas with their own attorney, and by early 1905 Ethel had moved out of the house and into a hotel. The court then appointed Dr. J.S. Bingham, brother-in-law of the deceased, as administrator. In the fall of 1905 there was a sale of much of the D.G. Colson property. The Circuit Court was called on in September of 1906 to settle a suit brought by W.G. Colson, David's only surviving brother, against the estate. It was some years before settlement was reached.

Ethel Colson must have had means, however, as she traveled and entertained a good deal for the rest of her life. She made her home for a time in Middlesboro and thereafter made regular visits until the early forties. During these visits, which usually lasted several months, she normally stayed at the elegant Cumberland Hotel. She exchanged "courtesies" with friends, gave teas and parties, and generally enjoyed the social life of the town. When she remarried in 1917, the local newspaper described her as "one of Middlesboro's most popular and charming society ladies." Her groom was Thomas Shepherd, whose father had been several times the mayor of Boston and was of a prominent New England family, important in the shoe manufacturing business. They soon divorced, however, and she took back the name Colson.

Ethel died in Texas in 1950 at the age of seventy-three. She and David had no children.

David Colson was a complex man, one who epitomized the contradictory character of Valley life. He was a shrewd politician and businessman, an urbane and cultured gentleman who was at home in the halls of power and influence in Frankfort, Lexington, and beyond. At the same time, he demonstrated much of the southern mountaineer's stereotypical clannishness and intense loyalty to family and friends, a penchant for taking offense at any slight and of holding tight to any grudge, and the pursuit of justice in the form of revenge above all goals. Those first facets of Colson's personality took him far; the latter were his undoing.

Footnote Twenty

The Smallpox Epidemic

March 1898: Middlesboro is totally isolated. No one is allowed to enter or leave the city. Train agents cannot sell tickets to or from Middlesboro. The states of Virginia and Tennessee have armed guards on all roads leading from the city into their territories. The city of Pineville has likewise closed the old Wilderness Road leading north into Kentucky. Even letters are quarantined—each is punctured and smoked with sulfur for five hours before being sent out. The smallpox epidemic has the "Magic City" totally in its clutches.

Valiant citizens were already battling an economic "bust" that had caused many to abandon the town and forced others to revert to the barter system to survive. The town treasury was empty and bondholders had first call on any stray penny that might be paid in taxes. It was almost inconceivable that yet another blow had fallen on Alexander Arthur's dream, especially this particular catastrophe, since Middlesborough's reputation for having a healthy climate was one of its early attractions. In fact, the clear mountain air, pure water, and mineral springs were considered so salubrious that a huge sanatorium had been built just across the Gap in Harrogate, Tennessee, though it had never really had an opportunity to prove itself before going under in the general economic depression.

The early developers arranged for most city services to be provided by subsidiary companies but made no special provisions for a hospital or medical care, though they did immediately address the need for sanitation and potable water.

A number of physicians were among the early "boomers," including Arthur's brother Macaulay, who first set up his practice in Harrogate. At the time it was normal to treat most illnesses at home, with the family as the primary caregivers. But with many single men living together in tents, this soon proved less than satisfactory. In December of 1889 a number of the ladies of town met to establish a "cottage hospital." The plan was that anyone subscribing 50¢ a month (equivalent to about $9.25 today) would have prior right to the "cots." Other sick persons would be accommodated only if a bed was not needed by a subscriber. Donations and the proceeds from benefits provided additional funds. Alexander Arthur's sister, Bertie Railton, was president of the organization.[1]

Middlesborough was lucky to escape any serious contagious diseases during its earliest years, what with so many people crammed into a relatively small valley under fairly unsanitary conditions. Doctors did report "considerable indispositions of a light manner," particularly fevers and bowel disorders, and warned residents to boil their water and take care with sanitation. And there was a short-lived outbreak of typhoid immediately following the great fire in May of 1890. In mid-1890 the newly chartered city took over responsibility for the hospital. The town continued to prove its claims as a healthy place to live, and in early 1892, with no patients in the city hospital and no funds to maintain it, the City Council ordered it closed.

By 1897, when the first intimations of the smallpox epidemic hit Middlesboro, it was a town of about 3,500, at least a fifth of them black. Housing was relatively integrated, but a disproportionate number of the African-Americans lived in the northeast section, often referred to as "the Rhine." It was there that the first smallpox case was discovered.

In mid-November 1897 Dr. F.P. Kenyon examined a black miner who had recently moved to the Rhine area from Birmingham, Alabama, to work at Mingo Mines. Although he had been sick for more than a week, it was not until the disease erupted in pustules that a doctor was called. The City Council acted rapidly when they learned of the dread diagnosis. That same evening the man and all those who had been exposed to him were strictly quarantined.

It appeared this measure had been sufficient, as no new cases were reported, and in mid-December the quarantine was lifted. The town breathed a collective sigh of relief. Smallpox was known to be highly contagious. Although the efficacy of Jenner's smallpox vaccination had been acknowledged for almost a hundred years, a large percentage of the population had not yet availed themselves of this protection. In fact, it was later estimated that when the first case was diagnosed, only 10 percent of the town's populace had already been successfully vaccinated.

The town's optimism was short-lived. In late December a second case was reported, then several others. The City Council decided stricter measures were needed. Even though the treasury was bare, they nonetheless set in motion plans to find a pesthouse where cases could be treated in isolation and a doctor to treat them, as well as guards to enforce a quarantine. This was accomplished by mid-January. Unfortunately, the pesthouse was located in a heavily populated area. To this point, all the cases had been mild and all had been African-Americans who lived "over the Rhine." There was apparently still some reluctance to identify the disease as smallpox, many hoping it was "Elephant Itch" or some other minor skin problem.

The physicians of the town, of which there were at least six, including those hired primarily by the railroad and the mines, turned to, working sixteen- to eighteen-hour shifts in an effort to immunize everyone. They had given more than a thousand vaccinations by the first week in February, but many in town still had not received the shot or needed a booster. The City Council then passed an ordinance making vaccination mandatory. They divided the city into districts, with a physician assigned to each to make a door-to-door canvas and vaccinate anyone, by force if necessary, who they felt was not sufficiently protected. The city agreed to pay for the vaccination of paupers, though with what, they did not specify. A second pesthouse was also authorized, and a general cleanup of the city undertaken by inmates of the city jail.

Despite all efforts, the epidemic seemed to worsen. In mid-February the first death was reported and the first white man, C.D. Ball, contracted the disease. On February 17, the tally stood at a total of twenty-nine cases, five of them white. The town redoubled its efforts. The Council ordered schools and saloons to close and forbade any gathering of crowds. No one under the age of fifteen was to be out in public at any time of day or night. The police chief was directed to go to all businesses and ensure that the employees were vaccinated. In one case, twenty persons in the Rhine area had to be handcuffed and vaccinated at gun point. The Council even posted a reward for reporting anyone concealing a case of smallpox.

Meanwhile the town was getting horrible publicity. In early February Dr. J.H. Albright of the Tennessee Board of Health had visited Middlesboro after inspecting Mingo Mine, which was just over the border in Tennessee. His report, which was reprinted in a number of newspapers, accused the town of being slow to respond to the epidemic and of releasing patients while they were still contagious. The town fathers were certainly not slow to respond to what they regarded as slander. They drafted a resolution, which they sent to the metropolitan papers and the railroad, refuting Dr. Albright's accusations and labeling them "unwarranted, uncalled-for, unprofessional, ungentlemanly, and unworthy."

Middlesboro's neighbor to the south, Claiborne County, Tennessee, was not to be fooled by the town's protestations. In response to a rumor that a miner with smallpox was about to be sent back to his home in Tennessee, the health authorities there stationed guards at the state line and vowed to stop the importation of the disease "if there is any virtue in a Winchester." Soon Lee County, Virginia, followed suit.

The *Claiborne Progress* seemed intent on whipping up even more hysteria. The paper reported an outbreak of smallpox in Morristown, Tennessee, supposedly the result of the laxness of Middlesboro's authorities. According to the story, the pesthouse guards had run out of whiskey and so had sent an infected inmate out for more. Instead of fulfilling his task, he was reported to have taken the money with which he was to purchase the liquor and instead bought himself a train ticket to Morristown. The L&N responded to this rumor by restricting tickets to those with written certificates of health and prohibiting their train crews from leaving the immediate vicinity of the depot. Later they refused to sell tickets to or from Middlesboro and would not allow passenger trains to even hesitate at the Middlesboro station.

Almost as pressing as the epidemic was the additional financial strain for the city. How were they to pay for the doctors, pesthouses, and supplies for the patients and guards? Not only was the town broke, it had already obligated itself for all "soon incoming" revenue to pay for expenses of the epidemic incurred through the first of March. The city applied to the county but was told that entity was in no better shape. Finally the county agreed to provide $1,000 if Mayor John Fitzpatrick would advance that amount from his own private pocket, for which the county would issue him warrants (essentially promissory notes which were at the time trading for 50-80¢ on the dollar.) He did so. The City Council also met with the businessmen in town and solicited their advice. There were pledges to pay some taxes in advance to get over the crisis. Meanwhile there were reports that some patients in the pesthouse were actually going hungry from lack of funds to provide sufficient food.

The city turned to the state Board of Health, but that body would do no more than send an inspector to investigate the situation. The Board said it could provide no funds and further, if the city would not take fiscal responsibility for dealing with the epidemic, then all health officers would be relieved of their posts and a strict quarantine of the city would be advised. In other words, Middlesboro would be essentially abandoned, left to stew in its own juices.

At this juncture, Congressman David Colson intervened with a request for federal aid. The Marine Hospital Service (later to be the Public Health Service) sent Dr. Wertenbaker to investigate. He arrived on March 13 to find 72 persons in the pesthouses and approximately 400 "suspects" (those who had been exposed but had not developed clearly defined symptoms) quarantined in their homes. He reported back that the town was demoralized and needed help.

At first it appeared that even the federal authorities might not help because of the wrangling with state and county health authorities. Once that was settled, Dr. Wertenbaker was joined by two other physicians and additional officers. They immediately set about finding a new pesthouse, one away from the most populated areas of town. For this they commandeered the Biggerstaff Boarding House, near the South Boston Gun Works (area of 38th Street), and renamed it the South Boston Hospital. All active cases were moved there and the old pesthouses fumigated. They also fumigated or, in the case of derelict houses, burned all places that had harbored a smallpox case. With their snappy blue uniforms and air of experienced authority, they began to give the town hope. This confidence was probably aided by the fact that the saloons had reopened, albeit with the proviso that no more than fifteen persons could be in any establishment at one time and no one could tarry more than fifteen minutes.

Actually, by the time the Marine Service took over, the efforts of the city fathers were finally bearing fruit, and the epidemic was abating. A careful canvas of the town revealed only thirty-five persons who had not yet been vaccinated. Just nine new cases of smallpox were diagnosed after the Marine Service took charge. And the Service found only three cases of other diseases, making Middlesboro, as the ever optimistic boosters claimed in the newspaper, "other than smallpox, the healthiest town on the globe."

Dr. Wertenbaker did continue the quarantine for a time. He was besieged by more than a hundred requests for permits to leave the city, but he denied almost all. Townspeople were also anxious for the fresh foodstuffs usually supplied by hucksters from Tennessee. Butter was unavailable and eggs were "a thing of the past." As the fear of contagion abated, the town chafed under its quarantine. But Middlesboro never lost its sense of humor. When the papers reported that its namesake in England was laboring under a smallpox epidemic with more than 500 cases, the papers asked whether it had been brought by "a Negro from Kentucky." And later, when

Dr. Will K. Evans and undertaker Hobert Cawood with the Evans Private Hospital ambulance. Courtesy of Phyllis Littrell.

smallpox was reported in Richmond, Kentucky, with the suspicion that it had come from Middlesboro, the papers replied that there could be "no doubt but what we had it to spare." Advertisements also began to play on the smallpox theme: "You can't catch smallpox if you eat Owsley's meat."

In early April there were definite signs that the epidemic had run its course. Churches were allowed to reopen and there were notices that the baseball season was about to begin with regular practices for the teams. Schools reopened. When the first passenger train in thirty-three days stopped at the Middlesboro depot on April 14, a large crowd gathered to cheer. In mid-April the Marine Service doctors departed after almost a month of successful labor.

The entire life of the town had been disrupted for five months, but luckily only two persons were known to have died as a direct result of smallpox. Middlesboro soon put its losses behind it, pulled up its socks, so to speak, and got on with its business.

Nevertheless, the smallpox epidemic had highlighted the need for a medical facility of some type. In 1899 the house built for the actress Lillie Langtry on Cumberland at 22nd was fitted out as a hospital. This did not work out, and the basement of the Methodist Church on 25th Street became the Epworth Hospital. In 1903, Drs. Buck, Curd, Arthur, Robertson, Brosheer, Howard, and Senter joined together to furnish an operating room at the Epworth Hospital. But more space was needed, and the King's Daughters, an organization whose membership was comprised of "a large number of the most prominent ladies of the Magic City," set to work. In 1910 they were able to obtain the large building on Cumberland that had originally been built as offices for the Middlesborough Town Company and was later used by the Elks organization. When the King's Daughters Hospital opened, it was the only hospital within seventy-five miles. This institution was short-lived, however, as it was sold by the Master Commissioner in 1914 to satisfy debts. (It was used as a private home until the First Baptist Church purchased the building for use as an annex, then demolished to make way for a modern addition.)

Meanwhile, in 1912 Dr. W.K. Evans opened his own twenty-bed hospital. He was later joined by his brother, Tom. This hospital was twice relocated and at its zenith had almost a hundred beds. Dr. Evans was very active in city politics; he was twice elected mayor and also served several terms as a city commissioner. His hospital last operated under Dr. Stellio Impresia. It finally closed its door completely in 1960.

The flu pandemic of 1918 hit rural areas like Bell County hard. There was an urgent need for further hospital beds, and the Elks came to the rescue by offering their large new home on Cumberland Avenue as a hospital. The three-story building was purchased in 1920 by Dr. C.K. Brosheer and Dr. Charles Brummet. They were later joined by, among others, Dr. Charles Cawood, Dr. Sam Flowers, and Dr. Arch Carr. The building was enlarged once, eventually having sixty-eight beds, with a surgery, x-ray facilities, and an accredited nursing school, the only one at the time in eastern Kentucky. In 1956, faced with the loss of patients to the new Miners' Hospital, the Middlesboro Hospital moved to a more modern, albeit smaller facility, still on Cumberland Avenue, but near 12th Street. It finally closed after the retirement of Drs. Cawood and Flowers in the mid-seventies.

During the twenties there was a separate facility, the Booker T. Washington Hospital, operated by Dr. I.H. Miller specifically for African-Americans. Dr. Miller, who had received his medical education in Nashville, came to Middlesboro from Nicholasville, Kentucky, in 1918. He had offices in the Ashbury Hotel on 19th Street. He stayed on into the forties, serving the community not only as a physician but also as an active participant in civic affairs.

In 1955 the United Mine Workers of America established a Miners' Hospital in Middlesboro. This metamorphosed into the present-day Middlesboro Appalachian Regional Hospital, with almost a hundred acute-care beds, multiple ancillary services, and a staff of more than thirty physicians. The beneficiaries of this modern facility can scarcely imagine what it must have been like for the citizens of Middlesboro during the smallpox epidemic of 1898.

FOOTNOTE TWENTY-ONE

Yellow Creek Politics

"When Middlesboro makes statewide news these days, it's usually because of the city's Byzantine political infighting." So said a *Louisville Courier-Journal* profile published in 1992 as part of a series entitled "Our Towns."

No one could challenge the truth of this characterization. In recent years, succeeding city councils had fought with various mayors. City officials had been summarily fired, then reinstated. Citizens' groups had formed with dizzying rapidity: Citizens for a Better Middlesboro, Yellow Creek Concerned Citizens, Time for a Change, New Direction. There had been reports of threats and counterthreats and even of guns in City Council chambers. So many legal actions had resulted that residents themselves referred to Middlesboro as "Sue City." Yet when reporters from the metropolitan papers tried to analyze the "Byzantine" political situation, they were defeated by connections and nuances that often went back many years, and by passions that seemed to have no rational explanation. One was almost tempted to ascribe the political infighting to something in the waters of Yellow Creek, particularly as the same scenario had played itself out many times since the town's founding.

Middlesborough was at its inception a company town, built and managed by the Middlesborough Town Company, Ltd., which was in turn largely owned by stockholders of the American Association, Ltd. The Town Company performed the usual duties of city government—laying out streets, providing for sanitation and public safety. Other companies, the stocks of which were owned in large part or wholly by the Town Company and its stockholders, were organized to furnish utilities and other services. The end result was that the American Association ran everything.

That changed when the city was granted a charter in March of 1890 and elections were scheduled for May. This meant that many matters affecting the American Association and its subsidiary companies would be settled by the newly enfranchised citizens of Middlesborough. W.C. Curtis had warned back in 1888 when the Town Company was first being organized, "It must be remembered that control of these matters will be taken out of the hand of the company and into the hands of the voters of the town, as soon as it is organized, and for that reason these plans should be so arranged that they would not be interfered with by the new residents."[1]

Part of the problem had been addressed by forming the subsidiary companies to provide water, electricity, and other services, thus keeping them under the control of the Town Company. But it was also imperative, insofar as the company was concerned, that the new city government be attuned to the interests of investors.

The city charter called for a City Council composed of five members elected at large who would then select from their membership a mayor. The Council would choose all city officials, including judges, tax assessors, etc., and would have complete control of city monies.

The Town Company first planned to run a mixed slate, the majority of whom would be company men, but including one or two from the "native" community. They approached David Colson (see Footnote Twenty), a dynamic, charismatic leader who had been born in the Yellow Creek Valley and still retained ownership of a large boundary of land within the new town. Colson had often worked with the American Association in obtaining property and could, they felt, be depended upon to keep the interests of the English investors in mind, while yet being a representative "native."

The English and their American allies had not taken into account the stubborn independence of the mountain stock from which Colson had sprung. He saw no reason to take a back seat to the foreigners. Before they knew what had hit them, the Town Company found itself facing an opposing slate of candidates headed by Colson himself.

One of their problems, of course, was that many of their natural constituency were not eligible to vote. Some were not even U.S. citizens. Arthur himself had gained citizenship only two years earlier. And many of the rough-and-tumble workmen, the bulk of the eligible voters, tended to identify more with the Colson ticket than with that of their bosses and the English investors.

The Town Company chose John Brooks to head their slate. He was a native of Knoxville, Tennessee, who had joined Arthur in his grand venture at its inception, when the future Middlesborough was mostly represented by a pile of ore on Arthur's back porch and a gleam in his eye. Brooks was a Confederate veteran who had served as a scout for General Joe Wheeler. He had been so severely wounded at the Battle of Chickamauga that the army physician ordered his grave dug. After a year in the hospital, he was able to rejoin his company and serve out the war with distinction. (It probably escaped the Town Company's notice that the mountains were the one place in the South where being a Confederate veteran was not a political advantage.) It was Brooks who established the military department of the University of Tennessee after the war. He was a stockholder and officer in several of the subsidiary companies formed by the Town Company, an urbane and likable man from all reports.

Also on the Company ballot was D.N. Mason, who was in the real estate business. The paper noted, in an ironic acknowledgment of the age of the city, that he was "one of the pioneers of Middlesborough having come here nearly a year ago." Hugh M. Rogers, another Town Company candidate, was also involved in real estate, probably as a speculator. He was a native of Lexington, a Confederate veteran who had joined General John Hunt Morgan's cavalry when he was sixteen. He had been wounded in an early battle, taken prisoner, and confined in a prison hospital for much of the war. He later became a U.S. marshall, serving in Harlan County, where he was shot in the lung by a moonshiner, a wound from which he never totally recovered. He had arrived in Middlesborough as the race for riches heated up. The ticket was rounded out by R.H. Fox, a contractor who was being employed by the Company to build streets and do hauling, and W.S. Worsham, also a builder, who had come six months earlier to take charge of the construction of one of the larger business buildings.

Colson's ticket was weighted with those who had no direct connection with the American Association. W.T. Davis was a native of the Pineville area. He later became a circuit judge for the Bell-Harlan circuit and was active in the Republican party. James Veal had also originally lived in Pineville but moved to Middlesborough in 1888. The others on the ballot were J.R. Young and a Mr. Ritchie. There was also one independent candidate, Louis Cohen.

The race was a hot one that engendered bitter feelings. Two polling places were selected, one at the Engine House, where the new fire engine was stored, and the other at the offices of the American Association. The election was held May 13, 1890, and set the tone for many to come. One man later described what he observed:

> As an innocent "Yank" hot for experience and observation, I have often been amused thinking of how I "washed back with the crowd" when Bob Fox, Dave Colson, etc. reached for their "pistol pockets." I saw the first election when locals and the "Town Company" fought for control of Middlesboro and its big improvement contracts. One of the "English" officials told me they had a job of fancy lying to do explaining to the London auditors the meaning of "away up in the thousands" charges to "expense" because of that important election. $40 a head was near the "high" and night importation of colorful citizens was an item of regular conversation. We "Yankees" enjoyed the discomfort of the "side" that lost almost 100 "importations," shipped in and stored (with eats and drinks) in the second story room of a Cumberland Avenue store, when the opposition punched in the rear windows and made a "plank runaway" for the compressed imported "citizens."[2]

Senator Joe Bosworth (who was to marry Veal's daughter) later recalled that there was actual auctioning of votes at the polling places. The Town Company men were the highest bidders. He estimated that the election cost the English company $15,000 to $20,000, roughly equivalent to $280,000 to $375,000 today, in an election in which the winner, Brooks, received 732 votes to Colson's 305.[3]

The new City Council met three times the next day, May 14. At the first meeting they elected Brooks mayor and named a city clerk. In the afternoon they appointed a city attorney and a city court judge. They met again at 7:30 p.m. that same day. The Council minutes explained the reason for calling the evening meeting: "there being some doubt as to the legality of the former organization of the Board of Council and in order to remove all doubts...it appearing from the poll books returned and certificates upon the poll books and comparison of the same that the following people received the following vote."[4] The minutes went on to enumerate the vote for each candidate, exactly as they had previously been reported. The Council then again elected Brooks mayor and again chose all the same officials as they had the first time.

It had to be admitted that the tally was a little suspicious, in that ballots voted at the American Association office were lopsidedly for the Brooks ticket, while the Colson slate won handily at the Engine House. Unfortunately for the latter, twice as many voters turned up to cast their ballots at the American Association office.

For a time the Council met almost daily. There was a great deal of work to accomplish. Having bought into Arthur's plans for his grand city, they set about establishing various offices as befit the city they envisioned, filled them with loyal friends paid good wages, and prepared to continue the work the Town company had started.

The services that had been provided by the Town Company would now have to be financed through taxes, never an easy chore. In addition, it was a priority of the Town Company that the city purchase the various improvements, such as the sewer system, which they already had under way, and that they move ahead with the company's plans for boardwalks, paving of streets, and the like, all of which would make town lots more attractive to would-be buyers. Therefore one of the Council's first acts was to fix a tax of $1,000 each on retail liquor dealers, to be paid in advance. With forty bars and saloons supplying the needs of a thirsty and growing population, this looked like a relatively painless way to finance city government. They then voted to buy from the Town Company the Engine Building, which had been designated the city hall when it was constructed by the company, and their fire apparatus. Before they could do so, there was a disastrous fire that almost destroyed the city and added to city expenses.

In September of 1890 the Council voted to issue $150,000 in bonds for public improvements. A general tax was levied to pay the interest and provide for repayment of principal. Other bonds were issued directly to the Town Company to pay for the city hall property and the sewer system. The city had managed to put itself deeply in debt just as the first blow that would foreshadow the "bust" was about to fall.

By this time the *Middlesborough News* was already complaining of "the raid on the city treasury" and proclaiming that it had been "well satisfied from the beginning" that the Council was "not made up of men who put the city's welfare first." The paper's accusations became more pointed as it reported that one member, who was chairman of the public works committee, voted on building contracts, then bid them himself, voting himself the jobs and later voting to pay himself. There were editorials pointing out "reckless extravagance" on the part of the Council. In January of 1891 the Council conducted an investigation of the police force for reported improprieties, and three months later the entire police force resigned. Councilmen began to bicker among themselves. Mason and Fox soon resigned. People began to talk about "reform" and taking over the Council in the next election. Within one year city government had played out most of the scenarios that would bedevil Middlesboro politics in the years to come.

Only two members of the original council, Brooks and Worsham, ran in the next election, which was held May 10, 1892. They were soundly defeated, and D.E. McDowell became the second mayor of Middlesboro.

The "bust" was already under way, and the new Council had its work cut out for it. City bondholders had already gone to the state legislature and rammed through the Roundtree Bill, which mandated that the city pay its obligations to its bondholders before it could make any other expenditures. At the same time, tax revenues were evaporating. City services were cut drastically, as were city jobs. Eventually the city would have to go to vouchers (IOUs) to pay employees.

David Colson was elected mayor in 1894. He came to office in the midst of a huge controversy regarding the police department and a deteriorating treasury. He resigned in 1895 to take his place in Congress, and Walter Bishop became mayor. The newspapers kept up a running critique of city government.[5] To cite just a few examples: "Election Fraud Perpetrated in Middlesborough....In keeping with the action of those who manipulate elections....Bishop sneaked into the Mayor's office." "We...hear the charge on every hand that the city government is as corrupt as the devil." And, reporting on the 1897 Republican primary:

> At about 10 o'clock orders were given from headquarters to stop buying votes....it was ascertained that the votes cast, and those left over exceeded the entire voting population of Middlesborough....One man...who knows everybody in the first ward said that he watched the polls for three hours and they were voting rapidly all the time, before he recognized a single face and that was a man who lived "way down in Middle Tennessee."

In September of 1898 the *Middlesborough News* opined that there were three competing factions in the city—Brooks-Fox, Saulsberry, and Colson—and "each has had a turn at the city treasury."

If anything, the political situation deteriorated in 1899. This was the year of the divisive, acrid statewide campaign that pitted Democrat William Goebel against Republican William Taylor in a race for the governorship and resulted in the assassination of Goebel. In Middlesboro the political struggle was no less bitter. Fanning the flames were two competing weekly newspapers, the *Middlesborough News,* which generally supported the Republicans, though often critical of local politicians of whatever persuasion, and the *Weekly Record,* which favored Goebel and pushed for "reform" of city government. In October of 1899 both Taylor and Goebel visited Middlesboro and gave campaign speeches at the Opera House.

Positions hardened as the election neared. The *News* reminded voters that the leading Democrat, "Boss" Ed Saulsberry, had served on the first council (he had replaced Mason), which had made "unjust and unfair contracts with various companies subsidiary to the Town and Land Company," thus throwing the city into an unhappy situation that forced well over half of every tax dollar to be sent to the bondholders. The *Record,* on the other hand, promised the Democrats would cut taxes and warned darkly of Republican plans: "Toughs, Ward Heelers and Disreputable characters to be stationed at polls to intimidate voters...(and to) destroy half of ballots."

Taylor forces were victorious statewide, but the election was immediately contested. In Middlesboro, the Democrats won by a small margin. Of the six Democratic candidates, the highest vote getter was R.C. Ford, with 311, while the lowest was C.N. Miller, with 297. The top Republican received 288 votes and the lowest, 276. The losers contested the election, claiming that votes had been bought with drink, money, and "other illegal means," that qualified black voters were harassed, and that men "of known and desperate character" from surrounding areas were parading with guns in the vicinity of the polling places, to say nothing of the mutilating of ballots and fraudulent counting. The Democrats countered that in view of what had happened in previous elections, the Republicans were in no position to throw stones.

The newly elected Council met on December 4, 1899. One of their first acts was to switch publication of official business from the *News* to the *Record.* The next action of the Council, taken while the mayor was away from the city and while meeting (according to the *News*) "in the dead of night in a secluded place," was to declare the office of Police Chief S.A. Ball and his assistant (the only two policemen the city could afford) to be vacant because of their "failure to suppress gamblers, enforce laws against gambling, failure to require saloons to close on Sundays and during elections," and because of interfering with the recent election. Rules were suspended so that a second reading and vote were taken that same night and a new chief, R.N. King, was chosen.

Next the Council turned its attention to other city officials. The city code had been previously revised so that there was a six-member Council who selected a mayor for a term of four years. Mayor W.H. "Uncle Bill" Turner had been named in 1898, so his term did not expire until 1902. The same was true of the city judge, Joe Bosworth. The Council's first move was to cut off their salaries entirely, while hiring Ed Saulsberry as city attorney at the large salary (for that time and considering the city treasury) of $100 a month plus fees.

When Turner and Bosworth did not resign as expected, the Council went further. On February 5, 1900, they passed this resolution: "Whereas there is no regularly elected Mayor of the city of Middlesborough, Kentucky Be it now resolved that the office of Mayor be and the same is now declared vacant."[6] Mayor Turner was present and protested, but to no avail. The Council selected R.C. Ford as mayor. The *News,* referring to the Goebel-Taylor controversy, in which two men had briefly claimed to be governor of Kentucky (until Goebel was assassinated and the courts settled the matter), sarcastically opined that "the fact that the state had two governors was too much for this city," since it had "always been the pride of Middlesboro that no place could get ahead of us," so now the town had matched the state with two chief executives of its own.

The next month the same maneuver was pulled against Judge Bosworth, and W.H. Rhorer, an associate of Saulsberry, was named to take his place, resulting in two judges for the city court. Legal actions were initiated. Special police and bailiffs were deputized by both sides. Both sets of city officials claimed authority. It would have been almost comical had not the controversy turned deadly. First shots were fired into city hall. Then a man lost his foot, and another forfeited his life.

Bosworth had possession of the city judge's chambers and had obtained a restraining order to prevent his removal, but the new city police and City Attorney Saulsberry refused to recognize him. When Bosworth attempted to hold court, the other officials would not conduct the prosecution. Matters came to a head in April when Bosworth ordered the release of a certain Charles Cousins because of the lack of prosecution. The Council debated the Cousins release at length during their next meeting, then ordered King to rearrest him.

That night in mid-April, Cousins was relaxing at the Keg House with his friends, among them H.E. Ball, the brother of the ousted Police Chief, and Ball's cousin Charlie Cecil, brother of the city jailer. In walked King, accompanied by three men he had just deputized, intent on taking Cousins into custody. Words were exchanged. Cecil later testified that one of the men, Will Mosley, had cocked his gun and had it pointed at Ball. Cecil said that he feared Ball was about to be shot, so he knocked the gun down. As he did so it discharged, shooting him in the foot. Cecil was rushed to the hospital, where his foot had to be amputated.

After the excitement, things had about returned to normal at the Keg House when shooting was heard in the alley to the rear. Patrons rushed out to find Mosley a victim of the gunfire. As he lay there dying, he was heard to whisper, "Don't blame me. Others made me do it."

The papers lamented that the town was "in a state of insurrection."

The Republican-dominated county court indicted members of the new Council's police force, King resigned, and the city soon had its third chief of police in five months. Meanwhile, Turner and Bosworth had been upheld in Circuit Court, but their opponents were threatening to appeal. On June 30, 1900, the *News* reported, "A condition of affairs exists here that is very demoralizing....The town is an arsenal. Firearms of the worse kind are seen on all sides. When armed bodies of men come openly on the streets in defiance of one another...when preparations go continually on for war...sooner or later the outbreak will come." Even the partisan *News* had to admit that both sides were "to some extent" to blame.

Happily for the town, the antagonists drew back from the brink and cooler heads prevailed. In early July there was a meeting of men representing both sides, intent on reaching a compromise. Turner was accepted as the only mayor. S.A. Ball would be chief of police, with John Turner, who had served with the new police force, as patrolman. All others, including all deputy sheriffs except one, would have no legal authority. The Republicans, in turn, would use their influence to get indictments against the King police force dismissed as well as those against various Democrats indicted for election fraud. Other matters of controversy were addressed, and it appeared that the city was embarked on an era of peace.

Appearances are often deceiving, however. City finances were still in desperate circumstances, and many old wounds continued to fester. The election of 1901 brought a new configuration to Council. Three councilmen, led by H.E. Ball, always voted as a block, while the other three also voted as a block. Mayor Turner had the tie-breaking vote, and he, without exception, voted with the Ball faction. The other side had a simple solution. They stopped attending Council meetings, so there was no quorum and thus no city business could legally be transacted.

From January of 1902 through August of that year, there were no council meetings for lack of a quorum. Finally the three dissident councilmen resigned and the city muddled on, helped by an improvement in the business climate of the city. But the mandates of the Roundtree Bill still meant there was little tax revenue left over after satisfying the demands of bondholders. Frustration with the seeming impotence of city government, particularly the small police force, led in 1905 to the formation of a Law and Order League, followed by martial law. It was only with the repeal of the Roundtree Bill, engineered by State Representative Joe Bosworth in 1906, that the city regained control of its finances. During the second decade of the twentieth century, with a general improvement in the economy of the area, there was a boom in building, vacant lots filled, a large city administration

Middlesboro officials and policemen, 1913-1915. Seated, left to right: unknown man, Mayor J.L. Manring, Police Judge Ed Evans, Councilman William Walbrecht, unknown man. Standing: Bill Lipps, George Fisher, Charlie Yeary, Night Chief of Police H.E. Ball, Day Chief George Vanbeber, Bill White, Lawrence Yeary, and Fire Chief Richard Knipp. Courtesy of the Bell County Historical Society.

building was constructed, streets were paved, and the city began to take on the look that Arthur had envisioned.

In 1915 there was a change to a commissioner form of government, then back to a city council form in 1920. Two years later there was yet another change, to a mayor and two commissioners. This would be the form for over thirty years.

The old pattern of reform-backsliding-reform continued. The mid-twenties were another time of uproar in city government. In 1928 there was a replay of 1900 when the city once again had two competing police departments. A new mayor had summarily dismissed one force and appointed his own. The old force sued, claiming lack of due process. For a time one group occupied the office with the phones while the other occupied the lobby of the police station. The newspaper reported it like a contest, as in "the new police force had four cases in police court while the old had three."

During the thirties, Floyd and Alvey Ball took control of city government and by mid-decade had also become political bosses in the county (see Footnote 29). There were sporadic efforts to challenge their power, but none was successful until the late forties. Gradually, beginning in the county, power was wrested from the Ball machine. The most telling blow came in 1953, when the city voted to change back to a mayor-city council form of government. The town went "dry" two years later.

Although the Ball machine had been defeated, political wrangling continued. The Democratic governor, reneging on an agreement made with reform Republicans, appointed twelve Democrats to the new Council. The Good Government slate, as they called themselves, set out to reform city hall. The new city clerk, Katherine Dance, found the books in total disarray, with almost no documentation of expenditures. There were invoices for items not received and for goods actually delivered to someone in the old political clique rather than to the city. Large amounts of petty cash were routinely kept on hand, and she was told that it was not unusual for the "in crowd" to use it as a bank, dipping into petty cash during poker games and "borrowing" a few dollars whenever they wished.[7] The city's credit was so bad that the reform councilmen had to go to a Tennessee bank for a loan to meet the city payroll and had to personally co-sign the note.[8]

In a replay of earlier days, one of the first actions of the Council was to suspend Chief of Police Guy Harrell. The charges against him included failure to enforce the laws against gambling. The court ordered him reinstated. A month later he was again suspended, then reinstated. Finally, in the fall of 1954 he was suspended, a trial was held at city hall, and he was fired.

The incumbent Democrats were elected to their seats in 1954, along with a Democratic mayor, F.R. Whalin. In 1955, however, Republicans carried the city, with only one exception. Nonetheless, the Council was usually split 6-6, and the wrangling continued. A Republican, Hubert White, took over as mayor in 1958. There was infighting between the mayor and Council, and the mayor even filed a suit against seven of the councilmen. Joe McCauley was the next mayor. In 1965 he was challenged in the Republican primary by one of his councilmen, who had also served on the school board, Chester Wolfe, an automobile parts dealer.

Wolfe was to serve as mayor for sixteen of the next twenty years. When he came into office, the town had been dry for just over ten years, but that was in name only. As has ever been the case in local politics, the reform had not sustained itself. Though there were no open saloons, liquor was readily available. In fact, it was later one of Mayor Wolfe's private boasts that when he came into office there were bootleggers on every corner, and he had reduced their number to six major players. A tightly controlled distribution system was instituted through the wholesale liquor houses in Lexington, and a "fee" charged for this service. College students returning from wet areas on the weekend were often used as the "mules" to transport liquor.[9]

The city administration could also brag of a safe city where there were few crimes other than victimless ones such as bootlegging. But during the late sixties and early seventies Middlesboro gained a reputation among the Kentucky State Police as a major conduit for stolen goods. For some residents, because the victims were not local, this did not seem so bad, and there were people in town who actually boasted of their purchases of "hot" jewelry. In one rather comical incident, a local store had bought some off-brand TV sets that did not sell well. When he was unable to sell the perfectly legal goods, the owner moved the TVs to a back room. He then put out the rumor that he was selling "hot" TVs out the back door. Although the price was the same as or higher than when he was offering legal electronics, his goods now moved like the proverbial hotcakes, and he rapidly unloaded his entire inventory.[10]

By the early 1970s a growing number of people expressed concern about the fact that the town seemed almost "wide open" again. Within a block of city hall and the police station there were places where liquor was easily obtained and even a semi-open bar, a gambling joint, and two houses of prostitution. Strangely enough, one of the latter operated out of the top two floors of the Majestic Hotel while the FBI maintained an office on the ground floor. In fact, the profession was so well protected in town that the working girls on the circuit were pleased to accommodate the Middlesboro establishments during the "Easter Rush" and the "Mother's Day Rush" (holidays that brought many of the men who had gone north for work back to town to visit their families) when extra personnel were needed.

Again there was a groundswell demand for reform, abetted by the ambition of the Democrats to retake city government. The campaign was bitter. As in previous reform movements, some Republicans joined to vote in the reform candidate, Crawford Blakeman. Blakeman's effort to "clean up" the city was aided by the state police, who attempted to enforce the federal mandate that anyone selling liquor must purchase a federal license. The same was required for gambling, even though both activities were illegal on the local level. Numerous raids began to have the desired affect.

Mayor Blakeman, along with some of his supporters, started receiving threats even before his election in the fall of 1973. Immediately upon learning of his victory, Blakeman had himself appointed a deputy sheriff so he

Chester Wolfe, ca. 1980. Courtesy of *Middlesboro Daily News.*

could carry a gun, and he carried a firearm with him the entire time he served. The state police and FBI advised him to have a steel plate welded under his car and always to check under the hood before starting it.[11] The stress of the job brought on warning signs of an imminent heart attack, and Blakeman's cardiologist insisted that he resign before finishing out his term. Troy Welch served as interim mayor until the next election.

Chester Wolfe won the 1977 race for mayor and served another eight years. This time there was care not to allow open flouting of the law and the city's sensibilities. But the Wolfe administration soon faced another type of reform. The town's oldest continuously operating industry, the Middlesboro Tanning Company (originally the Vaugh & Hall Tannery), was accused of polluting Yellow Creek. A citizens' group organized to demand that the tannery clean up its effluent and that the city improve its sewerage system. Council meetings began to be shouting matches as the Yellow Creek Concerned Citizens (YCC) demanded action. Soon came law suits.

In an effort to finance mandated improvements in the city's sewerage system, sewer charges were increased precipitously. Residents angered by the new sewer rates formed the Citizens for a Better Middlesboro (CBM) to try to oust city government, particularly Mayor Wolfe. Adjustments were made, the sewer charge reduced somewhat. But a new reform group, many of whom had been active in YCC and CBM, formed. Calling themselves "Time for a Change," they took on city hall. The Change candidates were successful in the 1983 election. One of their first actions was an effort to oust the long-time chief of police, James Pursiful, and several other officials, which they eventually managed to do. There was also an effort to impeach Mayor Wolfe, which was unsuccessful. For months it was "standing room only" at Council meetings, and the big-city media began to report regularly on Middlesboro's "Byzantine political infighting."

The city appeared to be saying "a pox on both your houses" when in 1985 it elected as mayor Raymond Walker, a businessman with no allegiance to either faction. But he found the partisan politics impossible and resigned before his term was half over. He was followed by an interim mayor, Betty Bell Peace, and then by Mayor Troy Welch, who spearheaded an effort to get successful business people in town to run for council. "New Direction" candidates were victorious at the ballot box and confidently expected their business acumen would carry the city beyond politics. One of their early actions was to form a search committee to find a new chief of police. The successful applicant was from out of town, a complete break with tradition and past practice. Soon Mayor Welch became unhappy with Chief Jerry Harris and dismissed him. When Harris contested this action in court, the New Direction people indicated their support for the chief. This led to a breech that never healed. Once again the Council chambers were the scene of bitter political struggles. The businessmen became discouraged and yet another reform movement faltered and faded.

It was 1990, and Middlesboro was one hundred years old. It seemed fated to go through the same political battles time after time. One really has to wonder if there is not something in the waters of Yellow Creek that forever pollutes the politics of the Magic City.

Footnote Twenty-Two

The Quarterhouse Battle

> A legal process took Lee Turner's team into Tennessee. Lee and Boone McCurry went after the team. Lee brot the team and McCurry bak. McCurry brot a load of buckshot. And there is blood on the face of the moon.[1]

What an accurate prophecy! Within a few days, anger and hostility culminated in the bloody Quarterhouse Battle in which at least seven persons lost their lives.

The scene of the Battle, the Quarterhouse, was located up Mingo Hollow, about three and a half miles southwest of Middlesboro and a quarter of the way to the huge Mingo Mines in Tennessee. The saloon was owned and operated by Will and Lee Turner, sons of Pres Turner, whose family had been among the first settlers in the Yellow Creek Valley. Erected by the brothers in the mid-1890s, it was a substantial two-story building constructed of heavy railroad timbers and surrounded by a log stockade much like those of frontier days, with portholes that could be utilized for defense. The Turners were careful to build it directly on the state line; thus half of it was in Kentucky and half in Tennessee. A white line was painted on the floor of the main room so there could be no mistaking the location of the state boundaries. When law enforcement officers arrived from Kentucky, everyone would be on the Tennessee side and untouchable. The opposite would happen should Tennessee attempt to police the establishment. Apparently the two states never coordinated their efforts.

There was plenty to attract the attention of the law. The Quarterhouse was a one-stop den of iniquity with a veritable smorgasbord of vices to entice the coal miners, who were the main customers. The large saloon provided liquor of all types, including that made in an on-premises distillery. A restaurant in an adjoining area provided meals, though doubtless not of the four-star variety. There were several rooms devoted to gambling. The Quarterhouse was also a house of ill repute, with rooms upstairs for the women. Then there was the staged entertainment—turkey matches, cockfights, even fights between a bulldog and a wildcat. Lee had his own wildcat caged nearby expressly for this purpose. The dangerous combination of liquor, gambling, and wild women often led to violent confrontations, and it was reported in the Lexington papers at the time of the Battle that well over fifty men had lost their lives there and another hundred had been wounded in the less than ten years of the Quarterhouse's existence. The paper went on to state that the Quarterhouse was "known throughout America because of the number who have been killed within its confines....it was a 'blind tiger' of the most revolting kind."

The Turner brothers were in their twenties when they established the Quarterhouse. "Wild Bill" was, as his nickname suggests, a rather fractious man in his younger days and had killed at least two men. At the time of his death in 1898 the paper stated that "of late years, with the exception of killing the negro, he had, to a certain extent, quit his wild ways." He was by then married, with two children, and had bought a home in Middlesboro, though he was rumored to have a second family in the mountains.

Lee Turner was a tall, handsome man with blue eyes and wavy reddish brown hair. He was said to be fearless, with a volatile temper, and handy with his guns. Despite his reputation as, according to the vernacular of day, "a bad man," he was also known as a charitable man who, with his brother, used a part of the Quarterhouse profits to feed and clothe widows and orphans and to help those in trouble.

Both Will and Lee rode coal-black stallions and were dashing and somewhat romantic figures. They displayed also a certain chivalry. One older resident recalled his mother telling of the time two men were using abusive language with her. Will Turner happened along and, realizing what was occurring, beat up both men, then took out his silk handkerchief and dried her tears.[2]

"Wild Bill" was killed at the Quarterhouse in October of 1898. He was apparently trying to break up a fight between Will Combs, who ran the restaurant, and another man by the name of Pridemore, when he was shot by Combs. Combs and Pridemore had been quarreling all evening, but it was later rumored that the quarrel was a ruse for the premeditated murder of Will. The paper reported that "Combs took to the mountains, but as he is a one-legged man, it is not believed he can get far." Turner's friends vowed revenge. They tracked him to South America, the area now called Frakes, but so named at that time because of its remoteness. Combs was captured and taken to Tennessee because Will had been killed on the Tennessee side of the saloon; he was sentenced to five years in prison. (Several years later Pridemore met a violent death, and Lee was charged with complicity. General Turner, Will's nephew, received a life sentence for the Pridemore killing, though he served little of that sentence.)

In an interview given the *Knoxville Sentinel* following the Quarterhouse Battle, Lee asserted that Will had been killed because the Turner boys led local Democratic forces, while the Balls and Colsons (see Footnotes Seven and Thirteen) were strong for the Republicans. In that interview he attributed the origins of the Battle to that same political animosity, and he further charged, "The Ball Brothers and their lieutenants had my brother Bill killed....Since that time they have been trying to kill me, and I have remained away from Middlesboro."

There were other aggravations. In a time when the local economy was not robust, the Quarterhouse, with its myriad of pleasures, drained away potential income from the saloons in Middlesboro, many of which were being run by the Balls, who were at the time allied with their cousins, the Colsons. Furthermore, there was a land title dispute between Turner and Gil (W.G.) Colson, who claimed he owned the land on which the Quarterhouse stood. Gil first had his case heard in Tennessee, but the decision went to the Turners. He then filed his case at the courthouse in Pineville. According to the Colson side, the case was decided in Gil's favor. According to the Turners, Gil, who was a lawyer, was the one who entered the judgment favorable to himself into the record book.

Gil Colson then insisted that Lee Turner pay rent on his establishment. As expected, Lee demurred. The next time Lee sent his wagon and mules into town to pick up a load of whiskey that had arrived at the train station, the Middlesboro authorities seized wagon, mules, and whiskey, claiming them as recompense for the rent Turner owed Colson. The wagon and mules were sold at a public auction at which Colson was the only bidder. There is no record as to what happened to the whiskey.

When Lee heard what had transpired, he took one of his men, Boone McCurry, and set off to reclaim his property. He was able to do so, but McCurry received a load of buckshot in the process.

Back to Pineville went Colson to get a warrant for the arrest of the men who had stolen "his" mules and wagon. William Thompson and C.D. Ball, deputy sheriffs, were instructed by Judge M.J. Moss to serve a warrant on Lee Turner. Just to sweeten the pot (and also because the theft had occurred in Virginia, where Bell County courts had no jurisdiction), the posse was also to arrest Lee on the charge that he had men stationed on the road between the Quarterhouse and Middlesboro, and that they would steal the liquor that had been bought at the Turner establishment and then take it back for resale. There was also the question of the illegal sale of whiskey, as Lee, though he purchased a federal license to sell liquor, never saw the need to purchase separate licenses from Kentucky and Tennessee.

The posse that formed on February 12, 1902, has been described as a mob of more than a hundred, but it probably actually numbered closer to forty or fifty. Among the members of the posse were Frank and Houston Ball and their cousin Charley Cecil. Charley had lost a leg in an earlier altercation with Ball opponents and had a peg leg; he was a long-time Middlesboro police officer and was deputy sheriff for the city. Also accompanying the posse was the Turners' old enemy, General Sowders.

Although a mine train ran up Mingo Hollow, the operators, fearing trouble, refused to transport the posse, so the armed men walked up the tracks the three and a half miles to the Quarterhouse. It was three or four o'clock in the afternoon when they arrived.

This was a quiet time at the Turner establishment, with few patrons gracing the saloon or gaming rooms in the mid-afternoon. Even so, it was later estimated that there were some thirty men, including several Turner employees, lounging around the place. Lee himself was in LaFollette, Tennessee, answering a legal charge. He later claimed that his enemies knew he would be gone and thus they would not have to deal with him, their goal not being the simple serving of a warrant but destruction of the Quarterhouse.

As the posse approached, it was apparent that they had not been expected, since the door to the stockade was open. Although phone communication was possible, the lines were apparently cut before the posse started up the Hollow.[3] The Turners and their allies had, however, been expecting trouble and were on the lookout. As soon as the large posse was spotted, the stockade doors were pulled shut and bolted.

The posse deployed around the building, surrounding it. Charley Cecil, accompanied by William Young, a one-armed African-American, banged on the door on the Kentucky side of the building, asking that Lee Turner come out. In answer, a shot was fired from an upstairs window, the bullet entering Cecil's shoulder and coursing down his body. Cecil slumped, and Young fled. Shots were exchanged as the posse attempted to rescue Cecil, who shortly thereafter succumbed to his wounds. According to Young, shots fired from the posse at almost the same time as the one that killed Cecil had hit someone inside the building, as he had seen someone fall in the few seconds that he was near the building.

After those first shots there could be no retreat. The Battle raged until dark with little advantage to either side, since the Turner faction was protected by the heavy timbers of the stockade and the posse was able to take cover behind rocks and trees. Then, as darkness approached, the Quarterhouse caught fire. Some say the posse set it on fire intentionally—a tactic frequently used in mountain feuds. Others say that those inside the Quarterhouse knocked over a stove and the resulting fire spread before it could be controlled. Still others believe the fusillade of bullets was somehow responsible. Whatever started the fire, it spread quickly to an area where barrels of liquor were stored. These blew up, their fury magnified by the explosion of ammunition that had been stored nearby. A sheet of fire engulfed the building and the occupants fled.

The women were allowed to escape, but several of the men were shot. Just how many will never be known. There were rumors of men shot as they tried to escape and of others who were handcuffed and then shot. In fact, the *Claiborne Progress,* in an article generally supportive of the Turner faction, reported that one of the wounded, Lee Hopper, had handcuffs on when he was found, and that he claimed the posse had captured and handcuffed the men, then deliberately blew their heads off. Members of the posse roamed the woods around the burning building for some time, firing sporadically. The night was pitch black by the time the firing ceased and the posse gathered their dead and wounded and returned to Middlesboro. John Doyle, another law officer, had been shot through the bowels and died a day or two later. The dead Turner men were left where they fell.

Early the next morning hundreds of people from Middlesboro trekked out to view the carnage. The Quarterhouse had burned to the ground, with only about fifty feet of stockade wall left standing. There were four bodies in the immediate vicinity of the ruins. One had been the Quarterhouse bartender; he had been shot in the back of the head. Another man had had his chin blown off. Still another man, who had been the "bouncer" for the establishment, had the top of his head shot off. His brain, almost completely intact, was found fifteen feet from the body. A fourth victim was a miner who just happened to be in the building at the time of the assault. He had been shot at very close range. A fifth dead man was found a little later at some distance from the burned building. The coroner found bones in the ashes but never determined whether they were human or, if so, how many individuals had been incinerated. In fact, he showed a remarkable lack of curiosity. When he was told of three bodies that were

Middlesborough News

A LOCAL WEEKLY

[illegible]isht 1889 MIDDLESBOROUGH, KY., SATURDAY, FEBRUARY 15, 1902 Number 62

BLOODY BATTL

Furius Fighting and Flaring Flame:
Deth and Destruction

TURNER'S NOTORIUS "QUARTER HOUS" IN ASHE

THE DETH ROLL

Sheriff's Posse	Turner's Army
CHARLES CECIL	FRANK JOHNSON
	JEFF PRATER
	PERRY WATSON
	MIKE WELSH
	JAY RUSSELL

MISSING, and believed to be Ded

CHARLES M. DRYE

INJURED

JOHN DOYLE

JAMES HOPPER

rumored to be further up on the mountain, he opined that they were probably in Tennessee and no concern of his.

The bodies had been robbed during the night of all usable possessions. There were rumors that families of other victims had come during the night and carried the bodies off to be buried secretly. Of the thirty men thought to have been in the Quarterhouse at the time of the Battle, only two are known to have escaped alive, and one of those (Hopper) had been wounded. Given the fact that only five deaths of those who had been inside were recorded, there were certainly some unanswered questions.

The only man from within the Turner stockade known to have escaped the Quarterhouse unscathed was Charlie Drye, an African-American who had run the restaurant and was, at that time, managing a secondary saloon and boarding house within the compound. He recalled there had been some anticipation of trouble ever since Lee had retrieved his mules, and he had been told to get his Winchester and be ready to help defend the Quarterhouse if needed. But he said that when he saw a large group of men with shotguns sneaking up the mountain, he decided that discretion was the better part of valor, and he took off across the mountain. He was about a fourth of a mile away when the shooting started. It was Dye who made the estimate of the number within the stockade at the time of the assault.

Lee Turner had returned home just after the battle started. The *Middlesborough News* reported that Lee, along with his nephew, "wer upon the mountain side and witnest the hole fight; sum think they wer amung the shooters....both wer at the upper end of the hollow very shortly after the batel." Lee returned to LaFollette, where he gave himself up to the Tennessee marshal. At the same time, he transferred his claim on the property to the American Association. He also arranged for burial of his slain men in the Turner family cemetery in Middlesboro, himself providing handsome caskets.

Lee had many sympathizers in Claiborne County, Tennessee. In fact, the *Claiborne Progress* claimed that 95 percent of the people in that county sympathized with Turner despite the unsavory reputation of the Quarterhouse. The paper described the killings as "foul murders" and the Battle itself as "one of the most diabolical deeds with which the pages of local history hav bin stained."

On the Kentucky side of the mountain the story was different. Governor Beckham offered a $400 reward for the arrest and conviction of Turner, Hopper, and Charles Drye. Drye was quickly located in Knoxville, extradited to Kentucky, and jailed for a time while waiting to be indicted for some crime related to the Quarterhouse Battle. No indictment was ever returned.

The reward for the capture of Lee was raised to $1,000, and his cousin, John "Popeye" Turner undertook to claim the prize. "Popeye" tried to extract information of his whereabouts from Lee's half-sister, Bets Turner. Unable to do so, he shortly thereafter happened on Lee riding along a road in the Yellow Creek Valley. According to Bets:

> Without warning, he opened fire, shooting Lee from his horse and shooting the horse in the neck. As he emptied his pistol, "Popeye" shouted triumphantly, "Eleven men dead and a thousand dollars." As Lee fell from the saddle his feet became tangled in the stirrups. He was dragged along the ground for some distance, but from this helpless position he managed to free one gun from its holster and poured its contents into "Popeye." As the latter was wearing a bullet-proof vest, the shots glanced off harmlessly. In the meantime, Lee had managed to free a German mauser, which he used with telling effect, killing "Popeye" immediately.[4]

Lee was arrested for this killing but quickly acquitted because of a plea of self-defense.

Ever the entrepreneur, Lee tried to capitalize on the wide publicity gleaned from the nationwide newspaper coverage of the Battle. It was reported in the Louisville papers in May of 1902 that he was about to take a drama on the road that would be called "The Battle of the Quarter House, or the King of the Cumberland Mountains" in which he himself would have the leading role. He had supposedly corresponded with the manager of Macauley's Theatre in Louisville and had a writer working on the play. Apparently nothing came of this. A reenactment of the Quarterhouse Battle was planned for Jellico in September of 1902, but it was stopped by the City Council, which felt it would be "grossly immoral." Town citizens were said to have torn the lithographs advertising the production off of boards and out of store windows. Lee then opened the Quarterhouse Saloon in LaFollette, Tennessee, started operating a small coal mine, and was again making money.

Meanwhile the two states were bickering over jurisdiction. Tennessee alleged its territory had been invaded by the Kentucky posse. Kentucky authorities claimed to have maps that definitively showed the entire incident happened in their state. Tennessee declined to litigate the matter, and Lee was arrested by Kentucky lawmen in June of 1903 for complicity in the killing of Charles Cecil and John Doyle. He was also indicted for complicity in the murder of Charlie Pridemore. Lee pointed out that he had been in Jacksboro, Tennessee, at the time of the Quarterhouse Battle. Public opinion in Middlesboro had shifted to the point that many felt he was being unduly prosecuted. The case against him was filed away in April of 1904, and in September of that year he opened a new saloon, this time in Middlesboro. Named "The Stag," it was located on the south side of Cumberland Avenue between 19th and 20th.

Lee Turner lived on until the late thirties, but he had increasing mental problems. Some said it was because he brooded too much on the past. Toward the end of his life he was approached by someone from Hollywood about doing a movie centered on the Quarterhouse Battle. According to his family, his mind "was too cocky" by then for any such effort. He died in a mental institution, leaving behind a wife and one child.

Footnote Twenty-Three

The Queen of the Rhine

Long-time residents still refer to a particular area of town in the northeast quadrant as "over the Rhine" or simply "the Rhine." They do so with a certain tone that suggests something a little disreputable, a little risqué, even though an elementary school and the town's softball field are located there and the principal street in the area, 15th, hosts rather mundane businesses: a print shop, a car wash, a small engine repair shop, and the like. Even the Super Kroger and the very modern and thoroughly commonplace Middlesboro Mall could be said to be "over the Rhine."

The term was in general use by late 1890. It is widely supposed today that the reference to the Rhine derives from the area being generally, though not exclusively, east of Yellow Creek and north of Little Yellow Creek. For earlier residents, however, there was a different reason to dub the area "the Rhine." There was a small brewery on the southern bank of Little Yellow Creek just north of where the football stadium is now located,[1] and the smell (some would say the fragrance) of fermenting hops permeated the air. The district was on the opposite side of the railroad tracks from the finer homes and businesses and was designed as a working-class neighborhood with many small rental houses. The laborers returning home with their lunch pails and the beery smell that greeted them reminded some of a similar German settlement in Cincinnati that was referred to as "over the Rhine." Thus the name.

Even in the earliest days there were saloons over the Rhine, but that was not unusual in any of the residential areas. In fact, the number of drinking establishments per capita in early Middlesborough was remarkable. When the population reached 4,000, there were more than forty bars, saloons, and "blind tigers" at which one's thirst could be slaked. Conditions were such as to encourage the indulgence. One early pioneer recalled:

> My tentmate...regularly imbibed something like a pint of whiskey before breakfast. On frozen nights—with snow aground and the wind churlishly beating the flaps of the tent, humming through its cordage and sieving up between the cracks in the plank floor—we slept under four or five covers that were as thick as horse-blankets....In such weather his "nightcap" became a busby—a tall one and straight. He would wake about daybreak, lean out from his cot, light the oil heater, and then reach under the cot for the "inner heater"—the quart bottle of Bourbon which he invariably placed there upon going to bed. There was a tart pop as he pulled the cork, and a familiar gurgle as the fiery liquid surged to the neck of the vessel. The process was repeated at intervals until at length he got up and drew on his boots. He was now primed for breakfast.[2]

The saloons on Cumberland Avenue tended to be rather elegant, while the ones on 19th and in the area of the Rhine catered more to a working-class clientele. Many of the workmen were single or had left their families behind. There was a natural tendency to carousing and rowdiness and a ready market for bawdy houses, for which the area became notorious. The delicate references in the newspapers to "soiled doves" soon became more pointed as conditions deteriorated.

On March 29, 1891, the *Middlesborough Daily News* editorialized:

> In the area known as Over the Rhine there exists a perfect hotbed of crime. Dives of the lowest order are to be found there where the most abandoned characters gather every night and indulge in scenes that are a disgrace to civilization. Women of the lowest stripe dance the hours away with men of damnable character, and every night or two we hear of these affairs ending in drunken boils [*sic*] in which someone is injured. It is as much as a citizen's life is worth to be found in one of these localities after dark, and those who, through circumstances, are obligated to live in the neighborhood are continually regaled with the most obscene language, curses and shrieks.

The paper could not, however, refrain from tweaking the police over their efforts to arrest certain residents of the Rhine: "Female denizens of Over the Rhine seem to think the police are 'good enough to eat.' Two of

The Chadwell Saloon on Lothbury Avenue, 1915. Courtesy of the Bell County Historical Society.

the boys have been badly bitten the past few days by female malefactors whom they were endeavoring to arrest, and the chief has posted a notice that the police department is not running a free lunch counter."

Things finally got to the point that the City Council passed a law that would make it illegal for any woman to be in any drinking establishment. Should a woman be in a saloon or bar for whatever reason, the presumption would be that the proprietor was running a bawdy house. There is, however, no indication that the law was ever enforced. There was also an effort to deny liquor licenses to any business east of the railroad tracks. This also failed.

One of the best known of the Rhine's early saloons was the Barrel House on Ashbury east of 17th Street. Originally owned by Harrison Ausmus, it was a relatively large two-story structure with the saloon in the front and a bowling alley in the rear. There was a gallery overhanging the main saloon which was on occasion used for political speeches. Upstairs was a pool and billiard room and also rooms for more private activities. The Barrel House was integrated, being regularly frequented by both black and white, as were many of the saloons in the Rhine area.

In 1899 the Barrel House was destroyed by fire. Its liquor license was transferred to a new saloon called the Keg House, which was built on an adjoining lot (just west of the present East End School). This was also two-story, though somewhat smaller than its predecessor. There was a saloon downstairs with private rooms above. The proprietors were J.L. Russell and John R. Ball.

One of the most colorful denizens of the Rhine was Alice Lamb, who was sometimes dubbed "the Queen of the Rhine." She was a local girl who came from one of the mountain families and had moved to Middlesborough to enjoy city life. Some called her "high-spirited" and others "a character." When the Overbeck New South Brewery launched their Pinnacle Beer, they turned to Alice to grace their label. She was depicted in a flowing toga-style garment, perched on the top of Chimney Rock (near the Pinnacle) with her arm outstretched, a bottle in her upraised hand—the picture of pure, unspoiled youth symbolizing the clear, pure beer that New South proclaimed.

Life, however, can be cruel. In 1894 Alice Lamb stood before the Criminal Court in Middlesboro accused of "disorderly conduct," which was usually a euphemism for prostitution. It could, of course, have meant just that she was drinking, dancing, and being disorderly, as an unusually high-spirited girl might do when seduced by the excitement of the Rhine. She was back in court in January of 1895, but the charges were dismissed. In July of 1895 she was found guilty of adultery (again, a term often used to indicate prostitution, especially as she was not married) and fined $25 and court costs. Alice was called to testify before the Grand Jury in October of 1896 in a case involving fornication, and the next month she was again charged with disorderly conduct.[3]

Local tradition has it that Alice continued along the path of a fallen woman, but she apparently managed thereafter to stay out of court.[4] There were rumors that she had a connection with a prominent man who could provide protection. She did have rooms in the Ashbury Hotel, which was not the best hotel in town but was still a reasonably nice hostelry at the time.[5]

In the spring of 1903 the following paragraph appeared in a newspaper article discussing the fate of a twelve-year-old girl charged with disorderly conduct whom the judge was considering sending to reform school: "Betsy Lamb was sent to reform school several years ago when she was 14 and now has a good position as a stenographer in Cincinnati having been thoroughly reformed. Betsy Lamb is the sister of Alice Lamb, a well known local character." Her sister was fortunate to have had this intervention, as life was about to catch up with Alice.

It was around 8:00 p.m. on a Thursday evening in October of 1903. There was the usual weekday crowd drinking at the Keg House, nothing out of the ordinary. Gradually the men became aware that something was dripping from the ceiling onto the bar, something dark and sticky. To their horror, they realized it was blood. The men rushed upstairs to find Alice Lamb lying in a pool of her own blood, her head almost completely severed from her body.

Almost immediately two men, Joe Brimm and Will Nelms, were arrested. Another man, identified only as Mottert, escaped. There was no explanation of a possible motive or why suspicion had fallen on these men. In January of 1904 the newspaper noted that John Ball, the proprietor of the Keg House, and his brother Frank had just arrived from North Carolina with Charles Nelms in custody. He too was charged with the murder. No notice of a trial nor any further discussion of the murder appeared in the papers. According to some, there was a man—no one recalled his name—who was tried and given eight years in prison for the crime.[6]

Another spin was put on the story by Arthur Rhorer, who was a college student at the time of the Lamb murder. His father was a lawyer who served at various times as city prosecutor and police court judge. The younger Mr. Rhorer, himself a lawyer, was well known as a raconteur in his later years. In speaking of the Keg House, he stated, "This saloon and brothel gained national notoriety when beauteous Alice Lamb was slain and no one was ever brought to trial for the murder. Rumor after rumor spread the act was that of a most prominent citizen jealous of his girl friend."[7]

There is a simple note in the records of Glenwood (now Lynch) Cemetery that Alice Lamb was buried on October 23, 1903, in grave 3 of lot 1 in block HH. No headstone marks her grave.

Over the years people continued to talk of the beheading of Alice Lamb as a gruesome example of how dangerous and "mean" was the Rhine. But at the time there was no great outcry in the city over Alice's murder. Though unusually brutal, it was but one of many acts of lawlessness that the city was trying to control.

Sporadic campaigns to "clean up the Rhine" were seldom successful for long, even though, as had always been true, large areas of the Rhine were occupied by law-abiding citizens and in 1908 a public school was built almost directly across from where the old Barrel House had once stood. In 1916 the city tried to clean up what was then referred to as "the red light district" by forcing property owners renting to "people of ill repute" to evict these tenants. For a few months this seemed effective, but soon everything was back to normal. Another doomed approach was tried in 1921 when the authorities rounded up some of the "disorderly women" and put them on the train to Claiborne County (just across the Gap in Tennessee) where, according to the newspaper, "they all will engage in gardening and poultry raising for the Middlesboro market." Despite all efforts, nothing worked for long, and older residents still talk about Nell Carroll's and other bawdy houses and "dives" that populated the Rhine of their youth.

Things began to change when the town went dry in the fifties, although several well known bootleggers continued to operate in the Rhine. Then came urban renewal, flood abatement projects, and the highway route change that converted 12th Street into Highway 25E, which attracted many legitimate businesses. But for many, the area will always be the Rhine and the story of Alice Lamb one of the city's enduring legends.

FOOTNOTE TWENTY-FOUR

That Peculiar Scottish Game

The founder of Middlesborough was an avid sportsman. In his grand plan for his city in the wilderness, he took thought to the importance of sports in the life of any proper Englishman and arranged that his metropolis would from its start have playing fields.

The area so designated was west of 25th Street and north of Cumberland Avenue. Though not identified as such on old maps, residents called it "The Commons." There Alexander Arthur had constructed a racetrack with chutes that allowed mile-long races, both for horses and for bicycles. A polo field was located in the middle of the track, and there were grandstands. He hired James Key as director of sports and entertainment. Key maintained a stable of hunters and a kennel of hounds, and arranged foxhunts for the Englishmen so they could "ride to the hounds" as they had done back home.

The Americans were partial to the game of baseball, and they organized a team in early 1891, issuing a challenge to "any team in the vicinity which wishes to give the Middlesborough club a trial." Many of the younger businessmen signed up, and they played teams from Knoxville, Barbourville, and surrounding areas. In 1908 the Middlesboro team had a particularly successful season and were named "champions of the mountains." They were even matched with the professional Louisville Colonels that year; unfortunately, they lost. In 1912 Middlesboro took over the franchise of Asheville, North Carolina, in the Appalachian League, but the league lasted only through 1914. Amateur teams composed of employees of various businesses in town and from the mines also did battle. There was lively competition, and it was not unusual for all the businesses in town to close for a game. The Middlesboro Boosters represented the city during the twenties,

The Middlesboro Junior Baseball Team, ca. 1902. In the front row, far left, is Doyle Colson, and at far right is Ed Ball. Courtesy of the Bell County Historical Society.

and in the forties the town had a semiprofessional team, the Lions. This was followed in 1949 by the Middlesboro Athletics, a semiprofessional team that was part of the Mountain League, with connections to the Cincinnati Reds. Just as Middlesboro climbed to the top of that league, it folded—a victim, according to a 1954 editorial, "of the major's farm system and TV."

From the twenties through the forties Middlesboro had a semiprofessional black baseball team, the Blue Sox. In its early years the team made month-long road trips into Alabama, West Virginia, Virginia, and Tennessee and played teams from many of the larger cities such as Birmingham, Charleston, Richmond, and Chattanooga. When the Great Depression hit, they stayed closer to home, no more than a day's journey, as most had other jobs. The team, sporting uniforms of gray and white pinstripes with blue socks, played for a cut of the gate receipts, with the winning team getting 60 percent and the losers 40 percent. According to the players, they always drew a good crowd, both black and white.[1]

Football got a later start in Middlesboro. The first recorded game was in 1893, with the Davis brothers as coaches. Owen Davis was a graduate of Yale and Bert of Harvard, and they were able to introduce locals to the finer points of the game. For two years the Middlesboro teams played those from surrounding areas. Then the Davis family, which had suffered reverses in the "bust," left town, interest waned, and football was played only sporadically until 1921, when the local high school fielded its first regular team. Since then, high school football has been an important part of Middlesboro life, with the local team winning several state championships.

Early residents enjoyed a number of other sports. Bowling was popular early on, with most of the early alleys attached to saloons. Separate bowling alleys appeared around 1900, and it became fashionable for the ladies to join in bowling parties. Fern Lake, originally named Lake Thirimere, provided not only good fishing but also boating. Early residents enjoyed regattas and single-scull races. In 1893 there was even a small steamboat on the lake. Lawn tennis was popular with both English and Americans, as was cycling. There were clubs for devotees of these sports, and regular competitions and excursions.

Two sports, however, were considered uniquely British. One was cricket, which was played exclusively by the foreigners. They had two teams, one from Middlesborough and the other from Harrogate. After the "bust" hit, cricket was no more.

The other, sometimes referred to as "that peculiar Scottish game," was to be more enduring and to give Middlesborough a place in the *Encyclopaedia Britannica,* which states that the city "may be" the home of the second oldest permanent golf course in the United States.

Golf is thought to have originated in Scotland in about the fifteenth century, though somewhat similar games were played as far back as the time of the Roman empire. It was popular in England during the seventeenth and eighteenth centuries but was only played sporadically in the new country until the mid-nineteenth century. The Foxburg Golf Club in Pennsylvania, established in 1887, is considered to be the first permanent course in the United States.

Golf was played in Middlesborough as early as 1889. A witness to the early emergence of the game was Livingston Satterlee, an attorney who came to Middlesboro in 1889 on a short fact-finding mission for some prominent would-be investors, including the famous English actress Lillie Langtry. He later recalled, "I found the little city teeming with excitement....[It] was full of remittance men from England, representing good families, some of them sons of lords and ladies. Many of these men brought with them their 'plus fours,' golf and riding togs and tennis clothes. Golf was already started when I was there, and there were only two or three places in the United Stated where golf had been introduced."[2]

Arthur Rhorer, one of the pioneer residents of Middlesborough, claimed that he caddied (or shagged, as it was then called) in the spring of 1890, and according to him the golfers were playing on a field that was already laid out, so he felt they had to have been playing on the same links in

1889.[3] The course was on part of the Commons, with the first tee at what is now 25th and Worchester. The first green was on Chichester, a little west of 25th. The remainder of the course, to the best of his memory, was just as it is today, though much rougher. The holes were baking powder cans and the greens were sand, but strict rules of golfing were followed. Most of the first players were English or Scottish, but as their numbers dwindled, more Americans took up the game.

Paul L. McKenrick was one of those Americans who enjoyed the new game of golf. He was a "boomer" who arrived in 1890 and stayed only a few years, but during that time he learned to play. He remembered that golf "was introduced when it was a decided novelty in America, and I believe 'our' course was the second oldest in the United States."[4]

Play on the course must have been fairly unorganized until July of 1894 when a group of golfers and would-be players met at the home of C.M. Woodbury to organize the Kentucky Golf Club. They elected P N. Cunningham president, H.W. Twiss vice-president, and Arthur Taylor secretary-treasurer. Committees were appointed for bylaws, grounds, and membership, and "all the usual business of organization was successfully and harmoniously transacted." It was noted at that time that there were a number of old and enthusiastic golfers who would be willing to teach and encourage the beginners.

In September of 1894 the newspaper described one of those beginners' sessions, with which anyone learning the game can identify:

> Older golfers gave illustrations of the use of "driver," "lofter," "nublick," "cleek," "putter," etc., and the beginners were convinced that it was like falling off a log until they tried it. One would "tee" his ball, draw back and swipe like Hercules. The ball, of course, would disappear from view, because the expectant gaze was directed to the far horizon. It would be discovered, however, calmly reposing status quo. Then came a little experimental playing. Prentice hands and practice hands alike made wonderful scores—several scores in as many hundred strokes. The balls, with good perversity, sought the ditches and high grass; the smoothest course that could be chosen developed "hazards;" balls were lost, clubs were shivered, golf filled the field; the excitement spread, the enthusiasm grew, and if golf doesn't grow in Middlesborough now the "De'll" himself is in it.[5]

The fate of the Kentucky Golf Club as an organization is not known, but golf did continue to be played on the same course, according to Rhorer

Golfers at the Middlesborough Country Club, ca. 1935. Courtesy of the Bell County Historical Society.

and other local golfers of the day.[6] Lots in the old Commons, however, were gradually being sold to private parties, and more houses were going up along 25th Street and on West Cumberland. There would also have been a problem with maintaining a course the golfers did not actually own.

A meeting was called in February of 1921 to again organize a golf club with the view of purchasing property for the course. J.L. Manring, Joe Bosworth, F.P. Scales, and Colonel John Miller headed the movement. At that first meeting, fifty "enthusiastic golfers" signed on, and committees were appointed to draw up bylaws and to choose the site to be purchased. By the end of March 1921 the Middlesborough Country Club, as the group had named itself, had almost a hundred members and had arranged to buy from Sam Weinstein the hundred-acre tract that encompassed most of the site that had apparently been utilized all along as a golf course. That this course had been allowed to deteriorate is evidenced by the fact that they expected it to take a "force of men" sixty days to get the ground ready for golf.

Meanwhile, this ambitious group started planning for a clubhouse and tennis courts. They also offered to give the city a corner of their recently acquired property for a free swimming pool and playground if sufficient money could be raised by subscription to construct them. This did not happen, though the Country Club was able later to construct its own pool.

In 1923 the Middlesborough Country Club celebrated new grass greens, and in 1924 the club began hosting the Tri-State Invitational Tournament. During the Depression of the thirties, the club was forced to reorganize but was able to maintain its course. One change came when Middlesboro built its floodwall. To that point in time the seventh hole was par six; in fact, some claimed it was the only par six hole in the nation. The building of the floodwall shortened the hole enough to convert it to a par five. Numerous famous players graced the greens, including the famed Babe Zaharias, who claimed she believed Middlesboro's boast of being the second oldest course in the nation because of the type and condition of the tees.

Today the players who enjoy the beautiful links of the Middlesborough Country Club, with its avenues of towering oak trees, can thank those intrepid Scotsmen and Englishmen who brought their sticks and balls with them to the wilderness of the Appalachians and laid out their course on the Commons of this foreign city more than a hundred years ago.

Footnote Twenty-Five

Lift up Thine Eyes

There is a morning in mid-winter when the sun rises directly behind the Pinnacle. As darkness fades, the majestic peak is silhouetted against the pearly blush. A few moments longer, pale gold tinges the mountain crest and the hills surrounding the Valley emerge, a rose-hued encircling wall. One cannot but join the psalmist in proclaiming, "I will lift up mine eyes unto the hills, from whence cometh my help. My help cometh from the Lord, which made heaven and earth."

Religion in the Southern Appalachians was historically an individual thing. Until the last century mountaineers were an isolated people for whom organized churches were not always available. They depended on the occasional itinerant preacher and spontaneous camp meetings. It was not unusual for a couple to live together as man and wife for several years and have a number of children before a minister came to the area who could bless their union. The majority of highlanders were illiterate, or close to it, and often could not read the Bibles that had been passed down through the generations. Religious beliefs and practices were based on oral traditions nurtured by separate families or inspired by itinerant charismatic preachers.

The Valley of Yellow Creek did not fit this mold; two churches had already been established in the basin by the middle of the nineteenth century. One of these was Bethlehem Methodist Church, also referred to as the Green Meeting House. A simple log structure built about 1845, it served the community until the arrival of Alexander Arthur and his developers. When the town sprang up complete with multiple churches, including two for the Methodists, the primitive building was abandoned. Over the years, even the nearby graveyard was neglected. In the late thirties a

Green Meeting House. Courtesy of the Bell County Historical Society.

group formed to preserve the few gravestones still remaining, but that effort came to naught. Today a city park called Ford's Woods marks the spot where early settlers worshipped.

The other early church was Yellow Creek Baptist Church, which was organized in 1842 by the Reverend Thomas Marsee and the Reverend William Williams, aided by the Reverend Ebenezer Ingram. The first church building was on the banks of the creek in the general area of the present-day airport. The Reverend Marsee served as the first pastor. Over the years the church moved six times but always remained in the western part of the Valley. It probably escaped extinction during the boom days because it was far removed from the center of town with all its churches. Today Old Yellow Creek Baptist Church occupies a handsome structure on West Winchester Street.

Churches were an important part of Alexander Arthur's grand plan for Middlesborough. Therefore the Town Company donated lots for sanctuaries to any religious group that organized, and often also provided free building materials and the services of a contractor. Already in 1890 the town could boast seven churches representing most of the major denominations, with others in the planning stage.

Most of the English founders of Middlesborough attended St. Mary's Episcopal Church, which was constructed in 1890 from blueprints of its namesake, located in a suburb of Middlesbrough, England. A magnificent stained-glass window was imported from England, and communicants made many generous gifts of furnishings, so that their sanctuary was a true reflection of their heritage. Today from the belfry of St. Mary's the original bell donated by Alexander Arthur still rings the call to worship.

The majority of the early churches survived the "bust" and went on to grow and later to construct larger buildings. One of those was First Baptist Church, which was organized in September of 1889. In 1908, as an outgrowth of a revival, the church sponsored a Bible study group. From seven men gathered under the tutelage of their first teacher, W.H. Gibson, the Baracas Men's Bible Class grew rapidly. There was a real growth spurt after T. Russ Hill, who is widely remembered as a dynamic, charismatic speaker, took over leadership of the class. Attendance reached more than nine hundred, which garnered it statewide recognition and led to a contest in the spring of 1925 with Central City, Kentucky, to set a record for the highest one-day attendance.

Many of the principal businessmen of the city were members of the Baracas Class, and they brought all of their organizational skills to the task. They made arrangements with the railroad to run a special train from Lynch, Kentucky, with stops all along the way at various coal camps and towns to pick up men from other churches. A volunteer crew, made up of members of the Baracas Class, ran the train at no cost to the railroad. All along the way careful plans had been made so that at each stop the men marched to the depot, where bands greeted them as they were ushered aboard lavishly decorated cars. Over a thousand men traveled this way, and the papers boasted that it was "the greatest special train carrying men only that any religious body ever sponsored so far as known records can be found." Other trains brought people from as far away as Knoxville, and the roads were clogged with those coming in from surrounding rural areas. The governor of Kentucky joined them.

Organizers expected a crowd of 5,000 and set about providing food for the multitude. J.F. Schneider, a local meat packer, donated five beeves and, with other members of the class, spent the night before the event barbecuing them. The men also prepared 5,000 ham sandwiches, three barrels of dill pickles, and gallons of lemonade.

As the morning of June 14, 1925, dawned, it became evident that the men had underestimated the crowd. Everyone was to meet at the railroad depot and march together to Ford's Woods, where the class would be held outdoors. It was a grand parade. First came Middlesboro's thirty-two-piece band playing "Onward, Christian Soldiers," followed by Governor William Fields and Congressman J.M. Robinson. In close formation behind them the men marched four abreast. They paraded south on 18th Street to Cumberland Avenue, down Cumberland to 24th, and then on 24th to Lynwood, and on to Ford's Woods. So large was the group that when the head of the parade was turning onto 24th, the end was still forming at the depot, meaning the column was more than a mile long. The Lynch Band marched in the middle of the parade to provide music for those behind.

Class was begun with a prayer offered by the minister of the Christian Church. Congressman Robinson spoke briefly before Governor Fields took over as the guest teacher. He taught a lesson on Barnabas, that early Christian missionary who accompanied St. Paul on his first journey. The regular teacher, T. Russ Hill, then dismissed the group with a prayer.

There was an immediate rush for the food. The mountains of barbecued beef and ham sandwiches vanished, leaving some with the fervent wish that the miracle of the loaves and fishes could be replayed. And in a way it was. At least a third of the guests did not make it to the dining tents before the food was all gone. But the townspeople immediately rose to the challenge, raided their own pantries, and saw to it that no one went hungry.

The official count for men attending class that day was 9,045. When women and children were included, the estimate was 12,000 or more. The paper boasted that no Sunday School "ever equaled that record in the South, and if the size of our city is taken into account, that record stands for the entire nation." And well into the forties the Baracas Class continued to be the largest men's Bible class in Kentucky.

As impressive as that multitude was, it cannot equal the imprint made by a man who worked almost entirely alone. Harrison H. Mayes was a coal miner—a short, slight man who worked long hours at a physically demanding job. To look at him was not to immediately see greatness. And in fact he did not aspire to greatness, only to spreading the message of Christianity. But his vision encompassed not just everyone in the country but the entire world, even outer space.

Harrison was reared in the coal camp of Fork Ridge, up Mingo Hollow. His father was a coal miner, and the family was not particularly pious.[1] But from an early age Harrison talked of being a missionary. His lack of an education and his family responsibilities prevented him from pursuing this dream in the usual manner, so he found other means. He taught Sunday School lessons at several churches and visited in the homes around his hollow, sharing Bible readings with the families. He tried his hand at gospel music, but though he could play several instruments well, his voice left something to be desired. He also began painting religious messages in red paint on the large boulders that were so plentiful in the area. But it was a serious mine accident in the 1920s that brought forth his true mission.

Harrison was working underground when a maverick coal car caught him against a wall, crushing him from the chest to the hips. His coworkers said he was almost mashed flat, and that his eyes appeared to "pop from the sockets." He was immediately transported to the hospital, but the doctors gave his family no hope for his survival. Although there were no broken bones, the trauma had been so severe and widespread that it was not thought he would last the night.

Harrison later told his son that he "went away and came back" that night. During that long night when he lingered near death, he promised God that if he were spared he would redouble his missionary efforts and

Harrison H. Mayes. Courtesy of Catherine Mayes.

would paint larger and more numerous signs. The next morning, the doctors were astonished to find their patient sitting up in bed and ready to eat. In only a few days, he seemed totally recovered. Harrison immediately set about fulfilling his pledge.

He originally had cardboard signs printed, but they were not sufficiently durable. Therefore he started making wooden crosses with messages such as "Jesus is Coming" and "Prepare to Meet God" painted on both sides. After he had a stack made he would find someone with a truck to drive him down some road, and he would stop about every ten miles and erect a sign. Gradually he expanded, so that within a few years his trips were taking him into distant states and eventually into almost every state of the union. He never asked anyone's permission before erecting a sign, and he was always receiving letters from state highway departments objecting to his cavalier methods. But far from being discouraged, he began to experiment with other vehicles for his messages.

At his home in Fork Ridge, he laid out a huge sign of whitewashed creek rock in his yard. Each letter was thirty-six feet high and ten feet wide. The message, which was aimed at planes flying overhead, proclaimed, "V. in God." The "V" stood for victory. His practical wife planted the family vegetable garden in amongst the letters.

Lillie, who had been just fourteen when she married Harrison, had to be practical, as they eventually had four children, and Harrison was financing his mission almost entirely from his own pocket. Occasionally his fellow miners would take up a collection or donate their pay for loading a car full of coal (miners were being paid at the time on a piece-work basis per coal car loaded) to help him buy supplies, but it took a good deal to build and paint the three to four hundred signs he made a year. And since he usually did not own a vehicle, he had to find someone to take him on his sign planting trips.

Harrison also began painting on oilcloth. These signs could be rolled into a tube and mailed all over the world. Once unfurled, they were easy to attach to a wall, tree, or whatever. Soon he was having nearby universities translate his messages into ten foreign languages, which he would then copy onto oilcloth and send to the appropriate foreign country. He always tried to include a brand new one-dollar bill for the person who was erecting the sign.

In the late thirties he started sending his messages in bottles. He would walk along 19th Street in Middlesboro and pick up discarded half-pint whiskey bottles. Harrison hated liquor as a sin, and one that had had a profound effect on his own family. Harrison's father and brother were both "bad to drink," and his brother had been killed in Chicago when he was accidentally run over by a truck while sleeping off a drunk in an empty box.

Harrison would put messages in the bottles and then drop them in rivers, especially ones leading to the ocean. Soon he was putting foreign language messages in the bottles and mailing them to missionaries, asking that they drop them in the Nile, the Amazon, and so forth.

He also began constructing signs of poured concrete and of corrugated steel, the latter usually salvaged from some wreck or dump. His concrete signs often weighed 1,500 pounds apiece and were a challenge to transport and erect. But they were certainly durable. In all, he tried about thirty different models and materials in his quest to proclaim his message to everyone in the world.

In 1948 he produced a particularly dramatic symbol for Middlesboro, a 140-foot lighted cross on a hill at the east end of Cumberland Avenue. At the time, the Dixie Highway, which was one of the major routes south, came down the avenue, so the cross inspired travelers as well as locals. The town literally stood at the foot of the cross and continues to do so to this day.

Harrison moved his family to Middlesboro in 1946. He built his house himself, choosing a lot that was on the beam airplanes followed when they flew into town so they would see the message on his roof, "Get Right with God." Later he changed the message to an even larger one, "Jesus saves." Because of its ministry to pilots and their passengers, he called his house the "Air Castle."[2]

Every part of his house was symbolic of his faith. The house itself was built in the shape of a cross, with four small rooms in front for living and a long workshop attached to the rear. He made the concrete blocks for the house himself, and each was imprinted with a small cross. The walk leading to the house was in the shape of an anchor, and a sign on the gate advised, "Anchor your heart to the cross." Twelve windows in the front of the house represented the disciples, while the ten in the back stood for the Ten Commandments. There were eight outside doors, one for each of the eight people saved in Noah's Ark. No doorknobs were visible. Where a knob would be expected was a wooden heart with the instruction "Notice—Open to God your heart and say." When the hinged heart was opened, there were the words "Jesus save me" and the doorknob. Even the fence around the house was symbolic. Harrison put up seven concrete posts to stand for the continents, a wooden one for the earth, and eight metal ones for the other planets. Seven strands of barbed wire in the fence represented the seven times

Jesus spoke from the cross, while the barbed wire itself recalled the crown of thorns. In the front yard were two huge concrete crosses, one of which read, "Thanks to God forever for landing me safely through the cross of Jesus Christ." The other proclaimed, "Lost forever because I forsakened the cross of Jesus Christ."

In the workshop behind the small living area, Harrison continued to turn out his crosses. When the mines closed in the mid-fifties he found that the merchants in town were willing to pay him well to paint signs for their businesses. But whatever he earned, after providing for his family, went into his mission. He eventually had crosses throughout the United States and in most foreign countries. He signed many of these "P.A.E.," which he said stood for his sacred name that was to be revealed only after his death.

Except for a very brief time, Harrison did not own a car, as he did not want to expend the necessary funds; he rode around town on a bicycle. It was a familiar sight to see him pedaling along, his bike basket filled with oilcloth scrolls which he handed out to anyone who would agree to pay the postage to mail the messages overseas.

He did not belong to any particular church or denomination. He attended various churches, often a different one each Sunday, and would describe himself as a Methodist-Catholic-Baptist-Presbyterian. Though he may have received some individual donations, he was never supported by any church or missionary society or other group.

Harrison had named each of his children for the continents (though his wife gave them more common names by which they were usually called) to symbolize his mission to the world. When his grandchildren began to come along, he called them by the names of the planets, thereby showing the scope of his vision. In 1948 he also started constructing wooden forms so he could pour in place even more solid concrete crosses, which were to be erected in the 1990s. He designated some for places on earth, but also instructed that others be placed on Venus, Mars, and Jupiter. This was, of course, years before space flight became a reality. For many years, these rows of crosses stood in battalions behind his home. He even made a small titanium cross that he sent to NASA in the hope that it would be included on one of the first space flights.

In the mid-seventies Harrison suffered a stroke and thereafter was unable to continue the strenuous work of building large crosses. But he continued, with the help of his wife, to fill his bottles with messages and to paint his oilcloth signs. And he never stopped talking about future projects, while he carefully followed the news of space exploration.

When Harrison died in 1986 at the age of eighty-eight, his sacred name was finally revealed: Planetary Aviation Evangelist.

Today at Ford's Woods, the site of the Green Meeting House and the huge Baracas Men's Bible Class meeting, a concrete bench in the shape of a cross welcomes those who pause to rest and enjoy the view of the Pinnacle and the Valley, lying protected within its surrounding mountains as if cradled in the palm of the hand of God.[3] The bench is inscribed with the signature "P.A.E."

Footnote Twenty-Six

The Ball-Colson Feud

One of the enduring legends of the Yellow Creek Valley is that of the Ball-Colson Feud. Older residents tell of a time when either a Ball or a Colson was shot every weekend and the streets ran with blood from multiple gory deaths. But the feud was never as deadly or as long lived as it is remembered.

The Ball-Colson Feud was primarily waged between two sets of brothers—Ira, Floyd, and Alva Ball and Doyle, Clay, and George Colson—though various cousins and friends, and even innocent bystanders, were sucked into the fray.

The Balls and Colsons were actually kinsmen. John and Polly Ball were the great-great-grandparents of both sets of brothers. In the early days their families were close allies and business associates. They had marched shoulder to shoulder on the Quarterhouse. George Colson was married to a first cousin of the Balls. An uncle of the Colsons, W.G., often served as lawyer and/or bondsman for the Balls' father and uncles. The boys grew up within half a mile of each other and, though the Balls were somewhat younger, were friends in their youth and early manhood.

As with most feuds, the underlying cause is difficult to nail down. The most commonly heard explanation is that it started with a quarrel over a poker game. Others say that the cousins, in the way of high-spirited friends, started playing practical jokes on each other and that things got out of hand when one of them cut off the mane and tail of another's horse. It is also said that Ira had harbored some resentment over the fact that George, five years older, had "slapped him around" as a child. Probably more than one single thing contributed to the ill feelings that developed between the two sets of brothers. Perhaps underlying all was a struggle for dominance, the universal conflict seen between the family or group that has had the power and/or money and the new group struggling to make it to the top of the heap.

In order to understand the feud, we must first get to know the protagonists.

The Balls

Ira, Floyd, and Alva were the sons of Frank Ball (see Footnote Thirteen). It could not have been easy growing up in a town that, at least in their formative years, reviled their father as a murderer. What would it have been like for the eleven-year-old Ira when the public schools were dismissed so all the school children could march in the funeral procession of the man his father had killed? Or to be the seven-year-old Floyd and hear the excited reports from the posse setting off to hunt down his father; or Alva, who was only two when his father entered prison and must have had to endure the taunts of his playmates over the years. To add to the family's difficulties, money was tight.

Predictably, Ira was soon in trouble. In June of 1909 the fifteen year old became embroiled in a quarrel over a game of pool at Nick Stone's Saloon on 19th. He pulled a knife and slashed his opponent across the side and back. The wounds were so serious that at first they were thought to be fatal, but the injured man survived, and Ira was sent to the House of Reform in Lexington. Sentenced to the reformatory at the same time was his cousin, fifteen-year-old Tom Manning, who would also later be involved in the feud.

Floyd Ball, 1917.
Courtesy of Edna Yeley.

Left, Ira Ball, ca. 1920. *Right*, Alvey Ball. Courtesy of W.W. Hoskins.

Ira was soon back in Middlesboro and at his old haunts. By 1916 he had opened Ira's Place on Lothbury Avenue in the building formerly occupied by Herndon's Saloon. Bell County had by then voted itself dry, and many of the old saloons had become soft-drink stands, though the drinks served were often not so soft. In August of 1916 the city revoked the licenses of a number of soft-drink stands, including that of Ira (also one belonging to his cousin Tyler Ball and one owned by a close friend, Wallace Gastineau) for substituting hard liquor for soft drinks. The next year his brother Floyd was in court, charged with violation of prohibition laws. Then in November of 1917 the *Pinnacle News* reported, under the headline "Like Olden Times," the fact that "two shooting affairs took place in the region back of the Huber and Phoenix Hotels. The first one was the shooting by Ira Ball of Will Evans." The cause of this shooting was not then known, but in March of 1919 Ira was acquitted of murder.

By 1920 Ira had, according to census records, already been married once and divorced. He was doing well financially and began building a row of brick houses on Cumberland Avenue near 15th Street for his extended family. He was free-handed with his money in other ways also. One younger cousin recalled that when Ira came to visit he would usually give each child a fifty cent piece—quite a handsome sum of cash for a youngster at that time.

While Ira was doing well in 1920, the town was not. Bootlegging and other crimes were on the increase. The Pineville newspaper reported in November of 1920 that the citizens of Middlesboro, "outraged at half a dozen murders in the past six months," had formed a Law and Order League with E.P. Nicholson as president and Dr. J. Archer Gray as vice-president. Three hundred people attended the first meeting of the organization. Speakers pointed out that the streets of Middlesboro had become dangerous and chastised the good citizens of the town for going bond for criminals.

In December of 1920 Tom Manning allegedly shot a certain Dan Marlow; Floyd and Ira were also involved. Manning escaped to Cumberland Gap, Tennessee, but was soon captured and lodged in the city jail. On December 14 Floyd was in police court charged with shooting inside the city, and Ira was placed under bond for malicious wounding. Soon thereafter, E.P. Nicholson received an anonymous letter warning:

> Dear Sir: I have been informed of your taking a great interest in the case of Dan Marlow against Ira Ball, and we don't want to hear any more of your talk, because we are running this town ourselves, and we will do what we think is according to the law....All we ask you to do is to nothing against us.[1]

Other prominent citizens received similar communications. The newspaper opined that the letters proved Middlesboro had two sets of officials, one elected and the other appointed by the criminal class.

The next day Ira's father, Frank Ball, offered a reward of $100 for the name of the person writing the letters, which he considered "an underhanded attack" on his son. Ira, however, was his own worst enemy. The next month he was in court charged with two counts of assault. According to the statement of an eyewitness, on a Saturday night in late February Ira beat and then shot Anna Parker Kirby, a widow with whom he had reportedly been living for three years. He then assaulted Harry Goodfriend as he was walking down Cumberland Avenue, beating him severely about the head with a revolver. No motive was given, but a witness heard Ira shout, "What's that you're trying to pull off," as he started beating Goodfriend. Both of Ira's victims were hospitalized but neither was fatally injured.

Rumors swirled about town that the police had made no effort to arrest Ira, even though the assaults occurred near the police station and the incidents were immediately reported to the officers. So incensed was Dr. Gray, minister of the First Presbyterian Church, that he devoted his entire Sunday night sermon to a condemnation of Ira Ball, whom he described as "one of the cheapest sort of 'bad men'...a common thug, bootlegger and gunman," and to a scathing rebuke of the city police department.

On Monday morning, having turned himself in to the police, Ira appeared in Police Court. He was ordered to post two bonds of $2,500 each and to go before the Circuit Court in Pineville. Instead, he simply walked out of the courtroom unmolested and was again at large. The newspapers reported that a public meeting had been called and that "public indignation is at a high pitch." Ira finally surrendered to the police two days later. Meanwhile two longtime policemen, W.B. White and George Fisher, had resigned because, they said, of the criticism in the press and from the pulpit. (Both were soon reinstated and were to continue their close friendship with the Balls for many years.)

Things apparently calmed down, and the papers had nothing more to report about the incident or its consequences. After the first fatality of the feud in November of 1921, the *Three States* stated that Ira had been in no trouble since he "made his famous confession to Dr. Gray and the Grand Jury scandal that followed," and that Dr. Gray believed he had reformed despite "constant rumors" to the contrary.

During the remainder of 1921, the Balls ran a restaurant near the railroad station and also had a grocery nearby. Ira was by this time twenty-seven, Floyd twenty-two, and Alva seventeen. Ira had taken a second wife, Lillian Beatrice Morgan, the day after his altercation with Parker and Goodfriend, and in April of 1921 Alva married Gladys Calloway. Floyd was already wed to Allie Herndon. They, along with their parents, were all living within a block of the corner of 15th and Cumberland.

The Colsons

Doyle, Clay, and George were the grandsons of John Colson Sr., the Patriarch of the Yellow Creek Valley. Their father was John Calvin Jr., who had been murdered in 1897 (see Footnote Seven). J.C. left a widow, the former Susan Cottrell[2] and nine children. At the time of their father's death, Clay was eleven, George nine, and Doyle five years old. Although the Colson family was relatively well-to-do, their life could not have been easy. In an addendum to her will, Susan was to lament, "My life has been very sad. I have been opposed and treated wrong, had to work sick, been faulted when I did the best I could. I forgive all. Carry no malice between any of you.

Life is too short for strife. Prepare for the great future. Your mother."[3] Susan died in 1915.

John and Susan had five daughters, two of whom succumbed to scarlet fever in 1900. Louise, who was ten, died at 4:30 p.m., and Cordie, age three, passed away at 6:00 p.m. on the same day. Their eldest daughter, Laura, married Charles Herd, a prominent lawyer, politician, and the editor of the *Pinnacle News*. Their second daughter, Mary Katherine, had to be institutionalized for mental problems and died at a young age. Another daughter, Lucy, married Dr. J.P. Brashear, a Middlesboro dentist who was active in civic affairs.

There were four boys in the family, none of whom took their mother's advice to avoid strife. She must have had premonitions of the problems her sons would have, as she directed in her will: "Treat Dave right and give him a chance in life. I do not want George, Doyle and Dave throwed out of a home. They can go back up to my home place and live and make a living if they will work."

David (John David), born in 1880, was the oldest of the brothers. He was somewhat of a recluse, living on the outskirts of Middlesboro and devoting most of his time to raising chickens. In May of 1914 he killed a Mrs. Sapp, who lived not far from him on Gum Springs Road, in a fit of temper over a property dispute. He escaped after the shooting despite a posse spending several days and nights combing the surrounding mountains searching for him. Four and a half years later he was arrested in San Antonio, Texas, and returned to Bell County. He was lodged in the Middlesboro jail for better than six months. When the case was first set for trial, it was found that several of the prosecution witnesses had disappeared, and the trial had to be delayed. Then on July 30, 1919, just as the jailer had unlocked Colson's cell, the fire alarm sounded. The jailer ran to check on the fire, forgetting in his haste to relock the cell door, and Colson made his escape. It proved to be a false alarm, and the *Pineville Sun* reported that it was "believed by many that a preconcerted plan had been formulated for the escape of Colson." To the best of anyone's knowledge, David never returned to Middlesboro. His nephew Calvin stated that he later tried to trace him and found that his uncle had apparently fled to Florida, where he again ran into trouble. He shot a man, and spent time in a Florida jail. When he got out he moved to Oregon. The family Bible records his date of death as 1965.[4]

James Clay was the next oldest son. When he was just fourteen Clay opened a newsstand in the lobby of the Middlesboro Post Office. In 1901 he went to Washington, D.C., with his sister Laura, whose husband was working for a congressman. He worked at the Census Department and then in 1902 took a job as an attaché to the U.S. Senate. Unfortunately Clay returned to Middlesboro the next year and was soon in trouble. One of the employees of the New South Brewery and Ice Company, which was very near his home, was found dead, the top of his skull blown off. In his right hand was a pistol with three chambers empty. The *Record* reported, "No one witnessed the killing, but suspicion points strongly to Clay Colson, who was seen on the company premises shortly before the discovery was made carrying a Winchester....The trouble leading up to the killing arose over Zuleger whipping George, a younger brother of Clay, for disturbing a picnic held in the vicinity of the brewery Sunday." Despite the circumstantial evidence, with no witnesses coming forward and the suspect from a prominent and influential family, the matter seems to have gone no further.

Clay served as an Internal Revenue officer in Nashville, Tennessee, from 1909 through 1914. He left the service after being injured in a raid on an illicit distillery. In 1917 he unsuccessfully ran for sheriff of Bell County. In his campaign ads he ran letters of recommendation from his superiors at the Revenue Department. One called him "a fearless officer with good sense" and another stated, "As a secret service man and general officer of the detection of violators of the Federal laws, he made a record that has not been excelled by anyone in my experience." Of course, "revenuers" were not always welcome in the mountains, and Clay was badly beaten. He spent the next few years managing his property, including rentals, and his name occasionally appeared in the social columns as one of the guests at some affair. He was still a bachelor.

The third son was George. In 1910 he married Minnie Cordia Ball, the daughter of C.D. Ball, and the couple set up housekeeping at the old farm that had belonged to George's father. Six children were born to them between 1911 and 1920. George ran a small coal mine and was reputedly also in the beverage business. He was known to enjoy his liquor and to be at least as hot tempered as his older brothers.

Harrison Doyle Colson was born in 1892, making him the youngest of the Colson boys, but still older than Ira Ball by two years. He too benefited from his family's political connections and by 1909 was working in Washington, D.C., for the Immigration Bureau. He was appointed Middlesboro City Clerk in 1913. Like the Balls, he once ran a soft drink stand in not so dry Middlesboro, and in 1916 his was one of the establishments raided for selling hard liquor. In July of 1918 the newspapers reported that Doyle, "who is one of our best known citizens," had been appointed deputy sheriff in the Middlesboro end of Bell County. He worked for the city of Middlesboro in 1920-1921 as a police officer and fire inspector. By then he was married to Lillie Dalton and had three young children, with another on the way. It is generally agreed by those who remember him that Doyle was the most easygoing of the brothers and was well liked by everyone. The fact that he was the first victim of the feud is thought by many to have been a tragic accident.

The other active participants in the feud were Bill and John Hurst, cousins to the Colson boys. Their mother, Eudoxia, was the youngest daughter of John Colson Sr. She was a musician, and her son John inherited her musical talents. "Big John," so called because of his unusual height, played the piano at the local movie theatre. His brother Bill was the more outgoing of the two and was already gaining a reputation as an outstanding pool player. They were, in common with their cousins, friends and companions of the Balls. In fact, when the feud first started, John owed Floyd money. When he immediately repaid his loan, the Balls knew he was taking the side of the Colsons.

By the fall of 1921 the stage was set for the first overt act of the feud. Two things happened that fall that were probably unrelated to the feud, except for the time frame. In September Ira Ball's home was destroyed by fire while he was out of town. The papers opined that the blaze had been set to cover a robbery. Then in early November a man by the name of Lloyd Robbins was shot and killed at Nelle Carroll's place, a house of prostitution in the Rhine area. In his deathbed statement Robbins said he had been shot by Tom Manning. There was no suggestion at the time, nor at any later date, that either of these incidents might be related to the antagonism that was by then simmering between the two sets of brothers. They were quarreling, at least ostensibly, over something that had happened during a poker game.

Bill Hurst left this description of the incident at the poker game:

> Late in the evening it was getting dark. There was a poker game in a house behind the old Ashbury Hotel, that I stood watching and Doyle Colson was standing near Ira Ball. He came behind Doyle Colson and stuck his pistol against Doyle's back and took Doyle's pistol and then started beating Doyle on the head with his pistol. I hollered at Ira and told him to stop. Then I turned my head and saw Floyd Ball with a pistol pointed at the back of my head and he told me to throw up my hands. I said no use. He said throw them up, you might have a pistol.

> Then I said I aint got nothing. Then Ira Ball hit me with his pistol on the head once while Floyd Ball had aimed at me. Then they went to the street around the old hotel and I cut thru back of the building and got ahead of them to a pressing shop where I had some stuff stored. But the shop was closed so I stood back in the front of the shop while the Balls went by and couldn't see me.[5]

The account does not indicate why Ira behaved as he did. Could it have been the suspicion of cheating, or an accusation of cheating, or some other real or imagined wrong?

A somewhat similar version was told by Floyd's cousin:

> Ira, Floyd, Bill Hurst and probably a Chadwell, I'm not sure about the 4th man, were having a friendly game of cards in one of the hotels. Doyle came in and Ira said to Doyle, I understand that you have been looking for me and carrying a gun. This led to an argument and Ira pulled a 38 squeezer and beat Doyle about the head and sending him to the hospital. Bill Hurst started to get in fight and Floyd told Bill to stay out of it. Bill left the way of the back steps and went away.[6]

On November 10, 1921, hostilities came to a head in the alley behind the Piedmont Hotel (also known as the Huber Hotel) on 19th. Ironically, Doyle was already in bed asleep that night when Clay dropped by and talked him into getting up and going out to a bar. What happened next is uncertain. All that is known for sure is that there was gunfire and when the shooting ceased Doyle lay dead and Ira and Clay were both wounded.

Although speculation and rumor ran rampant, no arrests were made. The morning after Doyle was found dead on the street, the county attorney and the coroner decided a finding by the coroner's jury would not be necessary. A grand jury met soon thereafter but adjourned without returning an indictment. The newspaper groused, "The same session of court that indicted 'Peanuts West'...for stealing a pound of butter, failed to charge anyone for causing the death of a man found dead in the street."

The assumption was that Ira had killed Doyle. Some, however, believed the actual shooting was done by a friend of Ira's from Harlan, Hugh Jones, who was on the second floor of the Piedmont Hotel and shot, it is said, from one of the windows when he thought Ira was in trouble.[7] Bill Hurst also left an account of this event, though there is no suggestion that he was actually an eyewitness. He does not so indicate, but presumably this version would have been given to him by Clay:

> Doyle and Clay Colson were in the Huber Hotel and they came out walking toward Cumberland Avenue. Ira Ball slipped out behind them and shot both Doyle and Clay in the back, killing Doyle Colson, and Clay Colson was able to fire one shot that just cut the skin of Ira's head and knocked Ira down.

Perhaps supporting this story is the fact that Doyle's sons related that their dead father's coat was kept hanging in the hall at their Grandfather Dalton's house and that it had bullet holes in the back.[8] It is also true that the bullet holes in the back could have been the result of someone firing from a hotel window that overlooked the quarrel.

The body was laid out at home, as was the custom. George came to the young widow and, as he said his final goodbye, asked for his brother's gun, which she gave him. With the corpse as a witness, George swore, "I'm going to kill that cur Ball with Doyle's own gun."[9]

Both Clay and Ira soon recovered from their wounds and rejoined the feud with even more bitterness. There was shooting back and forth, and one resident, a young girl at the time, can recall thinking that they must be terrible marksmen for there to be so many bullets let loose with no one hit. Unfortunately, on February 2, 1922, the bullets did reach their mark. Ira was shot through the abdomen and ten days later succumbed to the wound. George was shot though the leg. Of course, there were varying accounts of the affair, both at the time and during the later trials.

The shoot-out occurred on Cumberland Avenue at about 15th in the vicinity of the Ball compound. It was evening, and Ira and Lillian were returning by car from a movie at the Manring Theatre. According to the Balls, they were followed by a car containing Clay and George Colson and their cousins, John and Bill Hurst, all of whom were shooting off their guns. Just before they got to Ira's house, George got out of the car, which continued on, and started walking up the opposite side of the street. Ira put his car in the barn and sent Lillian into the house for his gun.

There is no way to determine who fired the opening volley. All accounts agree that George Colson was behind a tree or telephone pole and Ira was beside a tree or the mailbox in front of his house, and that they were shooting back and forth at each other. One who claimed to have been an eyewitness[10] stated that George had fired five times, and Ira thought he was having to reload. When Ira stepped out from behind the mailbox to take better aim, George pulled a second gun and shot him.

The Ball version, as related by the family genealogist and historian, William Hoskins, is that "Geo Colson ran and Ira Ball ran after him. He

Geo. Colson fell over behind a bank and yelled don't shoot any more Ira you have killed me. Ira thinking he had lowered his gun and walked up to where Geo. Colson lay in ambush. That was the awful fatal mistake my cousin Ira made."[11]

In the Colson version there is no carload of cousins firing off their weapons, just George walking home from town. Bill Hurst left this account:

> George Colson lived out in East end of town and walked thru east end of town to go home and had to pass by Ira's house and the shoot-out started as Geo passed Ira's house. They were both behind two small trees in the shoot-out. Ira didn't know Geo had Doyle's pistol and his own and when Geo fired 5 shots which emptied his pistol then Ira came out from his fort and was shot by Doyle's pistol who Ira had killed and was shot thru the stomack [12]

At a hearing in March of 1922, Bud Yoakum testified that he was driving home from town on Cumberland Avenue and was between 17th and 18th Streets when he first heard shots. As he drove by, Colson tried to stop him, but he was afraid of being shot and so drove on, later returning to pick up Colson and take him home. Another witness was Will Venable, who lived across the street from where the shooting took place. He said that he was awakened by the gunfire. When he looked out he could see by the light of the street lamp that Ira was beside the mailbox, George behind a tree, and a third person was shooting from near the Ball house. He assumed it was Alva, as he later saw him with a gun in his hand. He saw Colson try to stop a car, heard him yell, "Boys, help me out. I'm in a fight." The car did not stop, and Colson ran east. Ira ran after him about fifty yards, then grunted and fell. Venable stated that Ira then looked up at Alva, who was just behind him, and said, "Kill him, Alva, he's killed me."

As is often the case, in the face of tragedy there was also comedy. At the time of the shooting the Lions Club was meeting on the third floor of the Gorman Building.[13] L.D. Rouser was being initiated. He had just taken the order and sat down in front of a window when a stray bullet whistled past, grazing his leg. At first he thought it was part of the initiation and "determined to bear it like a man." Then he saw the bullet hole in the window and the one in his trousers and shouted, "I'm shot." The newspaper reported that in the excitement the "most notable feature was the way these Lions scattered." It took a while for them to regroup and get on with the election of officers. Rouser was elected treasurer, but when he

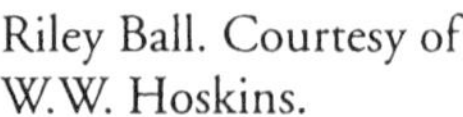

Riley Ball. Courtesy of W.W. Hoskins.

was called on to speak he declined, saying, "No boys, the pep is all shot out of me."

Ira died on February 12. He was buried in the Ball Cemetery, only a few hundred yards from the Colson homeplace and just across the road from the Middlesborough Cemetery, where Doyle had been laid to rest. In another irony, his funeral service was preached by Dr. J. Archer Gray, the Presbyterian minister who had reviled him from the pulpit a year earlier. (Ira's mother, Sallie, attended the Presbyterian Church.) Residents recall that it was one of the biggest funerals ever seen in Middlesboro, with great quantities of flowers everywhere.

In March of 1922 the grand jury met, with Tip Ball (a cousin to Ira) as foreman and George Fisher (a close friend and pallbearer at Ira's funeral) as a member of the panel. Although the papers reported "evidence to the affect that Colson was not the aggressor," the jurors discounted George's claim of self-defense and indicted him for murder. The same jury also indicted Clay Colson for a murder said to have been committed some eighteen years earlier, based on the testimony of Riley Ball, a cousin to Ira, who had just come forward claiming to have been an eyewitness to that crime. Court dates for both George and Clay were set for the May session.

On May 17 the courthouse at Pineville was crowded. Court Day was always an exciting social time, with whole families on the grounds as well as in the courthouse. It was common, incredibly, for the men, even those under indictment for violent crimes, to come to court armed. George Colson later claimed that he had asked the authorities to disarm both the Balls and the Colsons, but his request was disregarded.

At ten o'clock that morning, George and Clay were in the entry room to the office of the Circuit Court Clerk, making out affidavits. George's trial was scheduled to begin shortly. A lawyer, R.L. Maddox,[14] was seated at a desk to one side helping with the affidavits, but he later claimed to have seen nothing, and according to him no words were spoken before the shooting started. The hallway outside the upstairs office was crowded, but no one else was actually in the room.

Frank Ball, Ira's father, entered the room, his hands in his pockets. Riley Ball was right behind him. Clay was later to testify that he saw Frank start to draw his gun, and he threw himself against him. Of course, it is quite possible with tempers at the boiling point, that he could have misinterpreted Frank's move. The latter claimed at his trial that he had done nothing to cause Clay to rush toward him suddenly.

Whatever the spark, guns started blazing. Riley fell dead, shot directly between the eyes. Both Frank and Clay were wounded. Frank was shot twice in the head, one shot a glancing blow and the other through his neck to his cheek. Clay was wounded in the right shoulder. Court Clerk R.E. Wilson rushed in and found Riley dead in a corner, Frank lying in the middle of the room, Clay backed into the record room, and George standing unscathed in the room where the shooting had occurred.

The courthouse erupted into general panic, with people jumping out windows and diving under chairs. In the melee more shots were fired—"a fusillade of bullets." John Hurst, who had been just outside the door in the hall, was shot in the head. Bleeding profusely, he started crawling down the steps toward the office of County Judge James Bingham, who was also a physician and a kinsman by marriage. He was shot four more times, in the back, arm, and hands as he dragged himself down. It was only when Dr. Bingham emerged from his office with a shotgun in hand that the firing stopped.

There were numerous witnesses to the Hurst shooting, but diametrically opposed testimony. Some witnesses swore it was Floyd Ball who raised a gun in both hands, pointed it at Hurst's back, and fired repeatedly, while other eyewitnesses swore just as adamantly that the man firing the pistol was not Floyd but someone they had never seen before. Amazingly, with all

William, John (seated), and Ernest Hurst, ca. 1919. Courtesy of David Hurst.

the confusion and shooting, only one innocent bystander was hit. Fred McDaniels was wounded in the foot.

Bill Hurst left this first-person account of the affair:

> I was day clerk at the Continental Hotel across the street from the court house. Some one at the front door of the hotel said about fifteen shots were fired at the courthouse and I told Dill Durman to watch the desk for me and I went over there. Alva Ball and Tom Manning were on the outside of the side door as I went in. A man was standing near the door inside and I asked him who the man was that I saw on the floor. And he said that is your brother so I went down the hall and found him still alive so I got help and took him to the hospital to Dr. Wilson. I was told after John was shot throu his face upstairs, he staggered down the steps and Floyd Ball shot him in the back as he came down.[15]

In another account of the same affair, Bill wrote that he knew his brother was in the courthouse to hear the trial of George Colson and that when he ran over there, "People were coming out of doors and windows like when horses were unloaded from a railroad car." John's index finger had almost been shot off and the doctors wanted to amputate. But John managed to persuade them to try to save something because of his musical career, and he was left with a contracted but usable stump. The doctors were unable to remove the bullet from his back, and he carried that to his death. As surgery was being performed, the rumor swept Pineville that the Balls had escaped and were returning to the city heavily armed. The Colsons hired an armed guard to stay in the hospital.[16]

George was jailed in Pineville. Frank, Floyd, and Alva, along with Tom Manning, were arrested and transported to Middlesboro. There was no indication in the papers that Clay, who was in the hospital in Pineville, was charged with anything. In fact, there is a note in the court records that the German luger pistol belonging to him "that was taken during the trouble at the courthouse" was returned to him on May 20, 1922. (Although this writer could find no record of it, at least one person familiar with the affair believes that Clay Colson was convicted of something in connection with the shootout and served six months in jail before appealing his sentence and being released.)

The Balls protested their innocence. It was claimed that Frank and Riley were the only Ball men inside the courthouse at the time of the shooting. The others said they were sitting in a car outside the courthouse when they heard the shots and, thinking Frank was in trouble, ran to help. Several witnesses claimed to have seen Floyd, Alva, and Tom Manning running toward the courthouse when the shooting started. John Hurst later testified that though he had not seen the man who first shot him in the head[17] and then shot him again as he staggered down the steps, he did see Alva Ball as he shot him in the hand. Alva, he said, was standing at the door of the courthouse. Others testified to having seen Alva backing out of the courthouse shooting. The pistols of the combatants were checked immediately after the shooting. It was felt that Floyd's gun had been fired and reloaded.[18] Alva had only one pistol in his possession, though he was wearing two holsters.

At his trial, Floyd pointed out logically that the Balls could only lose by causing trouble. He stated, "Papa told me fifty times to let things alone and let the law take its course. We had nothing to gain. It was a Colson who was on trial and on the defense." When asked why the Balls had gone to court armed, he replied, "It would be suicide for us to go to Pineville without being armed. At any time, though, that the authorities will disarm the Colsons we are more than willing to put up our guns and never carry them again."

It should be pointed out here that while the Balls had a presumed ally in the Middlesboro justice system (Frank's brother H.E., who was chief of police) and were strong in the city, the Colsons had as their brother-in-law Charles Herd, the prosecuting attorney for the county, and were connected by marriage to many prominent families in Pineville and Bell County. Also, the father of the Hurst boys was on the Middlesboro City Council.

In retrospect, it is most probable that the whole affair at the courthouse was a tragic error for both sides, brought on by heightened tempers, suspicions, and fears, and the fact that everyone was armed and ready for the other side to make a misstep. The only fact arguing against this thesis is that the shooting of Riley once directly between the eyes looks more like an execution than a heat-of-the-moment effort at self-defense. Especially as, according to those who examined his gun, Riley had not fired a shot.

Although indictments were handed down against Floyd, Alva, and Frank, the trials did not take place until the next year. Meanwhile, in May of 1923, George Colson went on trial for the killing of Ira Ball. The trial had been delayed several times because of the absence of witnesses, and when it was finally held, there was a notable absence of those who had testified for the defense before the grand jury the year before.[19] The jury deliberated a long time before convicting him. It was thought they were convinced by what was said to be Ira's dying statement to the effect that Colson fired the first shot. George was sentenced to seven years in prison. He appealed and in October of 1923 the sentence was put aside on the grounds of new evidence concerning threats that were alleged to have been made by the Balls. George was freed on bond pending a new trial.

The first Ball trial was that of Floyd, held in June of 1923, for the malicious shooting and wounding of John Hurst. A change of venue had been granted and, to prevent a reoccurrence of a tragedy such as had happened in Pineville, everyone entering the courthouse was searched for weapons. Although there was much conflicting evidence, the jury deliberated only thirty minutes before convicting Floyd and sentencing him to five years in the penitentiary, the maximum punishment under state law for the crime with which he was charged. Frank's trial was scheduled for August, but he failed to appear, as did Alva, and both forfeited their bonds. Their trials finally took place in November of 1923. Alva's was first, he being accused of shooting Hurst. He was acquitted. Then Frank was tried for the shooting of Clay Colson and sentenced to six months in prison.

On the night before he left office, Governor Edwin Morrow pardoned Floyd Ball. George was also free, awaiting a new trial date.

As soon as possible, Clay Colson left Bell County and moved to Washington, D.C., where he worked for the Internal Revenue Service until his death in 1934. His obituary, probably supplied by his family, recalled the incident at the Pineville courthouse and stated, "Clay had been desperately wounded in that fight, and...when he was reached he was standing with a gun in each hand, although paralyzed in each arm and unable to shoot. His guns had not been fired during the shooting fray." He never married and, as far as anyone can recall, never returned to Middlesboro. His cousins John and Bill Hurst also left town soon after the shootout.

Meanwhile, the Balls and George Colson were at large on the streets of Middlesboro, still armed and still eager for revenge. George was said to have been drinking quite heavily by this time. On Saturday, June 14, 1924, he had a taxi take him to Gastineau's Drug Store on Ashbury Avenue. He was very drunk. Some say he was so far gone as to be almost in a stupor, and one version of the story is that he was so drunk he did not know where the taxi was taking him, that he asked to be taken home but was instead transported to the store owned by the Balls' good friend Wallace Gastineau. George was, as always, armed with two pistols.

There were only four people in the store, including Gastineau. One witness stated that Colson was so drunk he could hardly stand and was leaning on the soda fountain. Floyd Ball entered the store and, according to Gastineau, George said "Hello, Floyd" and began to quarrel. The witnesses were vague about what happened next, but they did agree that George was menacing Floyd. Floyd stated that George actually pulled his guns and started to shoot. With that, Floyd shot him five times, hitting him in the shoulder, the side and near the heart.[20] George was not killed immediately, and one resident can recall seeing him with his head propped on a Coke case, bleeding profusely. He was taken to the hospital and did regain consciousness but made no statement. He died shortly thereafter, but before he did he begged Floyd to have no more troubles with the Colsons in consideration of his wife, Minnie, who was Floyd's cousin.[21]

George was survived by his wife and six young children ranging in age from thirteen to four years old, and his four remaining siblings, brothers Dave and Clay and sisters Laura and Lucy. The papers reported that large crowds attended the "beautiful and impressive funeral services."

The overt feud was over.

George's widow, Minnie. was left in financial straits, and for a short time the children were sent to an orphanage in Louisville. It was assumed that Minnie's mother, who was separated from C.D. Ball and had some resources of her own, then helped the family. The children grew up in Middlesboro, and most stayed on as adults. One of the boys, Calvin, even worked for Floyd Ball. He said that Floyd told him how sorry he was about the whole affair.

Doyle's young wife, Lillie, was unable to hold her little family together. She moved to Louisville and later remarried. Doyle's sister Lucy and her husband adopted the youngest child, who was still an infant. The other children lived with first one and then another of their Dalton relatives. All eventually moved away from Middlesboro.

John Hurst, the cousin who was twenty-four years old when wounded at the Pineville Courthouse, moved to Chicago, where he spent the rest of his life. He was able to resume his musical career, playing in cocktail lounges and hotels, often as an accompanist, working with many of the well known artists of the day. He and his first wife were divorced, and she later married a Ball cousin. His son Ray lived with various of his Colson relatives. In 1924 John remarried. His second wife was a Middlesboro girl, a first cousin to Lina Smith, who was Floyd's second wife. Because of the feud, they kept the marriage a secret until he could arrange for her to join him in Chicago. They had two children and divorced, and much later he remarried. His children remember him as a rather distant, reserved man who worked all night and slept during the day. They recall he was fluent in seven foreign languages, all self-taught, even doing crossword puzzles in German to amuse himself. John seldom returned to Middlesboro and then only secretly. Whenever he visited his hometown he would stay in the Bruce Hotel. By that time it was a second-rate establishment, but, according to one of his nephews, "he knew the layout of the building and considered it a safe haven." He died in the late sixties.

Bill Hurst, the cousin who had been present at the ill-fated poker game, stayed out of town for some time, drifting from one job to another in various places. Gradually he came to depend on his expertise as a pool player, hustling games, as he later said, "from California to Michigan." Even after he returned to Middlesboro he took frequent trips to play pool, often with such world champions as Ralph Greenleaf, Earl Ruby, and Willie Mosconi. He ended his handwritten reminiscences by saying, "After learning to play pool and dice the best of others and winning money from players I went back to my Dear Mothers church and started leaving all pool rooms and gambling rooms and asked god forgiving and started the Christian life. I had lived thru a period of danger while the Ball Family controlled the City of Middlesboro."

Alva and Floyd went on to become the kingpins of Middlesboro during the "Little Las Vegas" days of the thirties, forties, and early fifties (see Footnote Twenty-nine).

In the next generation, according to both the Colsons and the Balls, there was not much evidence of the feud, and everyone was anxious to put it behind them. It was, after all, a small town. Balls and Colsons went to school together and played on the same sports teams. The son of Bill Hurst recalled, "I do remember that we did not own a car and that many times Floyd Ball would stop and give Dad a ride as he walked to town. Dad told me that on the first few occasions both Dad and Floyd had their hands near the pistol each was carrying, but as time went by neither felt the need of such precaution." But John Hurst's son Ray said that he always was very careful and had the feeling that the Balls kept a close watch on what he referred to as "the Colson orphans" for signs they might be tempted to rejoin the feud.

Yet the feud lived on in the collective memory of the town, and the general wisdom of the old-timers is that a certain amount of "bad blood" existed for many years between the two families.

And what of the two pistols—his own and Doyle's—that George Colson always carried? They were stolen from his house while his funeral was being held and were never seen again.

Footnote Twenty-Seven

The Chicago Connection

The Jewish Cemetery sits on a quiet knoll, known as Maxwellian Braes, in the southwestern part of Middlesboro, a silent testimony to the Jewish community that helped build Middlesboro. Here lie the Horrs, the Ginsbergs, the Eusters, the Goodfriends. Among the tombstones is one inscribed simply, "Jack Zuta—Born 2-15-88 — Died 7-31-30."

Many Jewish merchants were drawn to the booming "Magic City" of Middlesborough. They set up their tents, worked hard, and soon were able to build substantial stores along the main streets. One of those was Ike Ginsberg. He had arrived in the United States from Wilno, Lithuania (later a part of Poland), in 1888. He was only fifteen years old and had made the crossing alone. After a year in New York, he heard from friends who had already settled in southeastern Kentucky and made his way to Pineville. In the fall of 1890 he moved to Middlesborough and found employment in one of the tent stores, Rick's Notion Store. The "bust" came, but he, like many of his Jewish friends, decided to ride out the bad times. Ike joined with another of the Jewish families, the Goodfriends, and together they opened a clothing store in 1893. He saved his money, learned the business, and soon was able to open his own store. In 1898 he married Sadie Horr, whose family was also prominent in the business community. Other Horr daughters married into the Goodfriend and Euster families, so that much of the mercantile business in the city was interconnected through marriage. Ginsberg prospered, was active in civic affairs and, in 1933, was elected mayor of Middlesborough.

Jack Zuta was Ike's first cousin, though younger by some fifteen years. He was still a teenager when he arrived in Middlesborough sometime between 1903 and 1905, an immigrant from Russia.[1] This was the time of the pogroms in Russia, and many Jews were coming to America. Others of his family had gone only as far as Poland and were still living there in the thirties. Zuta himself was an orphan and apparently came to this country alone, but with arrangements made for him to stay with his cousin. Ike was quoted after his death as saying, "We had raised him from the time he came over from the old country."

Jack went to work for his cousin in his mercantile business and later tried his hand at selling insurance. He then joined with one of the Goodfriend boys, and together they owned and managed the White Elephant, a saloon on the south side of Cumberland Avenue between 19th and 20th. In early June 1908 the newspaper reported the rumor that Morris Goodfriend was about to be "led to the altar" by a Knoxville heiress and that "Jack Zuta, proprietor of the White Elephant will be the best man when the event is pulled off." Then in July of that year there was a notice that "The firm of Goodfriend and Zuta has been dissolved. Mr. Goodfriend, it is understood, will continue business at the same stand." Jack, meanwhile, moved across the street to the Mecca, which was located between

The Mecca Saloon on Cumberland Avenue, prior to 1915. Courtesy of the Bell County Historical Society.

19th and 18th and had originally been owned by Charlie and H.E. Ball. The Goodfriends also had an interest in this saloon.

Middlesboro went dry in 1915, and soon thereafter Zuta moved to Chicago. The exact circumstances of his move are not known, though the newspaper after his death explained that "with little to beckon ahead he was caught in the drift of a sordid stream, and then later came Chicago." Chicago at the time had one of the largest Jewish communities in the world, and a large percentage of the Jews there were from Russia, so it was a natural destination for Zuta, who was then twenty-seven years old. Additionally, the elder Horrs, in-laws of his cousin and of his erstwhile business partner, had moved back to Chicago. Perhaps he chose the Windy City because of that connection.

It is likely that he settled in the Jewish area. Describing that part of Chicago in the twenties, one author noted, "The main outline of the life of the European ghetto and the Russian pale have been transplanted almost in their entirety."[2] These recent immigrants often felt powerless and tended to believe they needed to rely on political "pull" and "fixes," which meant the ghetto gave birth to powerful political machines. Any lessons that Zuta had not already absorbed in Middlesboro about the ins and outs of politics and the importance of political influence he would certainly learn during his days in the Chicago ghetto.

Liquor was still legal in most of the country, and Zuta secured employment in a saloon or cabaret. Already by 1915 several vice rings existed in Chicago. They worked out of the cabarets. Ed Weiss and other later associates of Zuta were a part of one of these early crime families.

These cabarets could be tough joints. Bartenders like Zuta had to be able to deal with all sorts of people, to handle the drunks and break up fights. One night while trying to subdue a customer, Zuta accidentally killed a man. The gang members hanging around the cabaret that night instantly classified him as "a heavy," and he was accepted as one of them. Gradually he was drawn into their activities.[3]

Prohibition arrived in 1919, and almost immediately the gangsters of Chicago responded with speakeasies, adding to their normal activities the transportation and distribution of liquor and the arranging of protection. Zuta had valuable connections through his friends in Middlesboro, the Balls. They already had developed a business relationship with moonshiners in Tennessee and were in a position to put him in contact with those processors of liquid corn. By 1921 Zuta was in the business of liquor running and was handling collections and payments for the O'Banion gang on the north side of Chicago.

One of the members of this gang was "Nails" Morton, who was a hero to the Jewish community in Chicago because he had organized a defense society to protect Jews from "Jew baiters." When he was killed in 1923, five thousand Jews paid tribute to Morton as the man who made the city safe for his people. It is easy to see how a young Jewish immigrant like Zuta could be drawn into such a gang.

Much of the business of the gangs had to do with giving protection money to politicians and public officials. After Zuta's death, strong boxes were found with receipts, canceled checks, and notations in ledgers showing that from his early days in the gang he served as a business manager and took on the responsibility for making these payments. He was also deeply involved with gambling and organized vice. In April of 1923, when the Chicago Crime Commission published its first list of "Public Enemies," Zuta was one of the twenty-eight named. Al Capone headed the list and Zuta was number nine. In 1929 a "Who's Who" of organized crime in Chicago listed Zuta twice, once under the category "vice" and again under "gambling," and noted, "No record in Identification Bureau, nor Other Record of Conviction, but Notorious in These Activities."[4]

Zuta continued his connection with Middlesboro. The *Middlesboro Daily News* in December of 1920 reported, "Col. Ike Ginsburg who was called to the bedside of his cousin, Jack Zuty, stricken with double pneumonia in Chicago, will return Saturday. Mr. Zuty is an old Middlesboro boy and his friends here will be glad to learn that his condition shows improvement." Throughout the twenties Ginsburg made regular buying trips to Chicago to stock his store and usually visited with his cousin while he was there. One of Ike's sons, Marcus, moved to Chicago and worked for a time for Zuta.

Zuta also made regular trips back to Middlesboro, especially for the high Jewish holidays. Residents remember that he "cut quite a swath" on these visits, bringing a long touring car on the train with him so that he would have suitable transportation while in town, and distributing lavish gifts, particularly to his cousins. To the Jewish community in Middlesboro, he was simply a wealthy businessman from Chicago.[5] After his death the *Daily News* explained that his friends here did not know about the life he led in Chicago, "only that he appeared to prosper, only that wealth glittered, only that the same generous, freehearted Jack Zuta appeared to have 'made good.'"

Ike Ginsberg gave another picture of his visits:

Jack was a peculiar fellow in ways. He made Middlesboro his home.

> When he came to see us he usually stayed at a hotel because—well, you know the way Jack was. He liked to have the service of porters and bellboys and such and a place to gamble—-to have a card game. That was just Jack's way.[6]

A story that ran in the Chicago newspapers after his death said that Zuta had brought Chicago's Mayor Thompson to Middlesboro in order to make payoffs. This was flatly denied by everyone in the city he called his hometown. There was no evidence that he ever let his life in Chicago touch the people in Middlesboro, except for the Balls. He did stop by to see them when he was in town, and it was not just a social call.[7]

Ike Ginsberg had some inkling of what was happening up north. He later told a Chicago reporter:

> We didn't know anything about his doings, but I became suspicious when I came up here to see him one time. I came to his room, right here in the hotel and he wouldn't open the door—said he'd see me later. When I went to his room later the telephone rang and he said: "Don't answer it." Then he pulled down the window shade of his room. I became suspicious then. Why, I wanted to take him on my back, even though I'm 60 years old, and carry him right back to Middlesboro and home with me.[8]

Zuta had reason to be worried. The great profits being made in bootlegging and associated businesses led to competition between gangs and to the infamous Chicago gang wars. Dion O'Banion tried to double-cross Al Capone in 1924 and was murdered. Hymie Weiss assumed control of the O'Banion gang and he, along with George "Bugs" Moran, attempted to kill Capone. They failed, and Weiss was killed. Moran became the acknowledged leader of the Northside gang, with Jack Zuta as his business manager. It was said that next to Jake Guzide, Zuta "probably had the best business brains in the underworld."[9] By the late twenties Zuta and his Northside gang were known to control 145 saloons, "vice dens," and roadhouses.[10]

Gang warfare escalated. It had become a battle between Al Capone's gang and the Northside gang. Capone struck a telling blow with the St. Valentine's Day massacre in 1929, when he had seven of Moran's men killed, but he failed to rid himself of either Moran or Zuta.

On June 9, 1930, Jack Lingle, a newspaperman with close ties to Capone, was assassinated. Final responsibility was never definitely proven, but immediately after the murder it was rumored that Zuta had arranged the killing because he believed Lingle was "stirring up" the police to raid the operations of the Northside gang. He was picked up by the police for questioning, along with three others.

Zuta was said to have a reputation, whether deserved or not, of being a "squawker" who might talk to save his own neck, so a wave of apprehension ran through the underworld when he was taken in for questioning. He did not, in fact, give out any information during the twenty-four hours he was in custody, but reports to the contrary "leaked" to the street. Zuta asked for a police escort upon being released, probably feeling he was in danger both from the Capone gang, which might try to revenge the Lingle shooting, and from his own gang, who might want to seal his lips. He was right. A blue sedan bore down on the police car. Zuta yelled, "They're after us!" and hit the floor. Bullets sprayed the vehicle but missed Zuta, hitting instead two innocent bystanders, one of whom was killed.

On July 2, 1930, the *Middlesboro Daily News* ran a report of "the gang battle," but it was not until the next day that the paper identified Zuta as the target of the gunfire. The article stated that the motive for the murder attempt was that he had evidence in the Lingle killing, but even then there was no indication that the local paper knew or believed Zuta himself was a part of the gangs. That only became common knowledge in his home town after Zuta was killed. Then all the big city papers headlined the news, and the local paper ran the United Press story.

After the attempted assassination, Zuta disappeared. It was later reported that Chicago police officers, and perhaps others from the opposite side of the law, had been in Middlesboro attempting to locate him. Zuta, however, was hiding out in a Wisconsin resort hotel, having registered under the name of J. G. Goodman.

On August first he had a swim in the lake with a companion.[11] That evening Zuta went into the barroom, where there was a player piano, and began feeding it nickels while several couples danced around the room. He had just put another coin in the slot, choosing to play a current hit, "Good for You, Bad for Me," when several men entered the room. As Middlesboro residents learned from the *Daily News* of August 2:

> While forty dancers looked on eight men believed to be Chicago gangsters late last night entered the Lake View Resort Hotel, near Delafield, Wisconsin, and shot to death a man who was today identified as Jack Zuta, notorious North Side gang lieutenant and alleged arch foe of Al Capone....Witnesses of the assassination said six of the eight gunmen

> entered the dance hall while two others waited outside in two high powered automobiles. While three of them stood guard at the doors, three others walked boldly across the pavilion, one carrying a riot gun, another a sawed-off shot gun and the other a pistol. The two more heavily armed men menaced the bartender while the third walked to the player piano, deliberately shot down "Goodman" and walked away. Witnesses said the other two men fired volleys into the man's body as they too walked from the room. Sixty bathers were on the beach a short distance from the hotel. Hearing the shots, they ran toward the dance hall but were threatened by the door guards and stood helplessly while the gunmen leaped into the two automobiles and escaped.

The papers reported that at the same time that Zuta "was being executed in front of the resort merrymakers, Capone was holding a reception...for 100 of his followers, celebrating his return from the south." Sixteen bullets were extracted from Zuta's body. It was later established that they came from guns that could be traced to the Capone organization. But there was other evidence that linked the killing to the Northside gang. Both had motives, and the case was never solved.

For the rest of the month, Zuta was headline news in Middlesboro as well as the rest of the country.

Colonel Ginsberg and his son Jimmie went to Wisconsin to claim the body. When the newspaper reporters hounded them, identifying his cousin as a "trafficker in women" and other equally derogatory epithets, Ike angrily retorted, "What they say about Jack's 'racket' and his record may be all true. But there are many wolves in sheep's clothing walking the streets who aren't worth the ground Jack walked on."

Zuta returned to Middlesboro for the last time by train, to lie in state at Callison's Funeral Home in an elegant black casket. Friends watched the night through, and all the Jewish stores in town closed in his honor. The curious flocked to see the remains, and many older men today recall how as young boys they "snuck up" to Callison's to see the bullet holes in Zuta's face. The local Elks Club, of which Zuta had been a member, had charge of the services, but the orthodox Jewish ritual was used. The Middlesboro paper explained that "Zuta often expressed the desire to be buried with his relatives in the cemetery here."

The funerals of gangsters in Chicago at the time were immense affairs, with literally hundreds of floral tributes and the entire underworld, as well as politicians and others, in attendance. Zuta's funeral was simple. Colonel Ginsberg had announced when he went to claim the body, "You can tell those Chicago hoodlums, and politicians, and city officials, that they won't be wanted." The papers reported no large crowds or strangers in town for the funeral, and people who attended remember none. A rumor circulated that "Bugs" Moran was sighted in Knoxville several days before and after the funeral, but he was not seen in Middlesboro.

In an editorial after the funeral, the *Daily News* expounded on the wages of sin, but went on, "The dark years of activity in a strange underworld business in Chicago are mercifully veiled....memory of the beautiful traits of character of Zuta relieves the pain and softens the sorrow."

Actually, the activity was not to be veiled for long. Law enforcement officials began to unearth Zuta's strongboxes. Good business manager that he was, he had kept careful records detailing gang enterprises. While Zuta rested in final peace on Maxwellian Braes, Chicago was thrown into turmoil by the revelations contained in those strongboxes. Canceled checks, receipts, and notes tied many of Chicago's most powerful politicians to the gangs. Typical was a short note from Evanston Police Chief William Freeman:

> Dear Jack,
>
> I am temporarily in need of four C's for a couple of months. Can you let me have it? The bearer of this does not know what it is so put it in an envelope and seal it and address it to me. Your old pal,
>
> Bill Freeman
>
> P.S. Will let you know the night of the party. So be sure and come.

The mayor of Chicago, a state senator, and others were soon sucked into the cesspool. There was also evidence of Zuta's dealings with various well known criminals from other gangs. A United Press story datelined Chicago opined:

> Zuta, alive, was a menace to gangland. Powerful, and known as a talker, he possessed knowledge that all gangland and...many officials...feared he might disclose....Zuta, dead, had become more of a menace to gangland and officials than he ever was alive. That he kept detailed records of the financial dealings of the Moran-Aiello-Zuta powerful Northside gang, was known to investigators and the underworld alike. After his death it was a race between investigators and the underworld for the records. The investigators won.

In the aftermath of Zuta's assassination, "Bugs" Moran abdicated in favor of Capone, who thereafter became the sole head of the Chicago's gangland. The papers explained that while Moran had been able to hold on and even become stronger after the St. Valentine's Day Massacre, "his downfall came as natural consequent to the death of Jack Zuta who shared the chieftainship with him and the Aiello brothers."

Another matter that preoccupied Middlesboro was Zuta's estate. The rumor flew about town that Ike Ginsberg was the sole heir. Actually, the will on file at the Bell County Circuit Court clerk's office named Ginsberg his executor and one of his largest beneficiaries, but also made numerous other bequests. There was also a listing of safety deposit boxes, one in the name of Ike Ginsberg. Until probate, however, the contents of the will were not known. Reporters from the metropolitan dailies prowled Middlesboro trying to unearth a story and even offered large sums of money in return for an exclusive. Nonetheless, it was the *Middlesboro Daily News* that scooped the nation on October 11, 1930, with a copy of Zuta's will.

Predictably, the will was contested in Chicago courts by distant relatives both in this country and overseas. Additionally the great caches of hidden jewels and cash that Zuta was said to have had were apparently never found, and the estate was worth less than originally assumed. The town lost interest in this most notorious of its residents, and Zuta was forgotten as everyone turned their attention from the Roaring Twenties to the Great Depression.

Footnote Twenty-Eight

King Coal

The United Mine Workers of America was formally organized in 1890, the same year the city of Middlesborough was granted its charter. The two entities have also shared an inexorable tie to the boom and bust cycles of King Coal.

The early settlers in the Yellow Creek Valley had "doghole mines," small diggings in the rich coal seams of the Valley that yielded sufficient fuel for home use, but with no means of transport the coal had no commercial value. Railroads were the key to potential exploitation of the area's natural resources. The incentive for this development would be the rapid industrialization of the South following the Civil War.

In 1870 only one railroad connected southern Appalachia to the outside world, and that ran southwestward through Virginia and terminated in Knoxville, Tennessee. But Union soldiers who had marched through eastern Kentucky and Tennessee, some even stationed at the Gap above the Yellow Creek Valley, brought back tales of the wondrous treasure of minerals and timber hidden in the mountains, just waiting to be exploited. On January 1, 1872, the *Cumberland Spectator* excitedly reported that a survey was being conducted for the proposed Bristol and Cumberland Gap Railroad with a view to coming up the Powell Valley to the Cumberland Gap. At the same time the newspaper reported that the Louisville & Nashville Railroad had pledged to extend the line from its junction at Lebanon, Kentucky, through to the Cumberland Gap. Although the Bristol plan did not materialize, by 1882 the L&N had their line laid to London, and the next year it was extended south to Jellico, Tennessee, with the expectation that rail would be headed east from London toward Barbourville shortly and would reach Pineville by early 1888.

Meanwhile geologists were surveying the region's mineral resources. In 1875 a Harvard University professor, Nathaniel Shaler, led a group of his students in a summer project to study the geology of the Gap area. Among their other findings, they cataloged twenty seams of bituminous coal in the Yellow Creek Valley. Less than ten years later Kentucky state geologist John R. Proctor touted the abundance of coal in the Valley and urged the development of its resources. In 1889 Alexander Arthur oversaw the completion of rail lines linking Middlesborough with the markets of the Northeast, Midwest, and South, and the reign of King Coal was under way.

There was already agitation in the coal fields in other regions, and in January of 1890 various miners' unions, notably the Mine Laborers Union and the Knights of Labor, met in Columbus, Ohio, to form the United Mine Workers of America, with the first district being #19, which covered eastern Tennessee and southeastern Kentucky, including the Yellow Creek Valley.

Coal was always considered one of the bedrocks of Arthur's grand plan. The American Association planned to lease its ore-producing lands and reap the profits from lease payments and from the industries and various businesses that development of the coal fields would engender. Already by 1890 several coal companies had been organized and small mines opened to the west of Middlesborough. With the "bust," production stuttered but did not stop. The "boomers" might abandon their get-rich-quick schemes, but sober-minded realists saw that transportation was now available to get coal to market. As one commentator put it in 1905 when lauding local coal operators who came during the "boom" days and stayed on to build solid companies,

> they kept their hands on the plow handles and did not falter or turn back when reverses came. After the storm had passed they were leaders in gathering the scattered remnants of broken business fabrics and took an active part in laying the solid foundations on which the present undoubted prosperity of this section now stands.[1]

In the earliest days of the union, there was little interest among local miners, but after the "bust" and the nationwide Panic of 1893, they joined their brethren throughout the country in protesting conditions. The mine operators, squeezed by economic conditions, fought back. In 1893 the newspaper reported that miners at Mingo Mine were afraid to attend union meetings, and in March of 1894, the year of the first UMWA general strike, there was an attempt to burn the tipple at the Mingo Mountain Coal &

Coke Company. Robert Ralston, superintendent at the mine, was shot at from both sides of the hill when he tried to put out the fire.

Mingo Mountain Coal & Coke had been the first coal company organized to operate in the Yellow Creek area. Its founder was John Ralston, a Scotsman whose family immigrated to Pennsylvania when he was five. His father, James, who was "keeper" for the Clyde Ironworks when the Neilson hot blast method for smelting iron was first introduced, was recruited by an American company to build and supervise the first furnace in the United States to smelt iron ore using anthracite coal. He brought over with him on the ship the hot-blast tubes, the first to be used in this country. John grew up in the business, running his own steel rolling mills and coal operations in Pennsylvania for twenty-five years. Suddenly, in 1889, he closed out all of his businesses in Pennsylvania and, without telling anyone, packed up his entire family, which included thirteen children, and left for Kentucky. The exact circumstances of his doing so are still a family mystery.[2]

Four of John's sons joined him in the local coal business. Robert became vice-president and superintendent of Mingo Mountain Coal. The patriarch also founded Ralston Coal Company with son Herbert as superintendent and son Joseph as mine boss. In 1902 he organized Stony Fork Coal Company with son Charles as his superintendent. Another son, James Howard, ran a general mercantile business at both the Stony Fork and Ralston Coal mines.

In the late 1890s, King Coal started into a boom cycle, with demand steadily increasing. By 1900 local coal operators began to see the rewards of their perseverance. The workers shared to some extent in their good fortune, but in the fall of 1900 District 19 came out in a sympathy strike in support of its union nationwide. The newspaper did not understand, pointing out that local mines were paying $1.20 a day for laborers, $1.62 a day for drivers, and 47¢ a ton for digging, so that many miners were able to make as much as $70 a month, and some even more. A family man would pay $1.00 to $7.00 a month for rent in a company house, $1.00 a month for medical care, and $.50 a month for fuel. The editor went on, "The miner in the Middlesborough district is an aristocrat, if he did but know it. Many of them do and are anxious to go to work, but are held back by their comrades who are wandering after fake gods."

The strike was short-lived. Soon other companies were opening mines. In March of 1901 Yellow Creek Coal and Lumber Company incorporated, with E.S. Helburn, Joe Bosworth, J.G. Fitzpatrick, and A.H. Rennebaum as the entire company. These men, who would be active in civic affairs for almost half a century, were often called "the Yellow Creek Crowd" and

One of the Ralston mines up Mingo Hollow, 1901. Courtesy of Henry Ralston.

were widely credited, along with Ralston, with the resurgence of the local coal industry. They were to remain steadfast comrades through various business and political ventures, their wives were friends and worked together in church and civic organizations, and their children intermarried. Each gradually brought partners from other businesses into their tight circle, and frustrated UMWA organizers often blamed this close alliance for their difficulty in organizing the Middlesboro area.[3]

By 1903 Middlesboro was home to thirteen coal companies. Mine camps sprouted in the hollows around the city. During 1902-1903 seven hundred houses were constructed near the mines up Mingo Hollow alone. More mines opened and some of the smaller ones consolidated, most on property leased from the American Association. The majority of newly hired miners were nonunion. Middlesboro rode the wave of the coal prosperity, and by 1906 there was not a vacant business house or store room in the entire city. In 1910, when the UMWA contract came up for renewal, operators in District 19 refused to sign, and the union district office was reduced to a skeleton staff.

The war looming in Europe brought an increase in the demand for coal, which the mines of Eastern Kentucky were anxious to fulfill. The federal government, concerned about rising coal prices, moved to establish price ceilings. Meanwhile, miners, finding their labor much in demand, agitated for higher wages and better conditions, while coal operators, seeing their profits squeezed between government price controls and worker demands, resisted mightily. In mid-1917 the UMWA called a strike. In response, 150 members of the Coal Operators Association of Eastern Kentucky met in Middlesboro and voted "not to recognize the union in any sense either directly or indirectly." The owners determined to turn the mines over to the government if so directed, "but under no circumstances to yield to agitators." Mingo Mountain Coal was one of those that closed, then reopened under federal receivership. As work was commencing, miners were fired on from ambush, supposedly by union sympathizers.

Throughout the war years there were intermittent problems in the coal fields and coal shortages in many cities, despite price controls and agreements signed by the unions that effectively froze wages. In 1919 the controls came off, price restrictions were lifted, and wages increased. In late 1919 came a strike to force recognition of the UMWA.

As would so often happen, the milk and honey days of 1919, when some miners were making extremely high wages, ended in 1920 with a bust. During the war many industries had weathered coal shortages by learning to use the fuel more efficiently, so that their postwar demand was less. This, combined with the resumption of production overseas, caused a sudden drop in prices, which in turn led to decreased wages. The miners turned to their union for help.

In 1921 the UMWA called a general strike, which dragged on through mid-1922. Twelve to fifteen thousand men from area coal mines were idled. Some moved away voluntarily and others were evicted from their mine camp homes. Those nonunion miners who tried to work were threatened or even attacked and fired upon by union members. State troops were ordered into the area to guard the miners and keep the peace. Eventually all the mines around Middlesboro were closed. Finally the strike was settled as coal shortages resulted in increased prices, so that the operators felt they had more of a margin to accede to some union demands. Times were, however, unsettled, and when supply caught up with demand in 1924, Kentucky coal operators insisted on wage decreases. District 19 broke with the union and accepted this reduction. There was a brief resurgence in the local market with the signing of a coal contract with the L&N Railroad in 1925, and another short-lived revival the next year resulting from a strike in England that restricted coal supplies. At the time, it was noted that there were seventy-two mines in the vicinity of Middlesboro, with a population in the nearby coal camps of 15,000, as compared to the city's population of 12,000. The businesses of Middlesboro were thus very dependent on King Coal and were hit hard by the deep recession in the coal industry that began in 1927 and accelerated as the entire country slipped into the Great Depression.

As always, the miners turned to the union when times got hard. In 1931, eight to nine thousand miners in the area joined the UMWA. There was also widespread interest in the National Miners Union, especially after the UMWA appeared unable to address the immediate problems of its members. The NMU had close ties to the American Communist Party and made some early inroads by operating soup kitchens. It had been reported that 3,000 people were starving in Bell County. Since this was considered to be largely a result of the UMWA strike in the area, the national office of the Red Cross refused to provide relief. The UMWA was essentially bankrupt and could not help, so the NMU seemed the answer to many. Throughout 1932 there was great agitation in Middlesboro over the NMU. Students from the Communist-allied National Student League tried to enter the county to support the miners but were turned back at the Gap by a group of local citizens led by the County Attorney, W.B. Smith.

The NMU proved no more potent than the UMWA in dealing with the miners' problems, partly because the coal operators were themselves caught in the jaws of the Great Depression and many lost everything. By the end of 1932 the National Miners Union had essentially folded.

Among the coal operators caught in the Great Depression was Craig Ralston, the son of Herbert and grandson of John Ralston. He was married to Emma Rennebaum, the daughter of A.H. Rennebaum, one of "The Yellow Creek Crowd." Craig, whose mine had gone bankrupt in 1930, and his brother-in-law, Lee Rennebaum, decided in 1933 to try to open up an older, waterlogged mine up Mingo Hollow. They had no capital but worked beside their men with picks and shovels to dig a deep trench to drain the mine. There was no money to pay their workers, so the miners were allowed to take a gunny sack to the old commissary and help themselves to whatever was left on the shelves. The gamble paid off; they were able to start producing good grade coal just as another war loomed on the horizon in Europe, bringing with it an increase in demand. The Ralstons always felt a special bond with those miners who had joined in the venture with them. The men reciprocated and were therefore resistant to the lure of the UMWA.[4]

The National Industrial Recovery Act of 1933 guaranteed workers the right to organize. UMWA president John L. Lewis seized this golden opportunity to increase membership, and in pushing the union he chose to embrace modernization of the mines, which would result in fewer miners working at a higher wage. But the NIRA was invalidated by the Supreme

A UMWA rally. Date of photo unknown. Courtesy of the Bell County Historical Society.

Court in 1935, and the thirties continued to be an unsettled time, with reports of peace in the mines supplanted by periods of chaos with strikes and violence. Publicity and the national spotlight centered on "Bloody Harlan," the county adjacent to Bell, but there were scattered incidents of shootings and beatings in Bell County that almost assured that the Yellow Creek Valley would not escape tragedy. And come it did one night in mid-April of 1941 in a hailstorm of gunfire that left four men dead and another nine seriously wounded.

Mountain people are superstitious; they believe that things happen in threes—if two chickens are run over in the road, a third will soon meet the same fate. Therefore it was only to be expected that the next calamity would occur in Mingo Hollow at almost exactly the same spot as two previous tragedies, the massacre of the Mingo Indians and the Quarterhouse Battle.

The UMWA called yet another strike on April 1, 1941, as the union and coal operators negotiated for a new wage contract. Most mines in twelve states closed after 400,000 miners walked out, but up Mingo Hollow the nonunion mines continued to operate. It was a situation the UMWA could not tolerate. On April 14 a large convoy of union men, many of whom were from "Bloody Harlan" and surrounding counties as well as from northern Bell County, met at Colmar Road just north of Middlesboro to organize. One witness put the number of cars and trucks at thirty or forty, while others have said it was closer to fifty. James W. Ridings, past sheriff of

Bell County and then the International Representative of the UMWA in the area, addressed the miners. He later claimed he had urged them to avoid liquor and violence. There were allegations, however, that Ridings himself gave out shotgun shells at this meeting and that another man had passed out whiskey. At any rate, a convoy formed and drove through Middlesboro on their way to Mingo Hollow, where they planned to meet the evening shift as they were getting off work and convince them to sign the "check-off," thus indicating their support of the union. Early news reports claimed that seven hundred union miners congregated in Mingo Hollow, though the actual number was probably closer to two hundred.

The mine operators had some advance notice that the union men would be picketing in an effort to get their workers to sign up with the union. Rumors flew about Middlesboro, where most of the owners and managers lived, that there would be trouble up Mingo Hollow. The nonunion mines being targeted were Rennebaum Coal Company, owned by Craig Ralston and Lee Rennebaum, Fork Ridge Coal Company, Motch Coal Company, and Premier Coal Company. The mines were all on property leased to them by the American Association.

When the rumors of trouble reached C.W. "Dusty" Rhodes, the manager of the American Association and president of Fork Ridge Coal Company, he determined to meet the situation head on. Rhodes was, according to his friends, a charming and urbane gentleman who was active in civic affairs. It was said that an unemployed man could always get food at his back door, and he never refused to help those in need. Many of the miners, however, felt he was "a stiff necked Englishman who did not understand miners."[5]

Rhodes drove out to the mines, where he met up with three deputies who, they later said, were in the vicinity at the time investigating an auto theft. Rhodes asked the deputies, at least one of whom had served under Ridings, to order the pickets to keep the road open so miners leaving work could get through to go home. The deputies did so but were ignored, and they were disarmed for their trouble.

Rhodes then went to the schoolhouse near his mines to meet with his mine superintendent and other company men. They were joined by E.W. Silvers, vice-president and treasurer of Fork Ridge Coal Company, whose brother-in-law, Craig Ralston, had called him from Middlesboro to warn him of the trouble that was brewing. Also present was John Rhodes, Dusty's brother, who had driven out to the mines to bring him a message. John had asked a friend, J.H. Woodson, the manager of Kentucky Utilities, to accompany him. After some discussion, the group decided to drive down to where the pickets were blocking the road to personally deal with the situation.

Accompanying Rhodes in his car was Bob Robinson, a former Tennessee Highway Patrolman who was serving as a bodyguard. This was unfortunate, as Robinson was something of a hothead. Rhodes's normal bodyguard was Hubert Ball, a cousin to the Balls who ran Middlesboro and a congenial, easy-going fellow who maintained a certain rapport with the miners. Some maintain that had Hubert been on duty that night, the entire tragedy might have been averted.[6]

Meanwhile the first miners were getting off work and starting down the road. When they saw the crowd of pickets blocking their way, they returned to the safety of the mines. A short time later three miners, either braver or more foolhardy than the others, decided to run the gauntlet. They were stopped, and two of them agreed under duress to sign the "checkoff." The third refused and was hauled from his car with shouts of, "Take him to the creek" and "Turn over his car," but the threats were not carried out, as the picketers' attention was diverted by the approach of several cars coming together from the area of the mines. Someone shouted, "Yonder comes three cars, boys. Get them!"

The pickets had the road completely blocked as the company cars approached. Silvers got out of his automobile and started walking toward the union men. Ridings turned to the man next to him and asked who he was. When informed the man was Silvers, he said, "He's a mighty fine man. I hope they don't hurt him." Silvers addressed the pickets: "We don't want any trouble; we want peace because this is a civilized country." At that point, according to some witnesses, four or five union men "yoked" Silvers and threw him to the ground.

At almost the same time, Robinson and Rhodes stepped out of their car. Everyone agrees Robinson screamed something like, "Turn them God dammed cars around and get out." Some union men claim he added, "Clear this road or I'll kill every damn one of you." Robinson headed to the front of the car, rifle in hand. Rhodes got out on the other side of the vehicle. The union men later claimed he had a machine gun, though none was discovered at the scene by the authorities. All that was found afterward in the vicinity of Rhodes's car was a pistol on the front seat and a rifle in the back; neither had been fired.

One miner, however, who was on his way to work on the next shift that night and so was at the scene almost immediately after the shootout, presumably before any stories or alibis could be formulated, claimed that he was told nothing would have happened had Rhodes not gotten out of his car with a machine gun in hand. He was told that "they had to get him before he cleared the car or he could have laid down a blanket of fire."[7]

A shot rang out, then two more, a hesitation, and then a barrage of gunfire. Who fired the first shot? Each side claimed the other did. The situation was tense, and everyone had some weapon, so that the smallest spark would have set off the explosion.[8] The firing went on for a minute or more, a hailstorm of bullets. The union men, who greatly outnumbered their opponents, also had the advantage of the high ground and natural cover. Three company men were immediately killed. The remaining company men took cover under their cars and returned the fire, killing one miner and wounding others.

As the extent of the carnage became evident, the firing ceased. The union men threw their wounded into their cars and sped back toward Middlesboro. Other miners fled the scene on foot, many hiding out in the mountains for several days. Woodson crawled from beneath the car and ran to the commissary to call an ambulance. It was no use. Rhodes and Robinson had both been killed by high-powered rifles, and Silvers had been gut-shot. A union man, Sam Evans of Middlesboro, also lay dead. Area hospitals admitted eight union men with serious injuries. A ninth came in the next day, having hidden out overnight in the mountains.

Middlesboro was in shock. For one segment of the population it had been a massacre with two highly esteemed members of "society," along with their bodyguard, shot "like fish in a barrel." For another segment it was a righteous battle that had yielded a martyr. Better than three hundred mourners attended the funerals of Rhodes and Silvers, both of whom were buried from the Episcopal Church. Three thousand mourners, many of them miners bused in from surrounding areas, attended the funeral of Sam Evans at the Old Yellow Creek Baptist Church.

Indictments were first issued for James Ridings, A.C. Pace (a UMWA auditor who was also present that night), the nine wounded men who were known to have been involved, and three hundred unnamed miners, the number assumed to have been on the mountain at the time. William Turnblazer, the president of District 19, was also charged with first-degree murder even though he was out of town at the time, the rationale being that he had encouraged an atmosphere of violence that had led directly to the tragedy.

After the "Battle of Fork Ridge," as the union men called it, or "The Mingo Massacre," as it was styled by many others, Lee Rennebaum and Craig Ralston insisted that their men join the union, as they wanted no more killing.

The first trial, that for the murder of Rhodes, did not get under way until the day after Pearl Harbor, when attention was riveted elsewhere. The UMWA imported two experienced, "high-powered" defense lawyers. It took four days to choose a jury (and this was before the days of jury consultants). A total of more than nine hundred prospective jurors was called. Some did not appear, others admitted to an opinion or were dismissed because of ties to some union or the mines. Finally thirteen farmers were selected and the trial was under way.

Testimony was completed in less than four days. A number of the witnesses who were expected to testify did not appear or were not called. The jury deliberated for five and a half hours before returning a verdict of not guilty in the case of every defendant. Trials for the murders of Silvers and Robinson were delayed and finally, in August of 1942, dismissed with a directed acquittal. The country was in the middle of a real war, and the coal industry was an integral part of the war effort.

The war years were ones of great prosperity in the coal industry. Although there was controversy over strikes called by John L. Lewis, president of the UMWA, when it was felt that all should be united in the war effort, it was a period of union strength. Lewis won important benefits for his miners, and in many homes in the Yellow Creek Valley a portrait of Lewis hung next to that of President Franklin D. Roosevelt and the picture of Christ at the Gate.

The height of coal production nationwide was in 1942, but the boom continued through 1947, when District 19 could boast 20,000 unionized miners. Strangely enough, despite these numbers, District 19 was still one of the "provisional" districts. Like twenty-one others throughout the country, its officials were appointed by the national union president rather than being elected by union members.

Lewis and the national union, perhaps recognizing the inevitability of mechanization in the mines, were pursuing a policy of having fewer men working for higher wages and of favoring the larger mines. In many cases the union negotiated "sweetheart deals" with some companies while making unreasonable demands on others. At the same time, overseas coal importations were becoming more plentiful while demand was rapidly falling. Smaller southern Appalachian mines were hit hard, and by 1953 nearly a third of Kentucky's miners were unemployed, while many of the rest were getting only part-time work. Five thousand people in Bell County were out of work, and many left the area to find jobs elsewhere. Although there was a major, and often violent, organizing drive in 1959, the number of union miners in District 19 had fallen to 4,589 by 1964.

At the time of the 1964 International national convention, the UMWA president was Tony Boyle. William Turnblazer Jr., the son of the man who had been president of District 19 during the thirties and forties, was president of his father's old stronghold, while Albert Pass served as secretary-treasurer of District 19.[9] Both were beholden to the national union leadership for their positions, so when Boyle asked for their assistance at the convention, they were happy to comply.

The convention was held at Bal Harbor, Florida, far from the coal fields. The International paid the traveling expenses of many potentially favorable delegates, but even so there was a dissident element that was determined to be heard. That is where District 19 came in. Wearing white hats with "District 19" emblazoned on one side and "Tony Boyle" on the other, these delegates served as ushers. When someone opposed to Boyle tried to speak, his microphone was turned off and he was escorted from the meeting hall, sometimes being manhandled or even beaten in the process.

Opposition to Boyle was quieted in 1964 and at the 1968 convention. But in May of 1969 Jock Yablonski, who was then a member of the International Executive Board, announced his candidacy for president as a champion of the working miners. He was removed by the hierarchy from his position on the Board but not before a confrontation with Boyle sealed his death sentence. On June 23, 1969, according to eyewitness testimony, Boyle turned to Albert Pass after the Board meeting and said, "We are in a fight. We have to kill Yablonski or take care of him." Pass responded, "If no one else will kill him, District 19 will."[10]

To carry out the plot, Pass and Turnblazer enlisted Bill Prater, a union field worker operating just across the border in Tennessee. Prater contacted Paul Huddleston, the president of local 3228, a small pensioners' union in his area. Huddleston in turn, contracted with his son-in-law, Paul Gilly, who lived in Cleveland, to do the actual killing.

Pensioners were particularly vulnerable to pressure from the union hierarchy. In large part their income and health insurance (the generous "hospital card") depended upon the whim of local and national officials. Rules were so complicated that a pensioner could easily be dropped from the roles or, conversely, could suddenly receive benefits to which he had previously not been entitled. In the case of Paul Gilly, in addition to a sum of money for his part in the crime, he was promised that his father, a disabled coal miner, would receive the pension that had previously been denied him.

To launder the money that would be paid the actual killers, District 19 pensioners were enlisted. Twenty-two men were appointed to a Research and Information Committee that was to promote the interests of the union in the area. But the men were told that the money they would be paid by the International for their nonexistent services was to be "kicked-back" to District 19 in order to defeat a Southern Labor Union organizer who was running for county judge in Bell County. Since the SLU was felt to be a company union that stole members from the UMWA, the pensioners agreed and did as they were told.

Gilly recruited two other men, both also displaced Appalachian natives, and they spent several cold days in late December staking out the home of Jock Yablonski. As they sat in their car watching their proposed victim, they warmed themselves with frequent draughts of beer and, as is unfortunately the habit in southern Appalachia, threw the cans out the window. Yablonski noted their presence and reported to the local police the suspicious car with Tennessee plates, but nothing was done.

On New Year's Eve 1969 the three men burst into the Yablonski house and murdered everyone within, including Yablonski's wife, daughter, and dog.

The scheme quickly came unraveled as fingerprints on the discarded cans led to the actual killers, and they pointed back up the tangled web. Eventually everyone confessed and pointed to the person higher up, except for Albert Pass, who was convicted and was serving a life sentence when he died in 2002, his lips still sealed. (Tony Boyle died in prison in 1985, while awaiting his final trial.)

Ironically, all of this was happening just as King Coal was embarking on what will probably be remembered as its last local boom, which was powered by the Arab oil embargo. Once again, men with blackened faces became commonplace throughout the Yellow Creek Valley. Once again with their high wages, union miners became "the aristocrats," and the highest a young girl could aspire was to marry a coal miner. The great-grandson of John Ralston, a lawyer by profession, quit his law practice to go into the family business and operate a coal tipple. Even men with little mining experience could find a place in the coal mines, and unskilled labor was in great demand in other businesses as many employees left lower paying jobs to enter the mines. Men returned from "up north" to claim jobs "at home," and the Valley of Yellow Creek took on the aura of prosperity.

Alas, the boom was short-lived and was followed by a long strike in 1977-1978. Nonunion mines, particularly stripmines, became a dominant feature in Bell County. Soon even some of those were reducing their work force, transferring their miners, or closing. Modernization and mechanization meant that far fewer men were needed to produce the same amount of coal.

Although mining is still an important industry to the Yellow Creek Valley and coal-laden trains still rumble through Middlesboro, King Coal no longer reigns supreme. Gradually the UMWA pensioners are dying off, and few remain who remember the battles fought in the twenties, thirties, and forties to unionize the coal fields of Appalachia. And the men who now wrestle the black gold from the surrounding mountains do so with computerized machinery rather than with pick, shovel, and dynamite.

Footnote Twenty-Nine

Little Las Vegas

"Little Las Vegas," "Little Chicago," "the hottest spot on the railroad line"—that was Middlesboro in the 1940s. It was a kingdom unto itself, an island of license set in the midst of the Bible Belt, and its undisputed rulers were Floyd Ball and his little brother Alvey.

The country was just staggering out of the Great Depression and into a world war, yet in Middlesboro the Balls did not count their money—they literally measured it. Other places might be just beginning to turn on the lights again, but on Middlesboro's 19th Street it was a twenty-four-hour-a-day party, with drink flowing freely, slot machines in every establishment, and prostitutes who considered Middlesboro the best and most profitable spot on "the circuit." The splendid Cumberland Hotel hosted multiple conventions, while the Marboro, Middlesboro, Bruce, Friends, Wabash, and Majestic Hotels provided a popular base for the many traveling salesmen who worked in the area, though several of the hotels were better known for their girls than for their rooms, and it was sometimes difficult to engage a bed for a full night's rest. African-American visitors to town found the same pleasures waiting only a couple of blocks away, with the Ashbury and Union Hotels, the Silver Slipper, and Josh Burnette's Place.

Many a long-time resident, watching Floyd Ball walking down the street handing out money and favors as an emperor would to his subjects, shook his head and asked himself how this had happened. How had a small-time bootlegger who had once sold you a pint of moonshine on the sly, and his fractious younger brother, now so dapper in his swank suits and spats, clawed their way to the position where they owned much of the city and essentially ran all of it. Oh, the "better" people still did not normally socialize with them, but most of the businessmen, even those of wealth and social prominence, joined them in various enterprises. It was well known that the Balls ran the political machines of both parties in the city and in Bell County, and it was rumored that their influence extended to the governor's mansion and perhaps beyond.

The Early Years

Going back twenty-five years, it was a totally different story. Certainly their growing-up years were not an easy time for Floyd, Alva (Alvey), and their older brother Ira. Their father, Frank, who had been in jail during much of their childhood, had gone bankrupt (see Footnote Thirteen). Floyd had to quit school after completing the fourth grade and go to work at odd jobs and as a laborer on the railroad. In a time before government social programs, they must have had to depend to some extent on their extended family, especially their uncles, who owned saloons and were involved in politics. The boys were naturally drawn to the area around the railroad terminal, the locale of most of their uncles' businesses, where there was always some kind of excitement and a little money to be made.

In 1915 Bell County voted to go dry. Although the people of Middlesboro went for the "wets," they were outvoted in the county. The town, with a fair amount of tolerance for the liquor trade, took on characteristics the country would later exhibit during the Prohibition Era. Where once there had been saloons, now there were soft drink stands that offered the same selection of drink as before. To add fuel to the fire, King Coal was in one of its boom cycles, so that money was plentiful. And there was the general excitement and unrest caused by rumors of war, first with Mexico and then as part of the Great War in Europe.

It was a milieu tailor-made for the Balls, who were then young bucks. Ira was twenty-one in 1915, Floyd was seventeen, and Alvey, just twelve. Already, through their uncles, they had connections with moonshiners who could readily supply liquor, among them the Russell family just over the border in Tennessee, who had long been known for the quality of their homemade brew. Soon regular "milk runs" were set up, with a milk truck leaving empty containers at the homes of various farmers in the isolated hollows of Tennessee and, at the same time, picking up the full bottles, which were painted so as to appear from a distance to contain milk. The "milk" was then delivered to customers in Middlesboro.

By 1916 both Ira and Floyd had soft drink stands on Lothbury, as did their cousin Tyler Ball, and both had already been charged with violating prohibition. As in any time when no single person or group is on top, there was a great deal of violence in the several-block area that surrounded the railroad terminal. Ira was known to have a quick and nasty temper. He had stabbed a man when he was just fifteen and had been sent to a juvenile reformatory, but the effort to reform him was unsuccessful. In 1917 he killed a man but was acquitted of murder. Ira and Floyd were both in court in 1919 for carrying concealed weapons. The next year brought the city six murders in as many months. The local citizenry took notice, but the brawling, fighting, and shooting continued.

The Twenties

The 1920s were an exciting decade in the business life of Middlesboro. Despite several vicious strikes, coal was in a boom cycle during much of the decade, and the town prospered. With a population of 12,000 and an additional trading potential of better than 15,000 in the nearby coal camps and rural areas, Middlesboro supported more than a hundred retail businesses, ten wholesalers, seven manufacturing plants (Big Ben Manufacturing alone had more than 500 employees), and two banks. Money and the opportunity of sharing in the wealth were there for the taking. And the Balls were not ones to let opportunity pass them by.

The political scene was volatile. In 1920, in response to the violence, there had been the Law and Order League and a change to the mayor-council form of government. In 1922 the city went back to the commissioner framework, and H.E. Ball, uncle of Floyd and Alvey and long a member of the police force, was named chief of police. In 1926 H.E. Ball was replaced, but there was constant controversy within the department, and two years later he was elected city police court judge, a post he would hold to the benefit of his nephews until the early fifties.

The Ball-Colson Feud got under way in 1921 (see Footnote Twenty-Six). At the time, the older brothers were operating the Railroad Restaurant near the train terminal, and Alvey was working for his father at a grocery he had on 19th. All three were married by mid-1921.

Floyd had married Allie Moran Herndon in January of 1916, soon after he turned seventeen. She was a tiny red-headed, green-eyed "knockout" who immediately started working with him in his business. Little is known of her antecedents. She told the census taker that she was born in Virginia, while she told her foster daughter that she came from a small town in Kentucky.[1] It is likely that she was related to B.P. Herndon, who operated Herndon's Saloon on Lothbury, directly across from Frank Ball's Shady Grove. (When the town went dry in 1915, Ira Ball converted

Herndon's Saloon to Ira's Place, supposedly a soft drink establishment.) Allie and Floyd lived next door to his family home on Cumberland Avenue near 15th Street.

Alvey was seventeen and not yet out of school when he married Gladys Calloway. She lived with her grandparents, John and Melvina Wyrick, on a farm a couple of miles outside of Middlesboro. The two teenagers were mostly together in groups, going to church, making candy at someone's house, or sitting on the front porch playing games. One night in April of 1921 they decided to elope, and the next day they slipped across the border to Cumberland Gap, Tennessee, and got married. They did not tell anyone of the wedding for a week, as they were sure their families would object because of their age.[2]

After they had announced their marriage, Alvey and Gladys moved in with his parents. Also living there were Ira and his second wife, Lillian (nee Morgan), who had married only a few weeks before. Though they were later quite affectionate, the two brides at first considered their mother-in-law to be "mean as a stripped snake," as Sallie put them to doing all the cooking for the family. As soon as possible Alvey and Gladys moved into an apartment over the store that was across the street from Frank Ball's residence.

Almost immediately Gladys was drawn into the family businesses, hauling produce to the restaurant and store and helping out there. It was only a little over six months after her wedding that Doyle Colson was killed—the first fatality in the Ball-Colson Feud. Gladys was an eyewitness to Ira's shootout with George Colson. Her first child was born soon thereafter. When the newborn was taken to the hospital for Ira to see, he lamented, "Well, it's not a boy, so we won't get to name it Ira." Floyd announced that the baby would be named for him anyway, so she was called Ira Beatrice. That evening Ira died.

Even before the feud ended, events had taken an interesting turn. The Volstead Act had passed in 1919 and Prohibition was the law of the land. The Balls already had their business relationship with moonshiners in Tennessee and their connections in Chicago through Jack Zuta (see Footnote Twenty-Seven). Soon they had a two-way trade set up, with moonshine from Kentucky and Tennessee being sent to Chicago, while bonded whiskey from Canada was made available to them through their friends up north. As they dealt with the Chicago gangsters, the Balls began to ape their methods, moving to control gambling and other "vices" while investing much of their profits in corrupt politicians and in various activities that seemed to benefit "the little people" in a Robin Hood sort of way. At the same time they were able to capitalize on their reputation as dangerous men whom one did not wish to anger. Alvey used to boast that he was just like Al Capone, only with a smaller territory in which to operate.

During the twenties the Balls, including their father, Frank, were frequently arrested for bootlegging, as were some of their friends, particularly Wallace Gastineau. Bootlegging was also rampant in the county, with a number of places selling liquor on the road between Pineville and Middlesboro. Gambling was common in these joints, mostly in the form of cards, dice, and tipboards.

Floyd Gilbert had one such place, which he called the Halfway House, undoubtedly for its location at a point roughly midway between Bell County's two towns. Gilbert was more a contemporary of Frank than of his boys. His grandfather, Alex Gilbert, had been the first blacksmith in the area and had done work on the wagon trains that passed through the Gap. Floyd was reared in Middlesboro and early on worked as a miner. When he was eighteen he got into an altercation at the Quarterhouse, which resulted in his killing a man in self-defense. He served at one time on the city police force and also operated a boardinghouse on 19th Street before opening the Halfway House. Reputedly he was the first person to bring slot machines for gambling into Bell County. He obtained twelve of them from a friend in Harlan and lent a couple to the Balls to try out. They were so taken with the possibilities that they immediately began to get into gambling in a big way.

By 1926 the slot machines were so widespread that County Attorney D.W. Bingham "declared war" on the slots and other gambling devices, which he claimed were available throughout the county. The raids he instigated netted fifty-four of the machines. It was noted at the time that some of the slot machines were owned by an operator out of Knoxville, but this would soon change as the Balls gradually worked toward their goal of controlling all the machine gambling in the county.

Their plan was simplicity itself. The Balls provided the slot machines and took 50 percent of the profits. It soon became apparent that if anyone bought his own machines, these would almost immediately suffer irreparable damage. Occasionally when someone wanted a particular type of slot machine that the Balls did not have in their inventory, he would be allowed to purchase it himself, taking the cost off the top. But it was understood that the machine belonged to the Balls and that after the purchaser recouped the slot's cost, the take was still to be divided 50/50 with the Balls. Sometimes the Balls insisted on their cut even before the cost of the machine had been amortized.[3]

As they tightened their control over Bell County, it became almost impossible to say "no" to the Balls. When the operator of the Garmeda Mine told the Balls he would not allow them to put slot machines in his commissary, one of his storage sheds mysteriously blew up. The next day the Balls returned, again politely requesting the privilege of providing his commissary with slot machines. When the mine operator again refused, a second storehouse was demolished. Finally, faced with ruin unless he acceded, he agreed to the slot machines.[4]

The 1920s were a time of laying the foundation for Ball power. The brothers had started the decade vying for a piece of the action. By the end of that ten-year period they had rid themselves of certain potential rivals and had intimidated others. Along the way they had gained a reputation for ruthlessness when they were crossed. Several incidents enhanced that notoriety.

Alvey was acquitted of shooting John Hurst during the Courthouse melee in 1922 that was a part of the Ball-Colson Feud, but many were not convinced of his innocence. He was known to be of a fractious nature, much like his late brother Ira. In the last few months of 1927 alone he engaged in two gunfights. In October he was shot in the thigh during an exchange of bullets at the Crystal Cafe. Then, in early December, he shot a railroad man while at the Old Dixie Club House on the Pineville Pike. At first it was thought the man's wounds would prove fatal, since according to the first reports he had been shot through the head, the bullet going in one ear and out the other, as well as twice in the shoulder and back. But no warrants were sworn out and, when the man's condition improved, the matter was simply dropped.

During this period Floyd was involved in a shooting with a fatal outcome. In 1929 he was on his way to a carnival in Pineville but decided to stop by the poolroom operated by one of his black associates, James Cunningham, for a quick game of poker. It was said that the only thing Floyd loved more than carnivals was gambling.

The trouble actually began with a jealous husband, J.R. King, who was quarreling with his wife, Mamie, over her familiarity with a man by the name of Giles "Curly" Golston. The altercation escalated, and King stabbed Mamie a number of times, then rushed to the poolroom, where he knew Golston to be. As King ran into the building, he managed to grab a colt revolver from under the counter in the front room, then darted to the back, where Floyd was seated with Golston and two other men, Conley Gibson and Charlie Sanders. When he reached the door, King started shooting. His first two bullets hit Golston in the shoulder and leg. The next bullet hit Gibson, killing him instantly. He then shot Sanders, only wounding him. His fifth and last shot grazed Floyd's shoulder blade, cutting his shirt and breaking the skin in several places. King fled the building, still clutching the empty revolver, and almost immediately ran into three patrolmen who were returning to City Hall with a prisoner. They stopped King, thrusting a pistol in his stomach, and making him surrender his own weapon. At that point the policemen did not even know what he had done. Suddenly Floyd Ball, who had been in hot pursuit of King, rounded the corner onto Ashbury. Although King was in police custody, Floyd fired a fatal shot, killing him instantly.

Floyd was taken to Pineville to be charged and then was released on bond. Nothing came of the case, it being dismissed on the grounds that Mamie had disappeared and King was "an Alabama Negro" who had not been in Middlesboro long and who had, after all, just killed a man when he met his own demise.

It was not unusual for Floyd to gamble with a group of African-American friends. Throughout their reign, the Balls always had close ties to the blacks in town. Joe McKinney, who ran the Silver Slipper, was considered a close ally and one of their right-hand men. Among the Balls' friends there was little discrimination. One comrade remembered that "Blacks and whites usually mixed, both in gambling and drinking. As long as you had money, it didn't matter what color you were."[5] The Balls are generally given credit for the fact that Middlesboro, even in the thirties and forties, had only limited segregation in housing. African-Americans formed one of their strongest voting blocks, and they encouraged their dissemination throughout the city's precincts, even to the point of buying houses for persons of color in order to increase their political control.

Even as the Balls secured their power in the city during the twenties, their private lives became more complicated. In August of 1924 a second daughter, Edna Floyd, was born to Alvey and Gladys. Two years later they had Frances Lorraine, followed in 1929 by Alva Franklin, who would always be known as Sonny. This was despite a rather stormy marital course. Alvey, long known as being fractious, was also a heavy drinker and a ladies' man with a wandering eye. He was the opposite of the relatively quiet, hard-working homebody he had married.

Indicative of their relationship is the story Gladys told of Alvey's homecoming from prison in 1931. Alvey had been in the federal penitentiary for a year (the only extended time in prison for either of the brothers[6]), and Gladys had no idea he was being released until her mother-in-law called and told her to cook chicken with dumplings and dressing, his favorite dinner, as he would be home that night. Gladys rushed about, making sure the house was just so, the children clean and prepped for the homecoming, and dinner ready to serve as soon as he walked in the door. In he came, barely pausing to greet her and ignoring the children. Alvey went straight to his room, changed his clothes, and went out again without any explanation. He did not return until the next day. Gladys later learned that he had been at an all-night party thrown to celebrate his release.[7]

Floyd's love life was even more complicated. His first wife, Allie, had female problems and needed to have an early hysterectomy, so that she was never able to have children. From the beginning she helped him in his businesses and did so even after their divorce in 1926. Allie continued in the liquor business, as well as having several "girls" working for her, most of her life. It was always said that as long as Floyd Ball lived, he protected her, and any time she was in trouble or needed anything, he was always there for her.

But in 1926 he had other things on his mind. Lina Smith was one of the most beautiful girls in town, tall and slender, the antithesis of Allie, who had gained a great deal of weight following her surgery. Lina was the daughter of one of the "better" families in town. Her father, a mine operator, had died in a work accident, leaving the family financially strapped. After his death her mother taught herself to sew and became an accomplished seamstress, supporting herself and her five children with her skills. She insisted that each of her offspring work hard and get a good education.

Lina was her second child and was said to be her favorite, the one who was always petted and babied by the others. Lina attended Lincoln Memorial University but quit when she married Tom Jasper. The marriage lasted only a year, however, and she came back home to live. She was working at the National Bank when she got to know Floyd, who would bring in large cash deposits. Even then he was known for his charm, and she was intrigued by the man and by all the gifts he showered on her. She was, of course, aware of his reputation, but a certain wildness is often very titillating to a sheltered, well-bred young lady.

At the time, Lina's older sister was working in Versailles, just outside Lexington, Kentucky. Lina suddenly announced that she wished to join her sister so that she could resume her college education, this time at the University of Kentucky. Her real purpose, however, was to be near Floyd, who had recently been incarcerated at the state prison. He was soon released, and the couple returned to Middlesboro, probably marrying soon thereafter.

They moved into a small house in the area of town known as the Rhine, which was less than half a mile from the family compound at 15th and

Cumberland. The house, really little more than a shack according to those who remember it, was across the creek from the road (15th Street), and it was necessary to cross a small, rickety bridge to get to it. This was not the life Lina had envisioned. To make matters worse, Floyd's charm could quickly turn to cold anger when he was crossed.

Lina's mother was heartbroken over the match. She would not allow "Mr. Ball" in her house and grieved constantly. No doubt Lina was also cut off from many of her friends and their social activities, since they considered Floyd little more than a thug.

One November day in 1927, while home alone in the little house by the creek, Lina put a gun to her breast and pulled the trigger. Floyd came home to find her lying in a pool of blood. She was taken to the hospital and was conscious for about three hours before she lapsed into a coma and died. Floyd was there along with her family. She was able to tell them that she was despondent over her marriage,which she felt was a grave mistake, and over her mother's pronounced grief and disappointment. Lina was just twenty-three.[8]

A year later Floyd remarried. His bride was Mary Lee Wilson, a Bell County girl whose father drove a taxi in Pineville. She was tall and dark-headed, pretty, though not unusually beautiful, with a pleasant disposition; she had just turned sixteen at the time of the wedding. The couple moved into one of the Ball houses near 15th and Cumberland, and on August 9, 1929, their first child, Wilma Lee, was born. She was joined by a sister, Sally Louise, two years later.

The Thirties

While the twenties had been a time for Alvey and Floyd to claw their way to the top of the heap, the thirties were the decade that saw the Balls consolidating their power, both financial and political.

From the time they first came to Middlesborough, the Ball family had been interested in politics. Alvey and Floyd simply built on the influence and experience of their uncles and father and expanded their power through a carrot-and-stick strategy, spreading around the wealth generated by their growing slot machine business and trading on the fear engendered by their own reputation for violence. In their political endeavors they were aided by their extended family and their wide circle of friends and allies.

At first they limited themselves to city politics, but by the mid-thirties Alvey and Floyd were deeply involved in county politics and had essentially taken control of both parties. They captured the County Election Com-

The southwest corner of 19th and Lothbury, ca. 1930. Courtesy of Don Carroll.

mission, thereby enabling them to dictate who would be election officers. It became accepted as fact that all elections were rigged. One independent soul who had the audacity to run for office without their blessing complained privately that he did not get credit for a single vote in his own precinct, even though he knew he had voted for himself.

Of particular help in the control of county politics was the Balls' alliance with Gaines Williamson. Gaines had learned at his father's knee a passion for politics and a love of the Democratic party. He cast his first vote when he was just fourteen. At the time, he was delivering groceries for Hyde's Grocery Store, which was used as a polling place, and on this particular Saturday in 1928 there was a school board election. Alvey and Floyd Ball came into the store. They were upset at how few people had turned out to vote, and they "jumped on" Henry Hyde, telling him to get out and round up some voters. Then they looked at Gaines and asked if he had voted. He said he was too young. Undeterred by such fine details, they registered him on the spot and had him vote.[9]

Soon thereafter Gaines developed a business relationship with the Balls. His brother Joe, with the help of other family members, produced a fine grade of moonshine. Each morning Gaines would drive to high school in the family's Model A Ford with eleven cases of moonshine stashed in the back. He'd park the car in the garage of someone who lived near the school. After classes, when he reclaimed the car, it would be empty.

By the time he was twenty Gaines was already deeply involved in politics, and by 1936 he was running the Bell County Democratic Party. The Republicans were by far the dominant party in the county, but since the Democrats were usually in power in the statehouse, the Democratic leader in a county had certain advantages of patronage and access that gave him an importance unrelated to the number of Democratic voters. Together, the Balls and Gaines were a powerful force.

Once the Balls were able to deliver the county to a favored candidate on the state level, they gained a certain amount of influence in Frankfort. This was greatly enhanced by the fact that, as the profits from their slot machine empire started flowing in, they began to make rather sizable contributions to those in power in Frankfort.

The money also went to purchase property, both rental houses and businesses—bars, a vending and music machine business (probably more slot machines than anything else), a billiard parlor, and roadhouses out in the county. In the mid-thirties Floyd and Alvey bought the Wabash Hotel on the corner of 18th and Lothbury, just across from the railroad depot, the same location that thirty-five years earlier had boasted the Shady Grove, owned by their father. Downstairs in the Wabash was a saloon with dance floor, slot machines, and food service. On the first floor also was the office of Middlesboro Wholesale Liquor and Wine Company, which was owned in large part by the Balls. Upstairs there were gambling rooms and girls. Behind the Wabash was a smaller building that housed a counting room and a place to repair the slot machines.

As the slot machine business grew, responsibility for maintaining the slots and collecting the proceeds was delegated to their close friend Wallace Gastineau, who was helped by Alvey's brother-in-law, Benny Gerstle. Wallace was somewhat older than Floyd, but they grew up in the same neighborhood, and Wallace's father had operated a store and restaurant near the railroad terminal, the area where several of the Balls had saloons. Wallace graduated from the University of Kentucky and went on to law school but never formally practiced law. No one seems to know the reason. When his son-in-law questioned him, he would always laugh and say, "I'm right on 19th with the whores where I want to be."[10] He did serve as legal counsel for the Balls throughout their careers, and it was rumored that he also provided legal advice to Merle Middleton, the boss in Harlan County, and served as a link between the two empires.[11] He also sold bootleg liquor from the drugstore he owned on Ashbury.

It was Wallace and Benny who devised a simple way of counting slot machine profits. They emptied the machines into cigar boxes and, with a sweep of the hand, leveled off the coins. One box went to the business owner and the other to the Balls. Often the Balls' share was sold back to the business, so there were plenty of coins for future players. Usually when the coins were rolled, there was a little in excess of what had been estimated for the box. This was an extra profit to the owner or manager, or sometimes to the person who did the counting and rolling of coins. This was not done with dimes, as they were harder to calculate. Half dollars and silver dollars were also usually counted.[12]

During the thirties Floyd seemed gradually to pull a velvet glove over his iron fist, so that as the decade wore on there were fewer reports of altercations, scraps with the law, or physical aggression. Alvey, however, continued to be known as fractious and often violent. He was also drinking heavily.

In June of 1933 Alvey shot and killed Jake Simpson at the Evergreen Inn, a roadhouse located just south of town on the old Wilderness Road. Simpson was twenty-five at the time and the father of three young children. The exact motive was unclear, although there had been some type of disagreement or altercation earlier between the two men. That night Simpson told his friend Axley Barney, "I've been having trouble with Ball and I do not mean to let him get the ups on me." The two men drove together to the Evergreen, which was owned by the Balls, and ordered beers to be brought out to the car. There was a dance going on inside at the time. As they drank their beers, Jake took out a revolver and laid it on the car seat. Alvey pulled up in a car behind them, got out, and headed for the Inn. Suddenly he wheeled around and came back toward the Simpson vehicle. Barney, anticipating trouble, started to get out of the car. Ball said something to Simpson, then suddenly poked a gun inside the car and started shooting. Four bullets hit Simpson in the head and jaw, immediately killing him. Barney was wounded slightly in the back. A customer coming out of the inn at the time of the shooting was hit in the arm by a stray bullet. Alvey calmly returned to the inn, telling someone who was running out to see what was happening. "It's all over." He then went to Middlesboro and turned himself in to the police.

At the trial it soon became apparent that no one had seen anything. The only other person present at the time of the killing was Barney, who said his back was turned. The undertaker, George Callison, who was the first person to handle the body, stated that Simpson was sitting behind the steering wheel and that his gun was on the seat under his leg. It had not been fired. But the prosecutor, Walter Smith, stated that he could not make a case, and Judge D.C. Jones dismissed the charge. (Both Smith and Jones were friends and longtime political allies of the Balls.)

In 1936 Alvey again killed someone. This particular shooting death stuck in the collective memory of the town and was recalled in later years more than any other, probably because it seemed to prove how very dangerous it was to upset Alvey. The night it happened, Alvey was in the Tropical Gardens, the nightclub operated in conjunction with the Wabash Hotel. His cousin Ed Ball was tending bar. Two couples had rented the front upstairs suite at the Wabash for a private party. But one of the men kept coming downstairs and "ragging" Alvey. Ed later recalled that he took the man back upstairs at least three times and told him to stay there, as Alvey "was getting higher and higher." Ed's shift was over and he was just starting home when he heard gunshots. He was later told that the man had once again come downstairs and had picked up a butcher knife that Lee Cosmos, the cook, was using to cut up steaks. He started toward Alvey, and Alvey shot him.[13]

The account in the newspapers and at the trial was somewhat different. It was reported that Carl Frederick, who had been in Middlesboro only a short time, was at the Tropical Gardens with his friends E.M. Ethridge and his wife. The three of them worked for the same photography firm. They had reportedly been drinking heavily and were rather noisy and boisterous, though it was early in the evening. Mrs. Ethridge perched on the piano, "mashing the keys" as Alvey put it at the trial. Alvey said he went over and told her to sit at a table and stop disturbing the guests. He went on to testify that while he was talking to her, Frederick grabbed him from the rear and threw him all the way across the room, where he landed on his knees between some tables. As Frederick then started toward him, Ball said he drew two pistols and warned him to come no closer. Frederick retreated, but as he did so, he was heard to threaten, "I'm going to cut his heart out and fry it on a hot plate."

Much later that night, Frederick and Mr. Ethridge returned to the Tropical Gardens. They were seated on stools at the bar when Alvey approached them. Frederick called out to Ball, saying he was "yellow" and, as Alvey testified at his trial, "referred to him in other uncomplimentary ways." Ball said he then drew his pistols and fired into the ceiling. Frederick rose from his stool and lurched toward him, shouting, "You're firing blanks, you yellow coward." Ball shot him in the head, killing him instantly.

There were many witnesses in the bar that night, and all corroborated the account thus far. The question was whether Frederick had a knife in his hand when he lunged at Ball, thus making the fatal shot self-defense. The bartender testified that Frederick had been whittling on the bar with his knife just before the shooting. Ethridge denied Frederick was doing so, claiming he had known him for years and that he never carried a pocket knife. He went on to assert that his friend had "made no move to harm Ball when Ball killed him." Some of the witnesses mentioned a knife in their testimony, but since many of these were employees of the Balls, there was some doubt about their credibility. The undertaker, Hobert Cawood, testified that P.L. Perry, the night chief of police, had taken charge of a knife that was found at the scene. The prosecuting attorney demanded that the knife be produced. The defense countered that Perry had stored it and that he was in an out-of-state sanatorium being treated for low blood pressure and could not return to testify.

The jury was out only a short time before returning a verdict of not guilty.

A somewhat different version is repeated by most people and may even represent a second killing at the Wabash. Toward the end of his life, Alvey used to boast that he had killed six men, but this author could find records of only the two (Simpson and Fredericks) given above.[14]

The local story of the killing at the Wabash has a traveling salesman coming into the dining area with some friends. He quite possibly did not know who Alvey was, yet for some unknown reason he kept trying to get Alvey to eat with him. He is also said to have made some disparaging remark about Alvey's size and suggested that Alvey was afraid to sit with him. Suddenly Alvey pulled a gun and shot him. He died instantly, his face falling forward into his plate of scrambled eggs.

Glen Weaver, who claimed to have been present at the time, set the date at 1938 or 1939. Upstairs, Floyd was involved in a poker game. When he heard the shots fired, his first reaction was, "What's Alvey done now?" He sent one of the men who was watching the game, Dave Crockett, down to see what had happened. When Crockett returned to report that Alvey had killed someone, Floyd handed him his cards to play and went downstairs to fix things. Crockett did not recall hearing anything further about the killing, other than that the man's family had come from Texas to claim the body.[15]

Whether it was one or two killings at the Wabash, Alvey was certainly gaining a reputation as a man one avoided irritating at all costs. Illustrating this, Alvey's son told of the time his father was playing pinochle with some friends. One of the men, "Pig" Wilson, was dealt the ultimate hand, one that would almost certainly win. But he was afraid to show his cards because of how Alvey might react. So without saying anything he gathered up his hand and walked out the door. He then mailed his hand to the other players.

While the thirties was a decade of increasing power for the Balls, it was not a good period in their home lives. Alvey was fractious not only in public, he was increasingly difficult at home. Lillie Banks, who worked in their home for Alvey and Gladys in the late thirties and early forties, recalled that he was "bad to drink," and when drunk would draw his guns on herself and Gladys. He had two .45s, "as big as he was," and "he liked to play with them all the time."[16] When he got bad, Lillie would mostly just leave, but she could recall that Gladys would sometimes give him shots to calm him down.

Another long-time resident recalled being awakened one night by a noise like someone running and then a pounding at the back door. It was Gladys, who cried out that Alvey was after her, threatening to kill her. Such was the family's fear of Alvey that rather than coming to Gladys's aid themselves, they let her stay outside while they called her brother, who lived nearby, to come get her.[17]

It was probably during the late thirties that Alvey became addicted to drugs. His problem began one night when he came in from a heavy drinking bout, shaking all over. Gladys called a doctor who lived nearby to come to the house. He gave Alvey a shot that stopped the shakes; then Gladys held him in her lap, rocking him like a baby until he calmed down. From then on he was on drugs as well as liquor.[18]

Floyd too was having trouble with alcohol during the thirties, but it was not he but his wife Mary Lee who was drinking heavily. One of their babysitters from that period recalled a number of times when Mary Lee became quite drunk and Floyd reacted violently.[19] One incident that stands out in the family's memory is the time Floyd called to tell Mary Lee that he wanted to bring a colleague home for supper, so she should fix something special. When he walked in with his friend some hours later, Mary Lee was sitting in the middle of the living room floor, a huge bowl of biscuit dough between her knees, and she was drunkenly plopping the dough around like a child making mud pies.

It soon became apparent that Mary Lee could not stay home alone and have the responsibility of her young daughters. One of the "working girls" at the Wabash had become quite friendly with Mary Lee, and Floyd asked her to come stay at the house. Verna Jo Daugherty was from Frakes, the area of Bell County that was then referred to as South America because of its isolation. In later years Jo was a gracious, reserved lady, but when Floyd brought her home she was one of the local girls who plied 19th Street, using the Wabash as home base.[20] Attesting to her skill at her profession is the story told by a local resident who was at the time a clerk in the Montgomery Ward store. She recalled how Jo would go shopping in the morning, select a dress, and put it on layaway. She would then be back several times during the day, paying some each time on the dress. Often by closing she would have made enough to get her dress out of layaway in time for "the evening trade."

Soon Jo had taken Mary Lee's place, and the latter had been sent to a sanatorium. Floyd and Jo were married on November 24, 1936. She was twenty-four at the time; he was thirty-eight.

In 1937 Floyd bought a house on 25th Street, moving for the first time away from the Ball enclave in the East End.[21] The house itself was a fairly modest bungalow with a good deal of property in the rear where Floyd built a swimming pool with a bath house that featured a juke box and a small soda fountain so his children and their friends could make themselves milkshakes and other treats. One feature of the stucco house was a wall of glass bricks in the living room that let in natural light but blocked visibility. Floyd placed his large desk in front of that wall and had several of the opaque glass bricks replaced with special clear bricks that allowed him to look out without any one being able to see in. He continued, however, to conduct most of his business in his offices in and behind the Wabash. He was home each night for supper with his family but then left soon afterward to head back downtown.[22]

The Forties

The 1940 census showed Middlesboro to have a population of 11,777. During the decade that would increase to 14,419 and the county population would reach 43,812, its highest point to date.

In August of 1940 Middlesboro celebrated its fiftieth year with a Golden Anniversary celebration. A special edition of the newspaper chronicled the progress of the city. Along with histories of businesses and industries and stories of early days were biographic sketches of the city's leaders. The one about the Balls stated, "The two brothers are extensively engaged in the real estate business and other enterprises....They are influential in the political, commercial and economic life of Middlesboro and Bell County, and their support is invariably sought for all projects designed to contribute to the betterment of the community." The article went on to point out that Floyd was past exalted ruler of the Elks and Alvey presently held that position. It continued, "Both Floyd and Alva Ball are among the most progressive and public spirited citizens of Middlesboro and their contribution to life in the city is daily felt by scores of people."

As the money flowed in from the liquor and slot machine operations, the Balls plowed it into more legitimate businesses. They already owned the Wabash Hotel, a number of roadhouses out in the county, a bar and billiard hall in Middlesboro, a filling station, and a large number of rental houses scattered throughout the city. They were also partners in a new car agency, the Ball-Cawood Motor Company, and a wholesale liquor company. During the early to mid-forties they invested in the Cumberland Hotel, the Middlesboro Stockyards, the Pineville Laundry, Ball's Motor Court (a tourist court just outside the city limits), the Greyhound Bus Terminal Building, Cumberland Homes (builder of prefab homes), the Middlesboro Gas Company, and the Reed Manufacturing Company, a maker of mousetraps. In many cases their partners in these enterprises were leading businessmen in town. They also continued to buy up real estate, mostly low-rent "shanty" houses. By 1943 they were the largest property holders in the city of Middlesboro.

Not all their business ventures were profitable. They lost money on mousetraps and prefab buildings. It was also discovered later that many of the deeds to the houses they purchased were faulty.

The Balls did have another source of income: the assessment. Whenever they needed a lot of cash to swing an election or for some other purpose, they would go to each bar owner and tell him what his assessment would be. If the cash was not immediately forthcoming they would send an associate (some said "a thug") around to pick up the contribution. This arrangement was later formalized as the Southeastern Protective Association, an organization of Bell County alcohol dealers, numbering forty or fifty, who joined together to protect their interests.[23]

Gaines Williamson, who by this time had his own bar, the Manhattan Bar & Grill, recalled one incidence in particular. He and Floyd were in Frankfort together. The court of appeals was about to make a decision on one of the wet-dry elections, and Floyd asked Gaines to see if he could find out what the decision would be, since Gaines was a close friend of the attorney general. Williamson was able to relay the information that the court would decide in favor of the "wets." When Gaines got home the next day, he found a notice of an assessment and learned that the Balls had let it be known that it was costing them $40,000 to ensure a vote for the "wets"

Cumberland Avenue in the 1940s. Courtesy of the Bell County Historical Society.

and everyone had to pay up. Of course, when the decision was announced, the bar owners felt the assessment had been justified.

The Balls did not limit their gambling income to slot machines. They also ran high-stakes poker games. In the early years these games were to accommodate the big-time bootleggers who, during the years of national Prohibition, came in from cities such as Knoxville or Kingsport to pick up a load of bonded whiskey that had come down the pipeline from Canada. But soon there were players who came to town just for the private high-stakes games, and at one time one of the biggest places for gambling in the country was the second floor of a building on Cumberland Avenue. Several of the gambling establishments operated twenty-four hours a day and also offered blackjack and dice. They mimicked Las Vegas in that the drinks and girls were on the house for the high rollers. The Balls themselves, particularly Floyd, loved to gamble and often participated in the action.

This love of gambling led, in late 1940, to the loss of one of their oldest allies, George Fisher Sr. Colonel Fisher had been in law enforcement most of his life, working both as a city policeman and in the county sheriff's office, and had always been supportive of the Ball family. A large hulking man with a huge handlebar mustache, he was known as the "Bull of the Town" or simply "Big Bull." As years went by he acquired the Fad Pool Room on 19th and a row of rental houses referred to as the "Stripped Six," as well as other property around town. It was rumored that some of his rentals sheltered prostitutes who worked under his protection. Fisher was killed by Clyde Buchanon on December 17, 1940.

The official story was that Buchanon was wanted for questioning, and when he did not answer a summons, Chief of Police Charlie Minton and officers P.L. Perry and George Fisher went to his trailer near Indian Rock to arrest him. He was at the table having breakfast when they arrived and asked to be allowed to finish. The moment the lawmen were off guard, he grabbed a pistol, shot and killed Fisher, and seriously wounded Minton. Perry ran off to get help and Buchanon, who had himself been seriously wounded in the exchange of fire power, escaped by walking, with the help of his son, through the railroad tunnel to Tennessee and on into Virginia.

Those once close to the Balls give a different twist to the story.[24] They say that Buchanon held himself out to be a traveling repairman of cook stoves, practicing that trade with some success, but was actually a professional gambler who used his cover to con locals into playing cards with him. One night he got into a poker game with Alvey, Floyd, and Walter B. Smith, the county attorney. He cleaned them out. When they found out the truth about him, the Balls sent their friends out to arrest Buchanon, planning to extract not only their lost money but also a little revenge.

Reaction to Fisher's murder was swift. A huge posse led by the county attorney and by Alvey Ball set out on a massive manhunt. Meanwhile Buchanon's son, who was nineteen, had managed to get him well into Virginia and hide him in a gully. His father was bleeding heavily, so the boy went to the nearest community to obtain bandages and medicine. Someone in the local store realized the young stranger fit the description put out by the Kentucky authorities and reported his presence back to those in Middlesboro. Heavily armed, the posse crowded into thirteen cars and sped to Virginia, unconcerned about such questions as jurisdiction. The posse surrounded Buchanon, who was lying by a small fire in the gully. Smith called for him to surrender, and at the same time Alvey Ball shouted, "Come out with your hands up." Buchanon, knowing his time had come, fired once. There was an answering volley of more than fifty shots from the posse. He was, according to reports, "chewed up like sausage." When the firestorm ceased, it was discovered that he had only one bullet left in his gun and no spare bullets on or around him.

In his will Fisher named Floyd Ball as the executor of his rather considerable estate and appointed Floyd and Alvey guardians of his two youngest children. Both George Jr., who was six when his father died, and his sister Thelma felt, with some apparent justification, that the Balls appropriated most of their father's estate to their own use.[25]

Although the Balls were aggressive in their pursuit of profits from gambling, liquor, and their business deals, they did eschew two sources of in-

Cumberland Hotel. Courtesy of the Bell County Historical Society.

come. They did not profit directly from prostitution. The town was truly "wide open." Professionals from elsewhere considered Middlesboro one of the best stops on the "circuit"—they were not hassled by the police and often the only split was with the hotel owner for room rent. The most successful girls, however, were the local ones. They ran around together, went shopping and out to eat like any group of friends, and were well accepted on 19th. Some would lease rooms full-time in one of the hotels and would only have to pay rent. They would run their businesses themselves, utilizing the hotel porters as needed. Others worked for nothing as waitresses and barmaids in the joints that lined 19th and Lothbury Streets as a way of soliciting customers.[26] Daisy Tamer, owner of the Majestic Hotel,[27] was one of the first to reserve several rooms to be rented on an hourly basis for the express purpose of prostitution; soon, she was running a brothel. As time went on some of the hotel owners demanded a split of the girls' income as well as rent.[28] And there were always a few, like Allie Ball and Fanny Fife, who "ran" a few girls, acting like the more traditional madam. The Balls, however, simply rented rooms in the Wabash to the girls and let them conduct their own business.

Alvey and Floyd also declined to involve themselves in another potentially profitable activity, chicken fighting. Middlesboro in the 1930s and 1940s had an international reputation as a center for this sport. In fact, one of the most famous breeds of fighting chickens, the Blue Boons, was developed in the Yellow Creek Valley and shipped not only to other parts of the U.S. but also to Hawaii, the Philippines, and various places in Asia.[29] Most of the big contests were held at Alvarado, a farm owned by Alva Campbell just outside the city, and drew participants from as far away as New Orleans. The Balls were often among the spectators and liked to wager on the results but did not participate in any other way.

As rapidly as the cash flowed in, it could go out just as fast. Perhaps because of his hardscrabble beginning, Floyd in particular enjoyed giving away money. Anyone could walk up to him on the street and ask him for a dollar or more and it would be forthcoming. He enjoyed driving up in front of houses in a poor section of town and simply throwing a handful of coins to the children playing there. It was well accepted that no one ever went hungry if the Balls knew about it. At Christmas they provided more baskets than did the Salvation Army and all the other charitable organizations put together. Undoubtedly some of what he did was political charity, like that practiced by many politicians, that resulted in owed favors. But much of the time it seemed Floyd genuinely loved playing the part of Santa Claus all year long, even when there was no political advantage. For example, once when he was in New York City Floyd was walking down the street and saw a poorly clad youngster with his nose pressed to the display window of a sporting goods store. Floyd took the lad in and fitted him out with a complete baseball outfit, including a uniform, ball, bat, and glove, with nothing expected in return.[30]

Floyd was not considered an easy man with whom to do business because he was notorious for being "slow pay." He might ignore a debt or a payment due for months, then when the person he owed finally ran him down, pull out a wad of cash and pay the whole amount at once.[31] He always dealt in cash, eschewing checks. He had a little office behind the Wabash where he would be once a week to pay off what he owed. There would often be a line of people waiting for payments, and he would continue until he ran out of cash. The owner of a furniture store on 19th recalled how Floyd would drop by the store and tell him to send a houseful of new furniture out to some family that was in need. The man said he would always try to be in front of the pay line the next week so that he would be sure to get paid before Floyd's ready cash ran out that day.[32]

At the same time, Floyd was not one to push if a debt was owed him. Alvey was of a different turn. He kept a black book with his debtors listed and the exact date they were to repay him. He was always quick to remind someone when they were overdue, usually checking his book and saying, "Haven't I got a piece of you?" Yet he too could be charitable. Once Alvey won a man's business in a poker game but then graciously gave it back, thus saving the man's family from ruin.[33] Alvey was also the more dependable of the two. If he agreed to do something, a person could bank on it. And if he said he would meet you somewhere at a certain time, he would be there at that exact time, while Floyd might turn up two days later.

Alvey and Floyd were night owls. It was not unusual for them to stop in one of the joints at midnight or 1:00 a.m. and order up a complete steak dinner. By the same token, they were often still in their pajamas at noon. Alvey's one distinction, outside of the obvious, was that he loved to roller skate and was very good at it. It was considered quite an honor and a privilege if he asked someone to skate with him.

Both men seemed to have a faculty for inspiring strong allegiance. As they gained and consolidated their power, they were ably helped by their friends, many of whom they had been close to since childhood. Some, like Floyd Gilbert and Jack Zuta, were more contemporaries of their father and uncles and had served as mentors. Others, such as Hugh Jones, Wallace Gastineau, Jimmie Ginsberg, and their cousin Tom Manning, had been their playmates. Then there was a younger group, men like Glen Weaver, Bob Hatfield, and George Philpot, who had started hanging around 19th Street as kids, picking up loose change for small chores, and had been befriended by the Balls and gradually incorporated into their organization.[34] It wasn't just the money, or even a fear of incurring their displeasure, that engendered their intense loyalty, but rather, at least in the case of Floyd, a certain charisma and generosity of spirit that charmed his friends and often neutralized his enemies.

In 1940 everything seemed to be going the Balls' way. Not only was the money rolling in but they had control of both county and city politics. In 1941 Floyd ran for state representative and beat his opponent by a margin of four to one. During the campaign Floyd was a prominent spokesman for his party, giving speeches throughout the county urging a straight Republican ticket vote. Alvey served as chairman of both the finance and the organization committees for the campaign. The Democrats mounted little or no resistance, at least publicly, and the GOP slate of candidates swept the local elections. But in a preview of the storm clouds that were gathering on the horizon, a fledgling Law and Order Party had formed out in the county. Though unsuccessful countywide, the reform group did get one candidate elected to the Pineville City Council.

Floyd went to Frankfort in January of 1942. He rented the biggest suite of rooms he could find and immediately set about cutting a wide swath with his freely flowing money and his charm. The business of government bored him, however. The legislature had not been in session long when he beckoned a young reporter, Clay Wade Bailey, down from the press box. "Boy, I sure like your hat," he said. "I'll give you $100 for it. Now I want you to keep wearing it. I don't have time to read through all these bills. When it comes time to vote, you leave your hat on if I should vote no, and take it off if I vote yes. Now don't steer me wrong, or I'll blow your head off." Bailey wore that hat from then on and carefully studied each piece of legislation before deciding whether to remove his hat or not. His efforts were appreciated, as frequently he would find a twenty-dollar bill stuck in his pocket, a gift from Floyd.[35]

As a freshman in the House, Floyd got no notice in the newspapers, sponsored no bills, and served on no important committees, but the one issue on which he had campaigned (besides voting a straight Republican ticket), the need for funds for the proposed Cumberland Gap National Historical Park, did show up in the governor's budget. There are some who credit Floyd with a large part in the realization of the dream of a national park at the Gap.

Floyd's stint in the Legislature was marred by the death of his father on February 16, 1942. Frank Ball had been in poor health for ten years but had continued until the end to be actively in business with his sons and to be a leader in the Republican Party. His counsel would be sorely missed.

All of the saloons and other businesses along 19th and up and down Lothbury, Ashbury, and Amesbury closed for the funeral. It was the first time the bars had been closed for so many years that at one, the B & W, no one could find a key, or even remembered if there had ever been one, so someone had to stay behind to guard the liquor.

Frank was laid to rest at the old Ball-Jones Cemetery next to his son Ira. Now it was up to Floyd and Alvey to run the empire.

The Kentucky General Assembly at the time met for just sixty legislative days every two years. Soon Floyd was back full-time in Bell County, which, like everywhere else in the country, was preoccupied with the war. Coal was booming and work plentiful. Those who were on the home front labored on bond drives, scrap collections, and other projects to support the war effort. Alvey and Floyd were often among those working on one of these enterprises, and they were almost always among the top donors of funds. Alvey was usually involved as the exalted ruler of the Elks, since many cooperative efforts were made up of representatives of various civic groups.

The Elks at this time could count among its membership almost all of the prominent businessmen and professionals in not only Middlesboro but also the surrounding area and even into Tennessee. The U.S. congressman for the district, John M. Robinson of Barbourville, was initiated into the local Elks lodge in April of 1942. As the Elks' exalted ruler Alvey could not be dismissed as a common bootlegger. Nor could his brother, the state representative, who was in the forefront of so many civic endeavors. Not only the men but also many of the prominent women who were active in civic and church organizations had occasion to work with the Balls on some project.

The people in Middlesboro seemed less affronted by the bars and saloons, the drinking, gambling, and other vices than were those out in the county. Perhaps it was a more cosmopolitan attitude, but it might also have been the fact that the vice, with the exception of the slot machines, was pretty much confined to a very restricted area along 19th street and the streets that crossed it. There are many older women in Middlesboro today who say that they never ever went on 19th or saw a drunk, even though they attended school at 20th and Lothbury, one block from the center of the vice district. There were simply some streets upon which "nice" girls did not venture. It was all right to have a Coke at Lee's Drugstore on the northeast corner of 20th and Cumberland, but one did not continue down the street eastward toward 19th. One woman recalls working in a dry goods store on 19th. Her father drove her to the front door each day and picked her up after work, as she was not to walk on 19th. If one of the "professional ladies" came in to shop, the owner, who always sat in front at the cash register, would bang with a ruler on the register, a signal that she was to go to the rear of the store and busy herself in the stock room until the coast was clear.[36] Although shootings might be common in the vice district, respectable citizens were not much bothered with crime in their own homes, and the streets were safe. At any one time there were sometimes only three or four police officers on duty to patrol the whole of the city, and this was felt to be adequate. It seemed at first that Middlesboro could reap the benefits of vice without penalty.

Out in the county, however, it was a different story. Roadhouses were scattered throughout the county as well as in Pineville. The combination of alcohol, easy money from the booming coal mines, and a wartime psychology of living for the moment resulted in a lawlessness that became ever more abhorrent to many county residents. In the two and a half years from Pearl Harbor to mid-1944, forty-five homicides occurred in Bell County, far exceeding the fourteen deaths suffered by Bell County boys in the service of their country during the same time period. Ironically, a number of the aforementioned homicides involved service men who were home on leave.

It had become too much for some Bell Countians, and they began to unite in various cleanup drives, mostly led by county preachers. At first they had little effect, but as the decade wore on the reformers became more of a problem for the Balls.

In the fall of 1942, Albert "Happy" Chandler was running for the U.S. Senate. Chandler had been governor of Kentucky and was at that time already in Congress, having had himself appointed to fill the term of his predecessor, who had died in office. (He would later be U.S. baseball commissioner and then have a second term as governor.) Chandler was a Democrat and would not normally have merited support from the Balls. But he had once spent an evening with the Ball crowd at the Blue Room, a private club on Lothbury over the Kentucky Cafe. It was a place where cronies could meet privately to gamble and drink with no chance of being hassled. All of the in-crowd had keys. Chandler spent most of the night at the Blue Room, charming everyone with his stories and down-home attitude, and he gained the support of the Balls.[37]

In the tabulation room that November of 1942, the usual parody was being played out, with the hand-picked candidates of the Balls winning handily. All of a sudden Alvey came in and ordered them not to show so many votes for Chandler. They wanted to carry Bell County for him as promised but not by so wide a margin that, as he put it, "It will show us up bad with the Republicans in the state."[38] Immediately, Chandler's majority was reduced by half.

It was easy for the Balls to dictate the results of any election down to the exact number of votes. Not only was Floyd chairman of the Republican Party, and his friends Karl Harris and Gaines Williamson in charge of the Democratic Party, but Alvey was chairman of the Purgation Board and the Balls named the members of the Election Commission, which was responsible for certifying officers for each voting place. It became a common practice to let people vote their paper ballots in one box, then switch boxes with one already filled with ballots marked for the preferred candidates. The Balls also controlled who counted votes, which, prior to the advent of voting machines, was of paramount importance.

Another indication of the Balls' dominance in all things political was the firing in 1944 of the principal of the Middlesboro High School. R.L. Hamblett had served as principal for fourteen years, and his wife was a teacher in the district. There had apparently been no complaints about either until Hamblett made some remarks critical of the way the school district was being run to a group of teachers. At 7:30 p.m. he was summoned by a phone call to the office of the Ball brothers. When he arrived

Playing the slot machines, 1940s. Courtesy of the Bell County Historical Society.

four members of the School Board (C.W. Bailey, Karl Harris, Lon Robertson, and Fred Seale) were present along with School Superintendent J.W. Bradner and at least one of the Balls. (The fifth board member was in the service, stationed overseas at the time.) Mr. Hamblett later claimed that on the table before them were glasses and a pint of partly consumed whiskey along with an empty quart whiskey bottle. Mrs. Hamblett had accompanied him, but Harris took her by the arm and told her to go to the car and wait, "insisting that all would be well with me." School Superintendent Bradner and the Board remonstrated with Hamblett for some time, but when he was adamant that he would not recant his remarks, he was told to write out his resignation. The Board then adjourned to the high school for a "regular" Board meeting, and by 9:30 that same evening had accepted his resignation. In less than a week, Hamblett and his wife had left town.

The Balls' very dominance, however, led to the first cracks in their empire. Total power is corrupting and leads to a belief in invincibility. Two things happened in 1945-1946, both at least partially rooted in the belief that they could not be challenged: The Balls broke with Gaines Williamson and they reneged on a deal to back Earle Clements for governor.

The breach between Gaines and Alvey came in 1945. Gaines' eleven-year-old-son, Rudy, had been sickly and seemed unable to gain any weight, so Gaines finally took him to a specialist in Knoxville, the nearest city of any size and more than fifty miles from Middlesboro. He was admitted to St. Mary's Hospital with a tentative diagnosis of chronic tonsillitis. Once he had Rudy settled, Gaines returned to Middlesboro, a trip taking almost two hours at the time. He had hardly walked in the door when Alvey called, saying that he had a party planned and Gaines was to deliver a case of Old Granddad whiskey, a case of Old Taylor, two cases of champagne, and two country hams, already baked and sliced, the next day. At 3:00 a.m. that night, the hospital called. Rudy's appendix had ruptured, and the physicians had just performed emergency surgery. Rudy was in critical condition. With no thought but for his son's health, Gaines rushed back to the hospital. For three days and nights he sat by his son's bedside. He completely forgot about Alvey's order for liquor and food for his party. Not only did he not take care of it himself, he didn't assign the job to anyone else.

When Gaines got back to Middlesboro he immediately heard that Alvey was "bitter" toward him. In fact, as soon as he arrived at the Manhattan Bar and Grill he received a call from Alvey. He was roaring mad and ranted on and on for half an hour or more. Gaines tried to explain, but it was only after Alvey had "sort of run down" that he was able to tell him about Rudy. Alvey's response: "When the hell is your family more important than I am."[39]

From that moment on, Gaines and Alvey were enemies. This was unfortunate for the Ball empire because, even with Gaines on their side, there had been rumbles from dissident Democrats who objected to the Balls running their party and who were bolstered by the law-and-order element in the county. Several times during the late thirties and early forties local option elections were held in Bell County. Each time the "wets" won, but there were always charges of corruption. In 1943 the votes were counted four times, with a different result each time. Finally the court of appeals threw out the entire election, declaring the process corrupt beyond redemption. Meanwhile a group of Democrats in opposition to Gaines Williamson and the Balls tried to put in their own candidate for the election commission. The entire affair ended in court in Frankfort, causing unwelcome attention to politics in Bell County. A series of articles in the *Louisville Courier-Journal* by columnist Allan Trout, based largely on the court testimony, further highlighted the activities of the Ball brothers.

Although the Ball machine continued to dominate the elections that year and again in 1945, there were many in Bell County who agreed with Army Chaplin T.C. Sizemore, who was quoted in the newspaper as proclaiming, "The criminal element...dominating the political machine was destroying all the things we are fighting to defend. The only way we can better the situation is to get rid of the Ball machine." These people joined together to form a countywide organization, the Citizens League, which drew crowds of up to 500 at their public meetings. Although unable to prevail at the polls, they were able to petition successfully for another wet-dry contest in the spring of 1945. The Citizens League had also railed against the slot machines, pointing out that, unlike the sale of liquor, the use of gambling devices was already illegal. All that was needed was for the law to be enforced. But the same edition of the *Three States* that carried the Citizens League's advertisement denouncing slot machines also printed an editorial suggesting that they were not so bad and that the city should capitalize on its biggest business by extracting a "cut of the take" via taxing the machines. It pointed out that "take" for a single, relatively small business (the Hub on Cumberland Avenue) was estimated at between $1,000 and $3,000 a week. The editorial went on to say, "And for all that, it was the cleanest take of the whole 'capoodle' of gambling and power politics. The machines set [*sic*] there and bothered no one."

The local-option election was held in May of 1945. State Attorney General Eldon Dummit was in the tabulation room as the votes were counted. The "drys" won the first count, 4,907 to 4,721. In a recount the "wets" picked up thirty-three votes. The election was immediately contested, and by May of 1946 the question of local option in Bell County was before the Kentucky Court of Appeals for the seventh time in less than three years. That fall the court ruled five to three in favor of the "wets."

Meanwhile, in Middlesboro the reformers regrouped as the Mop and Broom Party. This started as a dissentient group of Republicans, tired of or perhaps embarrassed by the Ball domination of their party for so many years. They believed, as Ed Hoe wrote in a letter to the editor, the Grand Old Party in Bell County needed "to clean house where a mop and broom is really needed." Society matrons tied cleaning rags around their heads and carried brooms, while their businessmen husbands wielded mops to publicize their cause. Nevertheless, the Mop and Broom Party, which fielded a full ballot of candidates in the fall elections of 1945, went down to defeat at the hands of the Ball machine and had essentially disbanded by early 1946.

It appeared in 1946 that the Ball rule would go on forever. Alvey's citizenship rights, which he had lost as a felon, were restored by the governor that year. Floyd and Alvey joined with a prominent Pineville physician, Dr. C.B. Stacy, to incorporate the Middlesboro Gas Company and bring natural gas to the county. Alvey was chairman of the Salvation Army Board and Floyd was serving on committees of the Chamber of Commerce. Alvey had a fine farm in Virginia and was the top buyer at the Russell Hereford sales that year. Best of all, that was the year that Alvey's daughter married Wallace ("Wah Wah") Jones, one of the stars of the revered "Fabulous Five" University of Kentucky basketball team, in perhaps the largest wedding ever seen in Middlesboro. Edna had ten attendants in addition to her flower girls and the ring bearer. Eight hundred guests, recipients of the much coveted invitations, attended the wedding and reception.

Things were never quite as smooth as they seemed, however. An audit of city funds in June of 1946 showed a shortage of at least $40,000, most of it dating from 1942, 1943, and 1945. Further audits increased the missing total to almost $60,000. Rumors flew. A Court of Inquiry was convened and took testimony from two former deputy clerks at City Hall, Alberta Yoakum Lee and Patsy Roberts. They reported that the city clerk frequently took money from the cash drawer without leaving receipts and that bank deposits were made only at long intervals, sometimes four to six weeks apart. They both admitted that they had bought fur coats for themselves from Chief of Police Charles Minton for $10 each. They claimed he had had these coats in the city vault for some time. Evidence was also submitted that tax bills were marked paid but no corresponding cash posted to city accounts. The grand jury met in early 1947, and H.H. Hutcheson, the city clerk since 1938, and John Wallbrecht, former city auditor, were indicted for embezzlement of city funds. The case dragged on for another year before Hutcheson was found guilty. There was a hung jury in the Wallbrecht case, and Mrs. Roberts and Mrs. Lee, who had been indicted for negligence, were found not guilty.

Meanwhile there were statewide elections in 1947. Earle Clements was the Democratic candidate running against Republican E.S. Dummit for governor. The Democrats in Bell County proposed to the Balls that if they would back Clements, as governor he would leave the slot machines alone. The Balls agreed, but two nights before the election they changed their minds. Floyd called his people to him one at a time, gave them literature and cash, and sent them out to work for Dummit.[40] Some say this was because the Balls had learned that Gaines Williamson was going to double-cross them. It was a little late in the game, though, and Clements carried Bell County by a small margin as well as winning the vote statewide. Now the Balls had to deal with a governor who owed them nothing and a Democratic Party in their county that was no longer under their complete control.

Another major blow to the Ball empire came when the Kentucky legislature decided to form a new judicial district for Bell and Leslie Counties that would be separate from the one they had shared so long with Harlan County. For many years the Balls had helped elect the officers of the Circuit Court and had been their close friends and allies. These officials were now sent to Harlan County, and it was up to Governor Clements to appoint the officers of the new Forty-First Judicial District. With no need or desire to gain the Balls' approval, Clements appointed as Circuit Court judge R.L. Maddox, a Democrat who had been active in the Citizens League. Another Democrat, Robert J. Watson, was named commonwealth's attorney. Maddox immediately set out to demonstrate that he was different from the compliant judges with whom the Balls had dealt for the past twenty years or more.

Maddox was a long-time resident of Middlesboro who was the veteran of many legal battles and political skirmishes. At the time of his appointment he was pushing sixty, a stocky, rumpled man with small blue eyes and white wavy hair neatly parted in the middle. He must once have been a dashing figure, as the romantics in town tell how years before he went to a local Chautauqua performance and saw the beautiful Sybil Sipher giving a musical performance, playing on water glasses. They say it was love at first sight, and after a whirlwind courtship the two married and lived happily ever after.

At the same time it was certainly not "happily ever after" for Alvey and his wife Gladys. The marriage had been strained for years. Alvey had his own apartment at the back of the house, and seldom did he do more than walk through the family's portion. He and Gladys essentially did not speak to each other during the last ten years of their marriage. Should he happen to grace the family table at a meal, it was, "Sonny, ask your mother to pass such-and-such. Tell your mother so-and-so." The Balls all had parrots, and the birds did more talking to the family than did Alvey.

As long as the children were in school, Gladys stayed at the homeplace on Cumberland Avenue near 15th. Over the years the small house had been remodeled, a second floor added, and also an addition made to the rear. The family areas were always full of teenagers during the children's high school years. Gladys welcomed them all. Sonny was on the football team, Lorraine and Edna were majorettes, and all the children were involved in various school activities. Each of the children was given a brand new convertible when she or he was of age to drive, and all had plenty of ready cash. The football stadium was only a block from their house, and after-game parties at the Ball house became a ritual.

Not that the Ball teenagers were accepted by everyone. While they had many friends, a certain element in town still looked down upon them and discouraged their children from socializing with the Balls. Ira, being the eldest, probably took the brunt of this prejudice. Although she was voted Harvest Festival Queen at age fourteen, the only time a high school sophomore had won this title, sons of some of the "better" families were warned not to date her.[41] When Ira graduated from high school, Alvey rented a large house near the school and threw a huge party. A number of mothers who considered themselves "society" got together and forbade their children to attend. Daughters obeyed, but most of the boys managed to go, even if they had to "sneak" to do it. The younger children had less to contend with, partly because Floyd and Alvey had become more acceptable as they involved themselves more in civic and charitable endeavors. And of course for most teenagers the fun-loving, free-spending Balls were more attractive than the bluebloods any day. So the front of the house at 15th and Cumberland usually resounded with the sounds of popular music and laughter.

The atmosphere at the rear of the house was totally different. Alvey was drinking heavily and using "yellow jackets" (amphetamines). When sober and not using drugs he was still a savvy businessman, but often one could not tell when he had been drinking or using drugs until it was too late. Once the intoxicants loosened his fractious nature, he could do anything. If he heard something on the radio he didn't like, he was likely to pull out his pistol and shoot the radio.[42] At such times nothing and no one was safe from his temper.

Behind the Ball houses were several small structures for "the help." By the late forties no one would go in to wait on Alvey except Joe Jackson. As Joe approached, Alvey's parrot would call out, "Hey Mis Ball, here comes that Nigger." Jackson would be muttering to himself, "Should I go or should I not," debating whether Alvey was in good shape or not.

Sonny, the youngest child, graduated from high school in 1946. Edna's marriage to Wah Wah Jones was in August of that year. Soon thereafter Gladys moved to Lexington. She bought a farm on the Paris Pike across from the Lexington Country Club. Actually, it was Ira who went with the real estate agent and chose the estate, which featured a two-story mansion. As soon as Ira and Gladys moved in it became a meeting place for the University of Kentucky basketball players, just as their home in Middlesboro had been for their high school gang. Edna's husband, Wah Wah, was at the University of Kentucky, as was Lorraine, and Sonny was attending college in nearby Georgetown. Coach Adolph Rupp, probably more important to basketball-crazy Kentuckians than their governor, was a frequent visitor.[43]

Coach Rupp had reason to be grateful to the Balls. Wah Wah was a high school legend who had set a national scholastic record in basketball for high-scoring during his years at Harlan High. He was also a two-year All State football choice and a star baseball player who had been offered professional contracts by the Boston Braves and the Chicago Cubs. All the colleges were vying to recruit him. He had all but signed with the University of Tennessee and was heading back to Harlan from Knoxville when he stopped over in Middlesboro to visit Edna. She was then a sophomore at U.K., and her father was a big U.K. fan. She was adamantly opposed to Wah Wah going with arch-rival Tennessee. Love prevailed, and the University of Kentucky had a key ingredient in one of the finest basketball teams ever to take to the floor.

Jones starred in football and baseball at U.K., but it was at basketball that he really shone. His first season at U.K. was 1946, and by the third game he was already starting as center. The team won the conference tournament that year and had five on the All-Tournament team, including Wah Wah. As they piled win upon win, the team was dubbed "The Fabulous Five." The year 1947 was a triumphant one, and sportswriters labeled the 1948 team "one of the finest sports units of all times," calling Jones "the inspirational spark necessary to pull the team through tough situations."[44] In 1949 the U.K. football team was in the Orange Bowl and the basketball team played in the Sugar Bowl. Jones starred in both. Lexington was ecstatic, and Middlesboro basked in the reflected glory.

The years 1948 and 1949 were a momentous period for other members of the family. In February of 1948 Floyd's eldest daughter, Wilma, married Coy Bays, who was from Corbin and worked for the L&N Railroad. Approximately 450 guests attended the wedding and reception. The latter was held at the Cumberland Hotel with the assistance of Mrs. S.H. Flowers, wife of a prominent Middlesboro physician and well known in her own right as a newspaper columnist and state officer in the Garden Club. She supervised the filling of the hotel lobby with baskets of roses and arrangements of white tulips. For the receiving line, she improvised a garden of greenery, yellow roses, and white tulips. Flanking the four-tier wedding cake on the bride's table were crystal bowls of gardenias and arrangements of white tulips. It was truly an elegant affair equal to any ever held in Middlesboro.

Alvey's first grandchild, the son of Edna and Wah Wah, was born in September of 1948. Floyd became a grandfather in January of 1949. That same year his daughter Sallie married Paul Parrott, and Alvey's daughter Frances Loraine married Hugh Jones Jr., the brother of Wah Wah.

But things were not going well for the Ball empire. Alvey had moved out of the homeplace and was occupying a suite of rooms on the third floor of the Cumberland Hotel. He continued his bad habits despite efforts by Floyd to get him off the drugs. The two still worked well together, sometimes using the good-cop/bad-cop approach, utilizing their perceived images in order to prevail. Ingrained in the town's memory of those days are the twin characterizations: "Floyd would do anything for you, like Santa Claus walking down the street," while "Alvey would as soon shoot you as look at you." Neither was entirely accurate, but both were useful.

They needed their combined strengths. Judge Maddox had moved rapidly following his appointment to the bench. Although the county was wet, the use of slot machines for gambling was clearly illegal. Even prior to his appointment, there had been raids by the state authorities on roadhouses outside the city limits. Such county hot spots as the Bloody Bucket, the Fuzzy Duck, Kilroy Club, Ball's Blue Moon, the Maryland Club, Idol Hour, and Flamingo Inn had their slot machines seized. Barely two weeks after his appointment Maddox had the Kentucky State Police offer the city their assistance in law enforcement. Middlesboro's officials refused this generous offer. Nonetheless, in November of 1948 indictments were issued for thirty-eight Middlesboro businessmen accused of having gambling devices on their premises. Chief of Police Guy Harrell (Minton had already resigned in 1947 and was under indictment for embezzlement from the city) was indicted at the same time for failure to do his duty and for perjury.

Since nearly every Middlesboro hotel, restaurant, and saloon, and even most of the grocery stores, had slot machines in plain view, it was easy to find targets for the continuing campaign. In February of 1949 Maddox fined a total of fifty persons for having gambling devices. Among the businesses named were the Cumberland Hotel, Majestic Hotel, Tri-Way Club, City Cafe, Sharp's Court, Silver Slipper, Tropical Bar, Lunetta Cafe, Blue Moon, Ritz Cafe, Lafser Cafe, Ball's Court, Cave Cocktail Lounge, Three States Cafe, Old Terminal Cafe, Manhattan Bar & Grill, B & J Bar, Hub Grill, Busy Bee Cafe, Senora Sanitary Cafe, Fad Pool Room, Colonel's Bar and Grill, The Diner, Wakin & Tamer Market, Rhodes Fruit Stand, Whited Tourist Park, Yoakum Drug Store, and the Noetown Sports Center. Maddox was certainly making it hard for the Balls to do business in their usual manner!

The authorities did not capture many of the slots, however. Most of them disappeared suddenly and overnight. Left in their place were a few broken-down machines. The good slots were stored in a large tractor trailer truck parked in plain view not far from the Wabash. Law enforcement did not think to look in so obvious a place; besides, at that time the slot machines themselves were not illegal; only their use for gambling was. The Balls were confident they could soon move them back into their usual spots. Meanwhile there were always back rooms for gambling.

At the same time, it was getting harder to make huge profits from the liquor business. During the war and immediately thereafter liquor was under price control. The Balls with their wholesale liquor distributorship and their continuing connections with moonshiners were in a good position to profit from this situation. It was not their fault that many were willing to pay double the federally mandated price for their liquor (their good friend Jimmie Ginsberg went to federal prison for violating Office of Price Administration controls), or that if good bonded whiskey was not available, many would settle for Tennessee corn in liquid form. By 1948, however, the only advantage they had was that Bell County was a wet island in a sea of dry counties, so that they drew from a wide area. Cash was still rolling in, but not in the same amounts as before.

Balls had always been behind-the-scenes rulers in city politics. With the changes that had come in 1947-1948, they decided to be more open with their power. They had one of the city commissioners, Fred Silhanck, resign (he was almost immediately appointed city manager) to make way for Floyd's appointment to the vacancy. In December of 1948 Floyd Ball was sworn in as a city commissioner. City government at that time consisted of a mayor and two commissioners; the other two elected officials, Mayor Sherman Chasteen and Commissioner W.K. Evans, were allies. The Balls may have been challenged but they were certainly not beaten.

The Fifties

Middlesboro entered the new decade a busy, prosperous trade center despite a deteriorating coal market. Population neared the 15,000 mark, and the town drew from a wide trade area. The streets were thronged, particularly on Saturdays, with farmers from Tennessee and Virginia, miners and their families from the surrounding hollows, salesmen and travelers, to say nothing of local townspeople. Stores routinely stayed open till nine or ten o'clock, and it was a tradition with many locals to go downtown just to socialize. Older people remember that in order to get a good parking place on a fine summer evening, a member of the family would drive the car down early, park it, and walk home for supper. The family would then walk back to town, ensuring that they had a prime spot from which to visit. The older folks would stroll along Cumberland Avenue, window-shopping and visiting from car to car while the younger ones would stop in the ice cream shop or confectionery.

Although gambling and prostitution were less in evidence, alcohol was still legal, and the multiple bars and saloons did a brisk business as always. As in the preceding decades, there was still a strict segregation as to the location of the drinking establishments. Coming out of Woolworth's Five and Ten on Fountain Square (20th and Cumberland), one could hardly miss noting the neon sign of the Manhattan Bar and Grill, which depicted a cocktail glass with a girl in it kicking her legs. Yet she did her kicking between 19th and 20th, within the informal zone for the bars.

In early 1950 the noted journalist Joe Creason did a feature story on Middlesboro for the *Courier-Journal* Sunday magazine section. He wrote of the city's history and of its present achievements, the various booming industries, the city's efforts to attract further businesses, its two hospitals and thirteen physicians (unusual, he noted, in that they outnumbered the lawyers), the fine educational system, its two newspapers, and the rich cultural life and recreational opportunities. Creason asserted, "There's something about Middlesboro that gives it a vital personality all its own. In many ways, it doesn't seem to be a part of Bell County at all, but the pulsating center of a special little county, going its own way and accountable only to itself."

But of course it *was* part of the county, and in April of 1950 the grand jury meeting in Pineville indicted the entire seventeen-man city police force for not enforcing the law against slot machines. The city was even featured in the national press when *Newsweek,* in an article entitled "Corruption—the Middlesboro Mess," stated, "In Middlesboro 176 people were under indictment...charged with offenses ranging from vote frauds and gambling to malfeasance and neglect of duty." The article compared Middlesboro to some of the large cities, like Dayton, where organized crime was being investigated.[45]

Middlesboro's city officials went on record as condemning the actions of the grand jury. Rumors swirled that "a fix" would soon be effected and the slots would be back out in the open. And there was a night in April of 1950 when the slots did magically reappear at their familiar spots. The *Daily News* reported they "were in full operation in several places and customers were standing two and three deep waiting to play....Places operating made runs on banks to get change and in walking up the streets you could not go a block but what someone would run up to you and whisper 'the slots are back.'" But within three days they were again gone; it was said the Balls had been double-crossed.

To make matters worse, Alvey was being sued by the state of Kentucky for back taxes and the IRS was also sniffing around. The Balls could hardly forget that the offense for which Al Capone was finally jailed was tax evasion.

Alvey's drug habit was also a problem, despite several stints in a Lexington hospital and at a rehabilitation center in Asheville, North Carolina. It was about this time that Middlesboro lost one of its physicians. Alvey had been going to Dr. J.N. Rose for drugs. Frustrated in his efforts to control Alvey's drug use, Floyd went to Dr. Rose and threatened to kill him if he wrote Alvey one more prescription. Alvey then threatened to kill him if he didn't. By the next morning, Dr. Rose and his family had packed up and left town, never to return. Another physician, Dr. Sam Flowers, explained the situation facing a physician. According to him, Alvey always had a loaded revolver by his bedside. "It was difficult for a doctor to have a patient demanding drugs with a loaded gun." Dr. Flowers said that he tried to get around the dilemma by avoiding housecalls whenever possible.[46] His position as chief surgeon at the Middlesboro Hospital and one of the town's most respected physicians also helped insulate him from the Balls' wrath.

But Alvey's habit was not to be denied. Although his brother was trying to watch him, he could still find ways to obtain what he wanted. He arranged with a teenager, Bob Hatfield, who was driving cabs for his father's taxi/bootlegging business, to pick up his drugs. Alvey would then call to have a taxi bring him a pizza or hamburger and deliver it up to his room. Hatfield would have the drugs in the pizza box or hamburger bag. Alvey gave the boy two guns and told him to kill anyone who got in his way. He also saw to it that Hatfield was well rewarded, slipping him a good sum of money and supplying him with a new car.[47]

During the summer of 1950 there was general unrest in the Ball machine. The natural order of things seemed to be coming unglued. Alvey blamed many of the problems on Gaines Williamson. He used to proclaim, "I've killed six men, and I'm going to live long enough to kill one more, Gaines Williamson." On the night of September 9, 1950, he dressed with his usual care, despite the fact that he had had a great deal to drink. Alvey always wore tastefully matched outfits, often in pastels, with spats. His hair was carefully combed to conceal his balding spot, and he completed his wardrobe, as always, with his two pistols. It was a single block from the Cumberland Hotel to Gaines' Manhattan Bar & Grill.

As usual, the Manhattan was packed, the floor covered with sheets torn off tipboards. Alvey walked purposefully in and demanded to see Gaines. When the bartender told him that Gaines was out of town, he

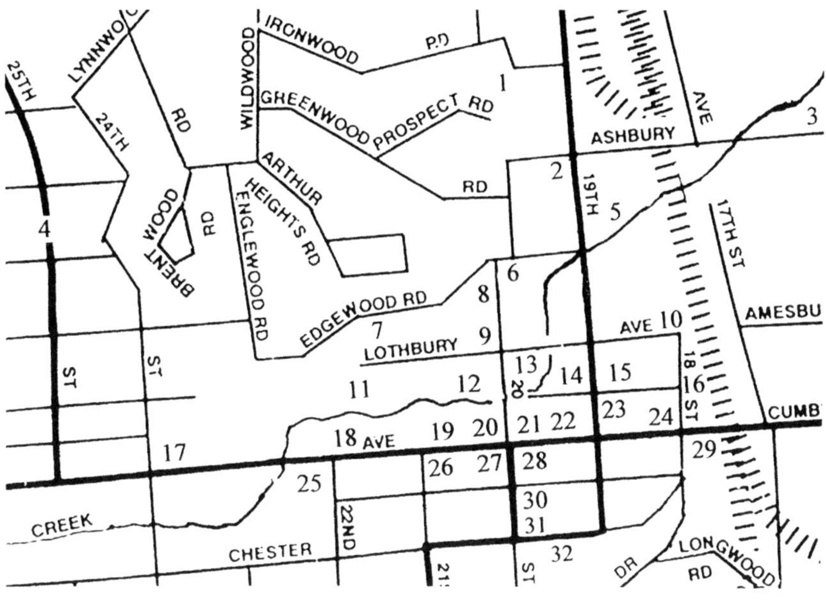

Downtown Middlesboro, 1950, showing the location of principal buildings. 1, Silver Slipper Club; 2, Thompson's Bar; 3, Lincoln School; 4, Dixie Highway; 5, Mt. Moriah Baptist Church; 6, Junior High School; 7, St. Mary's Episcopal Church; 8, First Presbyterian Church, Public Library; 9, Post Office; 10, Wabash Hotel; 11, High School; 12, Central School; 13, City Hall, Police Dept., Fire Dept.; 14, Majestic Hotel; 15, Empire Hotel; 16, Train Depot; 17, First Baptist Church; 18, First Christian Church; 19, Manring Theatre; 20, Montgomery Ward; 21, Lee's Drug Store; 22, Brownie Theatre, Manhattan Bar & Grill; 23, Middlesboro Hotel; 24, Cumberland Hotel; 25, American Association Building; 26, A.D. Campbell's; 27, Woolworth's; 28, J.C. Penney's; 29, Middlesboro-LaFollette Bus Line; 30, Bruce Hotel; 31, Park Theatre, Greyhound Bus Terminal; 32, St. Julian's Catholic Church. In general, most of the "nicer" stores were west of the midpoint on Cumberland Avenue, between 20th and 19th. East of that point and all up and down 19th, and to the northeast on the streets that crossed 19th, there were numerous bars, restaurants, pool rooms, and honky-tonks, with a smattering of small groceries and dry goods shops, service stations, hardware and feed stores, etc. Map produced by author.

started shooting, smashing whiskey bottles, scattering stacks of coins, and shattering the long mirror over the back bar. Patrons poured out of the building, and the Manhattan Bar & Grill was closed, at least temporarily.

When Alvey got back to his hotel, he found that his son Sonny had just arrived in town with his new bride, the former Willie Evans, who as a baby had been nicknamed "Wiggles" by her older sister. A strong bond of affection was to develop between Alvey and his somewhat overawed seventeen-year-old daughter-in-law. She saw him as "the smartest man" she ever met. She recalled he always had a dictionary nearby and would look up any word he came across that he didn't immediately recognize. He was careful with his own use of the language and did not hesitate to correct family members who made grammatical errors. Alvey returned her affection and often called her to come up and visit. The three of them—Alvey, Wiggles, and Sonny—frequently went out to dinner together. It impressed the teenager that Alvey would just call up the police and have them send a car to chauffeur him wherever he wanted to go.

The year 1950 was also notable for another marriage and a divorce. In May of that year Alvey's oldest daughter Ira married William King. This was her second marriage, the first having been to Warren Campbell. In December of 1950, Gladys Ball was granted a divorce from Alvey. She estimated in a deposition at the time that he was worth nearly a million dollars. In the final settlement, however, she received only some property in Middlesboro, $2,000 in cash, and her attorney fees.

Another event occurred in 1950 that would have a profound effect on the Balls, though at the time it seemed totally unrelated. In January of that year W.B. Bingham began his ministry at the Binghamtown Baptist Church. W.B. was a grocer who had started out by carrying his family's farm produce to mining camps to sell. He was manager of the Kroger store in Middlesboro from 1944 through 1946, then had his own grocery in Pineville. At the same time, he was pastoring at his home church in Knox County. He later recalled how he prayed, "Lord, let me go where I can do the most good, where I can win the most people." It was at that juncture that he received the call to preach at the Baptist church on 25th Street in Middlesboro. The church was directly across the road from Floyd Ball's home, and the two men frequently exchanged greetings.

In January of 1951 Sonny Ball got a draft call. Alvey certainly had the power to keep him out of the military service, but, as he told his daughter-in-law, he felt it would be good for his only son. Sonny had been in and out of a number of colleges and universities without effect. Perhaps Alvey could already see that the Ball empire would not last forever and that Sonny

Left, Alvey Ball, ca. 1950. Courtesy of Randy Ball. Right, Floyd Ball, ca. 1950. Courtesy of Sallie Ball Henson.

needed to experience more of the real world, where he could not depend on the Ball power and influence.

Storm clouds were definitely building on the Balls' horizon. Besides the attacks on liquor and gambling, the reformers were also beginning to focus on the drug problem. In February of 1951 the Bell County Grand Jury recommended that a special effort be made to find the source of distribution of amphetamines and barbiturates, which were commonly referred to as "Yellow Jackets" and "Red Devils." Later that year Judge Maddox wrote to the Senate Crime Investigating Committee asking that federal officers be sent to Middlesboro to investigate the "dope peddling ring" in the city.

In the fall of 1951 the national magazine *The Reporter* ran a three-part series by William S. Fairfield entitled "Bloody Harlan and Corrupt Bell," in which he described the regimes of the Balls and "their good friend," Merle Middleton, in Harlan County. In one article he described an interview with Floyd Ball, first explaining:

> On neither of my trips to Middlesboro last summer did I see Alvey Ball. "He's pretty fractious," I was told. "Might up and do you some harm if you just happened to touch him off the wrong way—especially if he's using those little pills he calls 'yellow jackets'." I decided not to take the chance, with the private rationalization that Floyd had always been the spokesman for both anyway....I called on Floyd Ball at his home, a moderately prosperous-looking residence of stucco and glass

> bricks on the outskirts of Middlesboro. Although it was early afternoon, I caught him at the breakfast table, in the company of two rather hard-faced men....Floyd's own face was in marked contrast—the face of a Sunday-school teacher, almost prissy behind the half rimmed glasses. The smooth complexion, the small pointed nose, the tight mouth, and the delicate chin all contributed to the impression, marred only by the faint gleam of two gold teeth as he greeted me....By common if unspoken agreement, the conversation remained general. Floyd talked quietly and intelligently. His grammar was not perfect but was far better than might have been expected. On local politics, he said the Democrats had been slowly gaining in strength in Bell County ever since the New Deal. On economics, he explained that his position with the natural-gas company precluded his discussion of the collapse of the local coal-mining industry and its effect on the people....While he talked, I took notes on his lounging attire: slippers, pale-green slacks, a grass-green belt, and red-striped pajama top. In this costume, it was easy to ascertain that he carried no gun—a fact which, according to others I talked with in the area, made me one of the few ever to see him in such a state of undress....Our interview ended with a brief outline of Floyd's business interests, most of which I had to pry from him with direct questions. When he saw me to the door, it was difficult to recall the many stories I had heard of this man's background.[48]

The writer went on, however, to say that "it was only necessary to stop in on Judge Maddox to get back on track." Maddox detailed the Balls' rise to power and the way they had corrupted the political process. Although the articles reported nothing that was not already generally known in Bell County, it was a little disconcerting to again see the area's dirty linen hung out to dry in the national press.

The year 1952 started inauspiciously for the Balls. In January ninety-one slot machines owned by them were seized by county officials. There was also a crackdown on "vice." Although prostitution was never a direct source of income for the Balls, the indictments of the proprietors of the Busy Bee, Canal Bar, and other establishments hit awfully close to home. To add insult to injury, the manager of their Tropical Bar was refused a liquor license because he had purchased a federal gambling tax stamp. Attacks on their power seemed to come from every direction.

Ironically, as the authority of the Balls was being challenged, the town seemed to become more dangerous. In July of 1952 a Middlesboro policeman, George Shelton, was gunned down in a gangland-style shooting. He was driving to Pineville with his brother and brother-in-law when another car pulled up alongside him and sprayed his car with machine gun fire. George was killed and his brother seriously wounded. The cause of the murder was said to be a feud between the Shelton and Smith families.

Willie Ball had good reason to remember this incident. She was a close friend of Shelton's daughter. George worked a split shift as a policeman and came home to sleep between shifts. The two young women would then slip out with his car and take a little ride without his knowing about it. Since his daughter did not know how to drive, Willie always drove. One day Alvey called and insisted she come to his suite immediately. When she arrived he was upset and pacing the floor. He told her there was something that was none of his business, a personal problem for someone else, but that he never wanted her to be in George Shelton's car again. He said, "It's none of my business, unless you get me involved." Willie had no idea what he was talking about but was always careful to obey him. A week later Shelton's daughter called and asked her to drive Shelton to Pineville, as he was not feeling well. Willie made an excuse. That was the day Shelton was killed.

Another murder the following year made an even deeper impression on the community. The scene was Ball's Court, a motel owned by the Balls and run by Andy Lowe, who had previously worked for them at the Wabash Hotel and who had also been involved with Merle Middleton, the "boss" of Harlan County. On July 2, 1953, a young waitress at the Court, Edith Hyleman, was found in one of the rooms, stabbed nineteen times. She died before she could give police a description of her assailant.

The investigation seemed to get nowhere, and six people associated with Ball's Court, including Andy Lowe, his girlfriend, Rosella Mason, and another girl from the motel, Pearl Moore, were charged with obstruction of justice. On July 30 they were cleared of the charge, and all celebrated at the home of George Philpot, who also worked for the Balls. Then on August 6 there was an accident at Lake Norris, which was a favorite place for the citizens of Middlesboro to boat, fish, and camp. Andy had taken Pearl and Rosella out for a boat ride. Suddenly the boat seemed to go out of control, and all of its occupants went overboard, all drowning. The strong supposition was that Andy had meant to drown the two girls, who had reputedly been witnesses to Hyleman's murder, but that one of them had grabbed him and pulled him overboard also. The murder of Edith Hyleman was never solved. It was, to quote one who should know, "very secret, very mysterious," and there was "deep cover."[49] Although it is unlikely that either Alvey or Floyd had anything to do with the murder, things had gotten to the point where the community tended to blame them for all unexplained crimes.

The year 1953 marked the beginning of the end for the Balls. In January there was another local-option election. The "drys" won by 70 votes. The "wets" contested the verdict, and the courts a year later invalidated the election; but each new challenge was getting harder to meet, especially as money was no longer coming in so fast.

The biggest threat was a movement to change Middlesboro's form of government to that of a mayor and a twelve-member council. With only two commissioners and a mayor, the Balls had controlled city politics for many years. In their weakened state, however, it was unlikely that they would be able to dictate to such a large, unwieldy body as the proposed council. Reform Republicans joined Gaines's Democrats to push for the change. They were promised that if the measure passed, the governor, who was charged with appointing the first council, would choose six Republicans and six Democrats. On November 3, 1953, the city voted to change its form of government, and the county voted in Democratic officials. Reneging on the informal agreement, the Democratic governor appointed Democrats to all twelve places on the newly organized council. For the first time in history the county and city were governed by Democrats.

Meanwhile another influence was making itself felt along 19th Street. W.B. Bingham, the minister at the Binghamtown Baptist Church, was taking his ministry to "the gangsters." He already knew many of the people in that part of the city from his days at Kroger in downtown Middlesboro. When he came back to town he made a conscious effort to preach to those who had mostly heretofore been condemned only by other churches. Not that he was any less opposed to liquor or the other "vices" identified by the churchgoers. In fact, he had been active in the Bell County Citizens League. But he believed strongly in loving the sinner while hating the sin. As he held services at the city jail and visited with those who made their living off liquor, gambling, and prostitution, it became his strong ambition "to fill the church with people off of 19th."

Floyd Ball had always respected churches and the ministry. Early on, when the first reform efforts started, some of those involved in the liquor trade and gambling suggested that they try to smear the reputation of the preachers involved. Floyd forbade it, saying that no one should touch the ministers or the churches, no matter what happened. So it was natural that Floyd would treat Preacher Bingham with respect and respond to his friendly gestures. Since Floyd lived directly across from the church, they saw each other frequently, and when Floyd was ill Bingham would visit him. Gradually Floyd started attending church.

In February of 1954, about six months after Floyd first started going to church, Binghamtown Baptist Church embarked on a week-long revival. The paper reported, "Each night penitents hit the saw dust trail and the Fire fell." One of those who was saved was Floyd Ball. On Sunday, February 28, twenty-one converts were baptized. Floyd and his wife, Jo, were among them.

Floyd turned to religion with the same dedication and energy that he had once applied to his less praiseworthy endeavors. He gave large sums to the church and became a leader in the Baptist Training Union, the youth group. Church members could hardly believe the humility that he demonstrated. When he first allowed a prayer meeting to be held at his house, it was a stormy night. Uncle Frank Baker, a crippled old man who sold pencils and razor blades on the street corner, arrived dripping wet. Floyd insisted on kneeling in front of him and removing his galoshes himself.[50] Floyd began witnessing himself and is credited by the Rev. W.B. Bingham with leading sixty people to the church, including most of the police force and many of those who worked along 19th.

Alvey was not one of those, though he did eventually make a profession of faith. He was battling his own twin demons of alcoholism and drug addiction. In 1954 he made one last attempt to dry out; he entered a hospital in Hot Springs, Arkansas. Alvey's son Sonny, along with his wife and their young daughter, Debbie, who was then two, accompanied him. He rented them a fancy house on a nearby lake, and the family settled in for the six-month "cure." By this time Alvey was regularly downing a fifth of whiskey a day. The theory was that he would "taper off" under medical supervision.

Alvey refused to give up his guns when he entered the hospital, and he insisted on leaving the hospital each evening to visit with his family. At the lake house he kept liquor and continued to feed his disease. He also kept a fifth in his hospital room. It was evident that he was not to be "cured," and after a few months he abandoned the effort, returning with his family to Middlesboro.

By 1954 it was apparent that the Ball machine was falling apart. In February of that year the Kentucky legislature passed a law declaring slot machines contraband. That meant that it was no longer necessary to prove the machines were being actively used for gambling in order to confiscate them. That same month Guy Harrell was suspended as chief of police. He was eventually reinstated, then suspended again, but meanwhile the charges against him made interesting reading in the newspapers. He was chastised for allowing illegal gambling in the city as well as turning a blind eye to all the "drinking, whoring, fornicating" and other bad behavior going on openly in the "joints," even on Sundays. Many managers of these maligned places of business were called to testify, and they could not deny that they had been allowed to do business largely unmolested by the police. It was generally acknowledged that Floyd and Alvey owned all the slot machines.

In September of 1954 there was another local-option election in Middlesboro, and again the "drys" won. The result was again challenged in court, but this time the "wets" were unable to prevail. Middlesboro would be officially dry in one year.

Further light was shed on the operations of the Balls when Hazel Shipman, who had been a bookkeeper at their Cumberland Hotel, went on trial for embezzlement in May of 1955. She evidently decided that offense was the best defense, and she talked extensively about their business dealings. Though her allegations were not uniformly believed, they again made interesting reading, and she was acquitted.

By this time, Floyd probably did not care. He had been diagnosed with incurable cancer and was developing painful boils all over his body. He gave his last testimony before 500 to 600 people, proclaiming, "They say I've got cancer—the doom of cancer. If I have cancer from the top of my head to the soles of my feet, you who sit here tonight are in greater danger if you do not know Jesus."[51] Preacher Bingham made a tape of his testimony and used part of it for Floyd's funeral, prompting people to remember in later years that "Floyd preached his own funeral service."

Floyd was by this time almost totally broke. He had given away a good deal of his money, and he had always been of the easy-come-easy-go school. People began pushing him to repay debts, and he borrowed more than $10,000 from his friend and business partner, Oscar Miracle, to settle up. Instead, there was a whole line of people wanting to borrow from him, and he lent it all out without ever paying his own debts.

When Christmas of 1955 came around, Floyd wanted to buy a new refrigerator for his wife. He was essentially bedfast by then, so he called on David Smith (the brother of his second wife, Lina) of Smith Electric to come out to the house with the G.E. catalog. Jo picked out one of the nicest appliances in the book, then left the room. Floyd asked how he could pay for it. David replied, "Why, just reach in your pocket and pull out the money." Floyd said he had none, and ended up putting it on a monthly payment plan.[52]

Alvey was now mainlining drugs as well as using pills and drinking heavily. Undoubtedly the terminal illness of his brother was affecting him greatly. The brothers had always been very close, and few had ever known them to even disagree in public. Floyd had devoted a great deal of time and money in the last few years of his life to trying to help Alvey overcome his problems, but to no avail. According to Alvey's daughter-in-law, he referred to himself as "the unhappiest man alive."

On January 25, 1956, Alvey was found in his hotel room, dead of an apparent drug overdose. Next to him was an empty syringe. He was only fifty-four.

Floyd was too sick to go out by then. He had his beloved little brother laid out at his own house and held the funeral there. Knowing his own death was imminent, he asked the funeral home to keep Alvey's body on ice so that they could be buried together.

Death came to Floyd on May 24, 1956. The brothers were buried together in a simple red brick above-ground tomb in the Hurst Cemetery on 19th Street. Alvey had always expressed a horror of being underground; it was the plan to build a large family mausoleum of glass and marble, to which the bodies of their parents and their brother would also be moved. But in the aftermath of the collapse of the Ball empire, nothing was ever done, and to this day the graves of Floyd and Alvey are not even marked with their names. Frank, Sallie, and Ira remain in the Jones/Ball Cemetery across the road, their graves overgrown with weeds and vandalized.

At the time the Balls died, Al Funk was their lawyer. His executive secretary at the time recalled that their finances were in a mess. Floyd had stacks of deeds to property, but many were faulty, and he had lots of debts. Many assets were held in the names of both Floyd and Alvey, but the debts were only owed by Floyd. It soon became apparent that Funk could not manage both estates. He handled that of Floyd while Walter B. Smith served as the lawyer for Alvey's estate, which was administered by his daughter Ira.[53]

Ira had always been the child most like her father, and it was the general consensus of the town that he was grooming her to take his place. Immediately after his death she did live in Middlesboro with her husband in one of the houses at 15th and Cumberland, while her mother and sister Lorraine moved back into the two-story house that had been the homeplace. Everything had changed, however, and they did not stay long, soon selling most of the property in Middlesboro and moving back to Lexington.

It took ten years to finally get Floyd's estate settled, and all his widow was left with was the house on 25th Street and a couple of small pieces of property. She was unable to retain even the stock in the gas company, which was one of Floyd's more successful investments. She was, however, guaranteed a job with the company, and she worked there until she became terminally ill in the 1980s.

Floyd's daughters both left Middlesboro soon after his death, and they never returned. The only direct descendent of Frank Ball to stay in the Middlesboro area was Alvey's son, Sonny. He and Willie had two children, Debbie and James Alva.

Frank Ball had been a force in Middlesboro's history almost from the town's inception, and his sons had essentially ruled Middlesboro for twenty-five years, yet not one history even mentions their names, with the exception of *History and Families: Bell County, Kentucky*, for which the family genealogist submitted short, one-sided biographies of the Balls. Older residents often talk of them in hushed voices, as if they were still to be feared, and this researcher was warned that she should not ask questions about the Balls, that another generation would have to die off before it was safe to say anything about them. Yet it is as likely, when people speak of them, that what they remember is the vibrant life of the city under their rule and the many things they did to help its citizens. Alvey and Floyd certainly proved the truism that there is good and bad in all of us.

FOOTNOTE THIRTY

Pioneers of the Air

Mesmerized, the four-year-old boy stared at the strange contraption being wheeled onto his father's field. All around him the crowd pressed. "He'll never get that thing off the ground," prophesied one. "If he does, it'll just crash." "Yeh, if God had wanted us to fly, he'd have give us wings." Others, more sagacious, claimed to have read of many successful flights, but few, if any, had ever before actually seen a flying machine.

It was May of 1912. Although the Wright Brothers' famous flight had taken place nine years earlier, this was the first time an airship had visited the mountains of southeastern Kentucky. The three-day event was sponsored by the boy's kinsman, Charles Herd, who was the editor of the local newspaper. Excitement had built as the advertisements proclaimed, "Positively...the Biggest Attraction ever pulled off...sights you have heard of and have always longed to see—Now is your chance!" Throngs poured into the Yellow Creek Valley from the surrounding hollows, coal camps, and towns, all anxious to see this new marvel.

At the appointed time, the Thomas Headless Biplane was rolled onto the field. The six-cylinder craft was twenty-five feet long and measured twenty-eight feet from wingtip to wingtip. It had been shipped by freight train to Cumberland Gap and then transported over the mountain by wagon. The plane's name came from the fact that its thirty-horsepower motor was mounted in the rear, as were all the steering and control gears, so that the aviator had only his steering wheel in front of him—thus it was "headless."

The pilot, Walter E. Johnson, had arrived in the city several days before his craft. A flying instructor from Bath, New York, he had been royally entertained by the city, and he reciprocated by giving talks to the children at school. As he strolled onto the field that Friday evening, adjusted his

Walter E. Johnson with a Thomas Headless Biplane. Courtesy of the Bell County Historical Society.

aviator's cap, and climbed into his plane, the crowd cheered. Then there was almost a palpable collective holding of breath as the plane roared down the field. Suddenly he was airborne! For six incredible minutes, the plane circled overhead, then landed somewhat joltingly but safely. So exciting was it that many returned the next day for his second flight. This time Johnson was in the air for eight minutes, demonstrating, as the paper reported, "that he was master of the air and was able to keep a machine weighing nearly 1000 pounds going in the air at the rate of 60 to 90 miles an hour." On Sunday afternoon he made two more flights, each lasting four minutes.

The crowd returned home believers in the miracle of air travel. But none was so affected as that four-year-old boy whose fascination with flight would be central to his life from that time on.

John Calvin "Jack" Colson was the youngest son of W.G. Colson. Although his was one of the most prominent families in Middlesboro, he was born and lived as a youth in Rose Hill, Virginia, where his father had a farm. Soon after that first thrilling vision of actual flight, he endured a great tragedy, the sudden death of his mother in a carriage accident. One of

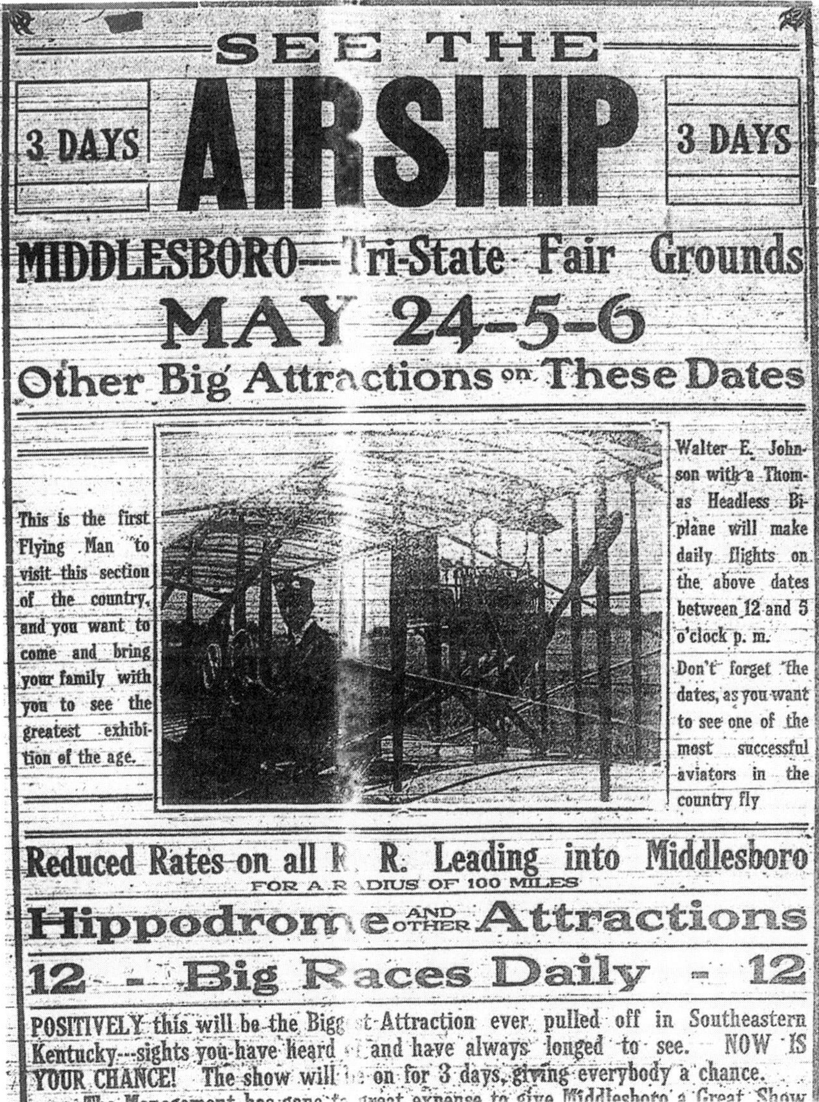

Newspaper ad for the first "airship" to visit Middlesboro. *Thousandsticks,* May 16, 1912.

Jack's earliest memories was of his mother hurriedly splashing water from a wash basin onto her face. She was in a rush to go somewhere, and as she ran out the door, she asked young Jack to empty her wash water. Sensing something was wrong, he instead followed her to the door and anxiously watched her drive off with her niece in the carriage, forgetting about the chore she had asked him to do. The next time he saw her, she was laid out in the parlor, dead. With a feeling of overwhelming guilt, Jack suddenly remembered that he had never emptied the basin, and ran to do so then.[1]

As Jack grew up it became common for one or more "barnstormers" to visit Middlesboro each year, usually in connection with a fair, and often billed as an Aerial Circus. The fairgrounds continued to be the large field east of the home his late uncle, David Grant Colson, had built during the "boom" days, where his grandmother continued to live for some years after her son's death, and where Jack himself would live for most of his adult life. Young Jack was always on hand to see any plane that visited the area. If he was lucky he would be allowed to carry water buckets out to those cleaning the craft.

When Jack was twelve the great barnstormer Eddie Stinson visited Middlesboro. Stinson was to fly with the National Air Tours and to become one of that era's best known pilots. He also designed and built his own planes and some years later developed a factory for building monoplanes. At the time of that first visit in 1919 he was mostly known for his daring air shows. His act often included a simulated dogfight with another barnstormer in which Stinson flew a Sopwith Camel. Colson would always remember his visit, as Stinson graciously spent time talking with the young boy about flying and allowed him to clean his plane.

In 1920 Stinson returned to Middlesboro with his wife for a stay of several months. They enthusiastically participated in the social life of the town, and he took passengers up for short rides at $25 each (a sum equivalent to what today would take one across country). Most of the "leading lights," as he later called them, went up with him. He also offered to give flying lessons. Undoubtedly Jack bitterly regretted that he was not old enough yet to be one of Stinson's students. His older brother Bill, who was somewhat of a mechanical genius, is said to have become friendly with Stinson during this visit and to have helped him with the wing design for one of his planes.[2]

Two years later Jack was finally able to start flying. He had to go to St. Louis, Louisville, or Cincinnati for lessons, which cost $45.00 an hour—a huge sum for the time, especially as lessons had to be purchased in five-hour blocks. But by the end of 1924 young Jack was a pilot. What had been known as the fairgrounds was now more commonly called Colson Field.

The year 1927 was a banner year for young Colson, as he eloped with Beulah McWilliams in January, and in November his first son, James Edward, was born. Their second son, John Calvin Colson Jr., arrived in 1930, and, quite possibly almost as important, that year Jack was finally able to purchase his own plane. By this time he was barnstorming all over the area, from Ohio and Pennsylvania to Virginia, West Virginia, North Carolina, Tennessee. and Kentucky. From the beginning Beulah, who was universally known in the vernacular of the mountains as "a pistol," helped him with his air shows. She would do the advance publicity, traveling by car to the towns where the show was to be held to give out handbills and drum up excitement.

The sight of an airplane was no longer so unusual, so it was necessary to do daredevil stunts to draw a crowd. Rolling, diving, wing-walking, and flying upside down were a usual part of Colson's repertoire. Another stunt was to throw a dummy out of the plane while banking, so that the crowd at first thought the pilot had fallen. In an interview, Colson recalled the first time they tried a more realistic trick:

> One day the barnstorming gang decided they wanted to try something different and decided to put a girl on a rope and let her look as if she were going to fall. A problem was created, however, when the wind from the flight made her fly in a horizontal position behind the plane. In order to draw her back into the plane the engine had to be slowed down and the plane just about dropped while a helper pulled her back into the plane.[3]

That daring Middlesboro girl was Bessie Welch. One day she and a friend went out to the airport just out of curiosity. They happened to start talking with Jack Colson, and he asked if they would like a little ride, and took them up. Bessie was hooked; she asked Jack if he would teach her to fly. He replied, "I don't know about that, but how'd you like to try some stunts?" With that, she was added to the barnstorming team and was soon doing wing walking and the like. After that first time doing the stunt simulating falling from the plane, when the plane nearly stalled, "the gang" rigged up a winch to haul her back in, and she repeated the stunt frequently.[4]

In recounting those days for a newspaper reporter, Jack later marveled, "We seldom went two or three days without an engine failure...and God always seemed to have a place for me to land....We flew because we loved flying and not because we saw a future in it."

Of course, there was definitely a future in flying, and it had almost arrived. Already regular passenger lines had been inaugurated between some of the country's major cities. In mid-1929 the vice-president of Mason and Dixon Air Lines, E.W. Savage, announced that he was planning to make the Middlesboro landing field an important part of the main air route from Cincinnati to Atlanta. He was quoted in the paper as saying, "Middlesboro is a strategic point since our pilots will obtain weather reports there for the mountain area. Middlesboro has an air field that will be entirely satisfactory after a few trees and fences are taken down." He went on to predict that eventually a network of airline routes would connect all parts of the country.

The town was galvanized into action by Savage's announcement. The airfield to which he referred was owned by the Colsons, who would make it available, but the contiguous property was also needed, so a committee was set up to secure sufficient land for a commercial airport. C.W. Griffith, a pilot who owned coal mines in nearby Pruden, was in regular contact with the officials of the Mason and Dixon Air Lines and served as an advisor to the committee. Because the airline was hoping to begin its flights in just two months, the city authorized work on the airfield even before contracts were worked out with property owners. By mid-October of 1929 the city had spent $350 to clear, fill, and smooth the runway, which was to run east and west between Petersborough (30th) and 35th Streets. The airline men were expected within days, but with the stock market crash, everything changed. At the end of November it was announced that the airline would be delaying their passenger service until March or April of the next year. Airport boosters were encouraged, however, as the company was also bidding on a route between Detroit and Atlanta by way of the Lexington-Middlesboro-Knoxville route. Alas, those plans, too, succumbed to the crash.

Interest in flight was not diminished by this turn of events. In July of 1931 the airfield was a stop on the National Air Tour. The contest began in Detroit with thirteen official contestants and more than twenty other planes. The Tour was due to stop in Middlesboro for several hours, and all participants were to be luncheon guests of the Kiwanis Club. The field was inspected by C.W. Griffith and another local aviator, Jack Cochron, who had attended Parks Air College of Aviation in St. Louis, and they pronounced it to be satisfactory. In fact, though the flyers on the Tour suggested the field was a little bumpy, there were no real complaints. The only one who even came close to having any difficulty in landing was the famed Major

James Doolittle. The papers explained that because he was flying a Lockheed "speed plane," he landed fast and needed a longer field than most.

Another of the flyers was Eddie Stinson, who was returning to Middlesboro as the president of Stinson Aircraft Corporation and was flying a plane produced in his own factory. The newspaper gushed that he had "practically got his start in aviation in Middlesboro."

Large crowds of locals turned out for this and other air shows, and there was a general fascination with all aspects of flight. Local boys, several of whom would become dedicated aviators, formed the Middlesboro Boys Aero Club. They hung around the airstrip all day just for the thrill of seeing a plane land or take off. The young teenagers vied for the opportunity to "flunky"—that is, to haul gasoline to the planes. There were no gasoline pumps, but Colson would supply visiting planes with fuel. The boys would run out to the field with five-gallon containers of gas, which the pilot would pour directly into the tank. Often they were allowed to look inside the plane, and sometimes even sit in the pilot's seat. A few of the pilots would occasionally take one of the older boys up for a quick spin with a turn at the controls.[5]

Despite disappointment over the decision of the Mason and Dixon Air Lines, the vision of a commercial airport continued. In point of fact, the grass strip between 30th Street and 35th, which had been owned for some years by Jack Colson's father, had been a recognized airstrip since 1918, quite possibly the second such in Kentucky.[6] Now the city laid plans to buy or lease several pieces of property, including that of Colson, for a public facility. This was done over a period of time from 1932 to 1934, and WPA (Works Progress Administration) participants were put to work to improve the field.

The airport was dedicated on September 27, 1934, with Robert Kincaid, chairman of the local airport committee, presiding over the ceremonies. Members of the Kentucky Airport Board attended, as did numerous pilots from other areas. Jack Colson continued to serve as manager of the field. He was by then giving flying lessons, and several locals were enthusiastic students.

In 1937 there occurred an event that seemed to have no connection with the local scene: the Army Air Corps circulated specifications for an aircraft that would become the P-38 Lightning. No one could have predicted that sixty years later tourists would be traveling to Middlesboro just to see this plane.[7]

Colson supposedly retired from barnstorming in 1937, though that did not end his daredevil flying. Residents still remember his exciting flights over their homes. His future daughter-in-law was a schoolgirl when he "buzzed" their school bus and flew too low, ending up in the top of a cedar tree. She said that he nonchalantly climbed out of the plane and down from the tree as if it were an everyday occurrence. There was probably no one in the Yellow Creek Valley or in the surrounding area that did not know the flyer. He was now devoting most of his time to management of the airport. A newspaper article in May of 1938 stated that it was the most active airport between Lexington and Knoxville. Colson had been flying passengers for four years already and could get someone to Knoxville in thirty minutes. It took two hours to fly to Cincinnati and a little over four hours to reach St. Louis. By this time Colson had 1,200 flying hours and had owned four different planes. He was qualified to fly by compass and at night and had taught more than twenty students to fly.

In August of 1938 Jack flew into the Detroit airport and was mobbed by a crowd of 30,000. It was a case of mistaken identity. One month earlier "Wrong Way" Doug Corrigan had made his famous flight. Corrigan had been refused permission to attempt a solo transatlantic flight because of the condition of his second-hand, much reconditioned and repaired plane. He took off on what was to have been a return trip to California, and was not heard of again until he stepped out of his plane in Dublin, Ireland, and asked, "Where am I?" He claimed to have gotten lost in the fog when his compass malfunctioned. No one believed his story, and both the Irish and U.S. governments threatened grave consequences. But his feat made him a hero to the common people on both sides of the Atlantic, who cheered him for his audacity and skill. His plane, besides being in such deplorable condition, was smaller than that of Charles Lindberg and carried less fuel, and he had no backers or careful preparation. In view of the fact that he was suddenly a hero, the two governments backtracked, and he was given celebrity treatment when he landed in New York—a tickertape parade, a meeting with President Roosevelt, and a triumphant tour.

Colson, flying a plane very similar to that of Corrigan, had landed at the Detroit airfield at about the time the latter was expected as part of his tour. The crowd awaiting the famed aviator broke through the police lines and rushed the startled Colson. All ended well as he was invited to be one of Corrigan's escorts the next day on his trip to Toledo.

In January of 1940, the city of Middlesboro finally purchased the land they had leased from the Colson heirs in the early thirties. In December of that year the city deeded half interest in the airport property to Bell County, and it became the Middlesboro-Bell County Airport.

By 1940 the war in Europe was looming ever larger on the horizon.

The young boys who had hung around the airfield waiting for a chance to "flunky" and who later had scraped together enough cash for lessons from Colson, sometimes being able to afford only fifteen minutes at a time, were now poised to be air warriors in defense of their country. The first to go was Dave Rogan, who in late 1940 traveled north to enlist in the Royal Canadian Air Force. He was probably the first person from the Yellow Creek Valley to see action in World War II, as he was already flying missions out of England at the time of Pearl Harbor. Other of Colson's early students—Gene Pattison, "Snooks" White, Joe Bosworth, and Jim, Joe, and Guy Iovine—joined the Army Air Corps after the declaration of war.

When Pearl Harbor was attacked there was the expectation of an imminent assault on the United States mainland, and all airports were temporarily closed. All active local pilots, of which there were five or six based in Middlesboro, were mobilized to guard the airport. The day after war was declared they were sworn into what was to become the Civil Air Patrol, and were charged with guarding the airport twenty-four hours a day. They constructed a small hut to serve as a guard house, but most of the night guarding fell to Jack Colson, since his home was essentially on airport property. Later on, the group was given regulation Army uniforms, and officers were commissioned. Jack was now Major Colson. Throughout the war the unit assumed responsibility for patrolling the area with particular attention to the sensitive TVA power lines (though, of course, they did not know the true importance of nearby Oak Ridge, Tennessee, at the time) and participated in a number of search and rescue operations. This dedication to the Civil Air Patrol was to continue after the war ended. In 1946 the local squadron had 160 members and was the second largest unit in the state.

Even before actual hostilities began, the United States had been preparing for that eventuality by trying to encourage the training of more pilots. In 1940 the Colson field was one of the airports selected to offer a Civilian Air Pilot Training Program (after Pearl Harbor it was called the War Training Services). Trainees were given an academic course in aeronautics at Lincoln Memorial University, just across the Cumberland Gap in Harrogate, Tennessee, and were lodged in that school's dormitories. Jack Colson was in charge of elementary flight training, which was held at the Middlesboro-Bell County Airfield. Any one who passed the rigorous three-month course was then sent elsewhere for further training in military air warfare. During the four years the program was in existence, approximately four hundred men took their elementary flight training in Middlesboro.

After the war ended there were numerous "GI Bill" programs to train returning veterans for civilian jobs and to avoid the unemployment that had occurred in the past when armies were deactivated. Colson, anticipating the market for domestic pilots, decided to continue his flight training school under the name Middlesboro Flying Service. He employed several additional instructors, including Joe Bosworth, and provided a program certified by the government. In addition he offered charter services and aircraft rentals and sales and did aerial photographs. The landing strips, one of which ran north-south and the other NNE-SSW, were still turf, but most of the crawdad holes had been smoothed over, so that landings were less rough than in earlier years. In 1948 the newly created Kentucky Department of Aeronautics designated Middlesboro as a Class I airstrip.

Interest in aviation was still high in the city. Many of the returning Air Force vets who went back to their civilian jobs in Middlesboro maintained their love of flying. In 1950 the Middlesboro-Bell County Airport Board was created to oversee the operation of the airfield. At that time four additional parcels of land were added to the airport property, and the main runway was changed from north-south to east-west and was paved. Gradually hangars were built, more local aviators maintained their planes at the field, and more businessmen began to realize the advantage of having a local airport.

At the same time, the U.N. police action in Korea was escalating into a full-scale war, and Middlesboro men again were serving their country as pilots. One of these was Jack's son James "Jim" Colson. He had learned to fly at age sixteen, and when he was eighteen he joined the Air Force. He embarked on a military career during which he flew 100 combat missions in the F-51 Mustang and taught Air Force Academy graduates to fly jet fighters. He distinguished himself in Korea and Viet Nam, earning the Distinguished Flying Cross three times and the Bronze Star twice.

Another was J. Roy Shoffner, who had learned to fly at the Middlesboro field when he was only fifteen or sixteen. When the Korean conflict began he enthusiastically joined the Air Force and was soon flying jet fighters. He loved piloting the F-89s and felt he had found his niche in life. He was planning a career in the Air Force when he received word that his father had had a heart attack. Because he was the only child, he decided that he had to return to Middlesboro to help his father manage his service station business. After a few years of working for his father and others, he went into business himself, manufacturing plastic pipe. A shrewd businessman, Shoffner looked for unrealized needs that his company could fulfill. He began by making innovations in his plastic products and went on to develop a product used to insulate fiber-optic cables. His company became the largest producer of fiber-optic interduct cable in the U.S. and was also

James, Beulah, and Jack Colson, ca. 1985. Courtesy of Jimmie Colson.

supplying it to overseas markets. At the same time, Shoffner branched out into other businesses: fast food franchises, a restaurant, supermarkets, and real estate. He also became a director of a local bank and was active in civic affairs. With all these irons in the fire he nonetheless never lost his enthusiasm for flying. He maintained a private plane at the Middlesboro-Bell County Airport and took off for the freedom of the skies whenever possible.

In the 1980s articles started appearing in aviation magazines about efforts to recover several antique airplanes buried under the snows of Greenland. Shoffner read with interest the story of the Lost Squadron, two B-17 Flying Fortress bombers and six P-38 Lightnings that had been forced to land on an icecap in 1942 when they ran out of fuel. According to the articles, the planes were new and in good condition when they were abandoned. Their crews had been rescued, but the planes had never been recovered. Two pilots from Atlanta, Pat Epps and Richard Taylor, had in 1980 become intrigued with the possibility of rescuing and restoring these planes and had made several expeditions to Greenland. Their original theory was that once they found the planes, they could simply shovel off the accumulated snow, gas up the planes, and fly them off the ice. After their first expedition the men knew it would not be so simple. Although the general location of the planes was known, they were deeply buried under layers of ice and snow. Perhaps if they had guessed how deeply, they would have quit then and there. As it turned out, more than 250 feet of ice and snow had covered the planes in the more than forty years they had been on the icecap.

It would take several more expeditions to Greenland, each dogged by its own combination of luck, poor planning, grand expectations, and personality conflicts, as well as various financial and contractual problems, before the planes were definitely located in the summer of 1988. Epps and Taylor, who had formed the Greenland Expedition Society (GES) to recover the planes, played up the "find" in the media.

It's doubtful that Middlesboro pilots spared much thought for the Lost Squadron that summer. In May of 1988 a tornado hit Middlesboro, seriously damaging the airport and a number of planes. Then, only a few days after that disaster, when a local pilot, Dr. Stanley Thompson, was taking off to ferry one of the planes to a repair facility, he crashed. He died instantly, along with his three passengers, the first fatalities that local pilots had suffered at the Middlesboro airport.[8]

During the summer of 1989 the GES was back in the news. They had actually been able to get down to one of the B-17s and to retrieve some artifacts. An expedition the next summer finally allowed the men to lower themselves through the narrow tubular opening they had been able to make in the ice and visually inspect the B-17. What they found was disheartening. The weight of the accumulated ice, along with the shifting caused by stress, had so crushed and mangled the plane that it was not worth trying to retrieve. If they were to bring up any of the planes, it would have to be one of the P-38s, since the fighters were heavily armored and would be more likely to have withstood the terrible force of the ice.

Shoffner had seen the various articles about the expeditions to Greenland and, finding himself in Atlanta one fall day in 1990 with some time to spare, dropped in at Epps' facility to view the artifacts that GES had thus far retrieved and to watch the videos of their efforts. He was intrigued. By this time Shoffner had sold his plastics business and had joined the ranks of self-made multimillionaires. GES was in desperate need of funding, and Shoffner was ready for a new challenge.

Over the next several months a deal was worked out for Shoffner to provide the financial backing for yet another effort to retrieve one of the planes. This was to be a businesslike venture that would build on the experience GES had gained and the technology they had developed. In the beginning it had taken the fly-by-the-seat-of-one's-pants type of adventurers to undertake the retrieval of the planes. Now, however, a different approach was needed. Joining the expedition as a key to that new way of working was Bob Cardin, a retired lieutenant colonel who had had extensive management experience in the military and was to bring a more disciplined structure to the enterprise.

Shoffner and Cardin arrived on the icecap in the spring of 1992 soon after the camp had been set up. Shoffner said he was only along to keep an eye on his money, but one has to believe he was drawn by a sense of adventure. From a purely business point of view there were better investments, but few business deals would provide the thrill of actually being lowered down the narrow 250-foot crevice they had drilled in the ice and being the first person in fifty years to sit in the cockpit of the P-38. That was the great dividend Shoffner realized on June 1, 1992, after first Epps and then himself strapped themselves into harnesses and descended through the thick ice walls to the cavity that had been melted out to reveal the plane.

Epps and Shoffner were relieved to discover that, in contrast with the B-17, the P-38 was basically intact and salvageable. Getting it to the surface would not be easy but was possible. It was necessary to dismantle the plane and bring it through the narrow passageway in small parts. Immediately the crew began that labor. By July 15, exactly fifty years to the day after the Lost Squadron had been forced to land on the icecap, they were able to celebrate the retrieval of a large portion of the plane. On hand for the ceremony was Brad McManus, the first of the pilots to land on the cap when the planes went down in 1942.

The most difficult part of the feat, bringing up the main section, was accomplished on August 1, 1992. The plane was, as Cardin put it, "out of the hole." But there were still logistic difficulties in getting it from the icecap to its final destination, Shoffner's private hangar at the Middlesboro-Bell County Airport. Once there, with Cardin still in charge, the painstaking process of putting the plane back together was begun. It soon became apparent that it would be a long, involved job, since almost every piece of the plane had to be repaired, reworked, or replaced. The goal was to return the plane to flying condition.

There was so much fascination with the project that Shoffner decided to open his hangar to the public as the Lost Squadron Museum. There would be not only artifacts and photographs of the planes and the various expeditions to retrieve them, but people could also see the work as it progressed. Interest was huge, particularly among World War II veterans, and there was a veritable pilgrimage of people who had flown the plane or had known someone—often a father or grandfather—who had piloted the P-38. Many of those who made the trip to the museum asked why it was in such an out-of-the-way small town rather than in a large urban center. Shoffner always replied, "Because that's where I am!"

The same could be said of the Middlesboro-Bell County Airport. Why should there be a modern airfield in this relatively small mountain town, especially in the very center of town in such a prime residential area? The answer: because that's where Jack Colson was.

In 1965 Jack was recognized as having more flying hours than anyone else in the state of Kentucky. He continued to fly for the airport and to give lessons until he was up in his seventies. Even at eighty he was still flying for pleasure. On his eighty-first birthday in 1989, Jack and his son Jim celebrated 100 years of combined flying.

Jack and Beulah Colson lived in the house at the edge of the runway until his death in 1994 at the age of eight-six. One likes to think he left this life with the music of the airplane roar in his ears.

On October 26, 2002, a crowd of more than 20,000 gathered at the airport to witness the maiden flight of the restored P-38, christened *Glacier Girl*, after fifty years under the ice of Greenland and another ten years of restoration work. In a scene reminiscent of that first flight of the Thomas Headless Biplane from the same field ninety years earlier, the crowd fell silent as the plane taxied down the runway. Then a loud cheer went up as it soared upward, silhouetted against the majestic Pinnacle, then circled and swooped over the Valley and into the pages of aviation history.

The maiden flight of *Glacier Girl.* Photo by the author, October 26, 2002.

Epilogue

As the Yellow Creek Valley meets the challenges of the twenty-first century, it can certainly look back on a colorful and exciting past. Middlesboro has had its share of difficulties, natural disasters, and economic setbacks. The advice given almost a hundred years ago by the city's founder, Alexander Arthur, in the last years of his life, after many disappointments, both personally and for his Magic City, still rings true today:

> You have come through years of depression and setback, but you have held to the faith that is in you, and I would say to you one and all, comrades, fellow citizens, set your faces to the front, take a new strong grip of things and the fruits of success we have so long waited for will fall into our hands fully ripe and pleasant to the taste. I have unlimited faith in your courage and go-aheadness and unbounded confidence in the resources in and around you that must create and sustain a big and busy city. Your climate is superb, your location strategic, your scenery—mountain, hill, dale, wood and stream—inspiring and exhilarating, and we invite the world to come and see and judge for itself. Verily 'tis the Mountain City of Kentucky, and a "city set upon a hill cannot be hid."[1]

Appendix I

Chronology

300-250 million years B.C.	Continents collide; earth's surface crumples to create the second-generation Appalachian Mountain chain
300-60 million years B.C.	Meteorite strike creates Yellow Creek basin
8000 B.C.	Earliest known human inhabitants appear in area now known as Bell County
1674 A.D.	Gabriel Arthur is the first white man to see the Yellow Creek Valley
1750	Dr. Thomas Walker and his party enter Kentucky through the Cumberland Gap
1769	Daniel Boone first passes through the Gap into Kentucky
1775	Daniel Boone and party open the Wilderness Road after Richard Henderson "buys" a large part of Kentucky from the Cherokees at Sycamore Shoals
1779-1800	More than 200,000 settlers pour through the Cumberland Gap into Kentucky and traverse the Yellow Creek Valley
Ca. 1790	Davis Tavern operates at the foot of the Gap
1792	Kentucky becomes the fifteenth state
1797	Dillon Asher becomes tollgate keeper at Cumberland Ford
Ca. 1800	Turner, Marsee, and Rains families move into the Yellow Creek Valley; a brick house (still standing) is built on the Wilderness Road by Clark Hunter

Ca. 1802	John and James Coulston (Colson) settle in Kentucky
1805	Arthur Campbell moves to the Valley
1810	The Valley is generally safe for settlers and is occupied by many small farms
1822	John Calvin Colson Sr. is born
1825	Eastbound traffic on the Wilderness Road equals that flowing west
1842	Yellow Creek Baptist Church is organized
1843	John C. Colson Sr. marries Mary Catherine Smith
Ca. 1845	Green Meeting House is built as both a school and a Methodist Church
1846	Alexander Alan Arthur is born near Montreal, Canada
Ca. 1850	John and Catherine Colson move their family to the Yellow Creek Valley
1861	David Grant Colson is born. The Civil War begins; the Confederates under General Zollicoffer invade Kentucky through the Cumberland Gap and skirmish with Colson's Home Guards
1862	Union General George Morgan occupies the Gap and forages supplies from the Valley; he is soon forced to evacuate
1863	Brigadier General Frazer takes command of the Gap, then loses the stronghold to Union forces
1864-65	The Union Army occupies the Gap and continues to forage in the Valley
1867	Josh Bell County is formed from portions of Harlan and Knox Counties
1871	The first fatality occurs in what was to become known as the Turner-Sowders Feud
1875	Harvard geology students are in area to study the geology of the Gap
1882	John Calvin Colson Sr. dies; Alexander Arthur marries Nellie Goodwin
1884	The Arthurs move to Newport, Tennessee; he is the general manager for the Scottish-Carolina Timber and Land Company

1885	The Turner-Sowders Feud is well under way; acts of violence continue through 1902
1886	Alexander Arthur first visits the Yellow Creek Valley; he forms the Gap Associates
1887	The American Association, Ltd. is established, with Arthur as general manager and chief American representative; the Watts Steel & Iron Syndicate, Ltd. announces plans to build a large steel processing plant in the Yellow Creek Valley
1888:	The city of Middlesborough is laid out by the Middlesborough Town Company; the Ball Boys move to the town
1889	The Valley becomes a tent city; the tunnel is completed through Cumberland Mountain; John Ralston moves to the Valley to establish the first coal company in the area; the Middlesborough Town Company holds the first lot auction; golf is being played on part of what is now the course of the Middlesborough Country Club; the Opera House is completed
1890	Middlesborough receives its charter and has its first city elections; Ben Harney arrives in Middlesborough; the United Mine Workers of America is organized; fires devastate the town; the population is 4,068 when the census is taken and almost 7,000 by the end of the year; in November the Baring Brothers Bank fails in England, the beginning of the "bust"
1891	In January, Arthur is discharged as general manager of the American Association, Ltd.; a man accused of ambushing the police is lynched; the public school system is established and Professor Bell arrives to organize a school for African-Americans; in November, the Middlesborough Town Company goes bankrupt, reorganizes as the Middlesborough Town and Lands Company
1892	The Four Seasons opens in Harrogate; Alice Woodbury organizes a literary club, the Wasiota Club
1893	The entire country slips into a Panic; the American Association, Ltd. is bankrupt, reorganizes as the American Association, Inc.; Ben Harney writes the first ragtime song
1894	Mayor David Colson is elected U.S. Representative from

	the 11th Congressional District; the UMWA calls its first general strike; the Kentucky Golf Club is organized by a group of Middlesborough men
1895	The population is 3,230
1897	The Arthurs are forced to sell their Harrogate home, Craig Neuk, and most of their possessions; Ben Harney publishes his *Ragtime Instructor;* John Calvin Colson Jr. is killed
1898	Middlesboro is in the grip of a smallpox epidemic; war is declared against Spain, and two companies of volunteers are quickly recruited in Bell County; David Colson vacates his congressional seat in order to command the Fourth Kentucky Volunteer Infantry
1900	The population is 4,162; Middlesboro has two competing sets of officials, including two mayors; David Colson is wounded in a shootout in Frankfort in which three men are killed
1901	Alex and Nellie Arthur move to New York State.
1902	The Quarterhouse Battle is fought
1903	Alice Lamb is beheaded
1905-1906	Middlesboro is in an uproar over Frank Ball's crimes; the town is under marital law
1906	The Roundtree Bill is repealed by the state legislature
1908	Lincoln School opens
1910	The population is 7,305; the Music Club is organized
1911	Alexander Arthur returns to Middlesboro
1912	Alexander Arthur dies; the first airplane visits town
1914-1918	World War I creates a strong demand for coal
1915	Bell County goes dry; Jack Zuta moves to Chicago
1918	The flu pandemic hits Bell County
1919	The Volstead Act makes Prohibition the law of the land
1920	The population is 8,041
1921	Doyle Colson is the first fatality in the Ball-Colson Feud
1922	A shootout between George Colson and Ira Ball results in Ball's death; a second shootout at the Bell County

	Courthouse results in the death of Riley Ball and the wounding of several other men
1924	Jack Colson is licensed as a pilot; George Colson is the last fatality in the Ball-Colson Feud
1925	The Baracas Class of the First Baptist Church is held at Ford's Woods
1929	Skyline Drive to the Pinnacle is dedicated; a commission is formed to work toward the establishment of a national park at the Cumberland Gap
1930	The population is 10,309; Jack Zuta is executed in the Chicago gang wars
1930s through mid-1950s	The Balls are "bosses" of Middlesboro and of Bell County; the town is "wide open" with liquor, slot machines and other gambling, and open prostitution
1932	The Book Club is organized; the National Miners Union circulates flyers in Middlesboro and attempts to organize nearby mines
1933	Phi Beta Kappa names Middlesboro High School one of the 1,000 outstanding schools in the United States; the Volstead Act is repealed, ending Prohibition
1934	The Middlesboro-Bell County Airport is dedicated
1936	Alvey Ball murders a man in the Wabash Hotel
1940	The population is 11,777; the airfield begins to offer a Civilian Air Pilot Training Program; Congress passes a bill creating the Cumberland Gap National Historical Park
1941	The Battle of Fork Ridge (also called the Mingo Mountain Massacre) takes the lives of several men; Floyd Ball is elected a state representative
1941-1945	World War II; coal production is at its height
1942	The Lost Squadron, including six P-38's, goes down on an icecap in Greenland
1943	Alvey and Floyd Ball are the largest property holders in Middlesboro
1946	H.H. Mayes moves into his "Air Castle" in Middlesboro to continue his ministry of producing and distributing

	religious signs; 3,000 Bell County coal miners on strike; an audit of city funds shows a large shortage
1947	The Middlesboro Little Theatre is organized
1948	R.L. Maddox is appointed Circuit Court judge of the new 41st Judicial District
1950	The population is 14,419; the entire city police force is indicted for not enforcing the law against slot machines; the Korean War begins
1953	The city votes to change to a Mayor-Council form of government; unemployment in Bell County is at an all-time high
1955	Middlesboro goes dry
1956	Alvey and Floyd Ball die
1959	The Cumberland Gap National Historical Park is dedicated
1964	President Lyndon Johnson announces his War on Poverty
1965	Lee Majors (Harvey Lee Yeary) becomes star of the TV series *The Big Valley;* the Appalachian Regional Commission is established; Chester Wolfe is elected mayor
1967	The Cumberland Hotel is demolished and a strip mall constructed on the property
1968	James Pursiful is appointed chief of police
1969	The murder of the Yablonski family is planned and executed by Middlesboro UMWA officers
1970	The population is 11,878
1973	The OPEC oil embargo creates a boom in the coal markets
1980	The population is 12,251
1983	Middlesboro Mall opens
1986	Fire destroys City Hall
1988	A tornado severely damages downtown Middlesboro
1990	The population is 11,328; Middlesboro celebrates its Centennial
1992	*Glacier Girl* is lifted from a Greenland icecap

1996	Twin highway tunnels are completed through Cumberland Mountain
2000	The population of Middlesboro is 10,384
2002	The *Glacier Girl* flies once more; the Cumberland Gap National Historical Park project to restore the Wilderness Road to its 1775-1800 era appearance is dedicated

Appendix II

Family Charts

The following are offered not as complete genealogies of any family but only as a way of showing the relationships between those people mentioned in this book. In cases where entries are incomplete (lack of dates, lack of spouse's name, etc.), the author was unable to obtain the information.

The Balls

(1) John Ball (1756-1809), m. Marry ("Polly") Yeary. Two of their children were:

(2) Mary Ball, m. Redden Smith. One of their daughters was:

(3) Mary Catherine Smith (1820-1914), m. John Calvin Colson Sr.

(2) George W. Ball (1787-1852), m. Sarah Moore. One of their sons was:

(3) Arthur Ball (1816-1865), m. Nancy King Daniels. One of their sons was:

(4) Phillip McNally Ball (1837-1927), m. Emeline Noe. Their children were:

(5) Charles Dudley Ball (1861-1956), m. 1) Matilda Yeary, 2) Evelyn Moore. Two of his children by Matilda were:

(6) Patton Ball (1884-1974)

(6) Minnie Cordia Ball, m. George Colson

(5) George Shelby Ball (1862-1911), m. Mary Marion. Three of their children were:

(6) Edgar Ball (b. 1884)

(6) Riley Ball (1886-1922)

(6) Rosa Ball, m. George Whited

(5) Sarah Ball (1864-1866)

(5) Rufus Harvey Ball (1865-1946), m. 1) Emma Burnett, 2) Dicey Turner

(5) Sillus Arthur Ball (1867-1902), m. Martha Sowder

(5) John Randolph Ball (1869-1912), m. Martha Gray. One of their sons was:

(6) Harry Ball

(5) Joseph Franklin ("Frank") Ball, (1870-1942), m. Edna Sallie Renfro. Their sons were:

(6) Ira Ball (1894-1922), m. Lillian Morgan

(6) William Floyd (Floyd) Ball (1898-1956), m. 1) Allie Herndon (Herdon), 2) Lina Smith, 3) Mary Lee Wilson, 4) Verna Jo Daugherty. His children by Mary Lee were:

(7) Wilma Lee Ball, m. Coy Bays

(7) Sallie Louise Ball, m. Paul Parrot

(6) James Alva ("Alvey") Ball (1905-1956), m. Gladys Calloway. Their children were:

(7) Ira Beatrice Ball, m. 1) Warren Campbell, 2) William King, 3) Joe Bosworth III

(7) Edna Floyd Ball, m. Wallace ("Wah Wah") Jones

(7) Frances Lorraine Ball, m. Hugh Jones, Jr.

(7) Alva Franklin ("Sonny") Ball, m. Willie Evans

[Gladys's half-brother was Benny Gerstle. Her nephew (her sister's son) was Tom Manning]

(5) Timothy Taylor Ball (1872-1890)

(5) Houston Edward Ball (1873-1965), m. 1) Hattie Turner, 2) Lola Daniels

(5) Margaret Loretta Ball (1874-1946), m. James William Grubb

(5) Delia Jane Ball (1876-1951), m. Wickerson Sloan

(5) Samuel Ewing Ball (1878-1880)

(5) Nancy Matilda Ball (1880-1952), m. 1) Henry Flannery, 2) Abner Fawbush

(5) Mary Magnolia Ball (1882-1964), m. Charles Rowlett

(5) Elizabeth Emeline Ball (b. 1884), m. William Snead Hoskins

(5) Hettie Rachel Ball (1886-1888)

For a complete genealogy of the Ball family, see William W. Hoskins, *John Ball Family* (Radford, Va., 1975).

The Colsons

[Spelled Coulston prior to 1834]

(1) John Coulston (1767-1860), m. Elizabeth

(1) James Madison Coulston (1770/75-1845/46), m. 2) Amelia Tinsley. One of their sons was:

(2) John Calvin Colson Sr. (1822-1882), m. Mary Catherine Smith. Their surviving children were:

(3) James Madison Colson (1844-1870), m. 1) Josephine Green, 2) Henrietta Barner

(3) Redden Taylor Colson (1847-1896), m. Marthena Moss

(3) Margaret Amelia Colson (1853-1913), m. 1) McCleaster Howard, 2) Jacob Slusher

(3) John Calvin Colson Jr. (1854-1897), m. Susan L. Cottrell. Their sons were:

(4) John David Colson (1880-1965)

(4) James Clay (Clay) Colson (1886-1934)

(4) George Colson (1888-1924), m. Minnie Cordia Ball

(4) Harrison Doyle (Doyle) Colson (1892-1921) m. Lillie Dalton

(3) William Gillus (Gil or W.G.)Colson (1857-1921), m. 1) Margaret Wheeler, 2) Cora Sawyers. His daughters by Margaret were:

(4) Mary Nora Colson (1880-1965)

(4) Verda Colson (1885-1962)

(4) Lela Colson (1887-1961)

Three of his sons by Cora were:

(4) William Gillis Colson (1896-1977)

(4) David Grant Colson (1898-1969)

(4) John Calvin ("Jack") Colson (1907-1994)

(3) Mary Katherine Colson (1859-1936), m. William Ball Moss

(3) David Grant Colson (1861-1904), m. Thishe Ethel Elliott

(3) George Sherman Colson (1864-1886)

(3) Laura Belle Colson (1866-1921), m. James S. Bingham

(3) Cordelia Violet Colson (1868-1924), m. John Glasgow Fitzpatrick

(3) Eudoxia Olivia Colson (1870-1943), m. William Dempsey Hurst. Their sons were:

(4) John Hurst (1885-1968)

(4) William Hurst (1899-1987)

(4) Ernest Hurst (1901-1920)

For more information on the Colson family, see Mary Neal Routzohn, "Colsons of Knox County, Kentucky," *Gateway* 5.3 (Winter/Spring 1987): 54-69.

The Turners

(1) Joe Turner (d. 1862 or 1863), m. Polly Massey (Marsee). One of their sons was:

(2) Thomas (b. 1832) (listed in 1850 census as "idiot")

(1) John ("Slicky John") Turner (ca. 1780-1881), m. Elizabeth ("Betsy") Massey (Marsee). Some of their children were:

(2) Nancy Turner (b. 1809), m. Need Rains. One of their daughters was:

(3) Lucy Rains (1839-1924), m. Thomas Turner

(2) Joe ("Pussyfoot" or "Hanc") Turner (1811-1891), m. 1) Patsy Rains, 2) Rebecca Hoskins. His children by Rebecca were:

(3) Levi ("Lee") Turner (1860-1887)

(3) Elizabeth Turner (1862-1944), m. General Sowders (ca. 1860-1914). Their only child was:

(4) Hubert Sowders (1887-1935), m. Annie Spears

(3) Harvey Turner (1867-1890)

(3) Gordon Turner (1869-1885)

(2) Sally Turner (b. 1818), m. Alfred Pierce. Three of their sons were:

(3) Richard Pierce (1841-1917)

(3) Joseph Pierce (b. 1843)

(3) Robert Pierce (b. 1847)

(2) Polly Turner, m. Demps King. Two of their sons were:

(3) John King (b. 1836)

(3) Jeff King (b. 1840)

(2) Robert Turner. Two of his children were:

(3) Margaret Turner, m. Jim Burch

(3) James Franklin Turner. Two of his children were:

(4) Monroe Turner

(4) Auxie Turner, m. ______ Vaughn

(2) Green Turner (1826-1865), m. Elizabeth Vaughn
When Green's widow remarried, it was to Pres Turner. Two of their sons were:

(3) William Walter ("Wild Bill") Turner (d. 1898)

(3) Lee Alfred Turner (d. late 1930s)

(2) Ben Turner (b. 1826), m. Cynthia Green. Their sons were:

(3) Silias Turner (1856-1940)

(3) Marcellus Turner (b. 1857)

(3) Marshall Turner (b. 1859), m. Martha Sowders

(3) John Turner (b. 1864)

(3) Green Turner (b. 1867)

(3) Franklin Turner (b. 1870)

(2) Emily Turner (1828-1905), m. James Henderson. Three of their sons were:

(3) Thomas Jeff Henderson (b. 1850)

(3) James Henderson (b. 1867)

(3) Joseph Henderson (b. 1871)

(2) Jack Turner (1839-1887). Two of his sons were:

(3) Alvis Turner (1868-1889)

(3) Proctor Turner

For a more complete genealogy of the Turner fmaily, see Trecia A. Northrup, *The Marsee Family of Yellow Creek Valley and Related Families: Turner and Rains* (self-published, 1998).

Appendix III

Historical Sites in and around Middlesboro Today

Those who have found something of interest in these "footnotes" are invited to enjoy the scenes of that past that are still easily accessible to tourist and long-time resident alike.

The Cumberland Gap National Historical Park offers an opportunity to walk the old Warriors' Path of the Indians (later the Wilderness Road of the pioneers), to explore the Gap Cave that Thomas Walker noted, and to gaze from various overlooks at the unique crater that is the Yellow Creek Valley. Civil War trenches and forts are still in evidence, and the quiet trails of the park allow one to experience to some degree the wilderness of earlier days. Hensley Settlement, an isolated, self-sustaining community on Brush Mountain, has been restored, giving the visitor a sense of what life was like in another era. The Park also has various exhibits in its Visitors Center to aid in understanding the history of the Cumberland Gap.

Middlesborough's wide Cumberland Avenue still welcomes visitors, and the downtown historical district, though devastated by fires and a tornado, still has a number of buildings dating from the time of the English founders. The old American Association Building, which has been restored as a museum, contains many artifacts related to the Arthur family. There is now a walkway along the canal built by the Italians. Just off the canal on 20th Street, the Coal House, constructed in 1926 with forty tons of bituminous coal, is a symbol of the importance of King Coal. Next to it is a small outdoor museum devoted to coal mining. Half a block down the street is the Bell County Historical Society Museum, which is located in the beautifully restored Carnegie Library building and contains an interesting exhibit of artifacts, photographs, and other items related not only to the Yellow Creek Valley but to all of Bell County. Just across from it is the Library and Exhibition Hall built by Alexander Arthur to showcase the area, and a block to the west of the museum is St. Mary's Episcopal Church, where the English expatriates worshipped. Overlooking the church is Arthur Heights, where the American Association developers built their fine homes. One of these lovely Victorian houses is now the Ridgerunner Bed and Breakfast.

A short drive to the north, down 19th Street, brings the visitor to John Colson's house, which was built on the Wilderness Road more than two hundred years ago. Across from it is the Middlesborough Cemetery, where Alexander and Nellie Arthur are buried.

West on Cumberland Avenue, taking 25th Street to Cirencester, one reaches the Middlesborough Country Club golf course. Further to the west, off Cumberland Avenue on 35th Street, is the Middlesboro Airport, with the Lost Squadron Museum. Just to the southwest of the main runway is the Colson House, built by David Colson and long the residence of Jack Colson.

Not far from Middlesboro are other scenes of historical interest. Traveling west on Cumberland Avenue will lead one to Highway 186 up Mingo Hollow, where there are still working coal mines and tipples as well as the remains of old mining towns. The state line marker is just off the site of the Quarterhouse.

South through the new Cumberland Gap Tunnel are the cities of Cumberland Gap and Harrogate, Tennessee. Lincoln Memorial University in Harrogate houses one of the country's finest collections of Lincoln memorabilia in its Abraham Lincoln Museum. The dormitory on the far hill contains part of the only remaining building of the Four Seasons, that extravagant but doomed resort.

Driving north on Highway 25E takes one along the route of the Wilderness Road to the Narrows and the city of Pineville at the Cumberland River Ford. The Pine Mountain State Park, the first of Kentucky's state parks, offers many attractions, including the famous Chained Rock.

All of these attractions are described in detail in Tom Shattuck's *A Cumberland Gap Area Guidebook*. For a professional tour of all the historical sites in and around the Yellow Creek basin, contact the Wilderness Road Tours (606-248-2626).

Source Notes

Footnote One. Fiery Genesis

1. Kenneth F. Weaver, "Meteorites—Invaders from Space," *National Geographic* 170.3 (September 1986): 394.
2. Paul Hodge, *Meteorite Craters and Impact Structures of the Earth* (Cambridge, England, 1994), 18-19. Other sources include the Kentucky Geological Survey website and its links; the U.S. Geological Survey and its links; lectures/correspondence with Donald Chesnut and William Andrews of the Kentucky Geological Survey and Keith A. Milan of the Department of Geological Sciences, University of Tennessee.

Footnote Two. Cherokee Traditions

1. Kincaid Papers, box 2, archives of the Cumberland Gap National Historical Park. Robert Kincaid, author of the definitive *The Wilderness Road,* was editor of the local newspaper and later president of Lincoln Memorial University. This writer could find no confirmation, but the stories are certainly reasonable, and consistent with the general history of the Cherokees, though some details, such as the scalpings and the size of the northern confederation, may have been embellishments.

Footnote Three. The First White Man

1. Clarence W. Alvord and Lee Bidgood, *The First Explorations of the Trans-Allegheny Region by the Virginians, 1650-1674* (Cleveland, 1912), 213. Almost all of the information about Gabriel Arthur comes from this lengthy letter sent by Wood to his friend John Richards.
2. Harriette Simpson Arnow in *Seedtime on the Cumberland* (Lexington, Ky., 1960), 2, notes that some historians disagree with this common assumption.

Footnote Four. The Davis Tavern

1. Ricardo Torres-Reyes, "Davis Tavern Site Study," 12-2-1969, archives of the Cumberland Gap National Historical Park.

2. Henry Harvey Fuson, *The History of Bell County,* 2 vols. (New York, 1947), 1:202.

3. Notes on file in the archives of the Cumberland Gap National Historical Park.

4. "Diary of Moses Austin, 1796," quoted by Robert L. Kincaid, *The Wilderness Road* (New York, 1947), 93.

5. *Ashers: A Family History,* 31. No author or place or date of publication given, but the information therein is generally accepted as accurate by the descendants of Dillon Asher, who have a large reunion each year in Bell County. One of the two cabins Asher built still stands. It has been moved just over the county line to Clay County and reconstructed at the Red Bird Mission.

6. Ronald E. Lee, "The Davis Tavern," *Gateway* 2.1 (Fall 1983): 3-5.

Footnote Five. Early Settlers

1. Robert Kincaid interviews over a period of some years with Judge Sam Turner, Marcelius M. Turner, and Sterling K. Turner, grandsons of "Slicky" Turner, as reported in columns in the *Middlesboro Daily News* in 1960. Also a personal interview by this author with Walter Turner, 4-5-1989.

2. Lewis Preston Summers, *Annals of Southwestern Virginia, 1769-1800,* 2 vols. (Johnson City, Tenn., 1992), 1: 16-17.

3. Henry Muhlenberg, *The Life of Major-General Peter Muhlenberg* (Philadelphia, 1848), 448.

4. The Wilderness Road followed the west bank of Yellow Creek and crossed the Cumberland River at the Ford, whereas the new 25E is partially east of Yellow Creek and crosses the river downstream from Pineville.

5. Kincaid, *Wilderness Road,* 183.

6. Ronald E. Lee, "Yellow Creek Settlers, Living on Indian Land," *Gateway* 2.2 (Spring 1984): 48. Lee researched the National Archives and found, in record group 75, file M0208-0002, an entire file of correspondence dated 1803-04 related to the Yellow Creek settlers.

7. Stella Miller, report of an interview with Amanda Miller, the 90-year-old granddaughter of Henry Parker, *Three States,* 11-3-1955.

Footnote Six. Arthur Campbell

1. Frederick Drimmer, *Captured by the Indians: 15 Firsthand Accounts* (New York, 1961), 26. James Smith was for five years a captive of the Mohawks. He was one of the first white men to explore southern Kentucky and Tennessee, and in 1788 he settled in Kentucky, later representing Bourbon County in the state legislature. He told his story in his memoirs, published under the title *An Account of the Remarkable Occurrences in the Life and Travels of Col. James Smith* (Lexington, Ky., 1799).

2. In fact, Green Clay, a land speculator who became one of the largest landholders and most powerful men in Kentucky, had laid claim to the tract in the Yellow Creek Valley. Campbell took him to court over the land in 1806. Clay was a second cousin to Henry Clay and the father of Cassius Clay.

3. William Kozee, *Early Families of Eastern and Southeastern Kentucky and Their Descendants* (Baltimore, Md., 1973), 114.

Footnote Seven. The Patriarch of the Valley

1. Their homestead is now under the waters of Cannon Creek Lake. When the lake was created, the graves were moved to the Middlesboro Cemetery. The date of their death has been given by other sources as 1843.

2. This house, identified by a historical marker, still stands, albeit altered by additions and stucco facing, on North 19th Street.

3. *Three States,* 6-30-1955, in a reprint of an interview with Robbins that had taken place some years prior to this publication of his reminiscences.

4. Memoranda written by W.E. Curtis, dated 10-24-1888, in a private collection of American Association papers belonging to Dan Johnson, Middlesboro.

5. Multiple deeds in boxes of American Association papers, Middlesboro-Bell County Public Library.

6. Author conversation with Susan Colson Garmon, 3-7-1989. Ms. Garmon is the great-granddaughter of Gillis and Cora. Some other members of the family deny that he was womanizer and doubt this story.

7. Harold W. Coates, *Stories of Kentucky Feuds* (Kingsport, Tenn., 1923), 195. In the foreword it is noted that Mr. Coates, who was editor of a Cincinnati newspaper, did extensive research in old newspaper files and court records to obtain his information. This author was unable to find other documentation, but the draft of an old legal document in the possession of the Colson family does give his place of death as Texas, and the family genealogy lists the place of death as Plain Oak, Texas.

Footnote Eight. War Comes to the Yellow Creek Valley

1. Robert Kincaid interview with John Spencer King, who was a teenager at the time of the Civil War, *Three States,* 8-3-1939.

2. Author interview with Henrietta Cole, 7-25-1991. Her grandfather's aunt was John Colson's wife. Ms Cole recalled many stories he had told her about his service as a Confederate soldier at the Gap.

3. Stella Miller column reporting on an interview with Joe Marsee, age 101, *Three States,* 9-1-1955.

4. A Robert Kincaid column reporting on an interview with Isaac Turner, who was an eyewitness, *Three States,* 8-10-1939.

5. Robert Kincaid, report of an interview with Bill Seabolt, also an eyewitness, *Three States,* 4-13-1939.

6. Robert Kincaid, report of an interview with Sill Turner, another eyewitness, *Three States,* 10-26-1939.

7. Robert Kincaid, interview with Bill Seabolt, *Three States,* 4-6-1939.

8. Author interview with Walter Turner, 4-5-1989.

9. Fred Boyles, historian for the Cumberland Gap National Historical Park, *Middlesboro Daily News,* 9-30-1986, based on information from the McEntire family.

10. A minority opinion among those searching for the gold holds that it was the Union Army of General G.W. Morgan that hid the gold before their desperate retreat from the Gap.

11. Stella Miller, reporting an interview with Bets Turner, the daughter of Green Turner, *Three States,* 10-6-1955.

Footnote Nine. The Turner-Sowders Feud

1. The 1880 census lists 1,112 persons living in 205 families in the Big Yellow Creek Precinct, but this includes a much larger area than just the Yellow Creek Valley.

2. Typewritten manuscript by Thomas Nelson Sowder, dated 1-27-1954, in the private collection of Earl H. Sowders Jr. of Lexington, Kentucky.

3. According to census records and Turner genealogy, Elizabeth did not have a brother Tom. She did have several cousins by that name living nearby, including an older second cousin who was said to be an "idiot" and who lived in various Turner households.

4. Several author interviews during 1989 with Linda Courtney, the great-granddaughter of General Sowders, who was repeating the stories told to her by her Granny, the daughter-in-law of General.

5. Author interview with Monroe Turner, 2-17-1989. He said he used to hide under the porch as a child and listen to the old people talk about the feud.

6. "Kentuckian, 102, Recalls Mountain Feud Between Turners and Sowders," *Knoxville Journal,* 8-19-1956, an interview with Joe "Pet" Marsee, who was kin to both the Turners and the Sowders.

7. Unidentified newspaper clipping, RG 10, Box 1, archives of the Cumberland Gap National Historical Park.

8. Sam J. Johnston, "A Forgotten Feud of the Kentucky Mountain," undated manuscript in the archives of Berea College Library, 4. The author is identified only as "a newspaper man" who "lost his life in some of the awful catastrophes that marked the route to Dawson when the gold fever first developed," which would date it prior to 1900.

9. Trecia A. Northrup, *The Marsee Family of Yellow Creek Valley and Related Families, Turner and Rains* (self-published, 1998), 53.

10. Marsee interview, *Knoxville Journal,* 8-19-56.

11. Author interview with Monroe Turner. The same information appears in the "Pet" Marsee interview.

12. Johnston, "A Forgotten Feud," 5.

13. Author interview with Auxie Turner Vaughn, 2-13-1989.

14. Tape made by John Sowders in 1981 and provided to the author by Brenda and Roy Marsee.

15. Charles Mutzenberg later wrote *Kentucky's Famous Feuds and Tragedies: Authentic History of the World Renowned Vendettas of the Dark and Bloody Ground* (New York, 1917), but he did not mention the feud in which he participated.

16. For more on these deaths and the Quarterhouse Battle, see Footnote 22.

Footnote Ten. Alexander Arthur and His Lady

1. Alexander Arthur to his wife Mary, February 1879, copy in the archives, Abraham Lincoln Museum, Lincoln Memorial University.
2. "Reminiscences of William Arthur," manuscript written for his family, supplied by his great-granddaughter Gail Burk.
3. Arthur to his wife, February 1879, archives, Abraham Lincoln Museum, Lincoln Memorial University.
4. Alexander Arthur, "The Scottish-Carolina Timber and Land Co.—Plans for the Development of the Company's Property," Boston, Mass., 7-25-1884, 13.
5. Wilma Dykeman, *The French Broad* (New York: Henry Holt, 1955), 166-77. Information about this time in Newport is based largely on Dykeman's interviews with Nellie Arthur, who was ninety-four years old at the time.
6. The Scottish Mansion stood proudly for many years as a Newport landmark and the home of Congressman W.C. Anderson. After being damaged by fire, it was demolished in 1974.
7. Alexander Arthur, "*Middlesboro in the Making,*" Middlesboro, n.d., n.p.
8. Ibid.
9. *Knoxville Journal,* 8-23-1889.
10. Nellie Arthur to Dr. Robert Kincaid, 3-31-1940, Kincaid Papers, archives, Finley Learning Center, Lincoln Memorial University. Emphasis is hers.
11. Much of the information about this period in the lives of Alex and Nellie came from their grandchildren Alexander Arthur II, Maggie Pickett, and Mary Stonecipher. They had been told these stories by both their grandmother and their father, P.M.
12. Receipts in family papers made available by Alexander Arthur II. Other personal information is also from this source.
13. The building the Arthurs constructed on this northeast corner lot is still standing and has been in constant use by various businesses since 1891.
14. RG 10, box 1, archives of the Cumberland Gap National Historical Park. This box is almost full of letters lauding Arthur.
15. Alan Arthur to Macaulay Arthur, 5-29-1893, archives, Abraham Lincoln Museum, Lincoln Memorial University.
16. The title for Craig Neuk was in Nellie's name only. In 1904 it was sold for use by the Grace Nettleson School for orphan girls. It then became a part of the new Lincoln Memorial University, where it was used as a guest house and then as a music conservatory. It gradually deteriorated and was finally demolished by the university in the 1960s. All that remains today is a portion of the stone water tower.
17. Rhonda Goodwin to Marion Arthur, November 1898, archives, Abraham Lincoln Museum, Lincoln Memorial University.
18. Nellie Arthur to Ruby Arthur, 7-13-1907, supplied by her granddaughter Maggie Pickett.
19. Ruby Arthur to Macaulay Arthur, 7-16-1907, supplied by Maggie Pickett.
20. C.B. Roberts papers, Box 1, Filson Club, Louisville, Ky.

21. Alexander Arthur to Marion, 12-19-1909, Arthur Foundation Papers, Middlesboro-Bell County Library, Middlesboro. Other letters from Alex to Marion quoted in the text are from this same source.

22. A copy Roberts made of his letter to Nellie Arthur, dated 3-11-1912, Roberts Papers, Box 1, Filson Club, Louisville, Ky.

23. Nellie Arthur to Roberts, 4-10-1912, Roberts Papers, Box 1, Filson Club.

24. Author interview with Alice Fuson, 2-12-1995.

25. Katherine Van Meter to J.T. Hurst (publisher of the *Middlesboro Daily News),* published in the *Daily News* 11-19-1993.

26. Information on this period in Nellie's life is based on the reminiscences of her granddaughters Maggie Pickett and Mary Stonecipher.

Footnote Eleven. Boom and Bust

1. James Lane Allen, "Mountain Passes of the Cumberland," reprint of an article from *Harpers Magazine* 81 (Sept. 1890): 2.

2. Ibid., 3.

3. Untitled pamphlet with reprint of a speech given by John Proctor to the British Iron and Steel Institute on 10-21-1890.

4. W.C. Golvard to the editor of *Three States,* 6-13-1940.

5. Willie Good, age 86, as interviewed by Stella Miller, *Three States,* 4-19-1956.

6. Charles B. Roberts, "The Building of Middlesborough," *Filson Club Quarterly* (January 1933), 22-23.

7. *Middlesborough Daily News,* 3-7-1891.

8. *Cumberland Gap: A Weekly Review of the Progress and Development of SE Kentucky, SW Virginia and Eastern Tennessee,* 10-9-1889.

9. Reporter interview with Mrs. Phil McKay, *Three States,* 9-12-1940.

10. W.C. Curtis, "Memorandum of Condition and Prospects of the Middlesborough Town Company," 10-24-1888, Knoxville, Tenn., in a collection of American Association papers belonging to Dan Johnson, Middlesboro.

11. Based on an inflation rate of 18.5 percent as determined from a *Wall Street Journal* article on 1-11-1999. All figures given in this and other chapters can be multiplied by this figure to obtain approximate values in today's currency.

12. Reporter interview with Mrs. L.L. Pumphrey, *Three States,* 9-19-1940.

13. Reminiscences of T.A. Lee, *Middlesboro Daily News,* 6-25-1926.

14. Average annual household income in the country at that time was about $418, which would be equivalent to $8,360 today. By way of comparison, average annual household income in 1999 was $40,816. From *U.S. News & World Report,* 8-6-2001.

15. Pamphlet, "Middlesborough, Kentucky as Seen by Noted Men," January 1891, n.p., n.d.

16. "Middlesborough and the Gap," an undated booklet containing a reprint of a speech made by A.A. Arthur, n.p., n.d.

17. Reminiscences of Herbert L. Satterlee, *Three States,* 6-20-1940.

18. This company continued to be vital to the local economy for years to come. Based in London, but with headquarters in Middlesboro, it continued Arthur's

vision of leasing its properties to coal and timber companies rather than developing them itself. When land was being acquired for the Cumberland Gap National Historical Park, the American Association deeded 2,005 acres to the federal government. In 1978 it sold all of its remaining 85,000 acres to J.M. Huber Corporation, a land management company based in New Jersey, and the American Association was no more.

19. Letter from Jim C. Bowling, who came to Middlesboro in 1888, *Three States,* 3-22-1934.

Footnote Twelve. The Melting Pot

1. Charles B. Roberts, "The Building of Middlesborough," *Filson Club Quarterly,* January 1933, 25.

2. Robert Kincaid interview with Herbert Livingston Satterlee, *Three States,* 6-13-1940.

3. Herbert Satterlee to Robert Kincaid, 6-10-1947, archives, Finley Learning Center, Lincoln Memorial University.

4. Copy of Charles B. Roberts to Sir Thomas Blake, 9-29-1914, Roberts Papers, Filson Club, Louisville, Ky.

5. N.A. Crippens, *Lincoln School and Its Community, 1891-1965* (Clarksville, Tenn., 1995), 34. Most of the information about Bell came from this book. Crippens based his biographical notes on an unpublished family history written by Elgetha Brand Bell.

6. Author interview with Wilbur Wade, 1-10-1991.

7. Author interview with Lillie Banks, 9-27-1995.

8. Author interview with David Weinstein, 7-26-1990.

9. Arthur Rhorer, "Paragraphs," *Middlesboro Daily News,* 8-28-1957.

10. Roberts, "The Building of Middlesborough," 27.

11. D. Adallis, "Historical Sketch of the Greek-American Colony of Middlesboro," *25th Anniversary Historical Sketch and Business Guide of Middlesboro-Pineville* (n.p, n.d.), 17.

12. Reporter interview with John Cakmis, who had recently visited Hill in Greece, *Middlesboro Daily News,* 10-30-1947.

Footnote Thirteen. The Ball Boys

1. Nelle Neikirk and Glen Shumate, "Ancestors and Descendants of Rev. Wm. Ewing Yeary of Bell County," undated manuscript, 10, private collection.

2. There is a marker noting his grave site on old Highway 58 near Ewing, Virginia. The grave itself is some distance off the highway and well up a steep hill.

3. Author interview with Ruth Ball McCabe, 7-26-1989.

4. *Bell County Citizen,* 5-12-1897.

5. William W. Hoskins, *John Ball Family* (Radford, Va., 1975), 9.

6. Frank Cecil and his brother Charlie were cousins to the Balls and were involved with them in many incidents over the years.

7. Records of the Bell County Circuit Court, 1894-96, State Archives, Frankfort, Ky.

8. Newspaper clippings, Roberts Papers, Filson Club, Louisville, Ky. Most are undated and unidentified as to source. Roberts, who had been Alexander Arthur's secretary, was living in New York City at the time. He clipped and saved items related to Middlesboro that he saw in the big city newspapers.

9. *New York Times,* 11-6-1905.

10. Author interview with Henrietta Cole, Frank's niece, 7-25-1991.

11. This house, albeit remodeled and with the exterior covered by aluminum siding, is still standing. Irene Ball Hargraves, Rufus's daughter, recalled that before it was remodeled you could see the bullet holes in the door jambs and stairs. She was told that Frank hid in the chimney. Author conversation with Ms. Hargraves in September of 1999.

12. The author has been unable to ascertain the exact date he was released. Relevant prison records have already been expunged. The newspaper did note in 1922, while reporting another problem Frank was having with the law, that he had previously spent ten years in prison.

13. *Jonesville Star* (Jonesville, Va.), 2-21-1907.

14. Hoskins, *John Ball Family,* 289.

15. *Middlesborough News,* 11-21-1908.

16. C.D. had a house at 16th and Ashbury (three blocks north of Cumberland Ave.) and owned property from there to about 13th. The area that is now East End School grounds contained his barn and field. Frank and his sons lived in the area around 15th and Cumberland. John lived on Cumberland close to 16th. H.E.'s property was on the hill just a block or so south of Cumberland, and went from 13th to 18th Streets.

17. Ernie Pyle, *Brave Men* (New York, 1944), 27.

Footnote Fourteen. Fire! Fire!

1. *Middlesborough News,* 6-1-1890. Apparent typos are actually the result of a newspaper fad of the day that promoted phonetic spelling as an aid to those who were barely literate.

2. Reporter interview with Mary Gagle, who was living over the Goan Clothing Store at the time of the fire, *Three States,* 6-18-1955.

3. Minute Book A, Middlesborough City Council.

Footnote Fifteen. The Magic City

1. A somewhat different slant on the mountaineers' savvy can be found in Robert S. Weise, *Grasping at Independence: Debt, Male Authority and Mineral Rights in Appalachian Kentucky, 1850-1915* (Knoxville, 2001). Mr. Weise's research studied a different area, but his conclusions might be valid for the Yellow Creek Valley.

2. John Gaventa, *Power and Powerlessness* (Chicago, 1980), 54. As a Rhodes Scholar at Oxford University, Gaventa did extensive research in the files of the American Association. He also did research in the Bell County area, both in court records and by recording family traditions and stories.

3. In addition to incidents of this type of fraud cited by Gaventa, this author has an example from her husband's family. His great-great-grandfather owned a

large boundary of land that straddled two counties (Campbell and Claiborne Counties, just over the border from Bell County, in Tennessee). On the day the patriarch died, the land was supposedly deeded to an intermediary (to later be transferred to a large land company) in two widely separated county seats. The deeds were signed with his name even though the patriarch had never learned to write and had always been known to just "make his mark." By the time the family realized what had happened, the patriarch's many children had scattered and had large families of their own, and sporadic efforts at legal redress collapsed under the weight of the process.

4. Gaventa, *Power and Powerlessness,* 54-55.

5. G.W. Easton, a lawyer for the American Association, to J.H. Bartlett, 7-13-1892. In a private collection of papers of C.D. Rhodes, a later manager of the American Association.

6. Report to the American Association, Ltd., dated 6-28-1887 and signed E.J. Bird, Ironton, Ohio. In a collection of Rhodes papers belonging to Dan Johnson, Middlesboro.

7. There were also intangible factors related to the habits and skills of the Watts sons, who were sent over to manage the project, and to an unfortunate accident involving one of the Watts sons. These are detailed in Footnote Eleven.

8. "Report of London Directors and Mr. E.F. Powers," submitted on 10-21-1891 to a meeting of the shareholders of the American Association in London. In a collection of Rhodes papers belonging to Dan Johnson, Middlesboro.

9. *Louisville Courier Journal,* 11-15-1894.

Footnote Sixteen. "Judge Lynch"

1. Reporter interview with Annie Hurst, whose husband, John, was on duty that night at the power plant, *Three States,* 5-17-1956.

2. The reminiscences of L.H. Park, who came to Middlesborough in the spring of 1890, *Three States,* 10-3-1940.

Footnote Seventeen. The Father of Ragtime

1. Isidore Witmark and Isaac Goldberg, *From Ragtime to Swingtime: The Story of the House of Witmark* (New York, 1939), 114.

2. William H. Tallmadge to author, 11-22-1993. Tallmadge was a professor of music at the State University College in Buffalo, New York (1949-1976), and at Berea College (1976-1986). He has done considerable research on Harney and exchanged information with this author over a period of years. Tallmadge is the one who uncovered most of the information about Harney's ancestry and his life prior to 1890.

3. William H. Tallmadge, "Ben Harney: The Middlesborough Years, 1890-93," *American Music* 13.2 (Summer 1995): 168.

4. *Louisville Courier-Journal,* 2-7-1899.

5. *Louisville Herald,* 4-23-1916.

6. *Louisville Courier Journal,* 2-7-1899.

7. Rudi Blesh and Harriet Janis, *They All Played Ragtime* (New York, 1950), 213.

8. *Louisville Herald,* 4-23-1916.

9. Blesh and Janis, *They All Played Ragtime,* 4.

10. Witmark and Goldberg, *From Ragtime to Swingtime,* 153.

11. Ibid.

12. Blesh and Janis, *They All Played Ragtime,* 226.

13. Dave Bourne, "The Ben Harney Years," *The Rag Times* 4.4 (Nov. 1970): 12.

14. Alec Wilder, *American Popular Song* (New York, 1972), 9.

15. Wayne D. Shirley, Music Division, Library of Congress, in a letter to the *Sonneck Society Newsletter* (Spring 1980), 14.

16. William J. Schafer, "Ben Harney and Ragtime Prehistory," *The Mississippi Rag* (July 1997), 22.

17. *Time,* 3-14-38, 7.

18. Blesh and Janis, *They All Played Ragtime,* 229-30.

19. Sigmund Spaeth, *Popular Music in America* (New York, 1948), 285.

Footnote Eighteen. The Athens of the Mountains

1. This building is today little changed on the exterior except that the entry has been enclosed and it has lost its original turret. Over the years it has been used as a high school, a meeting hall, and an office building.

2. Author interview with Louisa Hoe Cawood, 2-12-1995.

3. Author interview with Faye White, Viola's sister, 5-29-2000.

4. Author interview with Juanita Smith, 1-12-2000.

5. Author interview with Dr. Sam Flowers, 9-21-1991.

Footnote Nineteen. David Colson

1. The house that David built is still standing just west of the airport terminal. It stayed in the Colson family until 1994.

2. C.B. Roberts papers, Filson Club, Louisville.

3. *Middlesborough News,* 10-1-1904.

4. Coincidentally, Ben Golden fathered James S. Golden, the only Bell Countian, other than Colson, to serve in the U.S. Congress. Golden's tenure was from 1949 through 1955.

5. This second gun may have been the deciding factor that allowed Colson to prevail in the fight that was to come, just as a second gun would give his nephew, George Colson, the advantage some twenty years later in the Ball-Colson Feud (see Footnote Twenty-six).

6. Watterson to Colson, 6-18-1900, copy in the private collection of Mary Routzohn of Harlan, Ky.

7. Thomas E. Stephens, "Congressman David Grant Colson and the Tragedy of the Fourth Kentucky Volunteer Infantry," *Register of the Kentucky Historical Society* 98.1 (Winter 2000): 99-100.

8. Information given by his wife and reported in the metropolitan papers,

though not in the local papers. The *Middlesborough News* stated only that "a fit of fury preceded the collapse from which consciousness never came and merciful death followed." The *Middlesborough Record,* which reported the death in a single column on the third page, along with local news, stated, "He was taken suddenly ill with nervous prostration, which was the cause of his death." That there may have been more to the story is evidenced by the fact that there was some talk of poison, and his internal organs were sent to Louisville to be examined by the state medical examiner (who found no abnormalities). In another intriguing twist, C.B. Roberts (who had been private secretary to Alexander Arthur and who continued a lively interest in Middlesboro even after he moved to New York) left this account: "Several years later [after the shoot-out in Frankfort] his mind began to fail....One September day he had been riding his horse, of which he was very fond, in the solitude of the mountains, alone. He was seen to return slowly along Cumberland Avenue. He dismounted in front of the building in which his office was located, drew his pistol and killed the animal by a single discharge. He then went upstairs to his office, and another report rang out. That shot ended his own life" (Roberts Papers, Filson Club, Louisville). The author could find no other source that suggests his death was the result of suicide, and his family is adamant that it was not. Roberts left no indication as to the source of this story; perhaps it was only malicious rumor. (At the time, there was no requirement that the cause of death be a matter of public record.) Another question (asked only by this author) is whether David could have become addicted to morphine, having been given large doses of it to control the pain in his splintered elbow. At the time, morphine was readily available, and its use did not carry the same connotations it does today. Perhaps this could account for some of his erratic behavior in the last months of his life.

Footnote Twenty. The Smallpox Epidemic of 1898

1. All of the information for this chapter was taken from contemporary newspapers: *Middlesborough News, Weekly Record, Pineville Sun,* and *Middlesboro Daily News.*

Footnote Twenty-One. Yellow Creek Politics

1. W.C. Curtis, "Memorandum of Condition and Prospects of the Middlesborough Town Company," 10-24-1888, Knoxville, Tennessee. In a private collection of American Association papers.
2. Letter to the editor from L. McKenrick of Kittaning, Penn., *Three States,* 2-24-1944.
3. Reprint of a reporter interview with Joe Bosworth that had appeared in the *Louisville Courier-Journal, Middlesborough News,* 1-27-1906.
4. Minute Book A, entry for 5-15-1890, Official Records of the City of Middlesborough.
5. Minute Book B has unaccountably disappeared, so the newspapers give the only hint of what was occurring in city government.
6. Minute Book C, entry dated 2-5-1900, Official Records of the City of Middlesborough.

7. Author interview with Katherine Dance, 10-27-1991.

8. Author interview with Etta (Mrs. Willie) Laymon, 1-19-1993.

9. Multiple author conversations with Jean and George Fisher Jr., 1972-1978. George was, among other things, a supplier of liquor, and Jean took over the operation of the Majestic after Daisy Tamer retired.

10. This, and much that follows, comes from the personal knowledge and experience of the author.

11. Author interview with Crawford Blakeman, 6-29-1992. As far out as this sounds for a small town, the authorities were at the time in Middlesboro investigating the murder a year earlier of "Tootsie" Asher, whose car had exploded when she started it. Although her murder was not related to politics, it did cause Mayor Blakeman to take the FBI's warning seriously.

Footnote Twenty-Two. The Quarterhouse Battle

1. *Middlesborough News,* 2-8-1902. What appear to be misspellings or typos were actually part of a short-lived movement at the time to spell phonetically.

2. Author interview with Monroe Turner, 2-17-1989.

3. Author interview with Axie Turner Vaughn, 1-13-1989. She recalled her mother, who lived in the far western part of the city, saying that she was talking on the phone when she saw the posse approaching her house and then the phone went dead.

4. Interview with "Aunt" Bets Turner as recorded by Stella Miller, *Three States,* 10-6-1955.

Footnote Twenty-Three. The Queen of the Rhine

1. This was owned by Jack Ray (or Lay) and a MacFarland and is not to be confused with the large Overbeck New South Brewery that was located in what is now the national park. According to some accounts, it was also a distillery. It was totally destroyed by fire in 1910.

2. Charles B. Roberts, "The Building of Middlesborough," *Filson Club Quarterly,* January 1933, 20.

3. Records from the Bell County Circuit Court Criminal Order Book and from a record book styled "Order, Criminal Causes, Middlesborough City Court."

4. A word of explanation: old city records were stored in the basement of the city hall building. When the building was destroyed by fire in 1986, it was felt that all of these record books were so damaged by fire and water as to be unsalvageable. A bulldozer was used, and all the debris from the fire was loaded up and taken to a dump. This author spent the better part of a day at the dump trying to find anything that was still readable. (Unfortunately, I had not previously looked at these records.) Luckily, among the things I pulled from the dump were books that cover 1894 through 1902. Not all of them were decipherable, but in the parts I could read there was no further mention of Alice Lamb. (These books are now housed at the Bell County Historical Society Museum.) Any records prior to 1894 were apparently destroyed, and the newspapers did not normally give the names of women charged with disorderly conduct, fornication, adultery, or keeping of a bawdy house.

No record of Alice was found in the Commonwealth Order Books stored at the Bell County Circuit Court Clerk's office.

5. Author conversation with Jack Sharpe, 1-8-1999. He stated that his father had known Alice Lamb well and had told him about her.

6. Reporter interview with C.D. Ball, who was at the time remodeling the building that had once been the Keg House, *Three States,* 4-6-1939. The author was unable to find any record of such a trial.

7. Arthur Rhorer in "Paragraphs," *Middlesboro Daily News,* 9-30-1957. Mr. Rhorer is the only source this author could find for this story, and he did not elaborate further.

Footnote Twenty-Tour. That Peculiar Scottish Game

1. Author interviews with Eugene Spriggs, 2-3-1991, and with James Hodge, 2-3-2000.

2. Column by Robert Kincaid reporting on an earlier interview with Livingston Satterlee at his home in New York City, *Three States,* 6-13-1940. In this author's opinion, Mr. Satterlee offers the best evidence for the date golf began to be played in Middlesboro because he made only three short trips to the city, each at a different period in the city's development, and for very important clients, so each trip stood out in his memory. This mention of golf was in the nature of an aside in the discussion of other matters. Because of what he saw and did on this visit, it has to have occurred in 1889 or, at the very latest, early 1890.

3. Arthur Rhorer, a prominent Middlesboro attorney, in a letter dated 7-12-1952 and in various interviews and newspaper articles over the years. His father came to Middlesboro in 1889, and the family followed in early 1890. Arthur was six at the time. In the letter he stated that he caddied in 1895 and 1896, while in some interviews he said that he began to caddie in 1890. Whatever his work history, Rhorer remains the best source for the exact location of the course in the early days, and for the fact that it remained approximately the same over the years and was in continuous use. In his letter he stated unequivocally, "the playing of golf over the same course under style of Middlesborough Golf Course has been indulged in without interruption from 1889 to 1952."

4. Paul McKenrick in a long letter to *Three States* (9-20-1940) in response to a request that early residents share their memories as a way to celebrate the town's fiftieth anniversary.

5. *Middlesborough News,* 9-8-1894. It is notable that there were a number of "old and enthusiastic" golfers at the time. With golf such a new sport for the general populace, it seems very likely that they would have been introduced to the game by the English and Scottish players and that they would have continued to play on the course, especially if they were anything like present-day golfers in their devotion to the game.

6. A dissenting view is presented by Dr. Kenneth Smith in "History of the Founding of the Middlesboro Country Club," *Gateway* 11.2 (Spring 2000): 11-13.

Footnote Twenty-Five. Lift Up Thine Eyes

1. Information about his early life came from the author's conversations with his sons James and Clyde Mayes and with his daughter-in-law Catherine Mayes. Ms. Mayes has recently published a book about H.H. Mayes entitled *A Coal Miner's Simple Message* (Three States Printing, 1999).

2. This house, albeit modified and remodeled, still stands at 409 Chester Ave. in Middlesboro. An exact scale model of the original house, constructed by his son Clyde, is on exhibit at the Museum of Appalachia in Norris, Tennessee, along with many other artifacts of H.H. Mayes's life and works.

3. Simile used by Romell Johnson in an interview with the *Louisville Courier Journal,* March 16, 1992.

Footnote Twenty-Six. The Ball-Colson Feud

1. *Middlesboro Daily News,* 1-7-1921.

2. Susan's brother was Meade Cottrell, whom C.D. and Patton Ball were accused of killing in 1902 (see Footnote Thirteen).

3. Book of Wills, entry dated 2-25-1916, Bell County Circuit Court Clerk's Office.

4. Author conversation and correspondence with Calvin Colson in December of 1989.

5. Private papers of Bill Hurst, made available by his son David Hurst. An article in the *Claiborne County Tennessee News* of 5-17-1922 stated, "The trouble between the Colsons and Balls started in a quarrel over a card-game about a year ago in which Ira Ball, Floyd Ball, Doyle Colson and William Hurst were concerned," which would seem to corroborate Hurst's story.

6. William W. Hoskins to author, 10-26-1992. Mr. Hoskins was a cousin to the Balls and heard the story from them.

7. This was first related to the author by William W. Hoskins, who was the family genealogist and ever a strong defender of the Ball name in general and of those of Alva, Floyd, and Ira in particular. But a number of independent sources also related this same story. In another twist, Hugh Jones's two sons were to marry two of Alva's daughters.

8. Author phone conversation with Leslie Stephens (granddaughter of Doyle Colson), 1-27-1991. Her version was told to her by her uncles and her Dalton relatives.

9. Leslie Stephens to author, 2-7-1991.

10. This person, who did not wish to be identified, was about ten years old at the time of the incident and was walking home from the movies when the shooting started. She said she ducked into the entryway of a nearby house and watched the whole thing.

11. W.W. Hoskins, undated manuscript.

12. Bill Hurst papers. Dave Hurst stated that when he met Mrs. Wallace Gastineau the first time, they started discussing the Balls and the Colsons. She said, "It was Ira's fault." It was only when he, puzzled, related the conversation to

his father that he learned that Mrs. Gastineau had been married to Ira at the time of the shooting and was probably an eyewitness.

13. The Gorman Building was located downtown on 19th between Cumberland and Lothbury. This gives some credence to the story of a car full of young men shooting off their weapons as a prelude to the actual shootout at 15th.

14. Maddox would, in the late 1940s, be one of principal architects of the collapse of the Ball Empire (see Footnote Twenty-nine).

15. Bill Hurst papers.

16. One of the guards was Maurice Tribell, who would later be one of the strong influences in bringing Floyd into the Binghamtown Baptist Church (see Footnote Twenty-nine).

17. John did leave a rather cryptic tape, made late in life, in which he lamented something to the effect, "If I'd only said, George, I'm coming in." Although he was rambling, it sounded as if George was in some type of office shooting. This was related by John's son, John "Lin" Hurst, in an author interview, 6-15-1991.

18. William Hoskins made a handwritten note of his own on a photostat he had made of the newspaper article about the Hurst shooting: "Floyd Ball was the one that poured the oil on John Hurst."

19. Among the missing was Bud Yoakum, who was shot in July of 1922 in the Palace Cafe. His killer was later involved in another murder, this one perpetrated by Joe Morgan, Ira's brother-in-law. There was no suggestion in the record, however, that these killings were related to the feud.

20. It may be that Wallace Gastineau was the one who actually shot George. When Floyd was on his deathbed, he told his former brother-in-law, David Smith, that he had taken the blame for Gastineau because he could easily claim self-defense, since everyone knew about the feud. Author interview with David Smith, 9-11-1994.

21. W.W. Hoskins to author, 12-1-1992.

Footnote Twenty-Seven. The Chicago Connection

1. Newspaper articles at the time of his death stated that Zuta immigrated in 1908. Statements by Ginsberg and evidence of Zuta's business activities indicate that he came over much earlier. His legal name, as given in his will, was John U. Zuta. Others in his family spelled the name Zoota; the newspapers sometimes used Zuty and other spellings.

2. Louis Wirth, *The Ghetto* (Chicago, 1928), 202.

3. Author conversation (date not recorded) with Bill Ausmus, who obtained his information from Jimmie Ginsberg, the son of Ike Ginsberg.

4. John Landesco, *Organized Crime in Chicago,* part III (Chicago, 1929), 197.

5. Author interview with David Weinstein, 7-27-1990.

6. *Chicago American,* 8-5-1930.

7. Author conversation with Gladys (Mrs. Alva) Ball, 12-6-1992.

8. *Chicago American,* 8-5-1930.

9. John Kobler, *Capone: The Life and World of Al Capone* (New York, 1971), 303.

10. Walter Reckless, *Vice in Chicago* (Chicago, 1933), 80.

11. This date appears to be correct, despite the date on his tombstone.

Footnote Twenty-Eight. King Coal

1. J.C. Tipton, *Cumberland Coal Field and Its Creators* (Middlesboro, 1905), unnumbered pages.

2. Author interview with Henry Ralston, John's great-grandson, 2-12-1998.

3. Author conversation with William Turnblazer Jr., 7-22-1998.

4. Author interview with Eugene Settles, 8-14-1998. Settles's father had worked on the draining of the mine and always said that, of the twenty-five different mine operators he had worked for, Craig Ralston was the best.

5. Author conversation with William Whitaker, 3-13-1990. Whitaker lived at a coal camp in Mingo Hollow in 1941. His father had been a miner and was, at the time of the Battle, operating a small store with a single pool table where the miners would congregate. In point of fact, Rhodes was not English but was as American as the miners.

6. Author interview with William Edward Ball Sr., 9-17-1994. Hubert's cousin Floyd Ball was the first to "go bond" for the UMWA men.

7. Author interview with Eugene Settles, 8-14-1998.

8. Over more than ten years of talking with numerous retired miners, this author found many who claimed hearsay knowledge and/or said they were at the site immediately before or after the Battle, but only one who admitted being present at the time of the confrontation, and he said that as soon as the shooting started, he "dived over the hill" and ran all the way home, so he "didn't see nothing."

9. In the interest of complete disclosure, it must be here noted that this author's back yard adjoined that of the Pass family for more than twenty-five years, and she considered Beula (Mrs. Albert) Pass to be not only a good neighbor and friend but also a very admirable woman. Beula devoted much of her life to the care of her severely disabled daughter. This author's husband was the Pass family physician for at least twenty years and made numerous housecalls on their bedridden daughter. Also, in the early seventies he was Mrs. Turnblazer's physician. But in no way has any information been used here that would be considered confidential because of the physician-patient relationship.

10. John Gaventa, *Power and Powerlessness,* 181, quoting from the testimony in the Tony Boyle trial.

Footnote Twenty-Nine. Little Las Vegas

1. Author interview with Anna Faye Sandifer, Allie's adopted daughter, 1-22-1994. Allie's last name is sometimes given as Herdon. She also reported her age differently to various sources. She told her daughter she was thirteen when she married, but on her gravestone her date of birth is given as 1-29-1900, which would make her sixteen when she married.

2. Author interviews with Gladys Ball, 12-6-1992 and 10-20-1994.

3. Author interview with George Philpot (a Ball associate) on 2-18-1993. Corroborated by other sources who wished to remain anonymous. This desire to remain anonymous is also the case with many of the citations and much of the information contained in this chapter.

4. Author conversation (date not recorded) with Juanita Green Smith, whose father operated the Garmeda Mine.

5. Author interview with Glen Weaver (a Ball associate), 10-2-1994.

6. According to the records of the Federal Bureau of Prisons, Alva was sentenced to two years in the federal penitentiary in Atlanta for conspiracy to violate the National Prohibition Act. He entered prison on 11-26-29 and was paroled on 10-31-30 (letter to author from Anne Diestel, archivist for the Department of Justice).

7. Author interview with Willie Ball, 3-28-1995, information as told to her by her mother-in-law, Gladys Ball.

8. The newspapers gave her age as twenty-five, but her brother, David Smith, said she was twenty-three when she died. Over the years there have been many rumors—that she and Floyd had never actually married, that she was not alone at the time of the shooting, that her death was not a suicide—but this author could find no confirmation of any of these. (The author has also been unable to find any record of her marriage.) Her brother, who said he was present at the time of her death, stated that it occurred in the hospital and that she talked to them all before she died and affirmed that she had shot herself.

9. Author interview with Gaines Williamson, 3-18-1994.

10. Author interview with Joe Bosworth, 5-17-1999.

11. Merle Middleton held somewhat the same position in neighboring Harlan County as the Balls did in Bell County. He got his start as a "gun thug" for the coal companies during the union battles and gradually gained in political power until he ran the county. He invested in some legitimate businesses, most notably a bus company, but apparently was not as involved in gambling and liquor as were the Balls. In contemporary accounts the Balls are referred to as his "good friends."

12. Author interview with Cora Edds, former manager of Indian Rock, 9-6-1992.

13. Author interview with Ed Ball, 9-17-1994.

14. A third killing could have been the Buchanon massacre described later—certainly Alvey had a part in this death. One of the more unlikely stories told to this author came from Jim Burke, who said he had been told by someone who wished to remain anonymous that he had prayed at the deathbed of a friend who related the following story: The man had become embroiled in a fight and had beaten a man to the point that he no longer seemed to be breathing. Fearful of the consequences, he went to Alvey and said he was afraid he had killed someone. He said that Alvey returned to the scene of the fight with him, and when the victim showed some signs of life, Alvey drew his own gun and shot him through the heart, saying, "He's dead now." The story seemed too far-fetched to repeat until the author found an article in a 1939 newspaper describing a victim who had apparently been beaten to insensibility and then later shot through the heart.

15. Author interviews with Dave Crockett, 2-11-93, and with Harold Barton, March of 1994. (Frederick's family was from Iowa.)

16. Author interview with Lillie Banks, 9-27-1995.

17. Author interview with Mary Porter Fletcher, 6-18-1992.

18. Author interview with Willie Ball, 3-28-1995, information as told to her by her mother-in-law, Gladys Ball.

19. Author interview with Shelva Marsee, 4-24-1994, information as told to him by his mother, Mary Minton Marsee.

20. The author's husband was Jo Ball's personal physician for the last ten years of her life. Many of the other people who are mentioned or cited in this chapter were also patients at his office, where the author worked as office manager for twenty-five years. But great care has been taken in this work to in no way breach the confidentiality of the doctor-patient relationship.

21. The house is still standing at 1202 North 25th Street, unchanged except for an addition to the rear. The swimming pool was on the hill behind the house, where a public housing project is now located.

22. Author conversation with Sallie Ball Henson (Floyd's daughter), 9-6-1999.

23. Author conversation with Opal Madon (who was secretary to the Southeastern Protective Association's lawyer, A.W. Rhorer) in January of 1994.

24. Author interviews with Walter Turner, 4-5-1989, and with Glen Weaver, 10-2-1994.

25. Multiple author conversations with George Fisher Jr. and Thelma Fisher Stalcup, 1974-1990.

26. Author interviews with Robert Hatfield, 2-15-1995, and with George Philpot, 2-18-1993.

27. The Majestic is the only one of the old hotels still standing. It has been gutted and remodeled with a grant for historic preservation and now serves as the Middlesboro Medical Mall.

28. Author conversation with Bill Ausmus, date not recorded.

29. Author interview with Bill Burch, 11-22-92.

30. Author interview with the Rev. W.B. Bingham, 1-21-1993, information as told to him by Floyd's son-in-law, Coy Bays, who had accompanied him to New York.

31. Author interview with Bert Paynter, 3-2-1995.

32. Author conversation with Ballard Cardwell, 6-20-1989.

33. Author interview with Sonny Ball, 6-29-1992.

34. There are also a number of older men in Middlesboro today who remember that when, as young boys, they tried to loiter on 19th or hang out at the pool halls, Floyd would grab them up by the scruff of the neck and tell them to get back in school and make something of themselves.

35. Author interview with Harry Hoe (former State Representative who was told the story by Clay Bailey), 3-26-1995.

36. Author conversation with Betty Hayes, 2-11-1995.

37. Author interview with Glen Weaver, 10-2-1994.

38. "Bossism, Disorder Grip Bell County," anonymous pamphlet (which liberally borrows from Allan Trout's articles in the *Louisville Courier-Journal* in September and October of 1944), undated, but probably from late 1944 or early 1945, 10, quoting from the case of Simpson vs. Hughes, Franklin Circuit Court.

39. Author conversations with Gaines Williamson, 3-18-1994, and with Al Funk, 1-21-1994.

40. Author interview with George Philpot, 2-18-1993.

41. Author interview with Dave Rogan, 4-24-1995.

42. Author interview with Sonny Ball, 6-29-1992.

43. Author interview with Gladys Ball, 3-29-1995.

44. Russell Rice, *Kentucky Basketball's Big Blue Machine* (Huntsville, Ala., 1976), 170-71.

45. *Newsweek,* 5-1-1950.

46. Author interview with Dr. Samuel Flowers, 8-22-1991.

47. Author interview with Robert Hatfield, 2-15-1995.

48. William Fairfield III, "Bloody Harlan and Corrupt Bell," *The Reporter: A Fortnightly of Facts and Ideas* (New York), 10-16-1951, 23.

49. Author interview with George Philpot, 2-18-1993.

50. Author interview with John and Edith Cawood, 7-15-1991.

51. Copy of tape provided by Sallie Ball Henson.

52. Author interview with David Smith, 2-10-1991.

53. Author phone conversation with Al Funk, 1-21-1994, and interview with Cora Edds (who had become Funk's executive secretary after her stint managing Indian Rock and Jimmie Ginsberg's business interests), 9-6-1992.

Footnote Thirty. Pioneers of the Air

1. Susan Colson Garmon to author, 5-15-1997. A further account of this accident and of Jack Colson's family is found in Footnote Seven.

2. Author interview with David Smith, 9-8-1999.

3. *Middlesboro Daily News,* 8-19-1965.

4. Author conversation with her great-nephew, James Carl Shumate, summer of 1999.

5. Author conversations with Dave Rogan, Senter Ely, and Joe Bosworth III during the summer of 1999.

6. David Atwell, *Masterplan for the Middlesboro-Bell County Airport,* 1977, offices of Vaughn & Melton, Engineers, Middlesboro. Atwell stated in this plan drawn up for a grant application that Bowman Field in Louisville was the first and Middlesboro's Colson Field was the second.

7. For a complete history of the P-38 and the rescue and restoration project, see David Hayes, *The Lost Squadron* (Toronto, 1994).

8. There was a fatal accident at the airport in 1944 when a pilot from St. Louis crashed immediately after takeoff.

Epilogue

1. Alexander Arthur, "Middlesboro in the Making," n.d., n.p.

Sources and Bibliography

Author Interviews and Personal Contacts

The following people have generously shared their memories with me. Some gave extensive and multiple interviews, while others reminisced in informal conversations over the past ten years and more. Sadly, some are now deceased. A few persons specifically requested that their names be omitted, which I have done, and I have undoubtedly left off a few unintentionally. To all who contributed their knowledge of the history of our region, I wish to say "thank you."

Wynunee Anderson
Alexander Arthur II
William ("Little Bill") Ausmus
Alva Floyd Ball
Alva ("Sonny") and Willie Ball
Gladys (Mrs. Alvey) Ball
Jo (Mrs. Floyd) Ball
Randy Ball
William Edward ("Ed") Ball
Lillie Banks
Harold and Betty Barton
W.B. Bingham
Delphine Blackburn
Crawford and Gertrude Blakeman
Larry Blondell
Margaret Blondell
Joe Bosworth III
Jane Brewer
Clinton and Dot Broadwater
Martha Locke Brock
Ann Brown
Bill and Mildred Burch
Jim Burke
Doug Campbell
Ballard and Treecie Cardwell
Don Carroll
Joan Asher Cawood
John and Edith Cawood
Louisa Hoe Cawood
Pope Cawood
Hagan Chadwell
Robert Chadwell
Debbie Ball Channell
Henry Chappell
Don Cole
Henrietta Hoskins Cole

Don Coleman
Greg Colson
Harrison Doyle Colson
Jimmie (Mrs. James) Colson
John Calvin Colson
Virginia Colson
Emma Coomer
Teddy Cornett
Anna Faye Sandifer Cosby
Chester Cosby
Linda Peck Courtney
Dave and Olive Crockett
Herman Cupp
Katherine Dance
Tom Dooley
Mitchell Duncan
Wilma Dykeman
Elsie (Mrs. William) Easton
Temp Easton
Cora Edds
Senter Ely
Betty Ridings Emmett
George and Jean Fisher
Mary Porter Fletcher
Sam Flowers, M.D.
Edith (Mrs. Fred) Foster
Al Funk
Alice Fuson
Ben Fuson, D.D.S.
Martha (Mrs. Joby) Gastineau
Keith Grubbs
Susan Colson Harding
David and Imelda Harris
Helen (Mrs. Roosevelt) Harris
Robert Hatfield
Betty Hayes
Buddy Helms
Damron Helton
Sallie Ball Henson
Charlie Hines
James Hodge
Harry and Mary Bob Hoe
Homer and Jesse Hoe
William Hoskins
Murrell Hughes
Virginia Huff
David Hurst
John ("Lin") Hurst
June Sowders Jacob
Curtis Johnson
Dan Johnson
Willie Jones
Ruby Kimsey
Robert Lambdin
Etta (Mrs. Willie) Laymon
Frank Welch Lee
Raymond Lovett
Daryls Martin Lynch
Opal Madon
Roy Marsee
Shelvie Marsee
Walter Marsee
Paris Martin
Jack Mason
Clyde and Catherine Mayes
James Mayes
Ruth Ball McCabe
Ernest Mike
George Miller
Foster Minton
Ann Motch
Virginia Hurst Mulhaney
Joe Nagle
Mildred Nagle
Charles Niday
Lynn Noah
Ethel Parker
Beula (Mrs. Albert) Pass
Bert and Thelma Paynter
Mike Paynter
George Philpot
Margie Arthur Pickett
Cecil Powers
Henry Ralston
Opal (Mrs. George) Ridings
Dave and Betty Rogan
Robert Rogan
Eugene Settles
Goble Shackelford
Jack Sharpe

Roy Shoffner
James Carl Shumate
Herbert Silvers
David and Elizabeth Smith
Dennis Smith
Emily Smith
Isabelle Fitzpatrick Smith
Juanita (Mrs. Kirby) Smith
Keith Sowders
Minnie Marsee Sowders
Eugene and Margaret Spriggs
James Spriggs
Thelma Fisher Stalcup
Helen and Charles Stapleton
Leslie Colson Stephens
Mary Arthur Stonecipher
Maurine (Mrs. Guy) Susong
Vernon Thompson
Maurice Tribell
Bill Turnblazer
Alvis Turner
Monroe Turner
Walter Turner
Auxie Turner Vaughn
Wilbur Wade
Raymond Walker
William Watson
Glen Weaver
David Weinstein
Pat Welch
Troy Welch
William Whitaker
Charlotte (Mrs. Raymond "Snooks") White
Faye (Mrs. Hubert) White
Vivien (Mrs. Junior) Whitmore
William Widener
Gaines Williamson
Lilliard Phillip Williamson
Buddy Yeary
Mildred Yeary
Warren Yeary
Thursia Yoe

Manuscript Collections

American Association Papers. Middlesboro-Bell County Library, Middlesboro, Ky.
Appalachian Feuds Collection. Berea College Library, Berea, Ky.
Arthur Family letters, documents, and photographs in private collections of various family members (Alexander Arthur II of Hockessin, Del.; Maggie Pickett of Birmingham, Ala.; Mary Stonecipher of Cleveland, Tenn.; and Gail Burk of Scotts Valley, Calif.).
Arthur Family Papers. Middlesboro-Bell County Library, Middlesboro, Ky.
Arthur Papers. Abraham Lincoln Museum, Lincoln Memorial University, Harrogate, Tenn.
Arthur Papers. McClung Historical Collection, East Tennessee Historical Society, Knoxville, Tenn.
Book of Wills, Step Docket, Bell Circuit Orders. Bell County Circuit Court Clerk Office, Pineville, Ky.
Davis Tavern Site Study. Cumberland Gap National Historical Park, Middlesboro, Ky.
Diaries of William Lattrell, 1862-63. Cumberland Gap National Historical Park, Middlesboro, Ky.
Elks Record Books, 1924-64. Private Collection.
Kincaid Papers. Cumberland Gap National Historical Park, Middlesboro, Ky.

Kincaid Papers. Lincoln Memorial University Library, Harrogate, Tenn.
Middlesboro City Directories for 1922-23, 1924, 1926, 1934-35, 1937-38, 1940-41, 1950-51.
Minute Books of the Middlesborough City Council. Middlesboro City Clerk Office, Middlesboro, Ky.
Oral History Project tapes. Middlesboro-Bell County Library, Middlesboro, Ky.
Orders, Criminal Causes, Middlesborough City Court, 1896-1901. Bell County Historical Society Museum, Middlesboro, Ky.
Rhodes/Bartlett Papers. Private Collection of Dan Johnson, Middlesboro, Ky.
Roberts Papers. Filson Club Historical Society, Louisville, Ky.

Other Primary Sources

Arthur, Alexander. "Middlesborough and the Gap." n.p., n.d.
———. "Middlesboro in the Making." Middlesboro, Ky.: Pinnacle Printery, n.d.
"Cumberland Gap." New York: South Publishing Co., n.p., n.d.
"Middlesborough, Kentucky as Seen by Noted Men." n.p., January 1891.
"Middlesborough Catechism." n.p., 1890.
"Picturesque Middlesboro, the Magic City." n.p., n.d.
"Report by Edgar J. Paine, Esq., on His Return from a Visit to Cumberland Gap, U.S.A.," n.p.: American Association, 1889.
"Souvenir of Middlesborough." Middlesborough, Ky.: n.p., 1890.

Secondary Sources

Adallis, D. "Historical Sketch of the Greek-American Colony of Middlesboro." *25th Anniversary Historical Sketch and Business Guide of Middlesboro-Pineville,* n.p., n.d.
Allen, James Lane. "Mountain Passes of the Cumberland." Reprint from *Harpers Magazine* 81 (Sept. 1890): 565.
Alvord, Clarence W., and Bidgood, Lee. *The First Explorations of the Trans-Allegheny Region by the Virginians, 1650-1674.* Cleveland: Arthur H. Clark, 1912.
Arrow, Harriette Simpson. *Seedtime on the Cumberland.* Lexington: University of Kentucky Press, 1960.
Ashers: A Family History. n.p., n.d.
Atwell, David. "Masterplan for the Middlesboro Bell County Airport." n.p., 1977.
Ayers, William. "Historical Sketches." Pineville, Ky.: Sun Publishing, 1925.
Ball, Joan Useman. *Ball Family History.* n.p.: Self-published, 1980.
Ball, Palmer R. *Ball Family of Southwest Virginia.* Big Laurel, Va.: Cumberlandcrafters, 1980.
Bell County Historical Society. *History & Families, Bell County, Kentucky.* Paducah, Ky.: Turner Publishing, 1994.
Berlin, Edward. *Ragtime: A Musical and Cultural History.* Berkeley: Univ. of California Press, 1980.

Blesh, Rudi, and Janis, Harriet. *They All Played Ragtime.* New York: Oak, 1950.
"Bossism, Disorder Grip Bell County." n.p., n.d.
Bourne, Dave. "The Ben Harney Years." *Rag Times* 4.4 (Nov. 1970): 11-12.
Bourne, David. "Touring with Ben Harney." *Rag Times* (March 1983), 2-3.
Caudill, Harry M. *Theirs Be the Power: The Moguls of Eastern Kentucky.* Chicago: Univ. of Illinois Press, 1983.
Coates, Harold. *Stories of Kentucky Feuds.* Kingsport, Tenn.: Kingsport Press, 1923.
Crippens, N.A. *Lincoln School and Its Community, 1891-1965.* Clarkesville, Tenn.: Jostens, 1995.
DeRossett, Lou. *Middlesborough: The First Century.* Jacksboro, Tenn.: Action Printing, 1988.
Drimmer, Frederick. *Captured by the Indians: 15 Firsthand Accounts, 1750-1870.* Toronto, Ont.: General Publishing, 1961.
Dwiggins, Dan. *The Air Devils.* Philadelphia: Lippincott, 1966.
Dykeman, Wilma. *The French Broad.* New York: Holt, Rinehart & Winston, 1955.
Eller, Ronald D. *Miners, Millhands, and Mountaineers.* Knoxville: Univ. of Tennessee Press, 1982.
Fairfield, William, III. "Bloody Harlan and Corrupt Bell." *Reporter* (Sept. 18, 1951), 17-21; (Oct. 2, 1951), 21-26; (Oct. 16, 1951), 20-24.
Fey, Marshall. *Slot Machines: A Pictorial History of the First 100 Years.* Reno, Nev.: Liberty Belle Books, 1983.
Forester, William D. *Harlan County—The Turbulent Thirties.* n.p.: Self-published, 1986.
Fox, Maier B. *United We Stand: The UMWA, 1890-1990.* n.p.: UMWA, 1990.
French, Bevan M. *Traces of Catastrophe: A Handbook of Shock-Metamorphic Effects in Terrestrial Meteorite Structures.* Houston: Lunar and Planetary Institute, 1998.
Fuson, Henry H. *The History of Bell County, Kentucky.* New York: Hobson Press, 1947.
Gammond, Peter. *Scott Joplin and the Ragtime Era.* New York: St. Martin's, 1975.
Gaventa, John. *Power and Powerlessness.* Chicago: Univ. of Illinois Press, 1980.
Guteri, Fred. "The Panther Mountain Crater." *Discover* 21.8 (August 2000): 53-59.
Hasse, John Edward. *Ragtime: Its History, Composers and Music.* New York: Schirmer, 1985.
Hayes, David. *The Lost Squadron.* Toronto, Ont.: Madison Press Books, 1994.
Hevener, John. *Which Side Are You On? The Harlan County Coal Miners, 1931-39.* Urbana: Univ. of Illinois Press, 1978.
History of Tennessee. Nashville: Goodspeed Publishing, 1887.
Hodge, Paul. *Meteorite Craters and Impact Structures of the Earth.* Cambridge, England: Cambridge Univ. Press, 1994.
Hoskins, William W. *John Ball Family.* Radford, Va.: Commonwealth Press, 1975.
Jasen, David A., and Tichenor, T.J. *Rags and Ragtime.* New York: Seabury Press, 1978.
Jillson, William R. *Tales of the Dark and Bloody Ground.* n.p.: C.T. Dearing Printing, 1930.

Johnson, L.F. *Famous Kentucky Tragedies and Trials.* Louisville, Ky.: Baldwin Louisville Book Co., 1916.

Kephart, Horace. *Our Southern Highlanders.* New York: Macmillan, 1913.

Kincaid, Robert L. *The Wilderness Road.* New York: Bobbs-Merrill, 1947.

Klotter, James C. *William Goebel: The Politics of Wrath.* Lexington: University Press of Kentucky, 1977.

Kobler, John. *Capone: The Life and World of Al Capone.* New York: Putnam's, 1971.

Kozee, William. *Early Families of Eastern and Southeastern Kentucky and Their Descendants.* Baltimore: Genealogical Publishing, 1973.

Landesco, John. *Organized Crime in Chicago.* Part III. Chicago: Univ. of Chicago Press, 1929.

Lasley, Rick. "Middlesboro: The City in the Crater." *Gateway* 4.1 (Summer 1985): 15-18.

Lee, Ronald E. "Colonel Arthur Campbell, Early Bell County Settler." *Gateway* 1.2 (Fall 1982): 55-60.

———. "The Davis Tavern." *Gateway* 2.1 (Fall 1983): 1-5.

———. "Tellico Claims in the Yellow Creek Valley." *Gateway* 3.1 (Fall 1984): 18-29.

———. "Yellow Creek Settlers, Living on Indian Land." *Gateway* 2.2. (Spring 1984): 46-55.

Levy, Elizabeth, and Richards, Tad. *Struggle and Lose, Struggle and Win: The United Mine Workers of America.* New York: Four Winds Press, 1977.

Mayes, Catherine. *A Coal Miner's Simple Message.* Middlesboro, Ky.: Self-published, 1999.

McNeil, Joanne Ralston. *The Ralston Family through Eight Generations with Ratcliffe, Johnson and Allied Families.* Boise, Ida.: Hathaway Lanes, 2000.

Milam, Keith A., and Kenneth W. Kuehn. "The Middlesboro Impact Structure and Regional Geology of the Pine Mountain Thrust Sheet." Paper presented at the 2002 joint meeting of the North-Central Section and the Southeastern Section of the Geological Society of America, Lexington, Ky. *Guidebook for Geology Field Trips in Kentucky and Adjacent Areas,* ed. Frank L. Ettensohn and Margaret Smith, 57-73.

Moody, Richard T.J., and Zhuraduler, Andrey. *Atlas of the Evolving Earth.* New York: Macmillan Reference USA, 2001.

Montell, William Lynwood. *Killings: Folk Justice in the Upper South.* Lexington: Univ. Press of Kentucky, 1986.

Muhlenberg, Charles. *The Life of Major-General Peter Muhlenberg.* Philadelphia, 1848.

Mutzenberg, Charles G. *Kentucky's Famous Feuds and Tragedies: Authentic History of the World Renowned Vendettas of the Dark and Bloody Ground.* New York: R.F. Fenno, 1917.

Northrup, Trecia. *The Marsee Family of Yellow Creek Valley and Related Families; Turner & Rains.* n.p.: Self-published, 1998.

Pearce, John Ed. *Divide and Dissent: Kentucky Politics, 1930-63.* Lexington, Univ. Press of Kentucky, 1987.

Pyle, Ernie. *Brave Men.* New York: Holt, 1944.

Reckless, Walter. *Vice in Chicago.* Chicago: Univ. of Chicago Press, 1933.

Rice, Russell. *Kentucky Basketball's Big Blue Machine.* Huntsville, Ala.: Strode, 1976.

Roberts, Charles B. "The Building of Middlesborough." *Filson Club Quarterly* 7 (January 1933): 18-33.

Schafer, William J. "Ben Harney and Ragtime Prehistory." *Mississippi Rag* (July 1997), 22.

Schafer, William, and Riedel, Johannes. *The Art of Ragtime.* Baton Rouge: Louisiana State Univ. Press, 1973

Shattuck, Tom N. *A Cumberland Gap Area Guidebook.* Middlesboro: Wilderness Road Co., 1991

Snalling, Landon. *Middlesboro and Before Middlesboro Was.* Louisville, Ky.: George Fetter, 1924.

Spaeth, Sigmund. *A History of Popular Music in America.* New York: Random House, 1948.

Stephens, Thomas E. "Congressman David Grant Colson and the Tragedy of the Fourth Kentucky Volunteer Regiment." *Register of the Kentucky Historical Society* 98.1 (Winter 2000): 43-102.

Tallmadge, William. "Ben Harney: White? Black? Mulatto?" *Sonneck Society Newsletter* 3 (Fall 1979): 16-17.

———. "Ben Harney: The Middlesborough Years, 1890-93." *American Music* 13.2 (Summer 1995): 167-94.

Tapp, Hambleton, and Klotter, James C. *Kentucky: Decades of Discord, 1865-1900.* Frankfort: Kentucky Historical Society, 1977.

Taylor, Paul F. *Bloody Harlan.* Lanham, Md.: Univ. Press of America, 1990.

"The Story of the Pinnacle." n.p.: Sky Land Company, n.d.

Tipton, J.C. *The Cumberland Coal Field and Its Creators.* Middlesboro, Ky.: Pinnacle Printing, 1905.

Verhoeff, Mary. *Kentucky Mountain Transportation and Commerce, 1750-1911.* Louisville: John P. Morton, 1911

Waldo, Terry. *This Is Ragtime.* New York: Hawthorn Books, 1976.

Weaver, Kenneth F. "Meteorites—Invaders from Space." *National Geographic* 170.3 (September 1986): 390-418.

Weise, Robert S. *Grasping at Independence: Debt, Male Authority, and Mineral Rights in Appalachian Kentucky, 1850-1915.* Knoxville: Univ. of Tennessee Press, 2001.

Wilder, Alec. *American Popular Song...: The Great Innovators, 1900-05.* New York: Oxford Univ. Press, 1972.

Wirth, Louis. *The Ghetto.* Chicago: Univ. of Chicago Press, 1928.

Witmark, Isidore, and Goldberg, Isaac. *From Ragtime to Swingtime: The Story of the House of Witmark.* New York: E.E. Furman, 1939.

Woodward, Grace. *The Cherokees.* Norman: Univ. of Oklahoma Press, 1963.

Woolley, Bryan. *We Be Here When Morning Comes.* Lexington: Univ. Press of Kentucky, 1975.

Newspapers

Bell County Citizen. Pineville, 1897.
Bell County Republican. Middlesboro, 1902.
Cumberland Gap: A Weekly Review of the Progress and Development of SE Kentucky, SW Virginia and Eastern Tennessee. Middlesborough, 1889-90.
Cumberland Gap Progress. Cumberland Gap, Tenn., 1888-89
Daily Democrat. Middlesborough, 1891.
Daily Herald. Middlesborough, 1891
Daily News. Middlesborough, 1890-91.
Evening News. Middlesborough, 1891-95, 1901.
Middlesboro Daily News. 1920-60.
Middlesboro Record. Middlesboro, 1902-07.
Middlesborough News. Middlesboro, 1891-1908.
Mining Journal. Middlesborough, 1891.
Pineville Sun. Pineville, 1908-30.
Pinnacle News. Middlesboro, 1914-19.
Thousandsticks. Middlesboro, 1911-13.
Three States. Middlesboro, 1920-56.
Weekly Record. Middlesboro, 1897.

Index

Numbers in italics refer to photographs.